UNCLE TOM'S CABIN

AND THE READING REVOLUTION

UNCLE TOM'S CABIN

AND THE READING REVOLUTION

Race, Literacy, Childhood, and Fiction, 1851–1911

Barbara Hochman

University of Massachusetts Press
AMHERST AND BOSTON

Copyright © 2011 by University of Massachusetts Press
All rights reserved
Printed in the United States of America

LC 2011015730
ISBN 978-1-55849-894-5 (paper); 893-8 (library cloth)

Designed by Sally Nichols
Set in Granjon
Printed and bound by Thomson-Shore, Inc.

Library of Congress Cataloging-in-Publication Data

Hochman, Barbara.
  Uncle Tom's Cabin and the reading revolution : race, literacy, childhood, and fiction,
1851–1911 / Barbara Hochman.
      p. cm. — (Studies in print culture and the history of the book)
  Includes bibliographical references and index.
  ISBN 978-1-55849-894-5 (pbk. : alk. paper) — ISBN 978-1-55849-893-8 (library cloth
: alk. paper)
    1. Stowe, Harriet Beecher, 1811–1896. Uncle Tom's Cabin. 2. Books and reading—
United States—History—19th century. 3. Literature and society—United States—
History—19th century. 4. African Americans in literature. I. Title.
  PS2954.U6H63 2011
  813'.3—dc22
                                                                    2011015730

British Library Cataloguing in Publication data are available.

*For Baruch, Mike, and Benjy—who know a good story
when they hear one.*

Contents

Illustrations

Preface

On Readers

When I began working on the project that became this book I thought that illustrations of *Uncle Tom's Cabin* would help me interpret one specific textual feature: scenes of reading. But dramatic differences between illustrations before and after the Civil War soon led me to think about a transformation in the reception of Stowe's book, and about ongoing changes in reading habits and print culture more broadly. As a result, *"Uncle Tom's Cabin" and the Reading Revolution* retrieves neglected aspects of the novel's appeal—for black and white men, women, and children—not only in the antebellum period but in the ongoing aftermath of slavery and the Civil War. *"Uncle Tom's Cabin" and the Reading Revolution* is first and last a book about reading in context.

Uncle Tom's Cabin gave many readers of the 1850s familiar satisfactions associated with sentimental fiction, reform fiction, sermons, and other genres. Stowe's narrative fulfilled readers' expectations not only about fiction but also about domesticity, race, child-rearing, and slavery. Yet the novel came as a surprise to many readers—absorbing them to an unprecedented degree while modifying well-worn sentimental images (dying child, grieving mother, fugitive slave). The initial popularity of *Uncle Tom's Cabin* had less to do with feeling "right"—morally and politically—than with the contradictory pleasures of absorption in a riveting tale that encouraged identification with otherness. What made the novel so compelling, however, changed with time. As racial tensions increased in the 1890s, many commentators read it nostalgically, as though it were a plantation romance, while others celebrated it as an agent of emancipation—as if the reunited nation no longer had to worry about the legacy of slavery. With the onset of segregation and the rise of literary realism, many white readers grew indifferent to Stowe's novel. At the same time marginalized readers, especially African Americans, found new uses for it.

Any history of reading raises questions about evidence and interpretation. Scenes of reading, prefaces, illustrations, and reviews do not control reader response; yet they reflect commonly shared interpretive norms. The decisions of illustrators, editors, and reviewers, no less than diary jottings, tell us what some readers had to say about a book—what they thought should be singled out, celebrated, or passed over. But written accounts also remake the initial reading experience, even when that experience is recent. Personal letters or journal entries, like the remarks of professional commentators, are shaped by generic conventions and by the image of an intended reader, however tenuous. Children leave few records of their reading, and retrospectives of childhood create additional problems of interpretation. Some African American responses to *Uncle Tom's Cabin* have been reprinted so often that they have lost their interpretive power; others have been neglected. Juxtaposed synchronically and diachronically, my diverse mix of sources helps us understand why hundreds of thousands of mid-nineteenth-century adults were as susceptible as children to a piece of fiction. I hope that *"Uncle Tom's Cabin" and the Reading Revolution* will also refine our grasp of what changed as *Uncle Tom's Cabin* became an American "classic," and "Uncle Tom" an epithet of contempt.

This book would never have taken the shape that it has without the responses of a great many readers who deserve my thanks. They range from intimate friends to complete strangers.

I am particularly grateful to several readers who have followed my project from its initial stages to the writing of this preface. Baruch Hochman, Ellen Gruber Garvey, John Landau, and David M. Stewart variously offered information, skepticism, humor, insight, and criticism, as well as tireless encouragement and indispensable support.

Incisive comments often came from anonymous readers of grant proposals, paper proposals, and essays submitted for publication. Enthusiastic readers are always gratifying; but those who were confused, unconvinced, even outraged by my claims have also been useful. Two particularly helpful comments made in passing came from women I cannot acknowledge because, not realizing how productive their suggestions would be, I did not register their names at the time: In 2003, after listening to a paper I gave at a Northeast American Studies Association conference, a Ph.D. student told me that although the Shakers did not approve of fiction in general, they read *Uncle Tom's Cabin* aloud in group meetings. On the same occasion a historian in the audience suggested that I look into the way Methodist reformer Phoebe Palmer attacked *Uncle Tom's Cabin* for promoting the frivolous practice of novel-reading. I soon began to keep a record of such tips, and I thank many people for specific references in my notes.

Wonderfully perceptive readers of a chapter or two include Joan Acocella, Eitan Bar-Yosef, Yael Ben-zvi, Shlomi Deloia, Tresa Grauer, and Sarah Robbins. For sharing knowledge and thoughts along the way I also thank Robin Bernstein, Elizabeth Freund, Robert Gross, Kathleen Hulser, James L. Machor, Lee Clark Mitchell, Claire Parfait, Stephen Railton, Barbara Ryan, Joan Shelley Rubin, Karen Sanchez-Eppler, and Barbara Sicherman. Questions and challenges from my students at Ben-Gurion University helped clarify some of my pet theories. Shlomi Deloia, Orly Perez, and Thom Rofe made bibliographic suggestions, tracked down obscure references, summarized material, scoured websites for neglected sources, and pressed me to rethink particular passages. Thom Rofe tirelessly combed through my prose. Michael Taber thoughtfully and efficiently made the index. Naomi Landau provided indispensable library help.

In the final stages of the project, ongoing meetings with Ellen Gruber Garvey and Susan K. Harris were invaluable in helping me tie loose ends, anchor, support, and better contextualize important points.

This project could not have been undertaken without the archives of the General Research Division of New York Public Library, the Rare Books and Manuscript Library at Columbia University, the New-York Historical Society, the Arthur and Elizabeth Schlesinger Library on the History of Women in America at Radcliffe, the Schomburg Center for Research in Black Culture, the Cotsen Children's Library at Princeton University, and the Harriet Beecher Stowe Center. Mary Schlosser generously gave me access to her large collection of Stowe materials. Most of all I thank the American Antiquarian Society, that hub of research where many of my ideas for this book germinated. Georgia B. Barnhill, Thomas G. Knoles, and

Laura E. Wasowicz directed me to valuable sources and often provided insight into them. Caroline F. Sloat and Joanne D. Chaison gave me the opportunity to co-chair (with David Stewart) a summer seminar in "Reading and Everyday Life" which deepened my grasp of the conceptual and historical difficulties in reconstructing reading practices.

Paul Wright, former editor at the University of Massachusetts Press, believed in this project from the start, and has been a pleasure to work with. So has his successor, Brian Halley. The readers for the press—Patricia Crain and Christopher Wilson—gave the full manuscript enormously careful and constructive readings. I hope my revisions have done justice to their probing questions. My warm thanks go as well to managing editor Carol Betsch, copy editor Kay Scheuer, and designer Sally Nichols for their efficiency, patience, and good cheer.

Without the funding and free time provided by the following institutions, this book could not have been written at all. I acknowledge with gratitude the generous fellowship support of the American Antiquarian Society, the Northeast Modern Language Association, the Gilder Lehrman Institute of American History, the Israel Science Foundation, and the National Endowment for the Humanities. I express appreciation to the Warner Fund at the University Seminars at Columbia University for their help in publication. My ideas have benefited from discussion in the University Seminar on Women and Society. The dean, rector, and president of Ben-Gurion University helped defray the expenses of book publication and provided matching support for an international Israel Science Foundation Workshop ("Literature, Book History and the Anxiety of Disciplinarity") which I hosted at Ben-Gurion University in 2008. Participants at that workshop provided welcome feedback for my project in its final stages. The Department of Foreign Literature and Linguistics at Ben-Gurion University has been a wonderfully supportive and facilitating home base.

Finally, I thank several journals and publishers for permission to reprint previously published material in revised form. Portions of the Introduction appeared as "The History of Reading and the Death of the Text" in *American Literary History* 21.4 (Winter 2009): 845–58. A version of Chapter 1 appeared as "*Uncle Tom's Cabin* in the *National Era*: An Essay in Generic Norms and the Contexts of Reading" in *Book History* 7 (2004): 143–70. Part of note 18 in Chapter 4 appeared as "Goethe's Mignon: A Source for Topsy and Little Eva,"

Notes and Queries 56.3 [New Series] (September 2009): 370–71. Portions of Chapters 3 and 4 appeared as Chapter 5 in *The History of Reading,* vol. 1, ed. S. S. Towheed and W. R. Owens (London: Palgrave, 2011). Portions of Chapters 5 and 6 appeared as *"Uncle Tom's Cabin* at the World's Columbian Exhibition," *Libraries and Culture* 41.1 (Winter 2006): 82–108, and "Sentiment without Tears: *Uncle Tom's Cabin* as History in the 1890s" in *American Reception Study,* ed. James Machor and Philip Goldstein (New York: Oxford University Press, 2008): 255–76. Part of Chapter 7 appeared as "Sparing the White Child: The Lessons of *Uncle Tom's Cabin* in an Age of Segregation," *Journal of the History of Childhood and Youth* 4.1 (Winter 2011). Part of the Epilogue appeared in "Devouring *Uncle Tom's Cabin:* Black Readers between *Plessy vs. Ferguson* and *Brown vs. Board of Education,*" *Reception: Texts, Readers, Audiences, History* 2 (August 2010): 48–94.

UNCLE TOM'S CABIN

AND
THE READING
REVOLUTION

The Afterlife of a Book

In a novel, people's hearts break, and they die, and that is the end of it . . .

—*Uncle Tom's Cabin*

Between 1851 and the centenary of Stowe's birth in 1911 *Uncle Tom's Cabin* was adapted for disparate ends by editors, publishers, and illustrators as well as other readers—men and women, Northerners and Southerners, adults and children, black and white. This study explores a transformation in the cultural meaning of one book. It contributes to a history of reading in the United States by tracing changes in reading practices and a shift in widely shared and deeply intertwined assumptions about literacy, fiction, childhood, and race. These assumptions reshaped interpretive conventions and generated new meanings for Stowe's narrative in the decades following emancipation and the Civil War.

When *Uncle Tom's Cabin* first appeared, as installment fiction in an abolitionist weekly paper, it was an ephemeral text in a rapidly expanding market. But Stowe's tale soon gained the formidable status that St. Clare ironically attributes to Tom himself: "all the moral and Christian virtues bound in black morocco complete."[1] The book's initial popularity can be understood only in relation to what reading once meant as both private act and social practice. Reading was a crucially important activity in the antebellum United States, a site of cultural enthusiasm, conflict, and anxiety. In the 1850s many ministers, educators, and other commentators had deep reservations about fiction, precisely because of its growing popularity. *Uncle Tom's Cabin* played an important but neglected role in the process by which the novel became a dominant genre in U.S. literary culture. In tracing that process I clarify the changing place of fiction in American society, and create an intimate view of the reading experience.

Uncle Tom's Cabin may have been the most widely read book in the antebellum United States, with the possible exception of the Bible. Over the last twenty-five years Stowe's novel has become one of the most often taught and written-about texts in the U.S. literary canon. Much of the discussion has focused on Stowe's essentialized understanding of race and the related problem of sentiment as an aesthetic and political strategy. Stowe's stated aim in the preface to the first edition—"to awaken sympathy"—continues to dominate accounts of the book's impact.[2] Yet sympathy for "the lowly" was only one of many responses to her tale, even in the 1850s. While many antebellum readers closely followed Stowe's instructions—using her novel to renew their Christian faith and sympathizing with the "poor slaves" (while maintaining their own sense of difference)—other readers violated her famous imperative to "feel right" by allowing a book to absorb them to a degree that (in theory) Stowe herself would not have approved. Such readers temporarily collapsed the imaginative distance between themselves and endangered slave figures. This kind of reading went beyond sympathy and contemplation; it violated Stowe's guidelines for reading and veered dangerously close to the loss of self and reality-sense that stirred anxiety in ministers, educators, and other anti-fiction commentators.

In 1852 *Uncle Tom's Cabin* was not only a novel that represented slavery as a moral and political atrocity; it was also an unprecedented publishing phenomenon. White Northerners wept and could not put the book down; they neglected work and other obligations to finish it. Southerners often went to some lengths to obtain the novel, and read it surreptitiously. Abolitionists considered the tale a significant asset, while Southern reviews and anti-Tom narratives expressed outrage, confirming the book's divisive racial, sectional, and political potential.[3] By the 1890s, however, *Uncle Tom's Cabin* had become a different story.

Between the Civil War and the 1880s, Stowe's novel was not much reprinted.[4] Immediately after the war slavery and sectional strife were unpopular subjects. The end of Reconstruction (1877) triggered hopes for social stability and the desire to look forward, not back. Writers, educators, and former abolitionists soon began to voice guarded optimism about developments in African American education and free enterprise in the "New South."[5] However, as discrimination increased in the North and racial violence in the South, optimism was replaced by anxiety about the long-term legacy of slavery and the war. Interest in *Uncle Tom's Cabin* revived in this context.

Uncle Tom's Cabin gained a new lease on life during the 1880s and especially the '90s. Historians, men of letters, and other commentators of the period praised the novel as an agent of emancipation—evidence of America's moral, social, and cultural progress. Abraham Lincoln's purported words upon meeting Harriet Beecher Stowe ("So you're the little lady who started this great war") were widely quoted.[6] At the same time, the novel was invoked to support what Nina Silber calls the "romance of reunion"—a sentimental vision of national peace and harmony designed to counter mounting evidence that emancipation and the Civil War had created complex new social tensions.[7] Diverse reading communities put the novel to new uses; sometimes these uses were at odds with one another.

Stowe's eightieth birthday was much publicized in 1891 and became the occasion for retrospectives that charted the genesis of the novel and its impact. In 1893 expiration of copyright made it profitable for publishers to issue new reprints. That year *Uncle Tom's Cabin* was also the linchpin of the Stowe exhibit in the Woman's Building Library at the Columbian Exposition, where the book was represented as a national treasure. At the same time, the para-textual material of new editions reinforced existing social and racial hierarchies: illustrations, commentaries, and heavily edited children's books played down Stowe's evangelical and polemical thrust, while projecting figures of entertaining and devoted servants into an open-ended future. Southerners began praising Stowe's representation of slave loyalty. Much of the novel's imaginative vitality leaked out of it as commentators displaced Stowe's tale of exploited slaves, separated families, and brutalized children with nostalgic images of the plantation South. These changes enabled *Uncle Tom's Cabin* to serve new cultural needs in the 1890s—the "nadir" of U.S. race relations in Rayford Logan's much-quoted words.[8]

Uncle Tom's Cabin was publicly lionized toward the end of the nineteenth century—republished, recommended, bought, and borrowed from libraries—but white readers of this period did not often read it with rapt attention and emotion. The novel's framing at the Columbian Exposition epitomized its paradoxical place in the culture at large: celebrated as evidence of American progress but displayed behind secure glass doors, it was a closed book in an unusable library conceived as a monument. In the course of the 1890s *Uncle Tom's Cabin* not only acquired a newly virulent racist subtext; it also lost much of its power to captivate and enthrall. While it was often reprinted and praised in the public sphere, white adults of the 1890s neither read Stowe's book with intensity, nor referred it to social issues of the moment. At the same time new readers, especially African Americans, often the children and grandchildren of former slaves, were powerfully drawn to *Uncle Tom's Cabin,* and found unexpected uses for it.

To access these changes I examine multiple forms in which Stowe's novel was issued and read during the nineteenth and early twentieth century: as newspaper installments, illustrated volumes, and adaptations for children. Editors, reviewers, and illustrators are readers themselves; their work implies their understanding of a book and their sense of its meaning for others. Editions reflect changing assumptions about readers' expectations and help shape reader response. Yet published words and images can tell us only so much about how antebellum or late nineteenth-century readers actually read. I therefore analyze *Uncle Tom's Cabin* not just in relation to printed discussions and the paratextual material of editions—introductions, illustrations, advertisements—but also with attention to unpublished readers' comments in letters, diaries, occasional marginalia, and other artifacts. This combined strategy yields a layered description of the way *Uncle Tom's Cabin* was read and used in its first sixty years of existence.

A children's edition of *Uncle Tom's Cabin,* published in 1853, raises methodological questions that are central throughout this study. *Little Eva: Flower of the South* is a direct response to *Uncle Tom's Cabin,* one that rejects and counters Stowe's image of slavery, rewriting Stowe's novel as a pro-slavery picture book. In this hand-colored text of eight pages slaves would rather hear Eva read than read for themselves, and when a slave character is offered his freedom, he refuses to take it. But, as often happens, one response triggers another: in an extant copy of *Little Eva: Flower of the South* someone has written the words "the happy land," in script, at the top of two empty pages in the middle of the book (fig. 1).[9] If we take this reiterated phrase as a response to the story—does it affirm the book's vision of a slave plantation as a "happy land"? The reader provides no details. The silence of the blank page beneath the penciled words seems to speak more loudly than the cheerful phrase, and

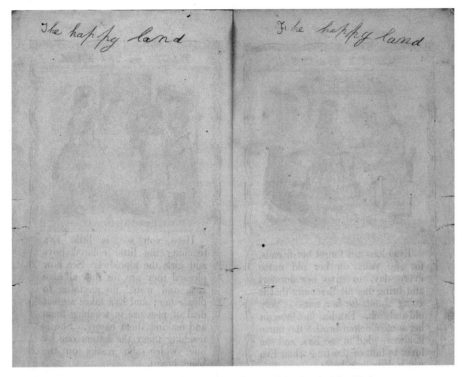

1. *"The happy land." Inscription in* Little Eva: The Flower of the South. *New York: Philip J. Cozans, 1853. Courtesy of the American Antiquarian Society.*

casts doubt on its meaning. Or perhaps a child merely used the blank pages to practice penmanship, when paper was scarce.

Interpreting children's responses to reading is a notoriously difficult enterprise, whether responses take the form of cryptic marginalia or more clearly formulated comments. All reading takes place "inside people's heads," as John Frow puts it, but the reading experience of children is even more difficult to document and interpret than that of adults.[10] Children themselves leave few records of their reading and, when they do, their writings are often tailored to adult expectations. The elusiveness of children's reading thus exemplifies problems of evidence and interpretation that often recur in the chapters that follow.

The unreliability of testimony is a problem for every history of reading. All readers' comments are designed with some audience in mind, self or other, real or imaginary.[11] "Private" remarks in letters and diaries are no more transparent than marginalia, or than published accounts by professionals.

Antebellum correspondents and even diarists knew that their words might be read by people they had not addressed.[12] This knowledge must have had some impact on their writing. Matters are further complicated by the difficulty of separating culturally typical responses from the pleasures (or conflicts) stirred by individual encounters with particular books. Readers' comments always trail behind the reading experience—they are produced when reading stops. In order to grasp what a book has meant to a reader of the past we must rely, as Frow puts it, "on secondary manifestations most of which consist of one or another form of self-report and all of which are dependent upon translation of the micro-processes of reading into . . . a time-bound critical vocabulary."[13] In fact, historically specific interpretive conventions and "a time-bound . . . vocabulary" shape not only all *reports* of textual encounters, but the initial encounters themselves. Yet precisely because the language that readers use to describe their experience changes over time, readers' comments provide insight into reading practices and response. Both published and unpublished accounts are rich sources, especially when juxtaposed and analyzed for their rhetorical strategies and their culturally specific vocabulary as well as for their basic claims. A reader's imagery and linguistic register, the representation (or misrepresentation) of texts read—these elements are all revealing. Eclectic sources are particularly useful when they confirm one another and suggest a pattern; in this study they disclose the powerful hold of *Uncle Tom's Cabin* on antebellum readers, its waning appeal for white readers at the turn of the century, its heightened appeal for African Americans of the same period, and the implications of that shift.

What Walter Benjamin calls the "afterlife" of a book begins as soon as a book is published; its very appearance reinforces or destabilizes generic norms and readers' expectations. When a book is widely read, the process involves ongoing aftershocks.[14] Stowe's narrative helped to shape its own initial position within an expanding print culture by providing a commentary on contemporary reading habits. *Uncle Tom's Cabin* is pervaded by images of books and reading, but they remain a neglected feature of the novel.[15] By rendering black and white men, women, and children examining Bibles, newspapers, placards, bills of sale, and other forms of printed matter, Stowe inscribed a diverse array of reading habits into her text. Representations of reading are no direct index of actual practices, but depictions of Bible-reading and slave literacy had implications in 1852 that were different in the 1890s and are not self-evident today. Stowe's recurrent focus on Eva and Tom bent over the Bible helped legitimize her novel for many antebellum readers who still disapproved of fiction-reading. The image of Tom and his Bible was also reassuring to readers who feared the consequences of allowing a slave to become literate. Nonetheless, a slave with a book was a provocative image throughout the nineteenth century. Hammatt Billings, Stowe's first American illustrator, understood Stowe's emphasis on slave literacy as an assertion of African American spirituality, interiority, and agency; his interpretation is apparent in the illustrations he created. By contrast, E. W. Kemble, Stowe's best-known illustrator of the 1890s, never pictured a black figure reading. Such differences reveal broad cultural tensions as well as changes in the meaning of Stowe's novel over time.

READING REVOLUTIONS

The "reading revolution" in the title of this book alludes to two transformations—one conceptualized by historians to explain cultural change, the other theorized by literary scholars to refine their own interpretive methods. Historians coined the phrase "reading revolution" to posit a transformation of reading habits in both Europe and the United States early in the nineteenth century when a significant "print culture" came into being with the help of new technology that facilitated paper-making, printing, distribution, and marketing. Robert Darnton, David Hall, and other historians have proposed that when people owned only a Bible, an almanac, and a devotional work or two, they read "intensively," reading and rereading a limited number of books. According to this model, reading habits changed in tandem with the proliferation of printed matter. By 1800 people began to read "extensively," consuming and discarding a wider range of material than ever before. Although this opposition is too neat to explain the diversity of reading practices, even in the northeastern antebellum United States, *Uncle Tom's Cabin* fits comfortably within the script up to a point.[16] The popularity of Stowe's novel could not have occurred without the factors that helped create the "reading revolution." Technological developments that enabled thousands of copies to be published and distributed within weeks, an unprecedented advertising campaign, the rising status of the novel as a literary form—these factors all contributed to the book's extraordinary circulation.[17] *Uncle Tom's Cabin* was read rapidly and widely in the 1850s; but many readers also lingered with it—thought about it, talked about it, wrote about it, and reread it—even in the South. Northern readers frequently consumed it with careful attention as well as emotion. Many passed the book on to friends and relatives.

The other "reading revolution" that informs my thinking and my methods throughout this work is "the return of the reader" to literary scholarship and pedagogy, a change that coincided with the Stowe revival of the 1970s and '80s.[18] In the early stages of this "revolution" the reader was a theoretical construct "implied" by the text itself; in the 1980s the idea of "the reader," or what Steven Mailloux calls a "reader vocabulary," did not substantially alter the methods or results of literary interpretation.[19] Attention to "the reader" in the first decade or two of response theory required neither historical specificity nor an interest in individual readers, still less in "non-professional" ones.[20] With the advent of the "new historicism," however, the imperative "always historicize" fueled a growing desire to reconstruct literary meanings and reading habits of the past.[21]

Over the last twenty years the history of reading has begun to flourish as an interdisciplinary field in which diverse scholars reconstruct lost reading practices and interpretive communities. Renewed interest in reading as an object of study has emerged hand in hand with rising anxiety about the future of books and reading in an electronic age. In both the academy and the press surveys proliferate, all designed to establish whether or not people are still reading (rather than watching a screen).[22] As a field, the history of reading is thriving, energized in part by these concerns.

The remaking of *Uncle Tom's Cabin* that was consolidated in the 1890s had had long-lasting effects that complicate the project of reconstructing the antebellum reading experience. When social change and a transformation of interpretive conventions remade *Uncle Tom's Cabin* toward the turn of the century, white readers found it increasingly difficult to identify or even sympathize with Eliza and Tom, not to speak of Topsy. To recognize this dynamic is to create historical perspective on both Stowe's text and its nineteenth-century readers. Neither the Stowe display at the World's Fair nor new editions of the 1890s set out to transform the meaning of Stowe's novel—but they did so. As a result an old book met changing cultural needs.

Fiction was already a popular form when installments of *Uncle Tom's*

Cabin began to appear. But there was a difference between the marketplace reality of fiction and its cultural respectability.[23] Attention to this difference qualifies a common assumption of literary history: the idea that, as Robert Darnton once noted, "the novel, like the bourgeoisie, always seems to be rising"[24] The rise of the novel was uneven. The inroads that fiction made into literary culture were fitful and intermittent throughout the nineteenth century and beyond. The emergence of fiction as a popular literary form plays an important role in the "reading revolution" that historians have explored; but interpreting watersheds in the history of reading, like interpreting marginalia, involves filling in blanks, many of which require imaginative leaps.[25] By analyzing shifts in the functions served by *Uncle Tom's Cabin* over time, I historicize and complicate both "the rise of the novel" and the idea of "the reader," while asking where textual meaning resides, how it is shaped, and how it changes.

When the idea of the reader entered discussions of literary theory during the 1970s and '80s it initiated a paradigm shift, raising questions about whether meaning is a function of the reader or the text. To put the opposition sharply: one relatively recent scenario ascribes a maximum of autonomy to readers who "poach" their way through texts finding what they seek, freely adapting and appropriating meanings as needed.[26] Another scenario identifies reading with the "discursive arrangements that constrain it and that impose on it a signification that is . . . independent of any deciphering."[27] By combining an emphasis on readers with an emphasis on books, I mediate between these two scripts (I do not choose between them). *Uncle Tom's Cabin* became a different book in the wake of the Civil War, the failure of Reconstruction, the start of legalized segregation, and the ongoing repercussions of slavery. By examining the genesis and implications of this process I situate my argument at the theoretical and methodological intersection where literature meets history. I offer insight into a social reality where printed matter was increasingly important but where its meaning for individuals and groups of readers was in flux. I use *Uncle Tom's Cabin* not only to disclose shifting assumptions about race, children, and fiction-reading, but also to gain a finer theoretical understanding of how Stowe's novel appealed to readers as what Charles Dudley Warner called "mere story."[28]

Uncle Tom's Cabin provides a particularly fine lens through which to examine cultural changes in the United States as well as theoretical questions about the dynamic of reading. Stowe's novel began as a book that was both loved and hated with intensity rarely seen on such a scale.[29] However, by the time Stowe died in 1896, a public consensus about the meaning and value of her book temporarily neutralized it as a trigger for either strong emotion or political controversy (at least among white adults). Other novels which began as popular successes have lost their appeal later on; conversely, some have found newly appreciative readers after a slow start. But few works of fiction can equal *Uncle Tom's Cabin* either for the intense feelings and polemics it inspired when first published, or for the way it continues to refract cultural tensions while raising questions about the unstable effects of a narrative.

INTERPRETING EVIDENCE OF READING

My combined focus on Stowe's tale, readers' comments, and the material forms in which *Uncle Tom's Cabin* appeared, distinguishes the present book from previous accounts of Stowe's reception. I draw on the work of many scholars who have already scoured the archive for evidence of how *Uncle Tom's Cabin* was conceived, published, reviewed, recast, and read. Some of the documents I analyze (illustrations, prefaces, reviews, and letters) have been made available by the work of Thomas F. Gossett, Joan Hedrick, Claire Parfait, Stephen Railton, Ronald J. and Mary Saracino Zboray and others.[30] But many of my sources are unknown or neglected. My analysis of both paratextual material and readers' comments is designed not only to clarify transformations in the meaning and cultural uses of *Uncle Tom's Cabin* but also to expose gaps between the consensus and responses that diverge from it. I follow Robert Darnton, Roger Chartier, Barbara Sicherman, Joan Rubin, and other historians by asking what we can use as evidence of reading from outside the text; but I am more willing than most to include evidence from within. I sustain a balance between attending to the multiple printed forms that make a text available as time goes on, to readings that "actually took place," and to the "protocol of reading" inscribed in the text.[31]

In 1896 the historian James Rhodes argued that emotional responses to *Uncle Tom's Cabin* had led to political change because masses of readers had reacted to Stowe's book exactly as she had intended. According to Rhodes's *History of the United States* the publication of *Uncle Tom's Cabin* was "one of the most important causes that led to [the success of the Republican party in 1860]. Of the literary forces that aided in bringing about the immense revolution in public sentiment between 1852 and 1860, we may affirm with confidence that by far the most weighty was the influence spread abroad by this book."[32] Rhodes invokes the popularity of Rousseau's *Nouvelle Héloïse* as a unique precedent for *Uncle Tom's Cabin*.[33] In alluding to Rousseau, Rhodes anticipates Darnton's influential discussion of the bourgeois French merchant Ranson, who sustained an ongoing correspondence with Rousseau's publisher while ordering books. Darnton suggests that Ranson followed Rousseau's "protocol of reading" to the letter, taking Rousseau's educational theories to heart and weaving them into his own life.[34]

Like Rhodes, many nineteenth-century commentators affirmed the idea of a close fit between Stowe's guidelines for reading and the antebellum response, asserting that white Northern readers reacted to *Uncle Tom's Cabin* with righteous tears, sympathy, and social criticism. The testimony of readers who did not follow this script is harder to locate and assess than the comments of readers who claim that *Uncle Tom's Cabin* changed lives and politics. Antebellum Southerners and African American readers provide some dissenting voices, but by now these too have been subsumed into a well-worn narrative: Southern readers were outraged and cried "libel"; angry black readers such as Martin Delany charged Stowe with racism.[35] Delany's criticism of Stowe remains important in any account of how *Uncle Tom's Cabin* was read, then and now. But the tenacious survival of *Uncle Tom's Cabin* in U.S. literary culture is still difficult to explain—the book has not been out of print since it was published.[36] From the 1890s onward, moreover, it seems that African Americans and other marginalized, "unintended readers" were among the most engaged consumers of the novel.[37]

Throughout this study, changes in the way *Uncle Tom's Cabin* was published and read raise the question: what constitutes evidence of reading? Readers' comments can help us understand transformations in the cultural function of a book, but only if we analyze both the language and the social contexts of response. Individual testimonies reveal the limits of a codified consensus and help us understand it. They add nuance and historical specificity to our idea of "reception" and complicate assumptions about sentiment as a monolithic genre and reading practice

The success of *Uncle Tom's Cabin* is not fully explained by the encomiums of readers who claim that they wept their way through the book and emerged with deepened moral and political insight. In a much reprinted account, Stowe describes her practice of reading completed installments of *Uncle Tom's Cabin* to her own offspring. She explains that when she read the scene of Uncle Tom's death to her two sons, the boys sobbed (the familiar prelude to changes of mind and heart throughout *Uncle Tom's Cabin*). They then drew the conclusion proposed by the scene: "Oh! mamma, slavery is the most cursed thing in the world!"[38] Stowe's vignette provides a prototypical narrative of the perfect fit between guidelines for reading and "real" reader response. But testimonies of reading are shaped by multiple factors, including their intended audience.

Stowe's description of her boys has been taken at face value by biographers and other commentators. We have no particular reason to doubt her claims, but in telling this story Stowe reinforced a set of instructions for reading her novel to which she was publicly committed: read, weep, and reflect. These instructions circulated widely through antebellum print culture—in ads, letters, reviews, and such artifacts as the *Uncle Tom's Cabin* handkerchief, issued by J. P. Jewett in 1852, and embossed with the famous scene in which Eva tells Uncle Tom that she will die.[39] Stowe's sons must have been particularly well prepared by their life in the Stowe family to respond as their mother claims they did. According to Elizabeth Stuart Phelps, when Stowe's youngest daughter was asked to write a school composition one day, she resolutely refused; later, she wrote the words "Slavery is the greatest curse of human Nature" on a "slip of paper" and submitted it to her teacher instead.[40] If this report is accurate, it too suggests how well the Stowe children had absorbed their anti-slavery lesson. But their readiness to confirm Stowe's expectations and convictions (in reports to their mother and teacher) does not explain the hold of *Uncle Tom's Cabin* on generations of children beyond the confines of the Stowe family.[41]

Stowe's sons were held up to the reading public as model readers of *Uncle Tom's Cabin*. Antebellum commentators asserted that adults enthusiastically accepted Stowe's guidelines as well—feeling for the "lowly" and following their feelings with renewed faith and political conviction.[42] The belief in a close alignment between Stowe's protocol of reading and the antebellum response is partially justified; it has certainly had a long life, even among scholars critical of sentiment.[43] Yet the emotional upheavals so often described by Stowe's antebellum readers deserve further scrutiny and historical contextualization.

Nineteenth-century readers, neglecting work or other duties, often put themselves in Tom or Eliza's place for a while as if there were no color line. "[I was] bound down captive" by the book, Carroll Norcross, a farm laborer and part-time writing-master in rural Maine, writes in his journal.[44] "I *could not* leave" the book, Stowe's friend Georgiana May reports in a letter to Stowe, "any more than I could have left a dying child."[45] The sense of being held "captive" by *Uncle Tom's Cabin* was widespread, but antebellum readers were bound to Stowe's novel not only by socially legitimate emotions (reflection, moral obligation, sympathy). They were held fast by dramatic dialogues, by a narrative voice that cajoled, exhorted, and threatened; and by a swiftly paced plot that includes slave suicide, a miraculous river-crossing, violence, and innocent deaths. This combination of rhetorical ploys elicited excitement and fear as well as tears and sublime feelings. Antebellum readers, especially those unaccustomed to giving themselves over to fiction, often express discomfort about their own responses.

Passionate immersion in a narrative does not necessarily lead to action; as Gillian Brown and others have noted, one can read a book and sympathize, then close it and think no more about the subject.[46] Even worse, in Lauren Berlant's words, the "political tradition of sentimentality [is]. . . . likely to justify ongoing forms of domination" by offering the short-lived satisfaction of tears rather than a radical critique of social structures.[47] My concern throughout this book is less with ethical claims and reasoned political alliances, more with subterranean and even contradictory responses that facilitated the blurring of boundaries—not only between fiction and reality but also between "races." The long-range effects of imaginative entry into a fictional world are hard to gauge, but after completing *Uncle Tom's Cabin* many antebellum readers were far from complacent. Their reactions often outstripped what Stowe had proposed or expected.

Between 1840 and 1870 Stowe frequently warned against the danger of excitement and over-stimulation caused by fiction.[48] Throughout *Uncle Tom's Cabin* Stowe's narrator urges readers to respond with an appropriate degree of sympathy and moral urgency—sentiments that, in Glenn Hendler's words required "the cultivation of a . . . proper repertoire of feelings" (2).[49] In the much-cited words of the novel's "Concluding Remarks," Stowe instructed her readers to "Feel *right*" (624, my emphasis).[50] Many readers claim to have followed these instructions; but a sizable gap remains betweens such assertions and other responses to *Uncle Tom's Cabin* often noted elsewhere in a single letter or diary entry. If Stowe had fully complied with her own stated views, she should have condemned the more extravagant claims of some readers.

READING VIA ABSORPTION AND IDENTIFICATION

Readers of the 1850s, deeply engrossed and moved by Stowe's novel, often consumed *Uncle Tom's Cabin* late at night, completing it in two or three days—or in one sitting, even in the South.[51] But many people who found themselves riveted to Stowe's tale were unaccustomed to being so "lost in a book," especially a fiction; *Uncle Tom's Cabin* provided release not only from gnawing uncertainty over slavery but also from strictures against novel-reading. Antebellum readers frequently claimed that the book led them to revise their view of slavery and renew their religious faith. By echoing Stowe's programmatic emphasis on the moral and religious value of *Uncle Tom's Cabin,* such readers rationalized their unprecedented experience of absorption in a novel.[52]

Up to a point many antebellum readers' comments conform to widely shared expectations for responding to *Uncle Tom's Cabin*. "Much have I heard and read about this same book," Carroll Norcross writes in his diary, "but never have I before had the pleasure of feasting, mentally, upon its enticing pages."[53] What Norcross "heard and read" surely prepared him to be absorbed by the book and to "feast" on it—"mentally," as he is careful to note. But the experience of reading *Uncle Tom's Cabin* went well beyond the "mental." "*Read* Uncle Tom, oh yes, literally devoured it," Maria Woodbury of Westfield, New York, writes to a friend in Holden, Massachusetts, on June 4, 1852 (emphasis in original).[54] "Charles bro't home 'Uncle Tom's Cabin' the other night, & the children are devouring it," Ellen Douglas Birdseye Wheaton notes in her diary in April 1852—with some envy perhaps, as she writes in the same entry that she "get[s] on very slowly with the life of Margaret Fuller."[55] Antebellum readers repeatedly speak of "devouring" the book; this trope repays attention.

The figure of the "solitary reader," freely indulging his or her appetite, was a common source of anxiety for cultural guardians in the eighteenth and nineteenth century. In the twentieth century this figure became a commonplace of fiction theory, aided in part by Walter Benjamin's influential essay "The Storyteller."[56] The novel reader, Benjamin writes, "is isolated, more so than any other reader. . . . In this solitude of his, the reader of a novel seizes upon his material more jealously than anyone else. He is ready to make it completely his own, to devour it, as it were. Indeed, he destroys: he swallows up the material as the fire devours logs in the fireplace."[57] In Benjamin's analysis of what it means to "devour" a novel, reading is driven by a destructive, "jealous" appetite and erotically tinged self-enclosure.

The metaphor of reading as eating was much in use by nineteenth-century educators, ministers, and other cultural spokesmen. In Stowe's words, if "stimulating condiments in literature be freely used in youth, all relish for more solid reading will in a majority of cases be destroyed."[58] Many commentators feared that novels would foster passivity and overindulgence (as in consumption of sweets, liquor, and other unhealthy food and drink).[59] Reading as "devouring" might seem to suggest considerable energy—not passivity—but such energy did not reassure those who distinguished "taste" from "appetite" and who promoted literacy to foster a sense of reality, order, and self-control.[60] Indeed, reading as devouring implies asocial, almost animal-like desire and abandon that was neither promoted by antebellum commentators nor proposed by *Uncle Tom's Cabin* itself. Time and patience to process and reflect upon a book was much recommended instead.

Northern ministers and educators feared that absorption in a novel would blur the boundaries between the fictive and the real, between text and reader, between self and other. Southern reviewers, worrying about the same incalculable consequences of fiction-reading that troubled Northern commentators, complained that by using fiction to make an abolitionist argument Stowe was hitting below the belt.[61] "It is a book to sink deep into the heart of all readers," Maria Woodbury notes in a letter, appropriating Eva's oft-repeated phrase. Many readers recycled Stowe's imagery to describe their experience of reading.[62] Such recycling suggests how deeply the words of the novel permeated readers' consciousness. More than any single character or scene it is the "book" that "sink[s] into the heart," the holistic experience of reading that entices, immobilizes, and impels some readers to express their responses by making Stowe's language their own.

In a speech before the Massachusetts Antislavery Society on January 27, 1853, Wendell Phillips suggested that the success of *Uncle Tom's Cabin* could be partly attributed to the "enthusiasm" generated by the work of abolitionists in the course of fifteen years.[63] However, as Phillips acknowledges, the Abolitionist movement was "unable to command a wide circulation for [its] . . . books and journals," even though it had set out the anti-slavery position "in a detail and with a fullness of evidence which no subject has ever received before in this country" (123–24, 118).[64] Stowe's "evidence" and arguments are much the same as those offered by Phillips, Richard Hildreth, Lydia Maria Child, Theodore Weld, and others. Why did she gain a wider hearing?

Phillips claims that *Uncle Tom's Cabin* would have "never been read" had not abolitionists already "raised up hundreds of thousands of hearts to sympathize with the slave" (131). Recent discussions of sentiment have repeatedly asked whether sympathy enables a reader to experience the pain of another, or whether it merely offers the pleasure of tears while heightening the reader's sense of superiority and personal safety.[65] To feel sympathy is not to confuse oneself with the sufferer. Sympathy facilitates, indeed requires, the preservation of distance between the one extending and the one receiving the benevolent or compassionate emotion. Philip Fisher's paradigm for sympathetic response is Rousseau's image of the distant spectator watching a lion tear a child from its mother. Susan Ryan suggests that "nineteenth-century benevolent discourse asserted the superiority (racial, regional, moral) of the helper and the otherness of the helped."[66]

I want to differentiate both sympathy and empathy from identification, which I take to be a more unruly and less moralized response to reading. Identification precedes empathy and sympathy. It may lead to both—or neither. Most significantly it blurs the distinction between self and other, which is exactly what worried antebellum reformers and other commentators. Empathy, as literary scholar Suzanne Keen points out, "like its semantic close relative, sympathy," is generally considered a "moral emotion." As such—and despite academic attacks on sentiment—empathy has acquired "widespread cultural valuation" in contemporary contexts ranging from psychological discourse through advice literature to science fiction and other popular forms.[67]

In an influential essay, the mid-twentieth century psychoanalyst Heinz Kohut defined empathy in terms that resonate strongly with beliefs held by Stowe and other nineteenth-century reformers who affirmed the potential of what they called sympathy for attaining social and moral goals.[68] Kohut takes empathy as an emotion that leads to introspection: an emotion in *the service of understanding*. By contrast, identification, whether temporary or permanent, may serve assorted ends, yield a variety of satisfactions, fulfill diverse needs (instinctual or emotional gratification, defense against anxiety, guilt, shame, etc.).[69] Identification then, as I will use the term throughout this book, is an effect of reading which is intense as well as unruly. By blurring the distinction between self and other, identification is more likely than sympathy or empathy to destabilize, even threaten, the reading self.[70]

According to Ryan, some benevolent antebellum reformers were fearful that a "too-thorough identification between helper and helped" would involve an unacceptable "degree of social leveling." Glenn Hendler notes that "the mediation between a distanced observer and the sufferer is always at risk of collapsing" and that the "fantasy of experiential equivalence has always caused unease in some of its readers."[71] However, such unease has had different sources at different times. Like feminist scholars of the 1990s, black antebellum readers such as Martin Delany or Frances Ellen Watkins Harper may have been troubled by Stowe's image of "the poor slaves" because of the potential cost to objects of sympathy who were misrepresented and further demeaned by the representation.[72] But white antebellum men and women were perturbed by *Uncle Tom's Cabin* for different reasons: intensely absorbed by Stowe's plot and characters, held "captive," and then "haunted" by Stowe's figures and events, many people were left with a residue of moral and emotional disturbance if not a revised political position.[73] The difference between Stowe and Phillips (or Hildreth, Child, and Weld) is precisely Stowe's success in going beyond sympathy or empathy by breaking down the imaginative distance between her white readers and the African American characters in her tale.

Stowe's idea of black subjectivity conformed to a middle-class domestic model. This is precisely what made it so compelling to white readers of the 1850s. Whether the image of Eliza or Tom was near or far from the reality of African Americans is a different question. The charges of distortion that Southerners often hurled at Stowe were meaningful only because so many readers accepted her story as a powerful kind of truth. Stowe responded to charges of exaggeration by citing "authoritative" sources in the *Key to Uncle Tom's Cabin* (1853); but the *Key* could not compete with the novel for the attention of the reading public. White antebellum readers who did not believe that African Americans were anything like themselves followed *Uncle Tom's Cabin* with rapt attention. As they did so, the emotional distance required for sympathy and empathy temporarily disappeared, and the idea of black subjectivity became imaginatively real. While "devouring" *Uncle Tom's Cabin*, or allowing it to "sink into" them, readers gained ideas and feelings about African Americans for which they were simply unprepared.

The meaning and function of racial stereotypes change with time; so does the meaning of sentiment. Stowe could not imagine a future in which African Americans would be full-fledged citizens of the United States, and her novel does not propose such a thing; some readers noted this as early as 1852.[74] But like Stowe's Senator Byrd, for whom a fugitive is at first no more than "the letters that spell the word" (155), white readers of *Uncle Tom's Cabin*, even those familiar with abolitionist rhetoric and sentimental fiction, were caught off guard, suddenly disarmed into entertaining the possibility that they were not as different from African American slaves as they had believed. Racist elements in Stowe's representation of Tom, Topsy, and other black characters have been much discussed and require no rehearsal here. However, recent work on "color-blind" language shows that racism persists in the absence of racist tropes and epithets. White children who learn not to say "nigger," even children who insist (in words) that all people are equal, may embrace, enact, and perpetuate racist assumptions. Some sociologists even suggest that color-blind vocabulary deprives children of a language with which to confront racial issues.[75] Conversely, Stowe's use of common racialized stereotypes may have reassured antebellum readers that otherness could be safely contained, while allowing them to engage her characters at a radical level of fantasy that sometimes produced feelings more complex than sympathy, and more benign than racism or romantic racialism.[76] Those feelings created surprise and consternation, intensifying the reading experience and destabilizing certainties about otherness.

When white antebellum readers plunged imaginatively into Eliza's or Tom's situation, they temporarily lost sight of the customary constraints of time, space, and other norms that reinforced widely accepted conventions of behavior and feeling. By drawing readers into her fiction so effectively, Stowe tapped into uncertainty about a series of boundaries—between North and South, self and other, black and white. In this way the novel may even have stirred doubts about how clear and strong racial difference really was. George Frederickson, Arthur Riss, Caroline Levander, and others have persuasively shown that Stowe's racial essentialism was a deeply rooted, unexamined, and culturally typical assumption.[77] I am not suggesting that Stowe questioned the naturalness of essentialized racial difference. However, *Uncle Tom's Cabin* went further than Stowe's theoretical commitments and beliefs—about race as about novels. It is not only that she planned "three or four" installments and wrote forty-one, but that the writing of her novel exploded some of her own clearly formulated ideas about slavery, race, sympathy, and fiction.[78] Because of the unpredictable dynamic of both writing and reading, her tale quite simply went beyond her.

Wendell Phillips was correct in suggesting that the moment was "ripe" for this book in 1852. Whether or not it directly influenced voting behavior or triggered political activism, it satisfied a deep hunger (and I use the word advisedly). The experience of reading *Uncle Tom's Cabin* left some readers with an admixture of feeling that allowed them to begin imagining slaves as people. Eliza, Tom, and Topsy were not real, but for antebellum white readers they were convincing. Fifty years later, the book's hold over readers had loosened—along with its moral and political thrust.

Late Nineteenth-Century White Readers: Detached

In the 1880s and '90s a new consensus emerged among white Northerners about what *Uncle Tom's Cabin* meant and how it should be read. Late nineteenth-century commentators assumed that contemporary readers would neither weep nor become unduly agitated by Stowe's text.[79] They did not expect or propose that white readers confuse themselves with "bound captives." Indeed, while many writers of Stowe's generation looked back nostalgically at the fervor with which antebellum readers had consumed *Uncle Tom's Cabin,* producing significant results for individuals and the nation, others asserted that "the great emancipation question of a few decades ago" did not sustain "all the old interest" for men and women of the 1890s.[80] But if contemporary readers did not devour the book with "the intensity of other days," at least they could enjoy it "without an expenditure of torture and tears."[81] In the last two decades of the century, Stowe's novel was understood to be a historical artifact, part document, part children's book, a novel that offered both a romantic and a realistic picture of the national past.

In 1892 lynching hit an all-time peak in the United States.[82] Four years later the court decision *Plessy vs. Ferguson* established legal grounds for making segregation a legitimate and widespread social practice.[83] *Uncle Tom's Cabin* served new functions in this context. As new editions proliferated during the 1890s and the turn of the century, adults were encouraged to read the book either for adventure and humor or by keeping their distance—historical, racial, emotional. New introductions, illustrations, and other paratextual material substantially recast Stowe's text, reinforcing racial binaries and neutralizing Stowe's religious, social, and moral emphases. Children's adaptations invited young readers to enjoy a story of white superiority and privilege by downplaying Eva's ethical and spiritual concerns, while making Topsy as incorrigible and purely comic as she became in late nineteenth-century stage productions.[84] Reworked and repackaged, *Uncle Tom's Cabin* turned into a virulently racist book.[85]

Southern commentators of the 1880s and '90s no longer express bitter outrage at the novel. In a characteristic article entitled "Mrs. Stowe's 'Uncle Tom' at Home in Kentucky," published in the *Century* in 1887, the Kentucky novelist James Lane Allen praises Stowe for her benign presentation of slavery. Validating her portrait of devoted servants and "excellent slaveholders," Allen asserts that "well-treated negroes cared not a snap for liberty."[86] In the words of one introduction to a full-length edition of the 1890s, the novel was a "homely plantation story."[87] Writing in *Scribner's Magazine* in 1893, Frances Hodgson Burnett looks back nostalgically at her own childhood reading of *Uncle Tom's Cabin*. Burnett recalls the "swarms of . . . poor slaves" on the plantations as "a picturesque and lovable feature" of the tale. Although she knew in theory that "the story itself demanded" tears, sympathy, and a desire that the slaves "be freed," these "demands" did not dictate her responses. On the contrary, Burnett explains that after reading the novel, she tied her doll to a candelabra stand and "brutally lash[ed]" it until she was red in the face. Her account thus exposes the book's potential for racist violence. Yet for *Scribner's* and its white middle-class reading public, Burnett's scene of childhood whipping was charming imaginative play.[88]

Burnett's description of reading Stowe's novel would have been outrageous, indeed unprintable, in a respectable Northern journal of the antebellum period. We can say the same of an idea proposed by Frank Norris, writing in the *World's Work* in 1902: "Do you think Mrs. Stowe was more interested in the slave question than she was in the writing of [her novel]?" Norris asks. "Her book, her manuscript, the page-to-page progress of the narrative, were more absorbing to her than all the Negroes that were ever whipped or sold."[89] Contemplating slavery through what James Lane Allen called the "telescopic remoteness of human history,"[90] white readers of *Uncle Tom's Cabin* often remained unmoved, or moved in a direction that Stowe had not proposed, and could not have anticipated. However, as the gap widened between Stowe's protocol of reading and the responses of educated white readers, others found new uses for the novel. While some late nineteenth- and early twentieth-century commentators celebrated Stowe's book for helping to abolish slavery, and some read it with nostalgia for gracious life on the plantation, African Americans and other disempowered readers—such as immigrants—reclaimed the book's socially radical potential.

TRANSFORMING UNCLE TOM'S CABIN

"Uncle Tom's Cabin" and the Reading Revolution complicates our understanding of Stowe's novel in cultural context, adding nuance and variety to the story of how it was read. To this end I analyze the responses of a wide range of readers while exploring the book's relation to the generic norms with which it was most associated—sentimental fiction, slave narratives, and children's literature in the antebellum period; history, historical romance, realism, and children's literature in the wake of the Civil War. I devote two chapters to *Uncle Tom's Cabin* as a children's book, and I do so for several reasons. Children have consistently been part of Stowe's audience—at times a significant part. Northerners recommended the book to young people from the moment it appeared. In the twentieth century *Uncle Tom's Cabin* became "a book for children," as Susan Belasco Smith has noted.[91] "No tenement baby should be without its 'Mother Goose,' and, a little later, its 'Little Women,' 'Uncle Tom's Cabin,' 'Robinson Crusoe,' and all the other precious childhood favorites," Dorothy Richardson wrote in 1905.[92] While *Uncle Tom's Cabin* was no "precious childhood favorite" in the South, it had a powerful if spectral presence there as well. Grace King,

a Louisiana writer, claimed in 1888 that Stowe's "hideous, black, dragonlike book . . . hovered on the horizon of every Southern child."[93] The tale appealed to children both before and after the Civil War. Finally, attention to children as readers not only foregrounds the central concerns of this study—reading habits, generic conventions, and race—but also highlights the question of interpretation, especially the role of sympathy, identification, and absorption in the experience of reading. There is good reason to suggest that the book's hold on many white adults has derived in part from the very narrative pleasures to which children and adolescents seem particularly susceptible—suspense, immersion in alternate worlds, identification with otherness.[94]

New prefaces, illustrations, and children's editions—like a new translation of any book into a foreign language—tell us less about the original text than about the culture for which the new version is prepared.[95] By analyzing published commentaries, paratextual material, and readers' accounts alongside neglected details of *Uncle Tom's Cabin,* especially Stowe's representation of reading and children, I raise formal questions that require historical answers. I uncover culturally specific meanings attached to literacy and fiction for both antebellum and turn-of-the-century readers—men, women, and children, black and white.

Chapter 1, "*Uncle Tom's Cabin* in the *National Era,*" begins by tracing the process that enabled Stowe to launch her anti-slavery attack in the form of a novel; it then examines the interplay between *Uncle Tom's Cabin* and the material that surrounded it when published as a series of installments. I argue that *Uncle Tom's Cabin* created its impact by giving new imaginative resonance to well-worn sentimental motifs—dying child, fugitive slave, grieving mother. The excitement generated by *Uncle Tom's Cabin* when it first appeared suggests that readers were as intrigued as discomfited by Stowe's modification of generic norms.[96]

Stowe's image of the literate slave is the focus of Chapter 2, "Imagining Black Literacy: Early Abolitionist Texts and Stowe's Rhetoric of Containment." The literate slave was a staple of early abolitionist texts. In recasting this figure for *Uncle Tom's Cabin,* Stowe on the one hand quieted fears that slave literacy would lead to disruptive desires and actions; on the other she employed scenes of reading to suggest that African Americans possess inner depth—subjectivity. The delicate balance between reassuring images and subversive ones was an important factor in the extraordinary popular success of the novel.

Another significant factor in the antebellum popularity of *Uncle Tom's Cabin* was Stowe's success in disarming a resistance to fiction that was still widespread in literary culture. In Chapter 3, "Legitimizing Fiction: Protocols of Reading in *Uncle Tom's Cabin*," I show that Stowe's model of reading—engaged, imaginative, and thoughtful—helped readers justify an emotionally overwhelming experience of absorption, one that educators, ministers, and others disapproved of. Stowe's scenes of reading, especially Bible-reading, helped legitimize the novel as a literary form at a time when being "lost in a book" was a dubious cultural practice.

Chapter 4, "Beyond Piety and Social Conscience: *Uncle Tom's Cabin* as an Antebellum Children's Book," examines *Pictures and Stories from Uncle Tom's Cabin*, a children's edition of 1853. As a children's book the full-length novel itself was a generic anomaly; respectable children's literature of the period was long on moral maxims and short on excitement or miracles. *Pictures and Stories* challenged interpretive norms more radically than its source, minimizing Stowe's racialized stereotypes and inviting children to identify directly with Harry's danger and rescue as well as Topsy's pain and misbehavior.

In the 1880s and '90s editors, commentators, and the Stowe display at the Columbian Exposition of 1893 showcased *Uncle Tom's Cabin* as a historical document, and as evidence of national achievement. Chapter 5, "Sentiment without Tears: *Uncle Tom's Cabin* as History in the Wake of the Civil War," analyzes the renewed appeal of Stowe's novel in the last quarter of the century. As fiction gained prestige, readers were freer to indulge in the pleasures of novel-reading. But with multiple titles to choose from, many white readers grew indifferent to Stowe's book. By contrast, African Americans read it for personal as well as historical significance.

Chapter 6, "Imagining the Past as the Future: Illustrating *Uncle Tom's Cabin* for the 1890s," focuses on the heightened anxiety about race that informs the very editions which present the novel as evidence of America's moral and social progress. Visual images of devoted servants and "picturesque" Southern scenes imply both a displaced ideal and a prescriptive model for postwar African American men and women. Read as a kind of realism, *Uncle Tom's Cabin* paradoxically offered a nostalgic image of bygone days, while providing white readers with a reassuring model of African Americans as loyal, dependent, and lacking in higher ambition.

By the turn of the century Stowe's text served new cultural ends in the form of a children's book. Chapter 7, "Sparing the White Child: The Lessons of *Uncle Tom's Cabin* for Children in an Age of Segregation," shows how textual revisions in one widely circulated children's edition support a secular, hierarchical, and racist status quo. The *Young Folks Uncle Tom's Cabin* reflects not only a changed understanding of race, but also a changed understanding of children and children's books, as amusement and imagination gained legitimacy in theories of child development. At the same time, this edition includes small but significant signs that black people are gaining limited acceptance as U.S. citizens.

African Americans were ambivalent about *Uncle Tom's Cabin* from the moment it first appeared. Yet, as I suggest in my Epilogue, "Devouring *Uncle Tom's Cabin:* Black Readers between *Plessy vs. Ferguson* and *Brown vs. Board of Education,*" African Americans were among the most engaged consumers of Stowe's book from the 1890s through the first half of the twentieth century. Indeed, at a time when information about slavery was scarce, they sometimes read *Uncle Tom's Cabin* as if their lives depended on it. From James Weldon Johnson and Mary Church Terrell through James Baldwin and Malcolm X, black writers have acknowledged their intensive reading of Stowe. The responses of such African American readers dramatize the cultural and personal significance of reading and help explain the continued vitality of *Uncle Tom's Cabin.*

Reading is shaped by individual as well as cultural history and by a person's experience of literature as well as life. An antebellum white Northerner's concept of a slave was generated primarily by reading. Generic norms and the experience of stories provided an important context for both the initial reception and the changing implications of *Uncle Tom's Cabin.* Between the 1850s and the turn of the century, print culture grew exponentially and, as Eric Lott, Linda Williams, and others have shown, Stowe's novel pervaded Anglo-American culture as theater, song, poster, and game.[97] But our keen awareness of *Uncle Tom's Cabin* as performance and visual artifact threatens to obscure our understanding of Stowe's book as a novel that was avidly read.

In the antebellum United States *Uncle Tom's Cabin* had a lively existence— as a book—in a vibrant culture of reading. Scholars who address the stage-life of Stowe's narrative have effectively traced its liberation from the printed page.[98] In a sense that liberation has been all too complete. Adam Sonstegard suggests that illustrations made Eliza's flight on the ice "an indelible image."[99] However, the episode that culminates in Eliza's escape on the ice would not have grabbed the imagination of illustrators and dramatists without the masterful pacing, dialogue, and verbal imagery of a long episode that only culminates in Eliza's river-crossing. Stowe's words inspired the visual and dramatic versions, not the other way around.[100] Many nineteenth-century readers experienced *Uncle Tom's Cabin* as larger than life—a "wonderful leaping fish," in Henry James's famous phrase—but at the time this experience was *generated* by reading (even for James).[101]

As print culture expanded and visual artifacts proliferated in the 1880s and '90s, advertisements, cartoons, illustrations, and posters heightened public awareness of select episodes and images from the novel, while displacing others. Isolated scenes of *Uncle Tom's Cabin* became increasingly familiar as performed on stage and screen, accompanied with song, dance, and spectacular effects. Readers in the second half of the twentieth century may more readily have associated "Eliza" with a scene from the *King and I* than with the episode Stowe created. Today getting "lost in a book" is no longer a common experience. *"Uncle Tom's Cabin" and the Reading Revolution* takes us back to a time when impassioned immersion in fiction was becoming such a typical reading practice as to be a cause of concern to many people. The history of *Uncle Tom's Cabin* in Stowe's lifetime is also a history of reading.

1

Uncle Tom's Cabin in the National Era
Recasting Sentimental Images

How we can become accustomed to anything!
—*Harriet Beecher Stowe*

Surprisingly little attention has been paid to the interplay between *Uncle Tom's Cabin* and the material that surrounded it when it first appeared as a series of installments in the free-soil weekly the *National Era*.[1] Publishing in that context, Stowe faced a formidable challenge: how to shape an account of slavery that would have a greater impact than the discourse already typical of the abolitionist press. In representing slavery during the 1840s, writers of slave narratives, sermons, poems, and other texts often sought to elicit sympathy from their readers. But abolitionists did not ask their readers to collapse the distance between themselves and the objects of their sympathy. On the contrary—reformers took it for granted that a proper sense of white separateness was crucial to benevolent feelings and actions.[2] *Uncle Tom's Cabin* established emotional identification as a widespread reading practice for consuming the story of slavery. How did Stowe's tale accomplish that end?

Stowe was well aware that neither her facts nor her arguments would be new to readers of the *Era*. In a sense they were all too familiar. By 1851, every issue of the paper included images of fugitives as well as political discussions, religious appeals, and other well-rehearsed attacks on slavery. Abolitionists such as William Lloyd Garrison complained that this flood of print was often greeted only by the "apathy of the people."[3] In designing her narrative, Stowe took up the rhetorical challenge that the Russian formalist critic Victor Shklovsky later called "defamiliarization": how to tell a well-known tale so as to "make it new."[4]

As we know from recurrent scenes of violence in today's news, outrages that cannot easily be remedied can often be ignored. "The best we can do is to shut our eyes and ears and let [slavery] alone," St. Clare remarks in Chapter XIX of *Uncle Tom's Cabin* (328). Earlier in the novel, when Haley the slave trader is unmoved by "the wild look of anguish" on the face of a slave mother whose child he has sold, Stowe's narrator adds: "You can get used to such things too my friend" (208). The numbing of sensibility required to "let [slavery] alone" was a specific obstacle to response that Stowe set out to overcome.

Abolitionist discourse unwittingly contributed to the making familiar that allows one to "get used to" atrocities. Slave narratives, as William Andrews suggests, sometimes "strained for shocking effects that would demand the attention of even the most indifferent reader";[5] yet this tactic itself inured some readers to scenes of violence, while impelling others to avert their eyes. In composing *Uncle Tom's Cabin,* Stowe was determined to break through what she saw as the defenses of readers who could hear about slavery every day, and never "listen." In the words of her narrator Stowe asked herself what the point was of telling "the story, told too oft,—every day told . . . the weak broken and torn for the profit and convenience of the strong! It needs not to be told. . . " (202). Stowe may have felt that the story of slavery was "told too oft" to bear repeating, but she was still impelled to publish her version of the tale. While composing *Uncle Tom's Cabin,* she gave careful thought to the problem of rhetoric: how could she subvert the complacency of contemporary readers, "accustomed to nap and nod under the pulpit," indifferent to sentimental appeals and abolitionist arguments?[6]

By the time Stowe decided to harness the power of fiction to the abolitionist cause, she had given considerable thought to the persuasive potential of imaginative texts, for good and ill. Fiction was not an inevitable choice for Stowe. Indeed, in some ways it was an unexpected departure. She had produced several kinds of writing by 1851—a children's geography, poetry, parables, sermons, literary commentary. She had often warned against the dangers of seductive, irreligious, even merely "amusing" fiction, especially for women, children, and other "impressionable" natures.[7] Stowe understood the lure of exciting tales and believed that the novel was a two-edged sword. This understanding led her to grasp fiction's latent power.

STOWE AND AMERICAN FICTION AT MID-CENTURY

Well before Stowe began to write *Uncle Tom's Cabin* she had read many novels. Her letters and the literary commentary that she published during the 1840s show that she was familiar with Scott, Bulwer, Dickens, George Sand, and others. While composing her narrative, Stowe wrestled with her own ambivalence—her strong reservations about novel-reading, and her passionate investment in it. Despite nagging doubts, she gradually came to believe that fiction had valuable uses under certain conditions.

Stowe had been an avid reader as a child. "At six years of age," Charles Stowe writes in his biography of his mother, "we find the little girl hungrily searching for mental food amid barrels of old sermons and pamphlets stored in a corner of the garret." In this account, "at the very bottom of a barrel of musty sermons" Harriet finds "an ancient volume of 'The Arabian Nights'" which, as Stowe's sister Isabella Beecher Hooker later recalled, Harriet committed to memory and regularly reproduced for her younger brothers at bedtime. "Story-books were rare in those days," Hooker writes, but "ransacking barrels in the garret" Harriet also found "a few odd pages of Don Quixote [a "delicious morsel," in Stowe's own words] which she devoured with eager relish."[8] The imagery of reading as eating in these biographical narratives is thoroughly conventional, but though Charles Stowe (like Carroll Norcross) is careful to mark Stowe's avidly consumed "food" as "mental," there is no mistaking the desire and intensity in his image of the "hungry" girl who "ransacks" the garret and eagerly "devours" what she finds.[9]

Stowe's relation to books and reading was deeply rooted in a concept of subjectivity and spiritual life derived from her literate, Calvinist childhood, where her beloved grandmother was a mediating presence between Scripture and her father's sermons.[10] Those sermons seemed "as unintelligible as Choctaw" to the young Harriet; it was her maternal grandmother who made the stories and characters of the Bible come to life.[11] Stowe's excitement at discovering *The Arabian Nights* beneath a pile of sermons neatly sums up the tensions between religious and secular reading that pervaded young Harriet's world. As Lawrence Buell argues, Stowe's attraction to fiction was complicated by "her evangelical conditioning."[12]

"You speak of your predilection for literature having been a snare to you," Stowe writes to her brother Edward Beecher at the age of eighteen in 1829. "I have found it so myself. I can scarcely think, without tears and indignation, that all that is beautiful and lovely and poetical has been laid on other altars."[13] Like many middle-class women of her generation, Stowe had been forbidden to read novels during much of her childhood. When her father made an exception for Sir Walter Scott, Stowe read him carefully enough to learn many passages by heart.[14] She continued to read him as an adult. In fact she was reading him just before beginning to write *Uncle Tom's Cabin*—only to feel "constantly pursued and haunted by the idea that I don't do anything."[15] Stowe shared many reservations about fiction that were common at mid-century.

During the 1840s Stowe gave considerable thought to the moral and spiritual functions that imaginative literature could serve. Writing in the *New York Evangelist* in 1842, she contrasts the "evil influence" of Bulwer or Byron with the pleasures afforded by Scott. For Stowe, Scott's virtues "almost seemed to redeem [his novels] from the class of lighter literature."[16] "Lighter literature" was a target of attack for both Catharine Beecher and Henry Ward Beecher in the course of the 1840s. But two years before the first installment of *Uncle Tom's Cabin* appeared in the *National Era*, Stowe had found a way to reconcile the idea of holy purposes with the use of fictional techniques. In her "Introductory Essay" to Charles Beecher's *The Incarnation* (1849), Stowe justifies her brother's imaginative reconstruction of Scripture, suggesting that a balance of "truth and fiction," will make the "Sacred Narrative" newly attractive to jaded readers.[17] She defends Beecher's invention of incident, dialogue, and descriptive detail, suggesting that devout, serious, imaginative literature, such as *The Incarnation,* will prevent fervent natures from being seduced by "the strains of a Byron, or the glowing pictures of a Bulwer or a Sue" (iv, ix). Addressing the dangers of reading the wrong kinds of books, Stowe suggests that it is "the want of some proper aliment" that impels young people to seek "strange fire from heathen altars, and cull . . . poisonous fruits and flowers from hot beds of the god of this world" (viii–ix). "There is . . . bread enough and to spare in a Father's house" (ix), she insists, tempering her own erotic imagery: substituting "a Father's house" for "hot beds," and plain "bread" for enticing, but "poisonous [,] fruits and flowers."

Stowe's attack on Byron, Bulwer, and Sue is unsurprising: these writers were much criticized on moral grounds. Henry Ward Beecher condemned

Bulwer "with utter loathing" for making "the English novel-literature more vile than he found it."[18] Using language that effectively competes with the novels he attacks, Beecher comments:

> Novels of the French school, and of English imitators, are the common-sewers of society into which drain the concentrated filth of the worst passions of the worst creatures. . . . These offspring-reptiles of the French mind, who can kill these? You might as well draw sword on a plague, or charge a malaria with the bayonet. This black-lettered literature circulates in this town, floats in our stores, nestles in the shops, is fingered and read nightly and hatches in the young mind broods of salacious thoughts. (210–11)

Beecher was on intimate terms with the texts he denounces—as was Stowe.[19] But in the course of the 1840s Stowe differentiated ever more finely not only between Sue or Bulwer and Dickens but also among the possible ends for which fictional rhetoric could be deployed. By the time she wrote her introductory essay for *The Incarnation* she had come round to the idea that fiction could be legitimate fare even for "many a youthful soul"—if clearly marked as "a proper aliment."

As Buell notes, the novel's uncertain position as a literary form made it impossible for Stowe to "think of herself as a novelist by *vocation*."[20] In justifying her brother's imaginative recasting of Scripture, Stowe anticipated one of the biggest problems she herself would encounter while writing her novel: how to treat serious problems of religious faith and historical reality in a narrative form widely presumed to encourage romantic fantasy, passivity, and idleness. *Uncle Tom's Cabin* was not designed for "the amusement of a passing hour," still less to offer pleasure and excitement.[21] Rather, like Charles Beecher's *Incarnation* it was to be fiction in the service of a higher purpose—religious and historical truth. Stowe took care to foreground that purpose at every opportunity, while freely adapting well-worn fictional strategies to her own ends.

Discussions of Stowe's novel over the last twenty years have emphasized the common ground between *Uncle Tom's Cabin* and other sentimental forms of middle-class culture. As that common ground has become increasingly visible, significant differences in emphasis have been lost.[22] *Uncle Tom's Cabin* echoed, even epitomized, the ubiquitous themes and images of sentimental print culture; but at the same time it modified firmly established reading conventions, as we have begun to see. Stowe wanted her readers to perceive slavery with "new eyes."[23] We might say that she tried to do for her readers what Beecher tried to do in *The Incarnation,* or what Eva does for Ophelia and what Tom begins to do for St. Clare: she offers them a fresh perspective on familiar terrain. For this purpose, Stowe recast familiar sentimental motifs (such as the beautiful moribund child) and reshaped the conventionalized images of fugitive slaves that dominated the news reports, political commentaries, and poetry of the abolitionist press. If we examine *Uncle Tom's Cabin* in the context of the political and literary material that appeared alongside it in the *National Era,* we will be in a better position to understand how Stowe's narrative challenged interpretive norms.

Fiction in the National Era

The *National Era* is not a faithful mirror of antebellum literary culture as a whole, but its potpourri of "high" and "low" genres was typical of abolitionist newspapers as well as periodicals that ranged from mass-circulation dailies to literary "annuals." A disparate array of texts, laid out side by side, was designed to attract a readership of men, women, and children.[24] The *Era's* format—four large pages, seven columns each—characterized many weeklies and dailies. But the place of "literature" in the *Era* was unusual. Garrison's *Liberator, Frederick Douglass's Paper,* the *National Anti-Slavery Standard,* and even the *New York Tribune* tended to print poetry, and sometimes fiction, on the last page of the paper. By contrast, the *Era* placed poems and serialized fiction in a prominent position on page one. Spread out over two, three, and even four columns, the fiction and poetry of the *Era* were not separated from the news in a clearly labeled column at the back; they were interlaced with readers' letters, congressional debates, political speeches and news reports.

What was the aesthetic and political function of literary discourse in the *National Era*? While its poetry sometimes took slavery for a subject, its fiction more often gave its readers a respite from the highly charged issues of the day. Within the abolitionist press generally, fiction played only a minor role in addressing the problem of slavery. In the *Era* itself, fiction assiduously avoided the subject—until installments of *Uncle Tom's Cabin* began to appear.[25] Stowe's novel altered the horizon of expectations for sentimental tales. By creating a dialogue with the texts that surrounded it, *Uncle Tom's Cabin* reshaped the relation between fiction and the network of ideas and images within which it was embedded.

The *National Era* had clearly defined ambitions as both a literary and a political paper. These aims coexisted but did not merge. In November of each year, Gamaliel Bailey, the editor of the *Era*, published an "Annual Letter" encouraging readers to renew their subscriptions. In 1851 Bailey's letter noted that "in conducting the *Era*, I have aimed to give it a two-fold character—that [of] a high-toned Literary paper, and that of a firm, consistent advocate of Human Rights."[26] To judge by the subjects dealt with by the "literary" discourse of the *Era*, Bailey's two aims had very little to do with one another. Although lofty poetry about the value of freedom was a staple of the paper, and satiric poems occasionally addressed the hypocrisy of the church with regard to the fugitive question, fiction only paid attention to "human rights" within the context of family relations: parents, or stepparents who are cruel to their children; children who break the heart of a parent by secretly meeting a lover, by running off to sea, or just by being untruthful or lazy.

Slave issues gained prominence in the *Era* during and after 1850. On January 3, 1850, the first number of the paper for that year, slavery was not mentioned until page 2; but attention to slavery steadily increased as the debate about whether and how to admit new territory to the Union intensified, and as the Fugitive Slave Law was debated, passed, enforced, and resisted. Nonetheless, as Stowe well knew, the fiction of the *Era* did not address and rarely even reflected social or political realities. By writing her anti-slavery work as fiction, she chose a narrative mode so familiar and disarming that it could create a popular sensation while obscuring the depth of the challenge it posed to both social and generic norms. She probably surprised herself as well as others.

If we consider *Uncle Tom's Cabin* in relation to the fiction typical of the *Era*, innovative and neglected features of Stowe's text become visible. With few exceptions the *Era*'s serialized fiction was set in a domestic space, implicitly in America but generally in an undifferentiated, unnamed locale. Cabins in "the woods," a little farm, or an elegant mansion provide the background for tales of saintly children, headstrong youth, or treacherous stepmothers. The fiction is didactic: it tells the reader to be diligent and patient; to obey one's parents, and trust Providence. It stresses the efficacy of individual will and the importance of emotional moderation, whether in love or death. To act impulsively is to court trouble. To mourn excessively is to forget that the dead parent, child, or lover has gone to a better world.

Such stories endorse piety, while suggesting that the realm of the family, like an individual's moral life, could remain untouched by ongoing political turmoil.[27] When the fiction of the *Era* did engage a social problem—such as poverty—it stressed the value of perseverance and humility.[28] If a story mentioned the situation of an immigrant or an abandoned woman, it always implied that the intemperate, careless, or otherwise culpable victim got what he or she richly deserved.[29] If a tale mentioned slavery in passing (which was extremely unusual), the institution was taken for granted as a given.[30] Since the *Era*'s abolitionist views were explicit and pervasive, their absence from fiction is striking.

Until the appearance of *Uncle Tom's Cabin,* a reader of the *Era* could turn to fiction for escape from complexity or doubt. "There is much loose talk about an overruling Providence," Stowe wrote in 1850.[31] Nowhere is such "loose talk" more evident than in the fiction (and poetry) of the *National Era,* where Providence is regularly seen to "work . . . all things well."[32] *Uncle Tom's Cabin* directly challenged the moral messages of the *Era*'s "high toned" literature; it ushered religious doubt, political conflict, and the problem of human rights into installment fiction.

Fictive Norms: Representing the Death of a Child

Untimely death is a recurrent motif in the *Era;* stories and poems repeatedly render a young person's death and offer a clear set of directives for making sense of it. This theme provides a particularly useful lens for reexamining Stowe because it enables us to see how she recast ubiquitous popular clichés.

The good and preternaturally wise child who dies young was represented in obituaries as well as poems and stories. The child who dies is always remarkable: "a child of the fairest promise," of "rare beauty and unusual precocity."[33] She (the child is generally a girl) is imagined as a precious "gem," a shining star, or, more often, a flower: "the fairest, purest, / the heavenliest flower of all."[34] This flower is "blighted" and doomed, but the reader is encouraged to see that the death of the child is for the best: she will be "glad to go where pain is o'er" and will partake of the heavenly glory.[35] Mourning is represented as an inappropriate response in this context.[36] The fact that the victim has achieved "immortal youth" in Paradise is easily borne in upon the bereaved family (or childhood friend).[37]

The very repetition of the dying-child motif suggests it had a wide appeal. One need go no farther than the obituaries of the *Era* itself to see that the stories and poems dealing with this theme drew on a common reality.[38] Stowe's image of beautiful, innocent Eva conformed to a well-known model. But Stowe reworked this popular image for new ends: unlike her analogues, Eva dies of slavery; and her death has significant consequences.[39] Stowe's focus on the reason for Eva's decline constituted a challenge to common assumptions about the appropriate subject matter for fiction. Her emphasis on the impact of Eva's death further complicates the sanguine moral messages of the serials published along-side *Uncle Tom's Cabin* in the *Era*.

The fourteenth installment of *Uncle Tom's Cabin* introduces Eva with an epi-graph that emphasizes her youth, freshness, beauty, and general superiority to the world in which she resides: "A young star! which shone / O'er life—too sweet an image for such glass! / A lovely being scarcely formed or moulded; / A rose with all its sweetest leaves yet folded" (226). A star, a rose, "too sweet" for this world—Eva, like many contemporary heroines, is doomed. Yet Stowe gives the figure of the moribund child additional resonance by raising a question never asked by the other fiction of the *Era:* how do wider social conditions shape the fate of this "scarcely formed or moulded" being?

From the beginning, Eva has the characteristic marks of a rare and other-worldly child whose "dreamy earnestness" and "spiritual gravity" (230) would have made her approaching death obvious to any informed reader of the period.[40] Eva exhibits the typical features of the exceptional child, untouched by her sur-roundings: "Dressed in white, [Eva] seemed to move like a shadow through all sorts of places, without contracting spot or stain" (231). But the similarity between Eva and the *Era*'s other saintly children comes to an end when Stowe shifts her attention from Eva as "unstained" by earthly things, to Eva as shaped by events in this world. This "rose" is "formed and moulded" by a social "blight." She is doomed by slavery, the cruelties of which she is repeatedly required to witness.

The symbolic implications of Eva's illness have been noted by Philip Fisher, Richard Brodhead, and others.[41] The point I want to emphasize here is that Stowe gives Eva's death a derivation unheard of in the stories from which she might seem to emerge. Moreover, while Stowe may have believed that a dying child was indeed going to "a better country" (416), she knew from her own experience that there was no death without suffering.[42] The fiction of the *Era* tended to note a child's suffering only to emphasize that death would bring welcome release. It never dwelled on pain. Stowe, on the contrary, makes Eva's anguish a central focus. With pale cheeks, and "her hands on her bosom," Eva listens to tales about brutally mistreated slaves and "sigh[s] heavily." As she tells Tom, in the recurrent formulation that explicitly links her approaching illness to slavery, "These things sink into my heart . . . they sink into my heart" (326, 347).[43] When, after hearing one such story, Eva "bursts into tears, and sob[s] convulsively" (347), St. Clare responds that "This child . . . ought not to hear any of this kind of thing"; but it is too late. Slavery, Stowe implies, cannot be kept away from Eva. And its consequences should not be kept out of fiction.

Stowe adapts the image of the dying child to new ends by giving Eva's death a social matrix; she also uses the figure of Eva to modify other typical features of the female child in popular tales of the period. Unlike many of her fictional antecedents—"sweet [and] frail," "dreamy, retiring . . . modest,"[44]—Eva is tough-minded when it comes to the most difficult subjects. She speaks frankly of her own death, though no one (except Tom) is willing to listen; and her questions are not "dreamy" or hesitant, but clear and sharp. When her mother complains about how much trouble the slaves cause her (" ' . . . as if we did it for our *convenience,*' said Marie. 'I'm sure if we consulted *that,* we might let them all go at once' ") Eva responds: "What do you keep them for, mama?" (260). This simple question, like the comment of the little boy in "The Emperor's New Clothes," calls attention to a bald fact, which an entire society attempts to deny.

The popularity of *Uncle Tom's Cabin* as a whole, and the figure of Eva in particular, suggests that Stowe's emphasis tapped a widespread desire to move beyond familiar stereotypes. Many readers must have welcomed the chance to hear more about the dying child than her humility and fortunate escape from this world. Stowe's perspective on the question of mourning deserves further attention in this context. In representing the moment of death, as in shaping the figure of Eva, Stowe radically revised familiar terms of discourse.

Just as Eva is initially presented to the reader in the conventional imagery of the too-beautiful-flower, so her death is rendered in language that would have been perfectly familiar to any regular reader of sentimental fiction. Chapter XXVI (installment twenty-five),[45] which describes the death of Eva, is preceded by an epigraph that exemplifies a characteristic perspective on death—there is good reason not to mourn: "Weep not for those whom the veil of the tomb / In life's early morning hath hid from our eyes" (412). Here as elsewhere the finality of death is redefined as a temporary removal from the sight of the living. In representing Eva's end, however, Stowe again recasts familiar tropes, shifting the focus from theoretical consolation to the problem of what remains to the living after the death of a child.

By 1850, as Ann Douglas, Karen Halttunen, and others have shown, representations of mourning often deflected attention from the bald fact of death itself. The fiction and poetry of the *Era,* like the visual iconography of the contemporary graveyard, stressed the regenerative potential of mourning and projected optimistic visions of the hereafter. In rendering the St. Clare household, however, Stowe explores the drama inherent in the very story that the fiction and poetry of the *Era* never pursued. Instead of tying up the loose ends of the episode with reassuring words about immortality, Stowe offers a sharp distinction between the blissful dead and the tortured survivors.

In the *Era,* stories and poems about premature death always ended on the upbeat with a benign plot development to balance the represented loss, or with a consoling message, akin to Stowe's epigraph. In the final lines of one typical poem about a dead girl: "When she wakes another morning / Angel hands will take her up."[46] By contrast, although Chapter XXVI of *Uncle Tom's Cabin* begins by instructing the reader to "weep not" for one who has died young, the chapter ends by underscoring the difficulty of accepting this advice. "Woe for them who watched the entrance into heaven," Stowe writes, "when they shall wake and find only the gray sky of daily life, and thou gone forever" (428). The exceptional nature of this emphasis can be seen if we compare it to the final words of a story that shared a page with Stowe's description of Eva's death.

"James McCary and His Boy" was a tale in two installments. At the end of the final episode the hero and heroine of the story find a poor young orphan who has been abused and abandoned to the cold. He dies in Molly's arms, the word "Mother" on his lips and, in the last lines of the story "when the morning dawned cold and gray, it was over plighted lovers, whose hope stretched goldenly down the future and the dead—untimely perished."[47] The concluding image of love, consummated in the presence of death, emphasizes "hope" and a "golden" future. This finale provides a sharp contrast to the "gray sky of daily life" which ends Stowe's episode. *Uncle Tom's Cabin* emphasizes that for those who remain behind, the sting of Eva's death is unrelieved. In the chapters that follow, moreover, Stowe questions the notion that conventional words of religious solace can be effective at such times.

Uncle Tom's Cabin suggests that Eva's own equanimity in dying will not easily compensate those who survive her. For St. Clare, after Eva's death, "the whole world is as empty as an egg-shell" (435). As the narrator notes, only "the cold mechanical habit of living remain[ed] after all vital interest in it [had] fled" (439). Such words must have come as a relief to many readers for whom—as for St. Clare—reassuring formulas about the immortality of a dead child were less than persuasive. Like contemporary mourning manuals, tales of "consolation" in the *Era* often emphasized that affliction "naturally . . . make[s] us Christians."[48] Stowe's narrative, on the contrary, asserts the lack of any such "natural" or easy quid pro quo. Although St. Clare's spirit begins to heal before his own sudden death, the installment format itself ensured that readers would linger with his pain and doubt. Stowe missed the deadline for December 18, 1851, and the *Era* appeared without an installment of her novel. As a result, readers found themselves with an additional week to contemplate the previous episode: St. Clare full of doubt and unable to pray while reading the Bible with Tom. It is tempting to speculate that Stowe purposely missed her deadline in order to intensify the effect of this installment.[49]

Uncle Tom's Cabin enabled its readers to feel that despair at the death of a child was a natural, rather than a self-indulgent response. If Stowe's representation of Eva's illness and death gave mortality a social frame, her representation of mourning reexamined the advice, at once so facile and so stringent, not to give way to grief. Tears had acquired considerable legitimacy in fiction, sermons, and mourning manuals by 1850; yet the imperative of restraint and resignation remained central, not only in the fiction and poetry of the *Era,* but in such widely read texts as Susan Warner's *The Wide Wide World.* Tears flow copiously in that novel, but the injunction to master one's emotions is emphatic.

Death is a great leveler, but antebellum mourning practices played a major role in middle-class self-definition. As a cultural form, mourning consolidated class distinctions, marked certain kinds of behavior as genteel, and served as a visible barometer of a mourner's moral condition. Unlike middle-class mourners, of course, slaves—who were dying or threatened with death every day—remained outside the loop of conventional behavior associated with burial, consolation, and other polite forms. Ritualized practices shaped the experience of white middle-class death in the antebellum United States. In this, as in so much else, slaves were different.

GENERIC NORMS/MORAL NORMS: REPRESENTING SLAVE MOTHERS

Stowe's representation of bereavement goes well beyond the Eva plot. It is central to her delineation of slave mothers. In depicting the experience of slave women in particular, *Uncle Tom's Cabin* makes the loss of a child the occasion for radical action. Such action ranges from escape to suicide and even infanticide. Stowe challenged both the generic conventions and moral norms of installment fiction with regard to this issue; in doing so she raised questions about the relation between black and white experience. *Uncle Tom's Cabin* thus fused the disjointed aims of Gamaliel Bailey's paper and opened a literary space for the meaningful representation of social and political turmoil.

Stowe's representation of mourning in *Uncle Tom's Cabin* addressed aspects of bereavement that most sentimental fiction avoided. St. Clare's dry eyes and lack of faith challenged religious clichés. Black characters whose responses to death were marked by a lack of restraint challenged social norms. Extreme behavior on the part of bereaved black characters also drew attention to the extraordinary circumstances of slave death. Stowe's rendering of unconventional mourners, especially African American ones, enabled her to defamiliarize mourning, as she defamiliarized the moribund child, and as, most radically, she would defamiliarize the figure of the fugitive.

Chapter XII of *Uncle Tom's Cabin* ("Select Incidents of Lawful Trade") began with the following epigraph: "In Ramah there was a voice heard— weeping and lamentation, and great mourning; Rachel weeping for her children and would not be comforted." This citation from Jeremiah gains its full resonance only in the context of what precedes and follows it, both in the adjacent columns of the paper, and within *Uncle Tom's Cabin* itself. On August 21, 1851, for the first time since Stowe's novel began to be serialized, the *Era* appeared without an episode of *Uncle Tom*.[50] Occupying the first 3 1/4 columns of the paper, in place of Stowe's tale, was the fifth installment of "Ill-Starred," by Patty Lee. This episode of "Ill-Starred" included the death of a

2. *Tom trying to comfort Lucy. From Harriet Beecher Stowe,* Uncle Tom's Cabin. *Boston: John P. Jewett, 1853. Collection of The New-York Historical Society. Negative #83643d.*

baby, accompanied by the narrator's comment: "I marvel sometimes when I see mothers who will not be comforted, mourning for the deaths of their children. They forget that the beauty of immortal youth is theirs. . . ."[51] In the next issue of the paper, the epigraph to *Uncle Tom* ("Rachel weeping for her children") creates a sharp comment on the moral bromides of "Ill-Starred." Stowe's citation implies that under certain conditions there is plenty of reason to be disconsolate.

The installment of *Uncle Tom's Cabin* which begins by referring to Rachel presents two cases of children lost to their mothers—not through death, but through slavery. While pursuing the fortunes of Tom and his new owner Haley, Stowe introduces two distraught slave women: Hagar (whose name with its Biblical source links her to Rachel) and Lucy. Early in Chapter XII, Haley separates Hagar from "her only remaining son" (194) by purchasing the boy at auction. As bystanders strive in vain "to comfort her" (198), the scene shifts to the boat which will transport Haley and his cargo to New Orleans. Here Haley sells Lucy's sleeping infant while her back is turned. As Lucy sits down dizzily, Haley philosophizes: "I know this yer comes kinder hard, at first, Lucy, but such a smart, sensible gal as you are, won't give way to it. You see it's *necessary,* and can't be helped!" When Lucy pleads with him to stop talking ("O! Mas'r, if you *only* won't talk to me now," [209]), Haley cannot fathom Lucy's feelings and does not anticipate her suicide. For J. P. Jewett's gift edition of 1853, the abolitionist illustrator Hammatt Billings amplified this scene with an engraving of Tom trying to comfort Lucy (fig. 2).[52]

Stowe's representation of Lucy and the accompanying illustration complicate two popular themes in fiction of the period: optimism about God's design and fortitude in the face of "necessity." The figure of Lucy justifies extreme behavior born of despair. As we have noted, representations of black children and mothers were conspicuous by their absence in the fiction of the *Era;* when Stowe made them central to her text, she suggested that contemporary tales did not reflect reality. She also extended her attack on facile images of suffering, death, and white mourning.

By sympathetically representing slave women who are driven to defy law and convention, Stowe presents despair and defiance as acceptable responses to injustice and pain. Like Eliza's famous escape over the ice, Hagar's or Lucy's inconsolability gains justification from the fact that slave children and mothers were more likely to experience prolonged suffering than death; even the theoretical comfort of heaven was denied them. In the story of Lucy, or that of Cassy, who kills her child to prevent him from remaining a slave (Chapter XXXIV), Stowe goes much further than she could have gone in representing white characters.[53]

Scholars such as Karen Sanchez-Eppler and Marianne Noble have explored the transgressive satisfactions of white middle-class readers who consumed narratives about the sexuality and abused bodies of black slave women. Given the religious and literary conventions of the period, narratives of African American experience indeed opened windows on events and emotions that were rarely represented as part of white middle-class life. It would surely have been impossible in 1850 to publish a sympathetic portrait of a white woman stripped naked and beaten. Neither a genteel periodical nor an inexpensive story paper would have been likely to print a tale that justified suicide (not to speak of infanticide) among white mothers. Stowe's emphasis on what black mothers could be driven to do needs to be seen in the context of generic expectations and middle-class reading conventions.

Stowe designed such figures as Lucy and Cassy to suggest—and explain, if not affirm—the intensity of violent emotional states. It is eminently likely that readers such as Anna Cushing or Maria Woodbury, schooled to faith and restraint, derived multiple satisfactions from Stowe's representation of slaves expressing anger, pain, despair, or aggression.[54] From alphabet books and conduct manuals through sermons and sentimental fiction, antebellum print culture endorsed the virtues of self-control and self-regulation, especially in women. Stowe's images of slave experience invited readers to identify with modes of behavior that were beyond the everyday experience of white middle-class readers. *Uncle Tom's Cabin* encouraged white mothers to circuit themselves through black ones in order to imagine states of feeling systematically forbidden to them. The pleasure derived from such identifications would necessarily be multiple and complex.

Slave characters such as Hagar, Lucy, Prue, Emmeline, and Cassy dramatize the disjuncture between black and white experience; but some of them also strike a balance between the extreme and the normative. Such a balance may have been designed to deflect the potentially prurient pleasures of voyeuristic identification. The extremes suggested by the most dramatic actions of Lucy or Cassy are contained by other aspects of their behavior. These characters take to drink, die, even kill, but they tend to remain highly self-possessed. Lucy is exemplary in her restrained and dignified mode of expression. Emmeline is exemplary in her modesty. Cassy speaks of having "raved and cursed" when her children were sold (519), but she shows no traces of madness while relating her life history to Tom. Her rhetoric is carefully modulated, often elegant. The most radical actions are offset by proper language. The figure of Eliza provides another counterweight to the unruliest implications of experience among Stowe's slave women. Eliza, intermittently present in the narrative from beginning to end, rarely sheds a tear and altogether behaves like the perfect model of true womanhood. Nevertheless, she breaks the law by running away from her legal owner. Stowe's portrait of Eliza and other slave mothers both fulfilled and challenged the moral norms of white women's behavior as represented in the *Era,* and throughout sentimental print culture.

Reportorial Norms: Representing Runaways

Uncle Tom's Cabin revised not only the sentimental themes and images of installment fiction but also the conventions for representing slaves elsewhere in the

National Era. Although the Fugitive Law was a common point of reference for reporters, editors, and other commentators in 1851, fugitive slaves were skimpily portrayed in the pages of the paper. Stowe believed that the truth about slavery resided in its concrete particulars; these were rendered invisible by the legalistic arguments, heavy-handed irony, and sweeping generalizations characteristic of much abolitionist rhetoric.

In the news reports, letters, and political articles of the *Era,* "fugitives" were constituted by a few fleeting details—the name of the slave's alleged owner, his or her place of capture, passing mention of the slave's activity prior to being arrested. These fugitives are abstract, barely adumbrated figures. They are often as stereotyped as the visual images in advertisements for run-away slaves which could be found in plenty on standardized specimen sheets.[55] Even when the case of a specific fugitive is discussed in the *Era* over a number of weeks—like a story in installments—the case is not presented as the experience of a differentiated human being capable of love, pain, or reflection.[56] Legal issues and the larger moral questions displace individuating detail about a specific man or woman.[57]

Occasionally, to be sure, a news report offers a more detailed account of a specific fugitive, real or imaginary. But with few exceptions, these accounts remain brief, generalized scenarios, which hurry to make a moral point: that a Christian nation should not treat human beings as chattel, or that a "higher law" should be acknowledged. Even when a specific incident is given extended coverage, the figure of the slave who is the occasion for the story remains anonymous, blank, a mere outline. Whether the report involves "a handful of poor negroes" "thirty or forty negroes," or "five persons, two white, Lewis and Hanaway, and three [nameless] blacks," the terms of reference effectively deprive the fugitives of individuality.[58] Sentimental fiction afforded Stowe a battery of rhetorical devices for defamiliarizing slavery. Central to this project was her effort to endow slave characters with voices and feelings—in short, subjectivity. Twentieth-century readers have become increasingly sensitive to the racist assumptions that inform Stowe's slave portraits and to sympathy itself as a coercive dynamic that appropriates and demeans its object.[59] But we underestimate Stowe's courage and originality if we fail to take account of the initial publication context within and for which she designed her plot and characters.

While fugitive slaves were often mentioned in the pages of the *Era,* their voices were almost as absent there as in the legal system. *Uncle Tom's Cabin,* by contrast, suggests that slaves have thoughts, feelings—and voices. Stowe's effort to attribute emotional depth and moral consciousness to the slaves she created relied heavily on white middle-class conceptions of subjectivity, moral norms, and family relations. In this way Stowe departed significantly from the representation of anonymous fugitives not only in runaway ads but in the news reports and political commentaries of the *Era* itself.

"Mr. Rust, who knocked the alleged slave Daniel down, and then chained him as a fugitive, is not yet in possession of 'his property' in spite of all aid rendered by Mr. Commissioner Smith and the Police Justices."[60] This sentence from the *Era* refers to "The Buffalo Fugitive" or "The Buffalo Outrage," an incident in which a fugitive was beaten senseless before being captured. The episode was the focus of considerable attention in the abolitionist press. The report in the *Era* consistently refers to the "alleged slave" in question ("the negro by the name of 'Daniel'"), using italics and inverted commas.[61] These devices are intended to suggest the injustice of the slave's treatment and the problems created by his legal status. The inverted commas around the term "property," and around Daniel's very name, direct irony against a law that defines a man as a thing. Yet these rhetorical ploys also have the effect of denying the fugitive all particularity, not to speak of subjectivity.

The case of the "Buffalo Fugitive" raises the question of whether a slave who escapes after having been brought into a free state by his master can be legally reclaimed or whether, having disappeared from a free state, the man is already free by rights. The editors of the *Era* believed that there were no grounds for returning such a slave to captivity: "undoubtedly by law [this slave] had a right" to leave the boat which had brought him to a free state (140). The cogent issue here is the surprisingly limited arsenal of rhetorical weapons that had become conventional in such reports: To assert the slave's "undoubted" right to freedom in this instance would not persuade anyone who (like Commissioner Smith) believed that *"a master has a perfect right to take his slave into or through a free state, and we as citizens of Free States are bound to protect the rights and the property of people in the South"* (140). The *Era* italicizes this statement by the commissioner in order to ridicule it—as if its absurdity is patently obvious. But its absurdity is obvious only to those who already agree with the *Era*'s view of the case.

The tactical use of inverted commas and italics as well as other modes of punctuation became routine in attacks on the legal commonplaces of slavery.[62] Another passage about "The Buffalo Fugitive" cites Commissioner Smith as follows: "*A man has a perfect right to bring his slave into a free state and it does not enfranchise him* (!)" (140). The exclamation point, placed in parenthesis after the commissioner's italicized statement is designed to mock his claim. Such devices implied irony; they were to trigger a familiar set of associations in like-minded readers. But the limited range of diacritical marks employed as a kind of shorthand for this purpose by the *Era* had little power in shaping an argument, and still less in creating the sense of a fugitive as a particular person.

We "are alternately shocked by the inhumanity of the commissioner and amazed by his ignorance of the law which he undertook to administer," the article notes. "The common reader will at once confess the inhumanity. The barefaced ignorance we shall easily expose" (140). Presuming the "inhumanity" to be self-evident to the "common reader" (apparent "at once"), the article passes over it, and proceeds to make a detailed case for the idea that local and municipal law should determine relations between owner and slave (140). "Daniel" himself, having been given no words, thoughts, or actions to begin with, now disappears from the report.

Stowe attempted to grab the attention of jaded readers by reshaping the horizon of expectations for fictions of black experience. Just as she created a new function for the image of the moribund white child and bereaved parent, so she transformed the perfunctory representation of slaves typical of the abolitionist press. Many images of slaves were clichés by 1850—the male fugitive with a bundle on his back, the female fugitive with a child in her arms, the dogs in pursuit of a slave at bay.[63] Stowe urges her reader to become acquainted not with a "handful of negroes" or a silent, depersonalized "fugitive named Daniel" but with "our old friend Eliza," and "our humble friend Tom." The most important black characters of *Uncle Tom's Cabin* embody ideals of white middle-class behavior, including gratitude and self-control.[64] However, many of these characters invite the reader's identification precisely where white norms of behavior are abrogated. As we have already seen, white antebellum men and women often accepted the invitation, becoming "bound captives" to the reading experience.

POETIC NORMS: FUGITIVES AND OTHERS

One additional framework for representing slavery in the *Era* repays attention. Well before 1851, poetry had become a forum for rendering imaginary scenarios that involved fugitives as well as slave-catchers and other representatives of the white community. The poetry of the *Era* was often as flowery, didactic, and pious as its installment fiction; yet the subject matter of poetry was broader. As the "highest" of the literary genres, poetry was widely presumed to be suited to lofty subjects—such as freedom. Poetic celebrations of freedom are frequent in the pages of the *Era* between 1850 and 1852, but the language of these texts remains highly abstract. Many a "Liberty Ode" castigates "foul oppression's night" and praises "freedom" without mentioning slavery at all.[65]

As Susan Belasco Smith has noted, one recurrent focus for the theme of liberty in this period was the revolution in Hungary, which brought Louis Kossuth to New York and stimulated much discussion of America as a haven for Hungarian exiles ("Ho! to the brave and noble band, / To Hungary's cause so tried, and true, / Columbia stretches forth her hand— / There's room for each, for all of you").[66] This theme became so pervasive in prose as well as poetry that some commentators, including Stowe herself, noted the ironic distance between the image of the noble European fugitive, and his persecuted American counterpart.[67] More often, however, this analogy was not underscored. In poetry, as in fiction, the *Era* refrained from addressing contemporary social problems directly, unless (as with events in Hungary) they could become the occasion for an expression of exemplary moral, spiritual, or patriotic ideals.[68]

However, the *Era* did publish some poetry that (unlike its fiction) directly addressed the problem of slavery. Such poems took a variety of forms. They ranged from urgent appeals to the North for political action ("Ho!. . . . New England's sons! /. . . . Come forth! ye chosen ones, / . . . to rend the curtains / Of slavery's brooding night"[69]) to satires of hypocritical clergymen. Poems in the former mode were often dominated by abstractions ("freemen," "battle for the right," "redemption drawing nigh"). Satiric poems, on the other hand, were often so coy or so broad that (like the rhetoric of news reports) they would appeal only to readers who were already convinced. In John Greenleaf Whittier's "A Sabbath Scene," for example, a minister throws a Bible at an escaped fugitive to trip her in the aisle of a church: "Of course I know your right divine / To own and work and whip her; / Quick deacon, throw that Polyglott / Before the wench, and trip her!"[70] This turns out to be a nightmare from which the speaker of the poem awakens at the end; the dream conceit made it all the easier for a pro-slavery reader to dismiss the represented events as exaggerated.

The anti-slavery poetry of the *Era,* whether exhortatory or satiric, formed a relatively repetitive array of verse. From within this array, however, a few texts stand out. Occasionally, poetic narratives created slave figures capable of thought and action. Some poems in this category even attempt to render a black character's voice. Such texts helped prepare the ground for Stowe, directly or indirectly.

The speaker of "The Slave—A Tableau" is a slave parent, on the verge of running away. He (or she; the speaker's gender is not clear) declaims a series of reflections as follows:

> The stream is free, that courses through our vales
> The waves whose music breaks upon the shore—
> Why should I be thus doomed to wear a chain?
> . . .
>
> What hopes and fears now crowd my aching brain?
> As by our sleeping breasts our children lie!
> To make us free, does Night now pour her strain,
> For which the stars are beckoning in the sky?
> . . .
>
> We snatched our babes, so young and fair. . . .
> O! keep the bloodhounds from our tear-stained track![71]

If this poem attempts to create the feel of spontaneous speech, it is hamstrung by the literary convention of dramatic monologue and the constraints of its rhythm and meter. The poem's elaborate focus on the backdrop of benign Nature further disrupts any sense of immediacy in the speaker's voice. Still, unlike news reports, such poetry did attempt to motivate the action of a fugitive from within. Relying on the sentimental image of a threatened domestic idyll, the poem proposes an analogy between black and white experience. It asks the reader to recognize the speaker's painful situation, to believe that a slave has words and feelings.[72] The elevated language itself makes a claim for the slave speaker as human and literate.

Occasionally, a poem about a fugitive went further in the direction that Stowe herself would soon take. One such poem was published in the *Era* on April 24, 1851, ten weeks before the first installment of *Uncle Tom's Cabin.* A forceful text in its own right, it deserves analysis because both its language and its themes may have inspired Stowe as she began to write her novel. "The Wanderer," by M. Hempstead was a narrative poem in twenty-one verses.[73] It creates an effect quite different from the *Era*'s bitingly satiric portraits of white hypocrisy, or its occasional poetic efforts to render a fugitive's voice. Unlike poems such as "The Slave—a Tableau" with its literate speech, high-flown rhetoric, and elaborate imagery, the language of "The Wanderer" is colloquial; its rhyme scheme is simple. Its primary speaker briefly sets the scene and proceeds to represent a conversation between a minister and his "little daughter." "Father," she asks, "When you told us about Daniel, / How he would not cease to pray, / Tho a law was made against it— / It was righteous, did you say?" (lines 7–12). The girl's question leads her father to affirm the notion of "a higher law than human" (line 25)—a familiar argument to opponents of the Fugitive Law. The child in the poem bows her head in silent understanding, and her voice disappears from the text at this point. But when a servant enters the room to tell the father that " . . . there is a stranger woman / Wants to see you at the door; / So forlorn a human being / Never did I see before" (lines 37–40), the little girl presses her cheek "close against the window pane" (lines 44) in order to observe the stranger. This child is more marginal to the action than the figure of Eva in *Uncle Tom;* but, like Eva, she is a witness to subsequent events and provides a kind of "natural" morality against which to evaluate them.

The minister sends for the stranger (" 'None have ever sought in vain / At my hand,' replied the master" [lines 46–47]). It soon turns out, however, that the stranger is a fugitive: "Save me! for the love of Heaven, / Save me!" (lines 61–62) the woman cries, as her "searching glance" discerns "moving figures in the distance" (lines 65–66). The minister now refuses to help her: " 'God protect you,' said the pastor, / 'For I cannot grant you aid; / Evil times are fallen upon us, / When such brutal laws are made; / But it is the will of Heaven / That our rulers be obeyed' " (lines 73–78). Unlike the self-righteous figures often mocked by the *Era*'s satiric pieces, this minister is torn: "O, the gaze of speechless anguish! / O the heart-wrung woman's wail! / As the hunted slave flew onward, / Made his very heart to quail— / Made his very hair to stiffen / And his face turn ashy pale!" (lines 77–84) The narrative now pursues the fugitive, introducing two additional characters, and adding another moral level with a few economical strokes: "When the moon arose that evening / On the evil and the good / Two poor tenants of a hovel, / That beside a forest stood, / Found the hunted woman lying / Where they went to gather wood" (lines 91–96). This couple takes the fugitive in, and tends her until she dies. The parish then provides a coffin and a grave. The pastor presides at the funeral but "his language fail[s him]" (line 110). In the last three verses, the narrator celebrates the actions of the poor couple and adjures the reader to have sympathy for the minister:

> In his ear a wail is ringing
>> And he hears it everywhere
> Hears it in his quiet parlor
>> Hears it on the pulpit stair
> O, entreat this pastor kindly
>> For he has enough to bear!
>
> But for that poor hovel's inmates
>> When they thither turned again,
> Well they knew it was an angel
>> That upon their bed had lain
> For it lighter seemed, and softer
>> To their weariness and pain.
>
> And their frugal bread seemed sweeter
>> To their hunger than before—
> Warmer was the sullen hearthstone,
>> Smoother was the broken floor,
> And they loved each other better,
>> Loved their God and neighbor more. (Lines 121–38)

Stowe was already working on *Uncle Tom's Cabin* when this poem appeared in the *Era* on April 24. In a letter to Bailey, written on March 9, Stowe explained that she had begun work on an anti-slavery sketch for his paper.[74] Bailey announced the forthcoming serial on May 8 (though the first installment did not in fact appear until June 5).

Whether or not Stowe read "The Wanderer," its innovations for representing slavery point in the direction of her text. Like *Uncle Tom's Cabin*, "The Wanderer" stresses the moral consequences of slavery for everyone involved. With its evangelical emphasis it attempts to create an empathic perspective not only on the fugitive, but also on the minister, and the poor couple. Stylistically, the poem has a simple and dramatic narrative line; its story is told alternately through dialogue and through the words of an omniscient narrator who (like Stowe) sometimes exhorts the reader ("O, entreat this pastor kindly" [line 125]), sometimes heightens the drama with vivid descriptions ("Made his very hair to stiffen / And his face turn ashy pale!" [lines 83–84]), and sometimes renders an action in succinct and prosey language ("but the door was shut and bolted / And the fugitive was gone" [lines 85–86]).

Unlike the minister, whose language "fails" him, this poem achieves some powerful rhetorical effects while anticipating many of the structural imperatives Stowe was in the process of grasping: the need to strip the slave situation of lofty generalities; to situate the action in a recognizable America rather than in Africa, Europe, or a dreamscape; to eliminate unrelieved caricature when representing those who uphold the fugitive law; to give ample time and space for developing the portrait of human relationships and dramatic conflicts; to differentiate among the voices of the actors in the tale; to leave certain problems unresolved, encouraging the reader to ponder.

"The Wanderer" challenged some conventional images and rhetorical strategies characteristic of the abolitionist press. Nonetheless, like most fiction and poetry of the *Era,* this versified drama is set in an unnamed locality, not a specific village or state of the Union. Moreover, the fugitive here remains a victim, dependent on others and unable to achieve her goal at any level. She is an occasion for demonstrating the appropriate behavior of the white world on which she is dependent.

It remained for Stowe to make the figure of the fugitive both more radical and more accessible in a work of fiction, thereby engaging the attention of undecided and even resisting readers as well as those with incipient or declared abolitionist sympathies. The popularity of *Uncle Tom's Cabin* sparked increased circulation for the *Era.*[75] Stowe elicited intense responses in a complacent reading public by making slavery "new" in multiple ways. In the course of an unusually long serialized narrative (*Uncle Tom's Cabin* ran for over ten months, when a two- or three-month serial was common), Stowe created a framework for complicating a set of political, religious, and literary norms. Devoting ample attention to the desires, pain, and doubts of her black characters, she modeled her African American figures on a familiar idea of human beings. Insofar as characters such as Eliza and George exemplify widely accepted virtues of white middle-class behavior, they were all the more attractive to white readers of the 1850s. But Stowe also allows them numerous thoughts and actions that violate civic laws and social norms.

Uncle Tom's Cabin ultimately affirms many of the moral, social, and rhetorical conventions that it challenges along the way. But it gave its initial readers ample time and imaginative space to contemplate destabilizing ideas and images. Stowe's emphasis on sympathy and religious faith kept the most radical implications of her vision in check. But in representing slave bereavement, language, and action, Stowe both catered to and radically revised the expectations of sentimental readers. It was this complicated balancing act which made her novel such a paradoxical institution: a popular sensation with a revolutionary impact.

Stowe employed one additional device for defamiliarizing slave experience as white antebellum readers imagined it: throughout *Uncle Tom's Cabin* the image of the literate slave complicates common assumptions about what a slave can do and be. Karen Sanchez-Eppler and Marcus Wood have argued that in *Uncle Tom's Cabin* the radical potential of imagining black literacy remains unfulfilled—while Tom haltingly begins to read and write, Stowe's valorizing of middle-class altruism and evangelical Christianity ensures that authority and agency remain in the hands of white characters.[76] But in representing slave literacy, as in representing slave bereavement, language, and action, Stowe at once catered to and challenged the expectations of sentimental readers. In order to appreciate the power of slave literacy as imagined in *Uncle Tom's Cabin,* we need to re-examine the figure of the reading slave, not only as Stowe presents him (the slave is generally a man) but as situated in the wider context of antebellum assumptions and anxieties about black reading. The literate slave deserves a chapter of his own.

2

Imagining Black Literacy
Early Abolitionist Texts and Stowe's Rhetoric of Containment

> "Give a nigger an inch, he will take an ell . . ."
> —*Frederick Douglass' Narrative*

This chapter examines Harriet Beecher Stowe's depiction of literacy against the background of widely shared antebellum assumptions about African American readers, and about literacy as a social practice. In *Uncle Tom's Cabin* Stowe revised several well-known images of literate slaves. Her representation of Uncle Tom's Bible-reading, George Harris's conversion to Christian and domestic literacy, and Topsy's evolving relation to reading all addressed growing fears that literacy was a Pandora's box,—"if you give a nigger an inch, he will take an ell" in the infamous words of Frederick Douglass's master, Hugh Auld.[1] Stowe's image of pious and peace-loving African American readers offered welcome reassurance to white readers in an increasingly polarized society, fraught with violence.

In abolitionist texts of the 1830s and '40s, literacy has distinctly disruptive consequences. By 1851, when installments of *Uncle Tom's Cabin* began to appear in the *National Era,* numerous slave narratives had established a link between literacy and escape or rebellion. Abolitionist fiction, such as Richard Hildreth's *The Slave* (1836), had reinforced the notion that the slave who learned to read and write would be "the first to run away."[2] In Frederick Douglass's *Narrative* literacy is crucially linked to individualism, but also to political goals. Stowe's emphasis on literacy as a "civilizing" practice that would serve the cause of faith and domesticity helped make *Uncle Tom's Cabin* far more popular than earlier abolitionist texts. At the same time, however, Stowe's representation of black literacy itself had a radical thrust: insofar as white Americans increasingly associated the act of reading with intellectual potential, moral depth, and meaningful interiority, Stowe's images of African American characters with books in their hands—and Republican as well as Biblical texts in their memories—suggested a link between literacy and subjectivity with important implications for the idea of slaves as people (neither beasts of burden nor property). As Christopher Castiglia and Julia Stern note, "the interior is not transparent, but is a construction that must be reached through the mediation of language and representation."[3] The image of a slave in the act of reading (especially reading the Bible) posited black interiority; at the same time it minimized the disruptive potential of this idea.

During the first two decades of the nineteenth century, Bible-reading was widely believed to encourage obedience and docility in slaves. Thus it was seen as a skill worth imparting to them (as to women and children). After slave rebellions of the 1830s, however, many people came to feel that literacy, even when restricted to Bible-reading, could have unforeseen results. Consequently, in many sections of the United States laws were passed making it illegal to teach a slave to read.[4] Representations of Tom with his Bible or George Harris among his bookshelves challenged the notion that African Americans were fit only for enslaved labor in the cotton field. The highly literate George Harris runs away from his master; he is prepared to kill for his freedom. Yet the image of Tom or Topsy with the Bible simultaneously told white readers that slave literacy would lead to faith and self-control, not violence. The competing implications of slave literacy played themselves out both in Stowe's language and in early illustrations of the novel.

Hammatt Billings, an illustrator with abolitionist sympathies, produced six illustrations for the first edition of *Uncle Tom's Cabin* (1852) and over a hundred for a lavish holiday edition that appeared in time for Christmas, 1852.[5] Billings's illustrations extended Stowe's emphasis on literacy, providing numerous images of black and white characters who write and read, sometimes seated together in close physical proximity. By repeatedly picturing Tom in particular with a Bible in his hand, Billings's much reprinted illustrations endorsed and elaborated Stowe's image of slaves as people who used the Bible as a guide not only to religious faith, but also to human relations and moral action. Like Stowe, Billings employed scenes of reading strategically as a way of rendering black privacy, subjectivity, and moral autonomy. Billings was in a sense Stowe's "ideal reader"— one who not only grasped her moral and political messages but also contributed to their circulation through print culture.[6]

Many of Stowe's scenes of reading dramatize the subordinate and "lowly" position of her slave figures. Little George Shelby and Eva are undeniably Tom's masters as well as his teachers.[7] Nonetheless, slave literacy had radical potential in 1852. Scenes of reading in which Uncle Tom ponders a text, even struggles with it, dramatize the obstacles under which he has labored to become literate. But when Billings shows Tom "sweating over his Bible," in Marcus Wood's evocative phrase,[8] it is neither to make a mockery of his desires and capacities, nor to put Tom's limitations on exhibit, but to ask whether barriers to learning are natural, just, and irrevocable. Such images invited white antebellum readers to think about why some people read while others don't, and to ask themselves why reading matters. For Stowe and Billings, at least, that was an important point.[9]

THE "DANGEROUS EXCITEMENT" OF LITERACY

Literacy was the linchpin of moral and economic self-improvement in the ante-bellum United States; it was a crucial component of citizenship.[10] Scenes of reading (and writing) throughout *Uncle Tom's Cabin* represent literacy as both a moral force and a practical skill. Stowe repeatedly cites and foregrounds the Biblical text as a touchstone to evangelical themes.[11] However, her representation of reading also has a place in a secular design, especially in the context of contemporary prohibitions on slave literacy. Not only freedom-seeking slaves, but also free blacks in the urban North believed literacy to be a powerful, even life-saving asset.[12] Indeed, as Dana Nelson Salvino notes, "at a time when literacy had become 'secularized' and magnified in its cultural efficacy. . . . then especially were blacks denied access to literacy."[13] A slave with a book was a provocative image in the antebellum United States.

One of Stowe's central aims in *Uncle Tom's Cabin* was to attack the slave system without inciting violence. The successful revolution that made Haiti an independent state in 1804 was taken as a grim warning by American slave holders. Bloody confrontations between abolitionist and anti-abolitionist activists as well as between slaves and masters increased in the United States throughout the 1830s and '40s. These conflicts provided an important context for reading about slaves and slavery across the United States. As Ezra Tawil puts it, "the specter of slave insurrection and 'race war' . . . haunted the discourse about slavery during the first half of the nineteenth century, and [was] a particularly menacing prospect after the Nat Turner rebellion of 1831."[14] Philip Lapsansky notes that graphics depicting "benign scenes of industrious freedmen" were among the rhetorical devices employed by abolitionists to "promote emancipation as safe, to counter the fears of slave violence raised by their opponents. Anti-abolitionists never let anyone forget that the decade of the 1830s began with the bloody Nat Turner insurrection, often attributed to the fiery pamphlet of black Bostonian David Walker."[15] In a lecture of 1853, Stowe's husband, Calvin Stowe, proposed promoting the sale of "only free-grown cotton" in order to abolish slavery by peaceful means. He emphasized that the alternative—which no one wants "to hear of"—is "a bloody revolution."[16]

Uncle Tom's Cabin went well beyond proposing economic boycott and passive resistance as responses to slavery—it advocated defiance of the Fugitive Slave Law. Still, the novel was to inspire men, women, and children with revulsion from slavery without promoting disorder elsewhere in the social scheme. "Violent rebellion," as Nancy Bentley puts it, "is precisely what the novel is meant to prevent."[17] If *Uncle Tom's Cabin* was a radical text, it was, as Jane Tompkins and others have emphasized, a utopian vision, not a political program.[18] Designed to instill or revitalize religious faith, it aimed to activate the white reader's emotions, moral imagination, and personal conscience through the experience of reading. Not surprisingly, the reading experience is also a recurrent theme within the book. Stowe's image of slave literacy contributes significantly to that theme.

In *A Key to Uncle Tom's Cabin* Stowe asserts that the set of laws designed to prevent slave literacy is "more cruel than any which ancient and heathen Rome ever knew. . . . The master in ancient Rome, might give his slave whatever advantages of education he chose . . . and the state did not interfere to prevent."[19] *A Key* explains the resistance to slave literacy as follows: "It has been foreseen that the result of education would be general intelligence; that the result of intelligence would be a knowledge of personal rights . . . [which] would be fatal to the system. . . . the example of educated and emancipated slaves would prove a dangerous excitement to those still in bondage."[20] *Uncle Tom's Cabin* is designed in part to counter arguments about the "dangerous excitement" of literacy.

Two texts published in 1836 provide a useful starting point for clarifying that dangerous excitement as represented in abolitionist discourse during Stowe's formative years as both fiction-writer and abolitionist. *The Slave's Friend,* a periodical for children launched by the American Anti-Slavery Society, and *The Slave; or, Memoirs of Archy Moore,* a novel published anonymously by Richard Hildreth the same year, gave literacy a central role in the case against slavery.[21] Both publications assert the intellectual potential of black men, women, and children by emphasizing the existence of black readers (and writers) in the United States, the Caribbean, and England. However, in both *The Slave's Friend* and *The Slave* (as in many slave narratives) literacy has unsettling results. It does not lead directly or exclusively to piety, nor is it confined to a supporting role in maintaining the order of the family or other patriarchal strongholds. Attention to early antebellum images of slave literacy can help us see how Stowe's redefinition of black literacy as a boon to religion and domesticity (rather than to autonomy or political action) assuaged mounting anxieties within the white reading public. Stowe's representation of slave literacy thus helps account for the popularity of *Uncle Tom's Cabin* in the antebellum period. At the same time, Stowe's scenes of reading harbored radical implications of their own.

The Slave's Friend: Literacy, Violence, and Disobedience

The short-lived children's periodical *The Slave's Friend* is especially useful in exploring the literary "horizon of expectations" shared by many of Stowe's first readers. Like *Uncle Tom's Cabin, The Slave's Friend* was an abolitionist text that made children a touchstone for the moral health of the nation. Like *Uncle Tom's Cabin, The Slave's Friend* directly addresses children, and amply represents them. Although there is no evidence that Stowe read *The Slave's Friend,* she very likely encountered it. As part of the American Anti-Slavery Society's pamphlet campaign, it was mailed directly to ministers and other individuals whose names and addresses were available on published lists.[22] But whether or not Stowe read the little journal, many themes and strategies of *The Slave's Friend* anticipate and clarify her rhetorical choices, especially her representation of black and white children using literacy.

The Slave's Friend promoted immediate abolition through nonviolent means. Violence, however, was generously represented in its pages. Through-out *The Slave's Friend* numerous stories and "eyewitness" accounts of the Caribbean attest to the benign results of interracial coexistence, but the question of whether vengeful violence will follow emancipation is consistently present in the background—and sometimes in the foreground: "Now I hear a little boy or girl saying 'What a dangerous thing that was—to set so many people free *all at once* [in Antigua]! They must have cut their masters' throats and killed all the children.' Not at all, my little readers! They went and shook their masters' hands and wished them happy day . . . went to meeting and praised God."[23] Fear of revenge, so graphically introduced, is not easily dispelled by the image of a handshake and a prayer. The alternative lingers in the imaginary field. Moreover, the reader of *The Slave's Friend* is never allowed to forget that the contemporary United States itself is the source of violent activity: slave traders throw starving boys and girls off a ship when supplies are low in the course of the middle passage;[24] traders who have stolen little children weigh them like chickens or coffee and sell them accordingly; plantation owners whip young slaves without mercy.[25] Anti-abolition violence also runs rampant.

Antebellum discourse did not lack chilling imagery or representations of violent events. News reports, story papers, and polemical abolitionist texts such as David Walker's "Appeal" or Theodore Welds's *Slavery As It Is* pulled no punches. These were not designed for family reading, however, and certainly not for children. *The Slave's Friend* blurred the boundaries between acceptable and unacceptable subjects for representation, especially for the young. Violence was common in children's tales of the 1830s and '40s, but it also elicited criticism. In one typical formulation the anonymous author of *The Mother's Friend* suggests that children should "as far as possible [be] guarded from everything likely to excite sudden alarm or to terrify the imagination."[26] The demise of *The Slave's Friend* was probably hastened by the economic depression and panic of 1837; but its violent content and controversial support for immediate abolition had limited appeal, and its framing of literacy as a tool of youthful rebellion probably did not help matters.[27]

Uncle Tom's Cabin too spoke to children, represented children, and emphasized the value of reading.[28] But *The Slave's Friend* went much further than Stowe would go in using a popular printed form to challenge authority structures at a time when obedience was a central aim of education.[29] Insofar as

3. Eva and Mammy reading. From Harriet Beecher Stowe, Uncle Tom's Cabin. *Boston: John P. Jewett, 1853. Collection of The New-York Historical Society. Negative #83644d.*

The Slave's Friend purveyed moral messages and information about the world while engaging children in an active dialogue, its objectives accord with the aims of many antebellum educators. However, *The Slave's Friend* is pervaded by a tension between two opposing scenarios—one that centers on dutiful, well-behaved boys and girls, and another in which both black and white children, using literacy, offer a serious challenge to things as they are.

In *Uncle Tom's Cabin,* Stowe walked a fine line, advocating the controversial practice of teaching slaves to read, yet reassuring her own readers that slave literacy would only strengthen the religious community and the norms of domestic life. When little George Shelby teaches Tom to read and write, it is with his mother's blessing. When Stowe first introduces Uncle Tom to the reader he is bent over his slate, writing with George's help. Later in the novel, Eva urges her mother to give the slaves on the St. Clare plantation direct access to the Bible. When Marie refuses, Eva quietly takes matters into her own hands and begins to teach Mammy her letters (fig. 3).

The image of Eva advocating slave literacy served Stowe's abolitionist agenda. However, it did not constitute a significant challenge to the status quo. The importance of children to the future of the nation was a commonplace of antebellum political ideology; the idea that children could teach adults certain things was an integral part of antebellum educational theory.[30] While Eva prods her father toward political activity by referring him to the Biblical text and disobeys her mother by coaching Mammy, Eva is never confrontational in relation to her parents. Like the Senator's wife, Mrs. Byrd, Eva trusts to the power of example and the influence of love to work moral transformations in others.[31] By contrast, *The Slave's Friend* urges its young readers to take an active, even aggressive part in social change.

The intended child readers of *The Slave's Friend* are repeatedly told that, unlike slave children, they themselves can do much; indeed, they can change the world. *The Slave's Friend* encourages white children to believe in their own creative agency; not to be deterred because they feel weak or small. Like a single raindrop which becomes a "cool refreshing shower" when merged with other drops, the activity of a child, especially when joined with the efforts of other children, can have a significant impact on a society (mis)shapen by adults.[32] Children are enjoined to organize in groups, spread the word, and raise money for the cause.[33] More than that: they are to seize the initiative and boycott the products of slave labor—a more radical suggestion when proposed in a children's periodical of the 1830s than in Calvin Stowe's British lecture of 1853.[34] Children are told to persuade their parents to buy beet sugar and other products which can be had "without making the poor slave work fourteen or eighteen hours a day to cut and grind the sugar canes."[35] They are told "[you can] influence your parents, and persons who are older than you"; they are even invited to correct their elders: "Did you ever hear any person say that negro children had no minds and couldn't learn to read and write? If you ever hear them say this again, you can *tell them that you know better,* and that if colored children can learn to read in Antigua, they can learn to read in America" (my emphasis).[36]

I do not want to overstate the threat of disorder posed by little white reformers. *The Slave's Friend* consistently promoted discipline and faith along with an end to the peculiar institution. Yet most children's literature stressed the importance of obeying legitimate authority and the dire consequences of disobedience, while emphasizing the sanctity and safety of the home. By contrast, the represented world of *The Slave's Friend* contains an ever-present specter of danger and disorder, for which adults, not children, are to blame. The threat of brute force is directed not only against kidnapped African children and American slaves but also against budding abolitionists. Although young readers of *The Slave's Friend* are reminded to be thankful that they themselves occupy a more privileged position than African children, they are primed to become supporters of the cause and so they too are in danger. *The Slave's Friend* devotes considerable attention to the story of the Reverend Elijah Lovejoy, whose printing press was destroyed and who was murdered by a mob because he "did his duty" and pleaded for "the poor slaves."[37] "God meant that [black people] should learn to read, and read the Bible, but the slaveholder says No, you shall not learn to read nor write. They whip anyone the first time he dares to teach them, and the next time they hang him!"[38] Recurrent illustrations include images of long Bowie knives inscribed with "death to abolition."

The Slave's Friend invites its young readers to join a righteous community unfairly threatened every moment from without. This community, held together by bonds of conviction and faith, is conceived in opposition to widely accepted authority figures. Abolitionist tales for children often emphasized the contrast between the servitude of slaves and the liberty of the white child. But, as Karen Sanchez-Eppler points out, the "liberty described is one projected into the future," not one available to white children within the hierarchical structure of the family.[39] On the pages of *The Slave's Friend*, the option of disobedience thus loomed large. Both black and white children might use their new-found knowledge and the practice of literacy itself to challenge conventional restraints. Who was to say whether such challenges to authority would stay within the confines of the abolitionist cause?

Throughout *The Slave's Friend* images of literate black children suggest that emancipation would bring benefits to all. Descriptions of peaceful, racially integrated cultural activities in the Caribbean provide a distinct counterpoint to what Anthony Maingot has called the "terrified consciousness of the Caribbean"—the widespread awareness of the bloody revolution that turned the French colony of Saint Domingue into Haiti.[40] As Franklin Knight points out, the "Haitian model of state formation drove xenophobic fear into the hearts of all whites from Boston to Buenos Aires and shattered their complacency."[41] Representations of assiduous black readers in Antigua or Barbados (where a major insurrection took place in 1816) endorse hallowed American values such as punctuality, diligence, and discipline, while suggesting there is no danger in freedom or education, whether in the Caribbean or in the United States.[42] "When people love to learn to read so well, how cruel it is to prevent them!"[43]

The Slave's Friend promotes the civilizing influence of literacy with numerous examples: "little negro children" who have recently been freed, and who read the Bible with devotion, are able to "tell about David and Goliath, and Jacob and Joseph and a great many other persons mentioned in the Old Testament." When these children read, they "hardly miss a word."[44] In Barbados black children arrive at the school house "an hour too early because they [are] so anxious to be instructed"[45] "Little reader! Do you love to go to school as the little children of Barbadoes do?"[46] Such idyllic examples suggest that those who prevent black children from reading are wicked—a strong word in 1836. "Is it not wicked . . . to deprive little slaves of books and bring them up in ignorance, and then say they are so stupid as not to know any thing?"[47] In *The Slave's Friend* the term "wicked" is reserved almost exclusively for slave owners and traders who exploit and abuse little children. Young readers are encouraged to draw an obvious moral from such stories: "would it not be best to have the slaves in the United States emancipated?"[48]

The central message of *The Slaves' Friend* was typical of many abolitionist publications of the 1830s.[49] But the idea of an unjust, cruel, and arbitrary world was assiduously avoided by antebellum fiction in general and by children's literature in particular. The representation of unjustifiable violence and the incitement to activism in the form of a miniature journal, written "so that very young children can understand it" made *The Slave's Friend* particularly provocative and formed an uneasy alliance with its promotion of faith and altruism on the one hand, its reassurance as to the peaceful consequences of emancipation on the other.[50]

HILDRETH'S *SLAVE*: LITERACY, ANGER, AND DEFIANCE

In 1836, the same year that *The Slave's Friend* first appeared, the white historian Richard Hildreth published *The Slave; or the Memoirs of Archy Moore,* one of the few works of fiction about slavery that preceded publication of *Uncle Tom's Cabin.*[51] (In a preface to a later edition, Hildreth claimed the novel was "the first successful application of fictitious narrative to anti-slavery purposes."[52]) Published anonymously, Hildreth's text was sometimes read as a slave narrative, but it was a novel, centered on and told by a slave figure, son of a white master and the master's favorite slave concubine.[53]

The Slave introduces the theme of literacy early in the book—Archy comes by letters easily. During Archy's childhood his time is spent mainly in attendance upon James, a sickly white half brother of his own age, who has difficulty learning. He and Archy thus devise a scheme: Archy will be present when little James is tutored, in order to help James master his A B C. The action is set in a period before anyone "had dreamed of those barbarous and detestable laws—. . . destined to be the everlasting disgrace of America—by which it has been made a *crime,* punishable with fine and imprisonment, to teach a slave to read" (12). No one objects to Archy's acquisition of literacy. James's father "obtained for him a large collection of books, adapted to his age, which he and I [Archy] used to read over together, and in which we took great delight" (12). Archy gains "some elementary knowledge of arithmetic and geography, and even a smattering of latin [*sic*]" (13). But he conceals some of his knowledge because the servants mock his accomplishments, which become a source of merriment for his master as well: "I was regarded as a sort of prodigy—like a three-legged hen or a sheep with four eyes; a thing to be produced and exhibited for the entertainment of strangers" (13). Archy's master takes delight in showing off his "learned nigger" at drinking parties (13). From this point on, Archy's situation deteriorates: his mother dies soon after telling him about his own origins; when young James dies shortly afterwards, Archy is left at the mercy of the system. He quickly learns to expect nothing but abuse from his father/master.

Once Archy recognizes his true position, his ability to read only intensifies his anger. Unlike the little black readers in *The Slave's Friend* (and unlike George Shelby, Eva, or the converted Topsy) Archy does not place literacy at the service of diligence, patience, or other "civilized" behavior. He reads and writes but he also expresses bitter resentment. As for piety, after learning who his father is, Archy reads the Bible—but not in order to study obedience. Instead, as if fulfilling the worst fears of those who advocated a prohibition on slave literacy, Archy turns to the Old Testament and extracts a moral that suits his pressing need. He "turn[s] with new interest to the story of Hagar, the bond-woman, and Ishmael her son; and as I read how an angel came to their relief, when the hard-hearted Abraham had driven them into the wilderness, there seemed to grow up within me a wild, strange, uncertain hope, that in some accident, I knew not what, I too might find succor and relief" (20). More like Nat Turner than the little Bible-readers in *The Slave's Friend,* Archy identifies with Ishmael. Far from learning patience or gaining faith from his reading, he imagines himself "wandering in the wilderness, every man's hand against me, and my hand against every man" (20). Indeed, Archy soon begins to enact this scenario.

In one of the more amazing episodes of the story Archy falls in love with Cassy, a slave woman, pleads with his mistress for permission to marry, and then—when his beloved is pursued by the unholy lust of her own father/master—plots their escape. Archy is Cassy's savior, a knight, a protector of true womanhood: "I knew well that Cassy's charms were too alluring not to excite a voluptuary, in whom a long indulgence had extinguished all the better feelings, and rendered incapable of controlling himself; and to whom neither the fear of punishment nor the dread of public indignation supplied the place of conscience" (43). Archy takes the moral high ground here, but he fails to tell Cassy that her master/father is also his own. In other words, he is prepared to commit incest with his half sister, while keeping her in the dark about her origin (38, 39). As Nancy Bentley puts it, "Hildreth condones—flaunts really—the transgressive passion of the sibling lovers."[54] These features of the narrative, all evident in the first eight chapters, undermine the idea that literacy will encourage obedience and loyalty or inculcate Victorian moral norms in slaves. The same set of issues must have prevented this book from gaining widespread attention. It was barely noticed when first published.[55] Nonetheless, Stowe read it.

Stowe may not have been acquainted with *The Slave's Friend,* but despite her often-stated reservations about fiction-reading she certainly knew Hildreth's book.[56] Indeed, *Uncle Tom's Cabin* can be taken almost point for point as a rebuttal of *The Slave.* George Harris is a modified version of Archy himself. In his anger, his intensity, and his articulateness, George shares many qualities with Archy (as with Frederick Douglass, upon whom George is more often thought to be modeled).[57] But the figure of George effectively transforms Hildreth's (and Douglass's) more radical emphases. The most disruptive implications of George's story are neutralized by Stowe's focus on his conversion to domesticity and religious faith (or at least practice).

George Harris is the one slave character in Stowe's text who puts literacy to secular uses. He speaks grammatical English, quotes the Declaration of Independence on the "consent of the governed," when reasoning the grounds for his escape (185), and invents a machine for the cleaning of hemp "which, considering the education and circumstances of the inventor, displays quite as much mechanical genius as Whitney's cotton gin" (54). Since this invention gives George's master "an uneasy consciousness of inferiority," George's achievement results in his being removed from the factory where he had worked and "put to the meanest drudgery of the farm" (56). George is only Stowe's "secondary black hero," as Robert Stepto notes.[58] Still, the figure of George affirms the innate intellectual capacity of African Americans and projects a powerful argument on behalf of slave literacy.[59] Stowe emphasizes George's self-culture against formidable odds and his creative use of the knowledge acquired. At the same time, she is careful to show that only peaceful, socially conservative results accrue from George's education. George runs away, and is willing to use force against the slave catchers who pursue him, but his accomplishments foster his piety and forbearance; they do not intensify his anger or encourage flagrant defiance of social norms. At the end of the novel, in a telling cameo, George sits reading "in a small, neat tenement, in the outskirts of Montreal, the time, evening":

> A cheerful fire blazes on the hearth; a tea-table, covered with a snowy cloth, stands prepared for the evening meal. In one corner of the room was a table covered with a green cloth, where was an open writing-desk, pens, paper, and over it a shelf of well-selected books.
>
> This was George's study. The same zeal for self-improvement, which led him to steal the much coveted arts of reading and writing, amid all the toil and discouragements of his early life, still led him to devote all his leisure time to self-cultivation.
>
> At this present time, he is seated at the table, making notes from a volume of the family library he has been reading.
>
> 'Come, George,' says Eliza, 'you've been gone all day. Do put down that book, and let's talk, while I'm getting tea,—do.'
>
> And little Eliza seconds the effort, by toddling up to her father and trying to pull the book out of his hand, and install herself on his knee as a substitute.
>
> 'O, you little witch!' says George, yielding, as, in such circumstances, man always must. (604)

This passage neatly summarizes George's exemplary status in *Uncle Tom's Cabin*. While his "zeal for self-improvement" is retrospectively invoked as justification for his transgressive "theft" of literacy, his willingness to put down his book at the request of his wife and child shows that George has become a family man, not a revolutionary. The volume he is reading, taken from his "well-selected . . . family library" is clearly a wholesome one; still, George lays it aside to embrace his daughter and affirms the claims of domesticity over intellectual (or political) urgencies.

As the scene continues, George asks his son, little Harry, how his arithmetic is coming along. When Harry responds that he "did it, every bit of it *myself*, father; and *nobody* helped me!" George praises his son's independence: "That's right . . . depend on yourself, my son" (605). Yet George's self-sufficiency is carefully qualified by both his domestic commitments and his religious faith. He asserts his willingness to be counseled by Eliza ("I have an eloquent preacher of the Gospel ever by my side, in the person of my beautiful wife. When I wander, her gentler spirit ever restores me, and keeps before my eyes the Christian calling and mission of our race" [611]); George subordinates individual to familial and communal needs. At the end of the novel, having "obtained a very thorough education" at a university in France" (608), he renounces the "wish to pass for an American" (608); and, in a plot development that has received much attention, Stowe, as Robert Stepto puts it, "sends [George] packing."[60] Before departing for Africa with his family George writes in a letter to a friend that he goes "to Liberia as to a field of work. I expect to work with both hands—to work *hard;* . . . and to work till I die" (611). Stowe's emphasis on George's capacity for tireless effort counters the common charge that freed slaves would be idle and self-indulgent. But the imagery of "a field" and of work "with both hands" is an odd way to represent George's intellectual achievements and moral autonomy. It anticipates the debate between Booker T. Washington and W. E. B. Du Bois about the ultimate goals of education for African Americans and further circumscribes George's personal ambition.

Stowe's strategies of containment were designed to tone down the disruptive implications of a text such as Hildreth's which, from Stowe's point of view, ill-served both the abolitionist and the evangelical cause while lowering the moral level of literary culture. But Hildreth's Archy was not Stowe's only model in shaping the figure of George. Frederick Douglass's *Narrative* also deserves attention in this context.

FREDERICK DOUGLASS: LITERACY AS SUBLIMATION

The first version of Douglass's autobiography appeared in 1845. This text avoids many of the pitfalls (especially the representation of violence, anger, and sexuality) which limited the audience of more radical abolitionist publications of the period such as *The Slave's Friend, The Slave,* or Theodore Weld's fiercely unsentimental *Slavery as It Is.*[61] Once again attention to the image of literacy in a text that precedes *Uncle Tom's Cabin* provides a useful way of isolating Stowe's shifts of emphasis and helps us understand the electrifying appeal of her novel in 1851.

Douglass's description of his first major encounter with the practice of reading occupies an important place in every version of his story. His account of acquiring literacy gained critical attention from the start and is regularly excerpted in condensed versions. In the *Narrative* of 1845, Douglass's initiation into literacy and especially his subsequent prohibition from it is framed as a "revelation" that explained "dark and mysterious things" to the young Douglass. His master's account of why it is "unlawful as well as unsafe, to teach a slave to read" (274) is well known and requires no rehearsal.[62] The point I want to stress is that even though Douglass derives an oppositional moral from his master's comments ("What he most dreaded, that I most desired. What he most loved, that I most hated . . ." [275]), the rage implicit in Douglass's new-found understanding is quickly muted or displaced not only by the rhetorical control of the well-balanced sentences, but also by Douglass's behavior: he channels his anger into the classic goal-directedness of the self-possessed and self-reliant man. Douglass's acquisition of literacy and the uses he makes of it are linked not to emotion or aggression but to hard work, self-control, even self-denial. Although Douglass uses his knowledge of letters to write a pass for himself and his friends, they fail to escape, and elsewhere in the narrative literacy mainly figures not at the level of events, but rather as proof, through Douglass's style, of his education—his sophistication, verbal proficiency, and range of reference.

Literacy is his most salient accomplishment, evident from the beginning of the narrative and visible on every subsequent page. Douglass consistently foregrounds the difference between his own rhetorical panache and the ungrammatical, vulgar language of his masters and overseers. "Now, you d—d b—h," his master shouts as he is about to whip Douglass's half-naked aunt, "I'll learn you how to disobey my orders!" (259). From the start Douglass's diction and syntax as well as his literary allusions demonstrate how far he has come from his origins as a slave child who did not know his own age or who his father was.

Throughout the *Narrative* Douglass's moral autonomy is more closely identified with rhetorical control than with force. Violence characterizes the brutal overseers; literacy is identified with more lasting and legitimate authority. Even the fight with Covey, presented by Douglass as an "epoch in [his] humble history" (294), "the turning point in [his] career" (298), almost immediately cedes its place to a display of his linguistic prowess. "It was a glorious resurrection, from the tomb of slavery, to the heaven of freedom. . . . and I now resolved that, however long I might remain a slave in form, the day had passed forever when I could be a slave in fact" (299). This is one of many passages praised for "great eloquence," that earned Douglass the label of "master rhetorician."[63] Douglass's rhetoric was regularly celebrated when his *Narrative* first appeared. His reliance on the pen (not the sword) quieted fears that might otherwise have been stirred by his representation of harsh realities and his own resistance to them. That particular quid pro quo—the way rhetorical flourishes absorb the fallout from Douglass's violent images—repays additional attention. As John Stauffer emphasizes, the second version of Douglass's narrative (*My Bondage and My Freedom*) smolders with anger.[64] But the first edition downplays it, soft-pedaling resentment and eliding any wish for vengeance.

The nadir of Douglass's slave experience as presented in the *Narrative* of 1845 is the point when, as he explains, "Mr Covey succeeded in breaking me. I was broken in body, soul, and spirit. My natural elasticity was crushed, my intellect languished, the disposition to read departed . . . the dark night of slavery closed in upon me; and behold a man transformed into a brute!" (293). The next paragraph describes a Sunday ("my only leisure time"), during which the brutalized narrator spends the day in "a sort of beast-like stupor" (293). What follows directly, however, is no image of "beast-like" behavior, but rather another widely praised passage in which Douglass, gazing at the white sails of beautiful vessels on the Chesapeake Bay, finds that his "thoughts would compel utterance; and there, with no audience but the Almighty, I would pour out my soul's complaint, in my rude way, with an apostrophe to the moving multitude of ships . . ." (293). Douglass's disingenuous emphasis on his "rude way" (and his lack of an audience) only foregrounds the fact that in the subsequent passage he pulls out all the rhetorical stops to persuade his readers that he is a sophisticated writer, not a dumb brute. His language here is precisely a substitute for the barrage of vituperation (or violent action) that his readers might legitimately expect at this juncture.

Douglass's poetic passage about the freely moving white sails on the bay reassuringly emphasizes not aggression against oppressors but Douglass's will to die himself if need be ("I had as well be killed running as die standing" [294]). In the Preface to the first edition of the *Narrative* Garrison singles out this "soliloquy" (249) as the most "thrilling" incident of the story: "Who can read that passage, and be insensible to its pathos, and sublimity? Compressed into it is a whole Alexandrian library of thought, feeling, and sentiment . . ." (249). Wendell Phillips also refers to this passage as evidence that Frederick Douglass is well qualified to be a literary man and a free one.[65]

Douglass's masterful rhetoric helped persuade Garrison, Phillips, and other white activists that he deserved support and would be useful to the abolitionist cause. His eloquence endorses the "ideology of literacy"—the belief in literacy as a conduit to "morality, citizenship, and prosperity" (Salvino, 147). But literacy does not automatically ensure freedom, still less equality. As Dana Nelson Salvino suggests, "literacy could lead blacks out of physical, but not cultural and economic bondage."[66] Douglass himself was increasingly aware of the gap between the high expectations attached to literacy and the limited value of skills acquired, often at a great price, by African American slaves—or free blacks, for that matter. But he wanted to be heard, and his endorsement of the transforming power of literacy helped to make him a striking example of self-improvement and the "civilized" virtues. In the first and still best-known version of the *Narrative* Douglass assiduously avoids any suggestion of a link between literacy and violence.[67] Even the restrained 1845 edition, however, was too radical a model for Stowe.

Insofar as the figure of George Harris is a response to Frederick Douglass as well as to Hildreth, George provides an example which, as we have seen, writes not only violence and defiant sexuality but even self-sufficiency out of the script. Through George, Stowe circumscribed Douglass's independence, muted his anger still further, and elided his prominent place in U.S. literary and political culture. One has only to compare the image of George at tea-time with Douglass's image of himself "at home" in the 1845 *Narrative* to see how wide a gulf remains between the two implicit outcomes. When Douglass describes his departure from Colonel Lloyd's plantation, he offers his reader a flash-forward: a glimpse of the free writer, Frederick Douglass "seated by my own table, in the enjoyment of freedom and the happiness of home" (273). "The happiness of home," however, gains no further elaboration in the *Narrative*. Douglass's wife is barely mentioned (as David Leverenz notes, she "seems an afterthought."[68]). "Home" is epitomized by and confined to an image of the independent Frederick Douglass at his writing table. The contrast between the image of the isolated writer and that of George Harris with tea cups, wife, children, and family library reflects the direction of Stowe's revisions: *Uncle Tom's Cabin* attempts to defuse the potential dynamite contained in narratives that associated black literacy with violence and illicit sexuality or even with black secular and political autonomy.

LITERACY AS RELATIONSHIP: INTERACTION AND INTERIORITY

In shaping the images of black characters who read, Stowe carefully unmade the association that we have been tracing between literacy and civil disobedience, unbridled sexuality, secular individualism, and violence. Stowe's association of literacy with piety, domesticity, and passive resistance helped earn her the growing contempt of twentieth-century readers, initiated most famously by James Baldwin in 1949. Nonetheless, Stowe's representation of Tom, Topsy, and George Harris as increasingly literate figures also helped insinuate the notion of black subjectivity into the collective consciousness of the white antebellum reading public—not by foregrounding the pragmatic uses of literacy, but rather by relying on an unspoken assumption indispensable to the "ideology of literacy": only human beings read.

Joanne Dobson and Marianne Noble have emphasized Stowe's belief in "human interaction" as "essential for human life."[69] Stowe's scenes of reading

4. Tom reading to two slave women. From Harriet Beecher Stowe, Uncle Tom's Cabin. *Boston: John P. Jewett, 1853. Collection of The New-York Historical Society. Negative #83649d.*

make a significant contribution to this emphasis; they repeatedly suggest that printed matter is a catalyst for interpersonal relations as well as moral and spiritual depth. As Sarah Robbins has shown, conversation and collaboration were increasingly valued as modes of pedagogy and "literacy management" in domestic culture during the 1840s and '50s.[70] Throughout *Uncle Tom's Cabin* Stowe's recurrent scenes of reading stress not only slave literacy but also warm and cozy human relations, which become the ground of learning. Little George Shelby helping Tom write, Eva teaching Mammy her letters, Tom reading his Bible to two slave women after a brutal workday (fig. 4), Uncle Tom and Eva poring over the Bible together—such scenes suggest both intimacy and intersubjectivity. They stress the fact that slaves speak, read, think, and feel. In early editions Billings and other illustrators elaborated such moments. A common practice emerged: in the 1850s scenes of reading were

LITTLE EVA READING THE BIBLE TO UNCLE TOM IN THE ARBOR. Page 68.

5. *Little Eva reading the Bible to Uncle Tom. From Harriet Beecher Stowe,* Uncle Tom's Cabin. *Boston: John P. Jewett, 1852. Collection of The New-York Historical Society. Negative #83640d.*

regularly included in illustrated editions, elaborating Stowe's emphasis on literacy as a practice rooted in dynamic interaction, a give and take that often crossed the color line.[71] Despite the "romantic racialism" evident in both Stowe's text and its visual accompaniments, the domestic and relational emphasis in scenes of reading throughout *Uncle Tom's Cabin* qualifies the widely shared perception of Stowe's African American characters as dehumanized "objects" of sympathy.[72]

Among the six illustrations that Billings provided for the first American edition of *Uncle Tom's Cabin* was the image of "Little Eva Reading the Bible to Uncle Tom in the Arbor." In this illustration Eva sits with the open Bible on her knee and points to the horizon across Lake Pontchartrain. She explains to Uncle Tom that she's going "*there,* to the spirits bright, *I'm going, before long*" (382) (fig. 5). This scene, repeatedly illustrated in the 1850s, can be taken as what W. J. T. Mitchell calls a "summary image," one that epitomizes a set of meanings which speak to a certain audience with particular force.[73] The image of Eva and Tom gazing at Lake Pontchartrain over the open book was the most frequently reprinted illustration of *Uncle Tom's Cabin* during the antebellum period.[74] In 1989, when Jane Tompkins explored the function of this moment, she examined it within the scheme of Stowe's religious typology. As I have already suggested, however, Stowe's scenes of Bible-reading also had more radical, secular implications.

In numerous versions of the scene, Eva and Tom sit by themselves, reading together. For the holiday edition Billings added not only other scenes of reading (and writing) but also images of Eva and Tom in close physical contact and a variety of moods. Undoubtedly neither Stowe nor Billings could have pictured the physical contact between a black man and a white girl unless such moments were rendered quite innocent. Marcus Wood suggests that in Victorian illustrations Tom "had become a harmless fiction, the ideal Christian house-slave, probably the only type of black male which Victorian society could imagine in physical contact with virginal white girlhood."[75] The ubiquitous presence of the Holy Book in illustrations of Tom and Eva helped ensure that the physical contact between them would not be taken amiss, especially by antebellum Northern readers who, like Ophelia, did not take interracial physical contact for granted. As we shall see in Chapter 6, illustrations of the 1890s and the turn of the century often eliminate all physical contact across the color line; children's editions in the age of segregation delete Stowe's descriptions of Eva embracing Mammy, and downplay her tête-à-têtes over the Bible with Tom.[76]

If the representation of black literacy in *Uncle Tom's Cabin* did not appear threatening to white readers of the antebellum period, this was because Stowe and her early illustrators carefully framed the act of reading as a domestic social practice rooted in family relations and religious faith. Some of Stowe's scenes of reading stress pedagogic exchanges; others stress individual meditation or contemplative interplay, such as that between Eva and Tom at the lake. All of these modes of "intensive reading" affirm the communal, relational, or spiritual values endorsed by educators, religious organizations, and literary commentators of the period.[77] In Wood's formulation, Tom is a model of "safe learning."[78] Confined to the Bible, Tom's reading is a source of faith and nonviolence.

Nevertheless, Stowe's scenes of reading harbored radical implications. These become visible when we consider reading and writing as independent practices with differential meanings in the antebellum context. The "value [of literacy] is seldom doubted," as Harvey Graff notes,[79] but reading often appears tame and passive by comparison with writing. As Jennifer Monaghan demonstrates, reading was understood to be a "lesser" skill than writing in the early republic because less important in the world of practical business.[80] Accordingly, Henry Gates, Robert Stepto, and others have argued that the act of writing becomes evidence of black agency in numerous slave narratives. "In the black tradition," Gates suggests, "writing became the visible sign, the commodity of exchange, the text and technology of reason."[81] Stowe complicates the privileging of writing over reading because insofar as the act of reading involves internalization, the figure of a black reader alone with a book, or engaged with others over a book, asserts the reality of black subjectivity.

The very association of reading with contemplation—with moral and spiritual qualities rather than professional or commercial activities—made it a perfect vehicle for representing interiority, the very thing white readers regularly denied black people. As Dana Nelson Salvino suggests, literacy in the early republic was understood to signify "moral accumulation";[82] it was thus inseparable from the idea of an inner space where a "moral accumulation" could be stored. For Stowe and her white antebellum readers the association of literacy with innerness went without saying; literacy could facilitate citizenship, self-improvement, or worldly success only for a person with a heart, mind, and soul. The prohibition on slave literacy was of a piece with the denial of black interiority, and both were indispensable conditions for seeing African Americans as objects or property.

Tom plays a particularly important role in Stowe's representation of reading. Tom embraces his Bible as true, incorporates its stories and images into his emotional life, and retains it as an aid to contemplation. "Scripture . . . seemed so entirely to have wrought itself into his being, as to have become a part of himself" (79). This process implies that Tom possesses a self, an imagination, a soul. It suggests that he is capable of reflection, introspection, moral seriousness. Both Tom's moral authority (with George Shelby, Eva, St. Clare, and even Ophelia) and his memory for the words of the Biblical text become evidence of his subjectivity, his possession of an inner storehouse of experience.

In Chapter XIV, Tom sits alone with his Bible on a cotton bale, on the deck of the ship that is taking him south to be sold. He drops tears on the Bible as he reads (228). Tom is depicted here as a sentimental reader—very like the ideal reader Stowe imagined for her novel. Jay Fliegelman has suggested that "sentimental readers" were beginning to constitute a "moral elite" in antebellum America.[83] While nineteenth-century critics of the novel-reading habit attacked fiction-readers for self-indulgence, isolation, and passivity, proponents of fiction stressed the value to be gained by a reader's active absorption and internalization of moral narratives. In this perspective, even novel-reading could make a contribution to meaningful inner depth. Conversely, insofar as the absorbed novel-reader was a source of anxiety to ministers, educators, and other commentators, this was precisely because of concern for the reader's moral and emotional life.

Cultural critics of the last twenty years have repeatedly linked the emergence of the novel as a genre—and scenes of reading within it—to the formation of bourgeois society and the consolidation of middle-class domesticity.[84] Tom's reading habits imply that he (like the middle-class lay reader) is to be seen as possessing an inner world. As a reader, Tom is active, even creative. His edition of the Bible "had been embellished with certain way-marks and guideboards of [his] own invention" (229). Through "bold, strong marks and dashes" (229) Tom indicates "the passages which more particularly gratified his ear or affected his heart" (229). Like the marginalia of many nineteenth-century readers, Tom's markings enable him "in a moment" to "seize upon his favorite [verses]" (229). Moreover, in a practice shared by St. Clare as well as other educated readers of the period, Tom uses his Bible to serve a function beyond the strictly textual: "and while it lay there before him, every passage breathing of some old home scene, and recalling some past enjoyment, his Bible seemed to him all of this life that remained, as well as the promise of a future one" (229).[85]

Tom's reading offers him a range of satisfactions: the sight of familiar passages and his own markings in the material book reconnects him to past experience; as he sits alone with the Bible on the cotton bales, the act of intense concentration takes him out of himself and attenuates his pain; the "sublime words" and the image of a heavenly home give him spiritual sustenance and emotional consolation. Tom's reading thus gives meaningful life to the book that he reads. But at the same time, Stowe's representation of Tom as a reader—memorizing passages, preferring some to others, connecting images with a remembered past and an imagined future—makes him the site of a complex innerness.

In *The Signifying Monkey,* Henry Louis Gates examines the trope of the book that does not come to life when opened by a black reader. Gates argues that the image of "the silent book"—the book that "did not reflect or acknowledge the black presence before it"—is central to James Albert Gronniosaw's slave narrative, a foundational text of the tradition.[86] Gronniosaw ascribes the "rather deafening silence" of a book to his own blackness; and when "the 'dialogue' that he records having observed between the book and his master eludes him," the silence of the book implies his own (136–37). Tracing this trope through subsequent slave narratives, Gates says of Equiano:

> Of course the book does not speak to him. Only subjects can endow an object with subjectivity; objects, such as a slave, posses no inherent subjectivity of their own.... When Equiano, the object, attempts to speak to the book, there follows only the deafening silence that obtains between two lifeless objects. Only a subject can speak....
>
> Through the act of writing alone, Equiano announces and preserves his newly found status as a subject. It is he who is master of his text. (156)

Unlike Gronniosaw, Equiano, Archie Moore—or Douglass—Tom does not confirm his relation to literacy by writing about his experience. From the scene in which little George Shelby teaches Tom to write letters on a slate, through the episode in which Eva tries helping Tom write a letter to Chloe, Tom's writing remains halting. However, Stowe's representation of Tom's dynamic interaction with the Biblical text and material book recasts the trope of the "silent book," by asserting that Tom's humanity, inner life, and cumulative memory are reflected in his capacity to make the book live. Recurrent images of Tom and the Bible affirm intensive reading while anticipating twentieth-century models of reading as transaction.[87]

Tom's Bible-reading has often been seen as evidence of the passivity and even complicity that made "Uncle Tom" a contemptible epithet in the twentieth century. Until the 1820s, as we have noted, Bible-reading for slaves was encouraged because it was presumed to promote obedience and docility. Nonetheless, for Tom, as for many slaves who (unlike Tom) acquired their freedom, the act of reading served a multiplicity of functions. In delineating those functions Stowe attempted to persuade her white readers that Tom had a familiar sensibility and moral imagination—a recognizable human shape. At times, to be sure, Stowe's representation of Tom as a reader reemphasizes his subordination to white masters, and sometimes children at that. Tom's reading is not only slow and laborious, but also often mystified. Like Eva, he is all the more "impressed" by the "wondrous imagery and fervent language" of Scripture when he does not understand it (he "questioned vainly of [its] . . . meaning" [380]). Nonetheless, the recurrent representation of Tom as a reader—reflecting, marking the text, and brooding over it—bolsters Stowe's claim for Tom's humanity while foregrounding the significance of the reading experience as such. Framed by Stowe's celebration of emotionally engaged reading, Tom emerges as a figure with more interiority than is generally attributed to him.

Literacy becomes a central element in Stowe's representation of Topsy, as it does in her image of George Harris and Tom.[88] Topsy's transformation, though predicated on Eva's love, is bound up with literacy; her conversion is sealed by the gift of a Bible. An episode which convinces both St. Clare and Ophelia that Topsy possesses a meaningful (i.e., *recognizable*) inner world occurs toward the end of events on the St. Clare plantation. After Eva's death Topsy conceals in "her bosom a little parcel" which turns out to be "a small book . . . given to [her] by Eva" (444). The book, which contains a lock of Eva's hair, wrapped in paper (444), also contains "a single verse of Scripture, arranged for every day in the year"—like a narrative in installments. When Rosa notices that Topsy is hiding something, she accuses the girl of stealing "and tried to force her hand into her bosom, while Topsy, enraged, kicked and fought valiantly for what she considered her rights" (443). For this book, hidden in her "bosom" (and identified with it) Topsy will fight. The book not only gives her a concept of "her rights"; it is also—like Tom's Bible for him and, later, Eva's for St. Clare—a token of love. Topsy's relation to her book implies a capacity for moral and emotional experience.

Stowe asserted the subjectivity of her black characters by representing them in terms that the white antebellum (especially Northern) reading public could understand. To adapt Huck Finn's famous phrase, she suggests that black characters are "white inside." This description may seem to reinstate Tom and Topsy as sentimental stereotypes, objects for condescension. Indeed, Stowe could imagine subjectivity only in terms that she (and her audience) already knew. She constructed her black characters on the model of white ones—which is precisely why they seemed so "real" to white antebellum readers. Since literacy was widely recognized as a practice that underwrote white subjectivity, it was perfectly suited for Stowe's goals.

6. *Tom reading on the cotton bales(unsigned). From Mary Low*, A Peep into Uncle Tom's Cabin. *Boston: John P. Jewett, 1853. Collection of The New-York Historical Society. Negative #83650d.*

In 1853 an edition of *Uncle Tom's Cabin* adapted for "youth" restructured the novel to begin with the figure of Tom as an engaged, contemplative reader. The first illustration in the text shows Tom with his Bible seated on the cotton bales (fig. 6). Whether Stowe had a hand in this recasting or whether we take the change as evidence of one reader's (and one publisher's) understanding of what was important (or would sell), the new opening of the story makes the image of black literacy particularly central to the narrative.[89] As I have been suggesting, Stowe's representation of slave literacy asserted that slaves could acquire (or already possessed) many of the virtues associated with reading in antebellum literary culture. But scenes of reading in *Uncle Tom's Cabin*—especially scenes that emphasized the value of communing with a text, absorbing it, reflecting upon it, and talking about it—served another function as well. They framed a protocol of reading for *Uncle Tom's Cabin* itself. We turn now to an examination of this "protocol."

3

Legitimizing Fiction
Protocols of Reading in Uncle Tom's Cabin

All through my duties this morning it haunts me.
—*Georgiana May to Harriet Beecher Stowe*

This chapter argues that throughout *Uncle Tom's Cabin* Stowe employed scenes of reading not only to make a case for black literacy but also to disarm a resistance to fiction that was still widespread in literary culture of the period. Although fiction-reading had become an extremely popular activity by mid-century, it was still regarded as problematic by many people. On the one hand, as an inferior literary form, fiction was deemed appropriate mainly for women and children, roughly equivalent to a taste for soap opera a hundred years later; on the other hand, it was considered especially dangerous for the dependent and vulnerable.[1] We have seen that Stowe was intimately familiar with the logic of the anti-fiction position, well versed in strictures against novel-reading from childhood. During the 1840s, while her brother Henry Ward Beecher addressed the subject of fiction-reading both from the pulpit and in print, Stowe herself warned against the dangers of "light reading." Genre was "the principal way books were marketed and consumed" in the antebellum period, as David Stewart points out.[2] Stowe was acutely aware that she was employing an "insignificant," much-maligned literary form to address the most contentious political and moral issues of the period. For a sentimental novel to serve such ends, some segments of the reading public had to modify their assumptions about the moral and literary meaning of fiction itself.

Emergent modes of middle-class domesticity in the 1850s gave fiction an important place within the family circle, as Richard Brodhead, Sarah Robbins, and others have emphasized. But readers in a variety of textual communities still saw the novel as an upstart in literary culture. Moral, religious, and aesthetic arguments were freely employed by commentators who sought to delimit the influence and attractions of fiction. Southerners saw Stowe's use of fiction as "unscrupulous" precisely because of its power to captivate readers.[3] Men of letters regarded fiction as aesthetically inferior to such literary forms as poetry, history, and classical texts. (Indeed, the low position of the novel in the hierarchy of generic forms lasted well into the twentieth century.[4]) Ministers, educators, and librarians were concerned with the ethical dangers posed by fiction, especially its impact on the young. The issue was not "immoral" fiction per se, but rather the habits of mind inculcated by texts that offered easy emotional satisfactions and diversion rather than encouraging self-scrutiny or developing the critical faculties.

Attacks on fiction, circulating widely in sermons, advice books, and periodicals, did not prevent novels from being avidly read by men, women, and children of the 1840s, and certainly the 1850s. Fiction flourished, not only in bound volumes but also in literary annuals, chapbooks, and the weekly press.[5] Yet the growing popularity of fiction in some quarters only heightened anxiety in others. Although literacy was widely celebrated as the bedrock of religious practice and civic education in the antebellum United States, the proliferation of reading matter—increasingly inexpensive and widely available—intensified concerns about selection, authority, and control. Commentators (both religious and secular) used highly charged language to dramatize the dangers associated with the irresistible flood of printed matter.[6] Distinctions between useful, beneficial works of the imagination and foolish, frivolous (even pernicious) ones appear not only in the evangelical press, but throughout antebellum print culture. In the 1870s, '80s, and '90s, advice manuals continue to stress the difference between frivolous passive reading and active, serious, useful attention to books. Guides to "home-reading" offer elaborate instructions about how to choose books, how to read them, and where to put them in the home.[7] Educators and men of letters regularly celebrate elevated, moral, or purposive reading, while denouncing books that encourage idleness and fantasy. Well into the twentieth century an unregulated taste for certain kinds of fiction was held responsible for everything from lagging cultural standards to increased self-indulgence, unbridled fantasy, and bad eyesight. Debates about the evil effects of television and the Internet are more recent expressions of related anxieties.

Uncle Tom's Cabin offered some persuasive reassurance about the function of the novel, and it did so in a register that spoke directly to some of fiction's firmest opponents. The protocol of reading that Stowe inscribed into her novel helped her mark out a unique cultural space for it. By suggesting that fiction could encourage active reading practices, benevolent emotion, and faith, rather than passivity and foolishness, *Uncle Tom's Cabin* became a significant factor in the complex process that made the novel an important cultural force by the end of the century. Of course Stowe was hardly the first novelist to elicit tears, celebrate religious feeling, and encourage social conscience. By 1851 the literary marketplace was saturated not only with sentiment, but with reform fiction that addressed social questions. Yet for many readers (including Stowe and the rest of the Beechers) the sanguine moral messages of sentimental fiction were almost as destructive of balanced thought and feeling as the violence and sexuality typical of temperance tales and crime novels.

From Stowe's point of view sensational plots were not justified by social criticism expressed along the way or by a moral tacked on at the end of the story. Indeed, reform fiction—despite its claim of moral purposes—was one of the greatest offenders of aesthetic taste and moral rigor for Stowe, Henry Ward Beecher, and others. Beecher addresses this problem in his sermon "The Strange Woman," where he attacks novels "of the French school and of English imitators" that "come to us impudently pretending to be reformers of morals and liberalizers of religion; they propose to instruct our laws, and teach . . . justice"; but flagrantly present "loathsome men . . . [with] their monstrous deeds, their lies, their plots their crimes, their dreadful pleasures."[8] Stowe shared Beecher's distaste for the disingenuousness of godless "reform" novels. Under cover of social criticism and ethical goals, the fiction of Eugène Sue or George Lippard seemed to legitimize narratives pervaded by sex and violence. Again like Beecher, Stowe celebrated those who used "plain words . . . to say plain things." To speak "plainly and properly" even if "rude and vulgar," Beecher insists, is preferable to speaking "by innuendo—which is the devil's language." Stowe attacked Byron and Bulwer on similar grounds.[9] Yet both Stowe and Beecher were keenly aware of the force of their own rhetoric—which was far less "plain" and transparent than they pretended.

Many of Stowe's rhetorical strategies in *Uncle Tom's Cabin* were conceived with the problematic cultural status of the novel in mind. Stowe shared the aims and adapted the narrative devices of sentimental novelists, temperance writers, and other reformers. But as we have seen, *Uncle Tom's Cabin* refused both reassuring celebrations of Providence and blatant shock tactics.[10] Grounding her attack on slavery in widely shared religious, domestic, and aesthetic values, Stowe employed Biblical allusions and citations as well as scenes of Bible-reading to give her narrative an aura of unimpeachable moral authority without insisting that everything is for the best in the best of all possible worlds. Attacking slavery as a sin, she forged an alliance between *Uncle Tom's Cabin* and the most respected (and best-selling) book in her world: Holy Scripture.

Scenes of reading throughout the novel privilege contemplative, intensive reading, especially Bible-reading. By celebrating engaged reading as an interpretive mode appropriate not only to Scripture but also to *Uncle Tom's Cabin,* Stowe attempted to neutralize the vociferous objections to certain kinds of fiction voiced by her father, brothers, sister—and often herself. The religious as well as the social importance of *Uncle Tom's Cabin* was much praised by early reviewers; this consensus was influential. Many readers abrogated their anti-fiction principles and made an exception for *Uncle Tom's Cabin.* Yet in doing so, antebellum readers went further than Stowe had proposed. *Uncle Tom's Cabin* disarmed the resistance of an influential segment of the reading public so as to open some well-guarded floodgates. As we shall see at the end of this chapter, the rising status of fiction is apparent in one relevant and conveniently circumscribed context: the abolitionist press. Changing publication practices in abolitionist newspapers of the 1840s and '50s clearly reflect the waning of the anti-fiction prejudice and help us recognize *Uncle Tom's Cabin* as a player in that process.

Antebellum Readers: Disarmed and Devouring

When *Uncle Tom's Cabin* first appeared, it straddled the divide that separated morally and spiritually serious works of literature from works that were frowned upon as foolish (even dangerous) amusements. It was read by many people who were strongly opposed to fiction in principle. The conservative abolitionists Lewis Tappan and James G. Birney, both opposed to novel-reading, made an exception for Stowe's book.[11] *Uncle Tom's Cabin* was the "one whole novel" read by Methodist reformer William S. Stockton (father of Frank R. Stockton—"The Lady or the Tiger").[12] Nineteenth-century readers in both England and America testify that Stowe's novel was the only "secular story" permitted in their family of origin.[13] Lucretia Mott also "yielded to its . . . influence," as her granddaughter wrote, even though Mott "condemned novels and wondered how anyone could find them interesting."[14] "When you meet with [a book] . . . you like," Lucretia Mott wrote to friends in 1848, "do recommend it. Not fiction, we have enough of that sort."[15] The writer of an unsigned newspaper article of 1868 recalls the impact of the novel on his family and neighbors in "one of the remote villages of Maine" whose inhabitants "had never before bowed down to any idols of fiction."[16] Although fiction-reading was generally forbidden among the Shakers, *Uncle Tom's Cabin* was read aloud to assembled Believers in 1852.[17] From the beginning Stowe's narrative belonged to a category of its own. Its religious content in particular gave it safe passage into many homes that had previously been inhospitable to novels.

Nineteenth-century readers of diverse religious and economic backgrounds express enthusiasm for *Uncle Tom's Cabin* in letters and diaries. Such enthusiasm is regularly accompanied by reference to the "good" the book will do. It is as if the moral and spiritual value of the book legitimizes the pleasure and excitement of reading it. But even those who recommend the book often express anxiety about the proliferation of fiction. "I think something good will come out of these book-making propensities of the age," the Reverend Lavius Hyde writes to his daughter after reading *Uncle Tom's Cabin*. But he adds: "I hope our darling Sarah will not neglect her Bible in this age of many books."[18]

Concern about the effect of novel-reading was not confined to the ministry or to fervent evangelicals. Antebellum men, women, and children who experienced *Uncle Tom's Cabin* intensely were subject to guilt for time spent—wasted—on inappropriate or selfish activity. "I have indulged myself in reading a good deal," Anna Cushing of Dorchester confides to her diary while reading *Uncle Tom's Cabin*, in April 1852. Cushing's entry reflects discomfort at what she seems to experience as self-indulgence; but this does not prevent her from finishing Stowe's novel in three days.[19]

Men as well as women consumed the book enthusiastically—and worried about the implications of their immersion in it. Carroll Norcross, farm laborer and part-time writing master of rural Maine, described his reading as follows, in August 1852:

> This morning . . . I took up a volume of Uncle Tom's Cabin. Soon I was all absorb[ed] in its interesting pages and was bound down captive by this ingenious production. . . . Eagerly I devoured the first volume regardless of the presence of those to whom at any other time I should have been happy to have tendered my whole attention. I disregarded all the rules of Ettiquit.

Norcross proceeds to the second volume, again "completely bound up," and disregarding propriety by reading "until nearly midnight."[20] Late-night reading was itself a defiance of social norms; proper young men were regularly urged to avoid it. "If exciting books are read at all," William Alcott warns, "they should be read in the forenoon, not in the evening." As David Stewart argues, Alcott's warning reflects common fears that late-night reading would lead to masturbation, "a practice luridly condemned in popular medical literature."[21]

Early reviewers often describe *Uncle Tom's Cabin* as exciting and moving, but it is the nonprofessional reader who expresses anxiety about the book's uncanny capacity to enthrall. An account by Henry Ward Beecher's wife exemplifies this process. One morning, she reports, after "rising earlier than usual and eating breakfast," her husband opened *Uncle Tom's Cabin*. He "threw himself upon the sofa, forgot his surroundings entirely and read until noon. He ate his dinner book in hand and during the afternoon frequently gave way to tears." As his wife tells the rest of the story:

> The night came on. It was growing late and I felt impelled to urge him to retire. Without raising his eyes from the book he replied:
>
> 'Soon soon; you go; I'll come soon.'
>
> Closing the house I went to our room. . . . The clock struck twelve, one, two, three, and then, to my great relief I heard Mr. Beecher coming upstairs. As he entered he threw 'Uncle Tom's Cabin' on the table, exclaiming: 'There, I've done it! But if Hattie Stowe ever writes anything more like that! I'll—well, she has nearly killed me anyhow!'
>
> And he never picked up the book from that day.[22]

This description evokes not only Beecher's experience of reading, but also his wife's reaction to that experience. Beecher's absorption elicits rising anxiety in his wife as she urges him to retire and watches the clock strike twelve, one, two, and three. When he finally leaves the book to join her upstairs she responds with "great relief." Antebellum readers often describe the way *Uncle*

Tom's Cabin elicited unexpected, even disquieting responses ("I have indulged myself"; "I was bound down captive"; "she has nearly killed me anyhow!"). In a letter to her sister, Mary Pierce Poor of Massachusetts explains that she has "been writing home to advise Elizabeth not to attempt [*Uncle Tom's Cabin*]. I am afraid it would kill her. I never read anything so affecting in my life."[23] Such comments suggest that readers of Stowe's book often went well beyond the guidelines for reading implicit in reviews, commentaries, and *Uncle Tom's Cabin* itself.

For readers who already associated fiction-reading with foolishness or self-indulgence, the intensity of response elicited by *Uncle Tom's Cabin* understandably created discomfort. Affirming Stowe's injunction to "feel right," such readers justified their unaccustomed dedication to a novel. "I hope the book will do good," Cushing notes, immediately after confessing that she has "indulged [her]self in reading"; Woodbury, who "literally devour[s]" *Uncle Tom's Cabin,* also claims "It has done me good. But, I still need some Christian patience and meekness, those qualities that shine so brightly in the life of the poor old negro."[24] Such explicit endorsements of Stowe's moral imperatives sometimes sound like afterthoughts. Deeply absorbed in *Uncle Tom's Cabin,* Cushing, Woodbury, Norcross, and others are threatened with the loss of their familiar sense of self and social positioning. Indeed, by completing the novel in three days—or one sitting—they maximize the threat to their customary sense of decorum and even reality. Consumed by their feelings while consuming a book, they ignore their friends and do not join their wives in bed. Such readers regain their composure only afterwards, as they formulate the moral meaning of their reading experience (or, like Mary Pierce Poor, caution others to avoid the book).[25] This dynamic implies just the kind of merger between text and reader that preoccupied commentators.

Although *Uncle Tom's Cabin* was publicly condemned and hard to buy in the South, Southerners often acquired it, and read it eagerly. "I have now finally managed to obtain *Uncle Tom's Cabin,*" Rosalie Roos of South Carolina writes in a letter on May 4, 1853. "In Charleston this book cannot be bought. . . . We have been able to borrow it from Mrs. Peronneau's sister and Eliza read it though in a day and has halfway become an abolitionist from it."[26] A resident of New Orleans writes to the editor of the *New York Independent* on August 18, 1852: "our citizens have [read it] . . . with avidity. . . . I sent to New York for the book, and when I carried it home and laid it upon the table, it was taken up and read by a young Southern friend then present, who has trafficked in slaves; . . . He asked and obtained the first loan of the book. Since then, it has been going the rounds, and before one is through, it is engaged by another."[27] Mary Boykin Chesnut's diary and letters show that she read it, reread it and "could not" read it ("too sickening") in the course of 1861 and 1862. Irresistibly drawn to it as well as repelled by it, Chesnut repeatedly mulls it over.[28] Southern reviewers too read the novel with intensity, as their often-cited outrage suggests.

In 1850 Charles William Holbrook, a young man from Massachusetts, took a job as a tutor to a planter's children in Rockingham County, North Carolina. He encountered *Uncle Tom's Cabin* when a visitor returned from a trip to New York, "bringing many presents."[29] Charles's diary jottings reflect the familiar pattern—absorption to a degree unusual in his experience, followed by expressions of inadequate piety and resolutions to do better. Charles—a young man who is "disgusted" at a public dance, "would not be seen" at the theater, and is committed to Temperance—begins to read Volume I of *Uncle Tom's Cabin* on October 1, 1852. He finds himself "much interested in it" and finishes the first volume by the next day (89). "Became much interested in it," he reiterates in his diary on October 2, adding that the book "relates some exciting scenes." On October 3, Charles records his emotional response to Eva's death ("The tears rushed into my eyes") and offsets his sense of the novel's excitement by "resolv[ing] to be more devoted" (89). By the next morning he finishes the novel, having taken it with him to school and completed his reading at recess. "I believe it to be the most interesting book I ever read," he comments (89). Although Charles occasionally mentions other reading matter in passing, Stowe's novel absorbs him to an exceptional degree and impels him to write at unusual and recurrent length. The day after completing the novel he begins to read it to one of his pupils, who confirms the brutality of slavery by citing instances from his own experience. On October 14, Charles notes that the planter, "Mr G. likes Uncle Tom's Cabin but Mrs G. is bitter against it." The next day there is "Great talk in the house about Mrs. Stowe" and the following day "Mr. Gallaway says he will burn 'Uncle Toms Cabin.' He has changed his mind on it. Mrs. G. thinks Mrs. Stowe is worse than *Legree*!" (90).

The only other fiction Charles mentions in his journal, in the weeks before and after reading Stowe, is *Aunt Phillis's Cabin*. This pro-slavery response to

Uncle Tom's Cabin arrives at the plantation along with Stowe's novel—but Charles either does not read it at this time, or does not comment on it. He notes in passing having read "Dr. Alcott's Young Man's Guide, Longfellow's poems &c," as well as a "paper from uncle Levi" with "most ridiculous resolutions by the South," and a "Review of Mexican War"; he also attends a lecture by Emerson (84–86). But Charles provides almost no commentary on these various encounters with literature. Immediately after mentioning Alcott and Longfellow, he notes "It has been very rainy. Been thinking of my future prospects. Rather dubious no mistake!!!" (84). Charles does not indicate whether his sense of inadequacy was intensified as a result of reading Alcott and Longfellow.

By contrast, Charles's reading of *Uncle Tom's Cabin* deepens and complicates his own growing experience of the South, of slavery, and of his work as a teacher. The novel becomes a kind of guide to his plantation experience and a source of understanding that he offers to others. Two weeks before beginning to read the novel, Charles had seen a slave trader for the first time ("one who can buy up and drive off coloredmen [*sic*] like cattle to a market" [89]). Four days after he begins reading the novel to his pupil, Charles writes that "Henderson [one of the slaves on the plantation] is sold from wife & children to go to N. Orleans!" (90).[30] Taking a leaf right out of Stowe's book, Charles notes that he "went down to [Henderson's] cabin and told him to become a Christian so as to meet his wife in Heaven" (90).

The image of Charles that emerges from these diary entries is of a young man who is uncertain of his future and curious about parts unknown (at one point he considers becoming a "missionary among the Indians at the far West" [85]). He is serious and disciplined. He worries about being "too indulgent" with pupils who whisper in class and who fail to "feel the importance of improving every moment" (86, 87). He is shocked and disapproving of things he sees en route to the plantation ("O! such profanity and drunkenness! I never before heard or saw. Nearly every man drinks, chews tobacco and swears!" [87]). He reports on a variety of indiscretions which seem to surprise him ("Mr. Gallaway said he lost 17 dollars once playing cards!" [88]; a man "in Madison . . . after living with his wife *seven* or *eight* months found her to be p——t and left her!!" (88). Throughout the diary he is a harsh judge of the behavior of others ("I see there *are* some *honest* men here as well as at home," he concedes at one point [88]). Within the framework of these diary entries, it is only reading *Uncle Tom's Cabin* that impels Charles to look inward ("to be more devoted") and extend to others spontaneous offers of information and insight. At the same time, his renewed commitment to spirituality and social action also serves to justify his fiction-reading pleasures. This dynamic was culturally typical.

Uncle Tom's Cabin appealed to an unusually wide range of readers. Reflecting on the novel's surprising success, Lydia Maria Child offered a witty theory about the strategic function of Stowe's religious emphasis: "I am glad [Mrs. Stowe] has written such a book," Child comments in a letter; "I am also glad that it has a moderate sprinkling of Calvinism in it. Not that *I* like that fiery medicine, even in homeopathic doses; but it will make it acceptable to a much larger class of readers."[31] Child suggests that by making a sweet pill somewhat bitter Stowe stimulated the appetite of many readers who would not otherwise have been willing to taste her concoction. The moral and religious earnestness of *Uncle Tom's Cabin* disarmed the resistance of many stalwart moral arbiters, enabling Stowe to bring a Trojan horse into a well-guarded camp. Phoebe Palmer, an influential Methodist speaker, writer, and humanitarian activist who vehemently opposed the Beechers' tolerance for "pious amusements" in general, attacked *Uncle Tom's Cabin* in particular because she feared just what Lydia Maria Child enthusiastically anticipated: that it would create a taste for fiction in "hundreds of families where novels had hitherto been prohibited."[32] Palmer may have been right: *Uncle Tom's Cabin* made novel-reading legitimate for many readers who had once resisted its lure altogether. The guidelines for reading that Stowe included in her narrative facilitated this process.

PROTOCOLS OF READING IN *UNCLE TOM's CABIN:* THE NOVEL AND THE HOLY BOOK

The protocol of reading inscribed in *Uncle Tom's Cabin* outlines the proper way to approach it. Stowe's narrator makes distinctions among different ways to read and suggests the moral and the social uses to which right-minded reading can be put. Relying heavily on citations from the Bible and discussions of Bible-reading, Stowe differentiates between interpretive practices worth emulating and others that should be resisted. The Bible itself was a pivotal resource in her narrative weave, but she is sparing in her use of quotation. Attacking promiscuous habits of citation, Stowe writes as follows to her son Charles during his studies at divinity school:

> The mere human brick laying of ideas torn from the Bible reminds me of those hovels which it is said the Greeks build from the ruins of the Parthenon and other temples. Fragments of beauty & glory made grotesque & absurd in their adaptation into a vulgar dwelling—A man gets a system—& builds into it texts of scripture torn from their original position and shorn of their glory.[33]

Instead of quotations, Stowe offers multiple scenes of Bible-reading and scenes in which characters discuss the text so as to open diverse questions about interpretation and the reading experience.

It would be difficult to overestimate the scale and intensity of Stowe's representation of reading in *Uncle Tom's Cabin*. Her emphasis on reading remains in the background when the novel is examined through the lens of sentiment or race alone but, as we have already seen, scenes of reading form an integral part of the text. When considered against the background of contemporary debates about fiction, Stowe's representation of books and readers emerges not only as a challenge to prohibitions on slave literacy but also as a strategy for repositioning the novel in literary culture. Stowe's representation of reading reflects her assumptions about the "long marginalized" genre that she used.[34]

Like any novelist, Stowe tried first and foremost to grab the attention of her readers—to engage their interest and sympathy, in short, to keep them reading. *Uncle Tom's Cabin* was offered to the public on familiar terms: part sentimental tale, part reform tract, part abolitionist appeal. But Stowe sought to encourage a mode of reading that was not conventionally associated with any of these forms. She urged her readers to approach her novel as Tom and Eva read Scripture—in an engaged, thoughtful, imaginative way, as if it were true. *Uncle Tom's Cabin* set out to modify the kind of reading widely associated with installment fiction, reform tracts, and news: speedily consumed, rapidly forgotten. At the beginning of Chapter XII Tom is said to be "thinking over some words of an unfashionable old book" (193). By celebrating Tom's relation to that book Stowe links her own "lowly" form of writing with another text that should, she implies, have more power and authority than it is sometimes given. Her practice of inscribing Scripture into her novel lent authority to her fiction; at the same time, the drama and vividness of her fiction lent new sex appeal to Scripture (that "unfashionable old book").[35]

The figure of Tom is central to Stowe's representation of the ideal reader—the kind of reader she desired for her own text, one who, she felt, would raise the moral level of American culture. Tom's reading practices are shaped by emotional responsiveness and faith; this way of reading is proposed as appropriate for two books that become linked to each other. Stowe's novel, like the "unfashionable old book" that sustains Tom, is accessible to the "lowly" as well as the rich or sophisticated.[36] Stowe's well-known valorization of simplicity and sincerity over sophistication—what we might call her hermeneutics of simplicity—is also an affirmation of Tom's style of reading. Tom becomes a model not just of black literacy but of all imaginatively engaged reading—including novel-reading.

Throughout the novel Tom derives comfort from the words of the Bible—an "ancient volume, got up principally by 'ignorant and unlearned men'" (193). *Uncle Tom's Cabin,* written not by "ignorant unlearned men" but by an "unlearned" wife and mother, is presented as another humble medium that represents truth. The opposition between high and low, educated and simple is also an endorsement of the novel itself. *Uncle Tom's Cabin* was offered to the reading public as a text that one could read literally—indeed this was a measure of its value. Such a book was to be its own best protection against both free-floating fantasy and skepticism.

As Karen Halttunen has shown, antebellum middle-class culture affirmed a "code of sincerity" or "transparency" which aspired to "truth and plainness in all our ways and doing." Joanne Dobson suggests that "transparent" language is a characteristic of sentimental fiction.[37] When Stowe represented Scriptural meaning as easily accessible to all, she drew on a long Puritan tradition and familiar assumptions of Scottish Common Sense philosophy.[38] When she implied that, like the Bible, *Uncle Tom's Cabin* was simple and true, she drew on firmly rooted values of antebellum middle-class society. Transposing a set of behavioral priorities into a protocol of reading, Stowe legitimized, even exalted, her own fiction. At the same time, she presented a carefully constructed argument as if it were artless. Stowe's narrative strategies, like her politics, were consequently naturalized. Her message was framed as both self-evident and sanctified.

Within *Uncle Tom's Cabin* numerous scenes privilege the kind of reading that leads to political wisdom, moral action, thoughtfulness, or faith, but only the Bible invites intensive reading and the habit of taking textual images for reality. *Uncle Tom's Cabin* presents fiction as generally false: "In a novel," Stowe writes, describing St. Clare's state of mind after he loses his first love, "people's hearts break, and they die, and that is the end of it; and in a story this is very convenient. But in real life we do not die when all that makes life bright dies to us" (241). Like many Anglo-American novels throughout the nineteenth-century, *Uncle Tom's Cabin* claims not to be a conventional "novel," but rather a picture of "real life."[39] Stowe further distances *Uncle Tom's Cabin* from "fiction" by avoiding any suggestion that readers might derive mere pleasure and excitement from her book. The kind of absorption that many antebellum readers of *Uncle Tom's Cabin* reported is not represented in the novel itself—with the possible exception of the scene in which Simon Legree, having picked up a book strategically placed on a table by his slave Cassie, finds himself "turning page after page," engrossed in "one of those collections of stories of bloody murders, ghostly legend and supernatural visitations, which, coarsely got up and illustrated have a strange fascination for one who once begins to read them" (568). Readers such as Woodbury, Cushing, Beecher, and Norcross violate Stowe's own protocol of reading, inscribed in her novel and elsewhere. They go beyond sympathy and contemplation, turning page after page, immersed, absorbed, strangely fascinated, giving themselves over to their appetites ("*Read* 'Uncle Tom's Cabin' oh yes, literally devoured it") and selfish needs ("I indulged myself), letting go of social responsibility ("I disregarded all the rules of Ettiquit") and enacting the very effects of 'bad' reading that cultural guardians warned against. At the same time, readers could turn to Stowe's novel itself for evidence of the novel's righteous aims and capacity to "do good."

Scenes of reading throughout *Uncle Tom's Cabin* explore contrasting modes of response, praising some, criticizing others. A multiplicity of printed texts vied for attention and authority in print culture of the period; reading practices were many and varied. Chapter XII of *Uncle Tom* ("Select Incidents of Lawful Trade") reflects this situation by representing a range of texts—handwritten and printed, public and private, worldly and spiritual: bills of sale, a slave-trader's ledger, newspaper advertisements, and Scripture. Each of these texts—like *Uncle Tom's Cabin* itself—implies a different perspective on the "peculiar institution." With the exception of the scene in which Simon Legree turns "page after page," engrossed in a ghost story, fiction-reading is never directly represented among these reading activities; but novel-reading is the necessary condition for accessing every image of print in the book. At stake in these competing perspectives is the meaning of Scripture, the meaning of slavery, and the function of the novel as a mediating text.

Chapter XII explores a question of reading in a much-cited scene where two "ladies," two parsons, and a variety of others engage in an impromptu debate. Both parsons rely upon Scripture to clinch their argument. At the climax of the scene two verses of Scripture are pitted against each other: "Cursed be Canaan" vs. "All things whatsoever you would that men should do unto you do you even so unto them" (201). Both verses were frequently cited in discussions of slavery. The first was widely used to suggest that slavery was justified by Scripture, the second to suggest the imperative of a "Higher Law"—higher, in particular, than the man-made "Fugitive Law."

The story of Noah and Ham ("Cursed be Canaan") required considerable unpacking before it could be used to justify American slavery. By contrast, "All things whatsoever . . ." is represented as a "plain . . . text" (201), one that conveys an undeniable moral imperative. Stowe argues that an elaborate mystification and distortion of "plain" facts is required before one can share the perspective of the pro-slavery parson. By contrast, "poor," ungrammatical fellows like John the drover, uneducated slaves like Tom, children like Eva, or women, become touchstones for a kind of natural epistemology in which simple truths, couched in transparent language, are recognized on sight. *Uncle Tom's Cabin* presents itself as appropriate to such reading practices.

When John "the honest drover" spits tobacco juice at a runaway ad, Stowe affirms spontaneous and direct responses to self-evident meanings contained in printed words (fig. 7). In a related sequence, Mrs. Bird (the Senator's wife) affirms the value of a "plain right thing" (145), over the reasoning of her husband, who has made eloquent speeches in the legislature on behalf of the Fugitive Slave Law. "Now John," says Mrs. Bird in Chapter IX, "I don't know anything about politics, but I can read my Bible; and there I see that I must feed the hungry, clothe the naked and comfort the desolate, and that Bible I mean to follow" (144). By validating the responses of John "the honest drover" and Mrs. Bird's literalist reading habits, Stowe suggests that no elaborate interpretive moves are required either to grasp the outrage of a runaway ad, or to see how "feed the hungry, clothe the naked" can be applied to the situa-

7. *John the drover spitting at a runaway ad. From Harriet Beecher Stowe,* Uncle Tom's Cabin. *Boston: John P. Jewett, 1853. Collection of The New-York Historical Society. Negative #83645d.*

tion of an escaped slave. The test of a "plain, right" perspective is precisely its accessibility to an unsophisticated reader.

Chapter XIV reinforces this argument. When Tom reads the Bible to himself, sitting on the cotton bales on deck, his laborious reading is presented as no disadvantage—indeed it is an advantage—to appropriation of the "book he was intent on" (229). "Having learned late in life, Tom was but a slow reader, and passed on laboriously from verse to verse" (228–29). Tom's reading practices—intense, emotional, trusting—are valorized in this scene. Indeed Stowe points a sharp contrast between Tom's way and a different approach: learned, sophisticated, skeptical.

> Cicero, when he buried his darling and only daughter, had a heart as full of honest grief as poor Tom's . . . but Cicero could pause over no such sublime words of hope, and look to no such future reunion; and if he *had* seen them, ten to one he would not have believed,—he must fill his head first with a thousand questions of authenticity of manuscript, and correctness of translation. But, to poor Tom, there it lay, just what he needed. . . . It must be true; for, if not true, how could he live? (229)

In the 1850s, the image of Cicero was routinely identified with manipulative rhetoric—deceptive, "mellifluous . . . eloquence."[40] Trading on these negative associations, Stowe turns Cicero into a figure for the quintessentially captious and resisting reader. The juxtaposition of Cicero and Tom implies diametrically opposed reading practices. Tom savors every "sublime" word, while Cicero "if he *had*" seen the Biblical text would have derived neither comfort, hope, pleasure, nor understanding from it. Distracted by "a thousand questions of authenticity of manuscript, and correctness of translation . . . he would not have believed" (229). It is as though Stowe here anticipates some of the criticism later leveled against her own book—for exaggeration, fabrication, imaginative extravagance, charges emanating with particular vehemence from the South where, as Thomas Gossett notes, even clergymen often "denounced Stowe almost in street language."[41] In the *Key to Uncle Tom's Cabin,* Stowe offered precisely what she criticizes Cicero for demanding: documentation, proof of authenticity. Yet the Cicero passage suggests that documentation is finally beside the point, and only hampers imaginative engagement with a narrative. Such engagement creates access to a kind of truth that is obscured by a preoccupation with what is "correct" or "accurate."[42] The emphasis on truth also justified the kind of absorbed reading practices that, under other circumstances, would have been suspect for many readers of the period.

By presenting *Uncle Tom's Cabin* itself as "plain" and "right"—like the Sacred Narrative—Stowe deflects attention from her own rhetorical strategies and implies that her novel too is to be absorbed and believed, not questioned. What is to be doubted is neither Scripture, nor Stowe's representation of slavery, but "the oft-fabled poetic legend of a patriarchal institution" (51). The idea of slavery as a benign "patriarchal institution" is lambasted here as pure fabrication: "fable ... poet[ry and] legend." This rhetorical move associates her novel (like the Bible) with the true and the real. The specious and even the fictive are located elsewhere, in novels where "people's hearts break, and they die" (241) or in those "stories of bloody murders, ghostly legend and supernatural visitations" that so fascinate Simon Legree (568). Thus Stowe attempts not only to counter indifference to Scripture but also to neutralize common doubts about the value of fiction-reading.

MODELS OF READING: TRUTH, REALITY, AND SUBJECTIVITY

Throughout *Uncle Tom's Cabin* the question of how to defamiliarize Scripture and make it imaginatively real is intimately linked to the question of how to do the same for slavery. Stowe's "Introduction" to her brother's account of *The Incarnation* directly addresses the problem of readers who fail to engage with the Biblical text, readers for whom Scripture does not come alive in the reading: "One of the principal difficulties" faced by many who begin to read the Bible, Stowe argues, is "that want of freshness and reality which is caused by early and long-continued familiarity with its language. . . . its reading is to them but a wearisome task. . . . their mind wanders in dreamy vacancy."[43] Stowe believed that abolitionist arguments had also grown too familiar to be meaningful in their present form; this idea is evident throughout the novel. *Uncle Tom's Cabin* asserts a recurrent analogy between readers who fail to engage actively with the Bible and those who fail to engage seriously with the realities of slavery. A woman on board the ship that is taking Tom south to be sold responds with a yawn to the passengers' debate about Scripture and slavery. When Eva quotes Scripture to Henrique after he whips his young slave he replies, "O, the Bible! To be sure it says a great many . . . things; but then, nobody ever thinks of doing them—you know, Eva, nobody does" (396). Eva's mother, who dozes over her prayerbook and "only imagine[s] she ha[s] been reading it" (405), fully accepts the claims of her pro-slavery minister. But St. Clare is the figure through whom Stowe most fully dramatizes the link between a failure to engage with slavery on the one hand, and a failure to engage with Scripture on the other. St. Clare's relation to both Scripture and slavery develops from a state of indifference to one of imaginative susceptibility. This development has received little emphasis in recent discussions of the novel. Still, Eva's father is a significant presence for approximately two hundred pages of the book. Nineteenth-century readers loved him.[44]

Stowe's emphasis on the regenerative potential of engaged reading is clearly reflected in her image of St. Clare, whose relation to Scripture figures prominently in his journey from "the habit of doubting" (435) to the possibility of belief. The incompleteness of the journey invites Stowe's reader to finish the process St. Clare has begun. St. Clare's changing relation to slavery and his changing relation to Scripture are closely intertwined, and both are offered as models for the skeptical reader of *Uncle Tom's Cabin*.

St. Clare is repeatedly seen with the Bible after Eva's death but, like the word "fugitive" in Senator Bird's newspaper, the Bible cannot speak to him. A scene that appropriately takes place in St. Clare's library foregrounds his inability to read. Tom enters the library to find his master "lying on his face with Eva's Bible open before him at a little distance" (435). "I want to believe this Bible,—and I can't," St. Clare says. For St. Clare, indeed, the Bible is no more than a fiction ("How do you know there's any Christ, Tom! You never saw the Lord" [436]). Tom explains that he feels the presence of Jesus in his heart and soul. "'Singular' said St. Clare, turning away, 'that the story of a man that lived and died eighteen hundred years ago can affect people so yet. But he was no man,' he added suddenly. 'No man ever had such long and living power'" (437). St Clare stops short of saying that Jesus was the son of God; indeed his emphasis on the powerful affect of the "story" and on Jesus as "no man" has more relevance to narrative than to theology. (After all, Tom and St. Clare are "no men" either.) St. Clare never loses his awareness of Scripture as "story" and "image." The issue of belief here crystallizes around a response to reading, one that problematizes the relation between reality and text. St Clare here shares Cicero's preoccupation with authenticity: "This is all real to you!" St Clare exclaims in amazement, as he observes Tom's response to the story of Lazarus. Reading the passage aloud, St. Clare himself "often paus[es] ... to wrestle down feelings which were roused by the pathos of the story" (437); he is mightily affected by "the story" but does not give free rein to his emotions. Ultimately, he comes to feel that the idea of "a last judgement" is indeed "a wonderful image" (450). By calling it an "image," however, St. Clare sustains the distance of the skeptic. As "image," the Last Judgment remains a rhetorical construct.

Nonetheless, St. Clare's incipient emotional response is represented as the beginning of a change in his relation to a book—and to life: "St. Clare was, in many respects, another man. He read his little Eva's Bible seriously and honestly; he thought more soberly and practically of his relation to his servants"; and (a detail often overlooked in discussions of *Uncle Tom's Cabin*) he begins to take "the legal steps necessary for Tom's emancipation" (440). Stowe places considerable emphasis on St. Clare as a reader, especially in the two chapters that end with his death. In the second of these chapters St. Clare reads—and rereads—a passage about the Last Judgment. Subsequently, he is "absent and thoughtful" (448); somewhat later he "seemed in a deep reverie" (448). Before his death at the end of this chapter St. Clare is well on the way to becoming a reader who immerses himself in a text, returns to it, reflects upon it, and applies it to his moral and practical life. He thus becomes a model for both the reader of Scripture and the reader of *Uncle Tom's Cabin*.

But Eva and Tom are the figures through whom Stowe most clearly suggests her understanding of the ideal way for a reader to approach and appropriate certain texts. Uneducated slave and little child are the antithesis of indifferent, doubting, captious readers. Eva and Tom read themselves into the Bible. As a result, Jesus becomes "a living all-surrounding reality" to them (400). Having embraced the text as truth, Eva and Tom find its images full of resonance and substance, directly reversing St. Clare's reading experience: "In that book which [Eva] and her simple old friend read together, she had seen and taken to her heart the image of one who loved the little child; and as she gazed and mused, He had ceased to be an image . . ." (400).

Attacks on fiction by ministers and educators often emphasized that readers took fiction as reality. From the point of view of those concerned with young people's reading in particular—Lydia Maria Child, Henry Ward Beecher, and others—the danger of corrupt and corrupting texts was precisely this: they offered seductive alternatives to common sense and plain language, to the moral and aesthetic imperatives of daily life. Stowe's aim, by contrast, was to turn the reader's imagination inward, not to fantasy, but to emotional and spiritual depths, as well as outward, to the world.

After Eva's death, a "softened" and "chastened" Ophelia is described "as one who communed with her own heart not in vain" (443). "Communing with one's

. . . heart" on the basis of a text: this is what Stowe invited her own readers to do—and many did. It is what St. Clare is presented as doing. It is what Tom and Eva repeatedly do. It is what even Topsy learns to do. After Eva's death, as we have seen, Topsy develops a passionate devotion to the book Eva has given her, and thus exhibits a capacity for moral and emotional experience. Between the 1850s and the 1890s these qualities were increasingly associated with secular reading, even novel-reading.

Stowe offered *Uncle Tom's Cabin* to the public not exactly as a secular analogue to the holy book, but as a transitional text: one that would ultimately lead its readers to the Bible itself—as her brother's fictionalized account of the *Incarnation* was designed to do. Like Scripture, as Stowe read it, *Uncle Tom's Cabin* was to provide food for "the faculty of the imagination" while provoking thought, faith, and moral action.[45] Stowe's novel at once promoted the reading of Scripture and invoked Scripture to legitimize sentimental fiction. (In 1870, Stowe justifies the legitimacy of fiction by asserting that "divine examples in the parables and allegories of Scripture" show "that this species of reading is not only lawful but necessary and useful.")[46] At the same time, *Uncle Tom's Cabin* itself vied with Scripture for the attention of the reading public.[47] Stowe may have succeeded in advancing a holy cause through fiction, but at the same time she made the pleasures of fiction-reading available to reading communities where fiction had previously met with sharp disapproval.

PROMOTING FICTION IN THE PARATEXT

Paratextual material for early editions of *Uncle Tom's Cabin* helped neutralize the stigma that still attached to fiction in 1851. Illustrations, prefaces, and advertisements reflect a clear understanding of both the lingering resistance to fiction and the marketability of religion. Illustrations reinforced the link between the Biblical text and Stowe's own. Hammatt Billings and other illustrators of the antebellum period elaborated Stowe's emphasis on the Holy Book by including numerous scenes of Bible reading and illuminated letters at the start of every chapter.[48] Illustrations of Tom and Eva, George Shelby and Tom, Eva and Mammy, Eva and Topsy, or Tom reading on the Legree plantation, all include the Bible in the background—or the foreground.

Illustrators are readers themselves, and Hammatt Billings was a reader particularly in tune with Stowe's stated priorities. His engravings for Jewett's lavish Christmas edition included not only numerous scenes of Bible-reading but also multiple images of Bibles, prayer-books, and open pages with such inscriptions as "feed the hungry, clothe the naked." Billings's illustrations reinforce the association of *Uncle Tom's Cabin* with the Bible and the idea of Stowe's novel itself as an "inspired" text. Stowe repeatedly claimed that *Uncle Tom's Cabin* had been written by God.[49] In 1852 George Sand classified Stowe's "genius" as that "of the saint."[50] James Sherman praised Stowe's "rare and sanctified talents" in "Introductory Remarks" to a British edition.[51] A review in *The Congregationalist* sees "the writing of this book as providential."[52] At the National Black Convention of 1853, *Uncle Tom's Cabin* "was celebrated 'as a work plainly marked by the finger of God' on behalf of black people."[53]

In the 1850s *Uncle Tom's Cabin* was much-advertised as "The Greatest Book of its Kind." But what kind of book was it? The category "fiction" or "novel" rarely appeared in antebellum ads or reviews. Early advertisements for *Uncle Tom's Cabin* referred to it as a book, a volume, a narrative, a work—anything but a novel. Given the low cultural status of fiction, this anomaly makes sense. The characteristic terminology is evident in the full-page ad with review-excerpts reprinted in Jewett's early editions.[54] These excerpts repeatedly stress the book's religious value, its "service [to] a holy but perilous work" (*Christian Examiner*).[55] In a phrase directly designed to counter the resistance to fiction, the ad for *Uncle Tom's Cabin* in volume two of the first edition notes that "Editors of Newspapers, Magazines, and even the staid Quarterlies have vied with each other in their eulogistic notices." The moral and religious seriousness of the book is restated on one cover for Jewett's gift edition: red leather, embossed in gold, with a figure of Christ standing above a prostrate Tom (a scene taken from the end of Chapter XL).

Jewett's foregrounding of religious themes was a crafty marketing tactic in a literary field where the status of the novel was uncertain, and as we have seen, this strategy was also Stowe's own. Yet from the beginning readers also praised *Uncle Tom's Cabin* in terms conventionally appropriate to secular literature, including fiction. Reviewers noted the "exciting interest," "spirit [and] vigor" of the book as well as its "thrilling contents" and "dramatic beauty."[56] There were abundant references to Stowe's "masterly genius," and "profound knowledge of the human heart."[57] These familiar terms told informed readers that *Uncle Tom's Cabin* was fiction. In the course of the 1850s this generic category became less and less of a liability.

FEAR OF FICTION: THE ABOLITIONIST PRESS

The *National Era,* where installments of *Uncle Tom's Cabin* began to appear on June 5, 1851, conceived of itself as "a superior family newspaper . . . [with a] literature department . . . inferior to that of no other weekly in the country."[58] Unlike *The Liberator, The National Anti-Slavery Standard,* or *Frederick Douglass' Paper,* where fiction appeared on the last page of the paper (if at all), the *Era* prominently showcased its serialized tales on page one, alongside congressional speeches, political discussions, and news reports. However, until the appearance of *Uncle Tom's Cabin,* as we saw in Chapter 1, the sentimental fiction published in the *Era* was confined to didactic tales of family life that rarely alluded to such vexed social problems as poverty or immigration, much less slavery. Until well after the success of Stowe's novel, *The Liberator* printed no serialized fiction, and almost no fiction of any kind. *The National Anti-Slavery Standard* and *Frederick Douglass' Paper* included some fiction, though rarely original American fiction that engaged contemporary social issues. A significant exception is Douglass's own tale "The Heroic Slave"—but Douglass's story was published almost a year after *Uncle Tom's Cabin* appeared in book form. Indeed, "The Heroic Slave" is a direct response to *Uncle Tom's Cabin,* a "countercomposition," in Robert Stepto's words.[59]

On February 5, 1847, *The Liberator* printed a poem that effectively explained the paper's rationale for avoiding fiction in its pages. According to this poem "true wisdom holds" that "the Press" should not provide "Trashy romances, cast in leaden moulds / Monotones, unnatural, and dull."[60] Three years later, "trashy romances" could still serve *The Liberator* as a whipping boy. A "Letter to Country Girls" makes a typical case against "these drawling concerns, who lounge around reading novels, lisping about fashion and gentility, . . . putting on airs to catch husbands, while their mothers are toiling and boiling in the kitchen." This "letter" goes to some lengths to criticize young city women who "spend their mornings lounging in bed, reading some silly book, taking lessons in music and French, fixing finery and the like."[61]

The grounds of attack here—fashion, false gentility, idleness, and self-involvement—are only some of the vices often associated with novel-reading in antebellum literary culture. Such charges were regularly echoed in literary journals, advice literature, and sermons for both men and women. Yet fiction was becoming a force that could not be ignored. Indeed, "A Letter to Country Girls" itself uses fictional techniques (description, dramatic situations, delineation of hypothetical characters). "Trashy" fiction continued to be criticized in *The Liberator*,[62] but certain kinds of fiction began to be praised.

One week after the appearance of "A Letter to Country Girls" a poem entitled "The Story Tellers" celebrates the European novel. In nineteen verses, the speaker proceeds to name names—Bunyan, Defoe, Swift, Sterne, Fielding, Richardson, the irrepressible Scott, and Dickens (who was reprinted in multiple contexts, including *Frederick Douglass' Paper*). Although no American fiction-writers are mentioned in "The Story Tellers," these verses suggest that novels have a role to play for American readers. As presented in this poem, fiction is largely for amusement and sentiment—"wit, . . . mirth, and feeling"—yet some fiction offers "wisdom" and "truth," especially to readers who "scorn / . . . more obtrusive teaching."[63]

The Liberator of this period displays growing attempts to rethink the function of novelistic strategies. Although fiction is still rare in *The Liberator* during the early 1850s, news reports become increasingly dramatic—even sensational—with headlines such as "Romantic Story" (January 4, 1850), "Horrible Doings up the River" (April 30, 1850), "Murder Most Foul and Unnatural" (February 27, 1852). Moreover, in a unique exception to *The Liberator*'s general policy, a (fictionalized) "Dialogue" among women in a "Sewing Circle" engages the Fugitive Slave Law, debating the question of what women can do about it.[64] Fiction does not appear in *The Liberator* again, however, until April 2, 1852, when it reprints a lengthy excerpt from *Uncle Tom's Cabin* "as a specimen of the dramatic power displayed in the remarkable and thrilling work by Harriet Beecher Stowe, entitled *Uncle Tom's Cabin* (just published and selling with great rapidity)." One week later, on April 9, 1852, *The Liberator* publishes a poem, "To the Author of 'Uncle Tom's Cabin'" (reprinted from the New York *Independent* and soon to appear in *Frederick Douglass' Paper* as well).[65] "To the Author of 'Uncle Tom's Cabin'" celebrates Stowe's book as the antidote to fiction that serves no moral or political end. Stowe is represented as the antithesis of those who dedicate their gifts to "thrilling tales that melt and enervate," or who "picture . . . / Passion, and pleasure, and unblest desire." Stowe has skillfully combined "Truth, natural wit, and love and piety" in order to "hold, with equal nerve and grace, / The damning mirror up to Slavery's Ethiop Face": "Hail Fiction's Better Mistress!"

Fiction plays an increasingly prominent role in *The Liberator* after this point. In 1855, the magazine took the unusual step of printing an excerpt from Hildreth's *Archy Moore* on page one. The reissuing of this early anti-slavery novel (like Frederick Douglass's composition of "The Heroic Slave") was itself a direct result of the changing conditions in the literary marketplace and changing interpretive conventions in the wake of the sensation created by *Uncle Tom's Cabin.* Slavery had become a far more legitimate—and popular—subject for fiction than before. An excerpt of Stowe's *Dred* appeared in *The Liberator* in 1856 ("Old Tiff"). Other extracts, fictionalized accounts of slave experience, and advertisements for fiction soon followed.[66]

Garrison's *Liberator* is not a faithful mirror of antebellum print culture as a whole. While many religious and abolitionist papers were already printing a certain amount of "light" fare (including fiction) by 1851, *The Liberator* was as virulently opposed to "mere amusement" as the *New York Evangelist.* Once *Uncle Tom's Cabin* was taken up in abolitionist and evangelical circles, however, its influence spread unimpeded beyond the confines of Stowe's initial reading public. When published in book form, *Uncle Tom's Cabin* rapidly gained favor among authors and literary commentators in the United States and Europe. It was the first American novel to have such wide appeal. As Meredith McGill has shown, pirated reprints of *Uncle Tom's Cabin* increased pressure for international copyright laws.[67] By the 1860s, Stowe was an international celebrity as well as a regular contributor to the prestigious *Atlantic Monthly.* Her voice was increasingly raised on behalf of fiction generally.

In 1865, in a chapter of *House and Home Papers* (first published in the *Atlantic*), Stowe asserts the value of fiction even though many religious leaders continue to condemn it, especially as Sunday reading. Novels vary, Stowe remarks: "Some are merely frivolous, some are absolutely noxious and dangerous, others again are written with a strong moral and religious purpose, and, being vivid and interesting, produce far more religious effect on the mind than dull treatises and sermons."[68] With Stowe's help, the advance of the novel continued. Writing in *The Nation* three years later, J. W. De Forest coins a phrase—"The Great American Novel"—which was to have considerable currency for decades. Apart from *Uncle Tom's Cabin,* De Forest claims, there is not "a single tale which paints American life so broadly, truly, and sympathetically that every American of feeling and culture is forced to acknowledge the picture as a likeness of something which he knows."[69] Prior to the unprecedented success of Stowe's narrative, "The Great American Novel" was literally an unimaginable phenomenon. But by the 1860s there was nothing surprising either in De Forest's appreciation of Stowe or in his view of the novel as an important literary form.

In 1873, in an "Introduction" to *A Library of Famous Fiction,* Stowe declared victory over lingering resistance to the novel. In her opening statement she asserts, "The propensity of the human mind to fiction is one of those irrepressible forces against which it has always proved vain to contend":

> In the strictest new England times Sir Charles Grandison was often recommended by clergymen, and lay on the toilet-table of godly young women, beside the Bible and Thomas Boston's "Fourfold State." Still, as a class, novels were considered a dangerous indulgence, and in our youth one of the stock themes for composition-writing was "On the disadvantages of novel-reading." (vi)

"For all that," Stowe adds, "there have always been, even in the strictest households, certain permitted works of fiction, which have taken such hold on the human heart that every member of the family . . . read them . . . as one of the choicest delights of life."[70]

The "9 Standard Masterpieces" reprinted in the *Library of Famous Fiction* range from *Pilgrim's Progress* to the *Arabian Nights.* No American texts are included in the volume. Fiction as a form, however, is fully endorsed by the collection and by Stowe's introduction. Neither the choice of texts for this "Library" nor the absence of American fiction among its selections is unusual. Although *Uncle Tom's Cabin* was De Forest's prime candidate for the "Great American Novel" in 1868, "great" American fiction remained a scarce commodity even at the end of the century. In the 1880s and '90s *Uncle Tom's Cabin* was invariably included on recommended reading lists or suggestions for "home libraries," but such lists still kept American fiction to a minimum.[71] When James Russell Lowell published a discussion of the "Five Indispensable Authors" in the *Century* in 1893, the only "indispensable" novelist on the list was Cervantes.[72] *Don Quixote*—one of the few novels that Stowe read parts of as a child—is a brilliant choice for Lowell to endorse in this context: one that offers the pleasures of fiction-reading while dramatizing its dangers.

Ambivalence about fiction and distinctions between morally "good" and "bad" fiction continued to inform literary reviews and other cultural commentary. Nevertheless, by the end of the 1890s, *Uncle Tom's Cabin* had become a "classic."[73] The widespread application of this term to Stowe's book reflects not only the status acquired by her tale, but the newly consolidated position of the novel in U.S. print culture. As Janice Radway has shown, the controversy about the function of fiction as a cultural form continued well into the 1920s and beyond.[74] Criteria for literary value were once again in flux at the end of the century. A new generation of readers resisted Stowe's didacticism as well as her narrative style. Her politics and evangelicalism had begun to seem dated; her prestige was on the wane.[75] But with invaluable assistance from *Uncle Tom's Cabin,* the novel as a respected form had arrived.

One sign of the cultural capital invested in *Uncle Tom's Cabin* toward the end of the century was its adaptation as a children's book. By the 1890s children's literature—like fiction in general—was increasingly popular. It was a valuable resource for publishers, and a growing presence in periodicals, bookstores, and libraries. Indeed, suitability for youth became a litmus test of literary respectability, and in this period *Uncle Tom's Cabin* both gained and lost by meeting that standard. Positioned alongside *Robinson Crusoe, Little Women,* and other "precious childhood favorites" on lists of recommended reading and elsewhere, *Uncle Tom's Cabin* might well seem tame enough for any nursery.[76] But as we have already noted, *Uncle Tom's Cabin* was read by children from the beginning; in 1851 it had considerable appeal for young readers—and not because it was harmless. Before turning to the way *Uncle Tom's Cabin* was read in the postwar period, we must look at its meaning and function as an antebellum children's book.

4

Beyond Piety and Social Conscience
Uncle Tom's Cabin *as an Antebellum Children's Book*

Charles bro't home 'Uncle Tom's Cabin' the other night, & the children are devouring it.
— *Ellen Douglas Birdseye Wheaton Diary, April 1852*

When the last installment of *Uncle Tom's Cabin* appeared in the *National Era,* on April 1, 1852, Stowe directly addressed the "dear little children who have followed her story" and from whom she now must part.[1] Her concluding words to children were deleted when the novel came out in book form, but *Uncle Tom's Cabin* featured children, spoke to children, and positioned both children and books as important grounds of domestic value. Stowe's thematic emphasis on child-rearing has been much discussed, but scholars have paid no serious attention to children either among Stowe's intended readers or as part of her real reading public.[2]

In 1852, after the first edition of *Uncle Tom's Cabin* appeared, advertisements and reviews noted its suitability for "every man, woman and child in America."[3] Throughout the nineteenth century *Uncle Tom's Cabin* was praised as "a capital story for the child as well as the adult."[4] Children devoured it, as Ellen Douglas Birdseye Wheaton of Syracuse, New York, notes in her diary in 1852.[5] Later, writers as varied as Theodore Dreiser, Frances Hodgson Burnett, Agnes Reppelier, Henry James, James Weldon Johnson, and James Baldwin express childhood fascination with *Uncle Tom's Cabin.*[6]

Less than a year after Stowe's book appeared, a children's book called *Pictures and Stories from Uncle Tom's Cabin* was published by T. Nelson and Sons in London and John P. Jewett in the United States. We do not know how many copies of *Pictures and Stories* were printed or sold, but the strategy of turning *Uncle Tom's Cabin* into a children's book persisted, as did recurrent emphases of plot and character created for that purpose.[7] Why was *Uncle*

Tom's Cabin so appealing to children and so often recommended to them? This question requires different answers for the antebellum and post–Civil War eras. I examine the postwar context for children's editions of *Uncle Tom's Cabin* in Chapter 7. Here, I attempt to explain why *Uncle Tom's Cabin* had greater appeal as an antebellum children's book than at any subsequent time, especially, though not exclusively, in the North (white children in the United States today rarely find themselves either shocked or engrossed by Stowe's novel).

Children's editions are a valuable and neglected resource for understanding the cultural work of a popular story.[8] Although textual analysis cannot tell us how a tale was actually read, children's editions foreground elements that are often overlooked in discussions of a lengthy narrative. This chapter considers *Pictures and Stories* as a gloss on *Uncle Tom's Cabin,* one that highlights the themes and narrative strategies that made Stowe's text so appealing to children—in part because the book violated widely shared conventions for antebellum children's reading.

Pictures and Stories from Uncle Tom's Cabin combines verses and illustrations with lengthy excerpts from the original. It is not clear who condensed *Uncle Tom's Cabin* for this adaptation or who wrote the verses for it. An editorial note saying the verses were "written by the Authoress" has led some scholars to assume that the reference is to Stowe, though others are doubtful.[9] Issued in the United States by Stowe's publisher, John P. Jewett, *Pictures and Stories* must have had Stowe's blessing; her poems of this period suggest she was certainly capable of writing the verses. However that may be, *Pictures and Stories* includes numerous passages from the original, making only small changes. It remains faithful to Stowe's text in many ways; at the same time it is quite a different book.

In abridging and simplifying *Uncle Tom's Cabin* it would have been easy to rely on the racialized stereotypes of the original to provide a kind of shorthand for characterization. Later children's editions often do just that, as we shall see in Chapter 7. But *Pictures and Stories* does the opposite, minimizing racialized language, while significantly restructuring the tale. *Pictures and Stories* was a well-constructed text. Thoughtful transitions and deft elaborations create a tightly woven narrative that reads smoothly, despite massive cuts. Brief interpolations explain the meaning of Canada for fugitive slaves, clarify the condition of the Ohio River, and provide details about Quaker practices. Parenthetical comments make the action comprehensible without slowing it down. Illustrations and verses break up blocks of prose, inviting "the youngest readers" as well as "their older brothers and sisters" to read, hear, and discuss the story.[10]

Pictures and Stories fulfills the didactic imperatives that shape most antebellum children's literature: it offers information about the world, provides an exemplary behavioral model, affirms sympathy, faith, benevolence, moral reflection, and the reading experience itself.[11] It reminds white children of their privileges and their obligations to the "lowly." But *Pictures and Stories* radicalizes *Uncle Tom's Cabin* in two ways: by minimizing racial markers and by maximizing the powerful motifs of fairy tale and legend that Stowe drew on in creating the figures of Harry and Topsy. More than *Uncle Tom's Cabin, Pictures and Stories* defies generic and pedagogic conventions of the period, both in its representation of race, and by offering substantial pleasures of absorption and identification. "A distinctive feature of reading," as Patricinio Schweickart notes, is "the willingness to be susceptible to another subjectivity."[12] This is all the more true of young readers, despite individual and cultural differences.

In what follows I argue, first, that *Uncle Tom's Cabin* itself was a generic anomaly among books read by children in the United States of the 1850s. I then turn to *Pictures and Stories* in order to explore a tension between the book's didactic emphases and the disruptive potential in its representation of children. The figures of Harry and Topsy in particular challenged common antebellum assumptions about racial difference, children's reading, and sympathy. Since *Pictures and Stories* relies heavily on *Uncle Tom's Cabin* itself, my analysis has implications for the impact of Harry and Topsy on readers of the full-length novel; I return to these implications toward the end of the chapter.

Uncle Tom's Cabin: Reality, Fantasy, and Identification

Uncle Tom's Cabin invited young antebellum readers to experience strong emotions across the line of propriety—and color. In representing Harry's midnight excursion and rescue, or Topsy's mischief and her struggle to be good, Stowe combined ingredients that were rare in children's literature of the period. Violence was rampant in antebellum print culture, and children's tales were no exception. Illness or death was the regular outcome of disobedience in moral tales. Temperance and missionary tracts describe the brutality of drunkards and heathens. Abolitionist stories depict cruelty to kidnapped African children or little American slaves, as we saw in Chapter 2. But some of these narratives were not welcome in the middle-class home; and most of them lacked in imaginative force what they provided in graphic detail.

Responding to such texts in the 1850s, writers for and about children criticized the use of fantastic events and frightening images.[13] They also cautioned against the representation of disobedience, for fear that it might be imitated.[14] Yet Harry's story blends the fearful with the miraculous. Topsy is a child who lies, steals, and outwits adults. In addition, Stowe attributed interiority (fear, anger, inner conflict) to black children.[15] *Pictures and Stories* intensifies the focus on Harry and Topsy and goes further than its source in presenting them as analogues to young white readers—not as sentimental or racial stereotypes. The Harry and Topsy of *Uncle Tom's Cabin* are already quite different not only from the typical white child in moral tales of the period, but also from the little slaves who populate most abolitionist narratives.[16] After passage of the Fugitive Slave Law, tales of children kidnapped and sold into slavery circulated widely both in the press and in a steady stream of abolitionist narratives, many of them designed for children. While most of these stories were told and forgotten, *Uncle Tom's Cabin* continues to be published in editions for children as well as adults.

Stowe took pains to stress the factual basis of her sources—including little Harry's rescue on the ice (*UTC*, 618).[17] Up to a point, Topsy's experience is that of many real slave children who were raised for the market, sold, and mistreated. Yet factual accuracy does not begin to explain the appeal of the narrative. The antecedents of Harry and Topsy are not so much in contemporary accounts of slave children as in fiction and fairy tale. Little Harry— awakened in the middle of the night and told he must flee from the "ugly man"—has more in common with "The Babes in the Wood" or "Hansel and Gretel" than with abolitionist reports of fugitive slaves. Topsy, appearing out of nowhere, bought by a stranger and abruptly thrust into his family, recalls such characters as Heathcliff or Goethe's Mignon—arguably the nineteenth century's most famous "child without provenance," in Carolyn Steedman's words.[18] Harry and Topsy also bring to mind the multitude of threatened, abandoned, or mysteriously acquired children—lost and found, bought and sold—that populate cautionary tales of this period. Many English and

American chapbooks feature children stolen by gypsies and otherwise removed from the safety of home, temporarily or permanently—often as a direct result of disobedience.[19] Neither Harry nor Topsy is endangered because they have misbehaved, however. Their experience invites complex, multi-layered responses.

I argue that Harry and Topsy gained a prominent place in the American imaginary because they became for white children not objects of sympathy, but subjects for identification. I use the term identification to mean a way of seeing oneself in the image of another, a temporary "detour through the other," in Diana Fuss's words.[20] Walter Benjamin suggests that "in their reading [children] . . . absorb; they do not empathize."[21] We need not take this idea as applicable to every child everywhere in order to see that a child's identification with a fictional character may not serve moral or social purposes such as those attributed to sympathy and empathy by advocates, whether in the antebellum period or in our own.[22] But at the same time it is important to see that identification, as Fuss notes, is not a historically universal concept.[23] Like fantasies and dreams, identifications are shaped in part by temperament and personal experience; in part they are culturally inflected. Harry and Topsy were clearly marked as different from the white antebellum children who read their story. Yet Harry and Topsy—playful, frightened, naughty—must also have seemed uncannily familiar to white antebellum children who were regularly urged to overcome thoughtlessness, fear, and anger, not to mention disobedience.

When read as the story of Harry and Topsy, *Uncle Tom's Cabin* is a fairy tale of rescue, transformation, and child agency. It encourages laughter while addressing children's vulnerability (to separation, to violence, to death). This mix of narrative components was unusual in antebellum children's books. In addition, Stowe's use of black children to enact behavior and emotions that were under-represented in stories written for white ones must have made Harry and Topsy especially attractive in 1852. Stowe may have intended Topsy's conversion to harness young readers' pleasure in mischief and defiance for specific moral ends. But children, like adults, read selectively.

Up to a point the idea that white antebellum children saw themselves in Harry and Topsy dovetails with that of postcolonial critics who suggest that white people routinely see their own repressed fantasies writ large in black figures.[24] It also recalls Karen Sanchez-Eppler's account of abolitionist texts that refigure "the sexual fears and desires of the white woman on the body of the black."[25] Indeed, Stowe could not have entertained her intended readers with the story of a white child exasperating adults—any more than she could have represented white women sold in the marketplace or committing suicide, not to speak of infanticide. Because Topsy was black, the conventions for representing white children did not hold. But the image of Topsy did not explore misbehavior only to reinforce the young white reader's sense of complacency and condescension. Topsy's actions and inner turmoil could not remain exclusively a function of blackness during a reading experience that invited a child to be lost in a book, absorbed in an alternate reality.

We cannot know for sure to what extent Stowe's racial stereotypes and minstrel effects (especially in the figure of Topsy) contributed to the book's popularity. Nevertheless, by examining *Uncle Tom's Cabin* as an antebellum children's book, we better understand Harry and Topsy's appeal for generations of readers—without attributing it entirely to racialized images on the one hand, sentimental tropes on the other.

Nineteenth-century ministers, educators, and benevolent reformers celebrated the moral significance of sympathy but they cautioned against the confusion that the reading of fiction might produce through identification.[26] *Uncle Tom's Cabin* encouraged such confusion and identification. This goal is particularly apparent in Stowe's targeting of white child readers. Insofar as Stowe persuaded white children to see themselves *as* threatened slaves—to feel not *for* but *like* Harry or Topsy—*Uncle Tom's Cabin* subverted the reader's customary sense of safety on one side of the color line.[27] By inviting readers to experiment with disparate subject positions, the tale challenged widely shared racialized assumptions. *Pictures and Stories* takes such strategies further. This will be clear if we begin by considering the difference between the image of Harry in *Uncle Tom's Cabin* and his role in *Pictures and Stories*.

What Happened to Harry?

Scholarly attention to Stowe's representation of children has focused on Eva and Topsy as racialized images, and as characters that exemplify Stowe's claims for the value of discipline through love in child-rearing. Little Harry has gained scant attention, and when he appears in discussions of *Uncle Tom's Cabin* it is usually with emphasis on the minstrel echoes of the opening scene, where Harry performs for his master and a visiting slave trader. He dances and mimics on demand, encouraged by raisins and orange slices thrown on the floor for him to pick up.[28] As a result of this performance the slave trader determines to buy Harry and sets the plot of *Uncle Tom's Cabin* in motion.

A hundred years later Ralph Ellison recast this scene for *Invisible Man.* Early in that novel the African American narrator and his classmates are forced by their so-called benefactors to perform a painfully degrading script; the black high school graduates are then told to get on their knees and scramble for gold coins as their reward. The white audience howls with laughter as the young men discover that the coins are fake, and the platform an electric grid. To see the connection between these two scenes is to see the potential for humiliation and violence in the opening image of little Harry. But these implications neither exhaust Harry's rhetorical function in Stowe's text nor explain his centrality in popular memory of the book.

Stowe knew a good deal more about children than she knew about African Americans. She was well aware, for example, that children are not always docile, loving, and pious. Thus the child characters of *Uncle Tom's Cabin* repay attention, not only for their resonance as symbols of race or nation,[29] but as figures that elicited intense responses from the antebellum readers who "devoured" Stowe's book. I suggest that white children (and perhaps adults) of the 1850s could see their own fear, anger, and mischief reflected back to them in Harry and Topsy. Thus, as we shall see, Stowe's representation of these two figures raises questions not only about the fixity of racial difference, but also about two governing ideas of antebellum educational theory: that sympathy should be the main goal of reform fiction and that a child's impulse to imitate is a formative element in the way that children read.

DELAYED RACIALIZATION IN *PICTURES AND STORIES:* INTRODUCING LITTLE HARRY

Unlike *Uncle Tom's Cabin, Pictures and Stories* is designed to propel a reader directly into the tale of a threatened child. It reorganizes Stowe's narrative so that it not only begins with Harry and Eliza but also stays with them until the Harris family is reunited in Canada. Eliza crossing the ice with little Harry in her arms appears on the cover of *Pictures and Stories* (fig. 8). In this illustration,

8. *Cover of* Pictures and Stories. *From Harriet Beecher Stowe,* Pictures and Stories from Uncle Tom's Cabin. *Boston: John P. Jewett, 1853. Collection of The New-York Historical Society. Negative #83651d.*

as throughout the book, the issue of slave labor is merely the background for dramatic events concerning children. Eliza's efforts, Harry's fears, and his miraculous escape dominate the entire first half of the text. The story expands only later to include Tom, Eva, Topsy, and an explicit concern with race.

The main events of the Harry plot are unchanged in *Pictures and Stories:* Harry is sold to a trader, and in the course of a dangerous escape he is saved. But the scene in which he dances and mimics is minimized, and race is barely noted in the course of his adventure. In the opening scene of *Uncle Tom's Cabin* the narrator describes Harry as a "quadroon boy, between four and five years of age"; Mr. Shelby calls the boy "Jim Crow" (43–44). But in *Pictures and Stories* Harry is referred to only as a child, a boy, or his mother's baby. The book here employs the tactic that AnaLouise Keating calls "delayed racialization." Harry and Eliza appear first as "people, marked by language, location, [situation, and appearance] . . . not by racial labels."[30]

The first section of *Pictures and Stories* is entitled "The Sale of Little Harry." Since Harry's slave status remains crucial to the plot—he is a piece of property, and can be bought and sold—the absence of racial markers is striking.[31] Illustrations of Harry minimize the stereotyped physical features associated with African Americans in paintings, illustrations, runaway ads, and cartoons of the period (fig. 9).[32] In *Uncle Tom's Cabin* Harry's "whiteness" is realistically motivated by his mixed racial origins, which are specified the moment he appears. But *Pictures and Stories* does not draw attention to this issue. Harry's light appearance, presented without comment, heightens the sense of incomprehensible danger while inviting white children to identify with his situation and feelings. Like Eliza, he is modeled on white middle-class conceptions of interiority—which makes him all the more accessible to the white reader. It also makes him an unusual African American character in antebellum children's books. In abolitionist narratives children are often described in terms of their African origins as well as dark color, partly in order to avoid the very moral and historical questions raised by the existence of mulattos and quadroons. Still, as Shirley Samuels suggests, the "ambiguity and instability of bodily identity" pervades antebellum discourse.[33] Harry's unmarked "whiteness" reinforces the proposed analogy between him and the white reader; it also lays the groundwork for making the same point about the intensely "black" Topsy later on.

Harry's story challenges not only racialized norms of description, but also

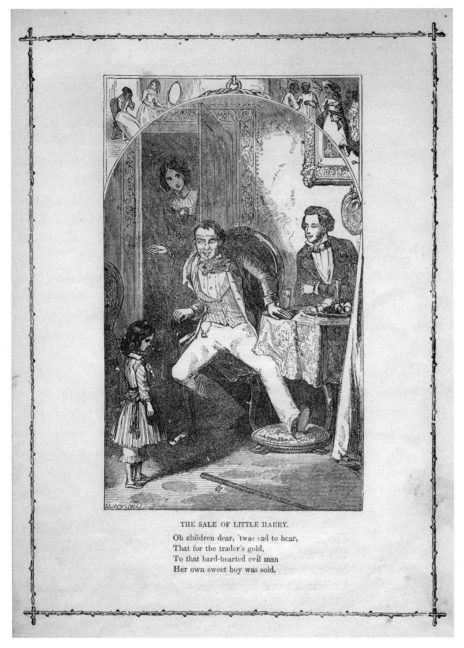

THE SALE OF LITTLE HARRY.

Oh children dear, 'twas sad to hear,
That for the trader's gold,
To that hard-hearted evil man
Her own sweet boy was sold.

9. *Little Harry with Haley and Shelby. From Harriet Beecher Stowe,* Pictures and Stories from Uncle Tom's Cabin. *Boston: John P. Jewett, 1853. Collection of The New-York Historical Society. Negative #83652d.*

generic prohibitions on the fearful or the incredible. Sold to a "cruel" and "wicked" stranger, he is threatened with abandonment and abuse. *Pictures and Stories* opens like a traditional fable. We are introduced to "A father and a mother . . . / Who had a little son" (4). In characteristic fairy-tale fashion Harry is an only child—and his parents' "only joy" (4). With his "thick . . . curls" and "bright . . . eyes" (4), Harry is both so "wise" and so "funny" that "all about the rich man's house / Were pleased to see him play, / Till a wicked trader buying slaves / Came there one winter day" (6). Fairy-tale echoes continue as "the trader and the rich man" decide the boy's fate in whispers. Little Harry is a victim of things he cannot understand: "It was a sparkling, frosty, starlight night, and the mother wrapped the shawl close round her child, as, perfectly quiet with terror, he clung round her neck" (*P&S*, 7; *UTC*, 88). Pursued by the "ugly man," Harry is spirited away to safety over "great blocks of the floating ice" and the "wild . . . water's roar" (*UTC*, 88; *P&S*, 7, 8). Frightened and uncomprehending, Harry is not only like the Babes in the Wood or Hansel and Gretel, but also like any child who is innocent of the meanings attached to adult words and practices.

Realistic details provide a conventional domestic context for extraordinary events. Harry's responses when his mother wakes him up and hurries him out into the darkness are not melodramatic, clichéd, or racially marked. Harry expresses his thoughts and feelings on appropriately childlike topics (such as where his mother is going in the middle of the night) and in age-appropriate language (most of it taken directly from the full-length novel). As Harry and Eliza hurry along, Harry finds himself "sinking to sleep," but resists the temptation and asks: "Mother, I don't need to keep awake, do I?" When Eliza tries to reassure him, Harry persists: "But, mother, if I do get asleep, you won't let [the ugly man] get me?" (*P&S*, 7; *UTC*, 105). Scared but trusting, Harry in this episode is a far cry from the minstrel image at the start of the full-length novel, and he has still less in common with slave children in other abolitionist tales, where African boys and girls are generally viewed from the outside, across a distance, and often marked as exotic. Even *The Slave's Friend*, a well-written children's periodical committed to immediate abolition, did not often dwell on the probing questions or internal states of black children.

Like every antebellum children's book, *Pictures and Stories* affirms good behavior. Yet the figure of Harry challenges the pedagogic and literary imperative that children renounce desire, comply with the demands of adults, and think first of others. While Harry does not lie or defy adults, he sleeps when he is tired and eats when he is hungry, even though his mother refuses the crumbs of cake that he tries to push into her mouth (*P&S,* 7; *UTC,* 107). The tale thus encourages children to enter imaginatively into the situation of a character who is accessible precisely because at some level of fear or desire he is already familiar. Any child who has been frightened and bewildered or has wanted to be rescued can appreciate little Harry. Insofar as a white reader is persuaded to participate in Harry's experience, the color line is temporarily destabilized.

"JUST LIKE . . . TOPSY AT THE LOOKING GLASS"

Nineteenth-century commentators often saw Topsy as a comic figure. Contemporary scholars more often see her as a racial stereotype or the key figure in Stowe's argument about child-rearing practices. In this script Topsy is a girl who does not know how to behave, but is finally converted and transformed by Eva's love—and death.[34] Like other children's editions *Pictures and Stories* deletes or revises the passages of *Uncle Tom's Cabin* that most dramatically foreground the abuse Topsy has suffered and that account for her rage and indifference. The welts on Topsy's back that make Ophelia turn pale do not appear in *Pictures and Stories;* nor does the speech in which Topsy wishes she "could be skinned, and come white" (355, 409). But unlike children's editions that appeared at the end of the nineteenth century, *Pictures and Stories* retains enough of Topsy's history and emotional suffering to make it responsible for her ignorance and defiance.[35] At the same time, *Pictures and Stories* makes that defiance look downright appealing. The book minimizes Topsy's racialized traits and invites the white child reader to share her experience.

Pictures and Stories presents Topsy only after Harry's story is complete. Introduced as "a poor negro child," the figure of Topsy immediately brings the issue of race into focus (20). One verse draws attention to her "bare black elbows" (22); another suggests that everyone except Eva would "call / her names, for being black and bad" (26). Yet *Pictures and Stories* eliminates Topsy's lies and acrobatics as well as other stereotyped features of slave behavior; it also elides racial markers such as animal imagery (a staple of abolitionist tales, to which we will return).[36] Topsy's misbehavior is confined to one playful prank (dressing up in Ophelia's shawl) that would be attractive to many a white child.

Topsy is presented as mildly disobedient and wanting to have fun, but also as a girl who has been "cuff[ed] and scold[ed] . . . all her days" (22). "Her naughty ways" are explained by her past (22).[37] The book stresses Topsy's difficulties adjusting to a new life in a white family; unlike the usual slave child in abolitionist tales, Topsy cannot effortlessly become a model of conventional traits.[38] But unlike *Uncle Tom's Cabin, Pictures and Stories* does not employ either the narrative voice or adult characters' conversations to elaborate the damage done to children by the institution of slavery. Topsy's actions make the argument in simplified terms.

Where the image of Harry challenges generic norms for reality-bound moral tales and gives a child reader emotional space to experience fear and vulnerability, the image of Topsy challenges the antebellum prohibition on the representation of naughtiness, inviting a reader's participation in mischief without providing the usual comeuppance for the offending character. Beyond that, *Pictures and Stories* changes the end of the Topsy plot as it appears in *Uncle Tom's Cabin:* it eliminates Topsy's conversion but highlights her inner struggle. Thus the image of Topsy not only violates the general reluctance to represent disobedience, but implies that being good can be extremely difficult. Only difficult for black children? White children must have known better.

In *Pictures and Stories* Topsy's mischief is limited to her appropriation of Ophelia's red shawl and ivory fan: "See little Topsy at the glass quite gay, / Her mistress has forgot the keys to-day, / So she has rummaged every drawer, and dressed / Herself out in Miss Feely's very best" (*P&S,* 22). With Ophelia's "shawl of gorgeous red / Wound like a Turk's great Turban round her head" (22, 23), Topsy contemplates herself in Ophelia's mirror. Illustrated as well as versified, this episode highlights the exotic and smacks of Orientalism (fig. 10). But it is presented as childlike fun with a hint of anxiety, not a minstrel act.

Topsy plays in secret, absorbed in her game; she does not perform for white characters here.[39] Her antics are designed to engage the reader of the book, but until Ophelia barges in on her, there are no onlookers in the represented world of the text. Decked out in extravagant folds of red cloth, Topsy is her own audience, testing the boundaries of a self-in-transition by dressing up, rather than wishing to be "skinned." *Pictures and Stories* adjures little white readers not to violate decorum like Topsy; it voices disapproval of children who pretend to be something they are not ("none can keep such borrowed plumes as these" [24]). Yet the book devotes more space to Topsy's experiment than to the proposed

TOPSY AT THE LOOKING-GLASS.

Mark where she stands! the shawl of gorgeous red
Wound like a Turk's great turban round her head,
A finer shawl for trailing on the floor,
Just shows her bare black elbows, and **no more.**

10. Topsy in Ophelia's shawl. From Harriet Beecher Stowe, Pictures and Stories from Uncle Tom's Cabin. *Boston: John P. Jewett, 1853. Collection of The New-York Historical Society. Negative #83653d.*

moral. In addition, Topsy's emotional suffering competes for the reader's attention.

Using the fairy-tale mode to address the white child reader, *Pictures and Stories* explores Topsy's ongoing rejection in the St. Clare household. When Topsy brings flowers for the ailing Eva, the "scornful" Marie (like a wicked stepmother) cries, "begone you nasty thing!" and Eva pleads with her mama on Topsy's behalf: "'Oh mother dear, let Topsy stay' / Says Eva in her gentle mood, / She brought such pretty flowers today, / Indeed she's trying to be good" (*P&S*, 25, 26). In the illustration for this episode Topsy is black in color; but she is also sweet and demure (fig. 11). Unlike most antebellum illustrations of Topsy, her body language here suggests internality—thoughtfulness, pain. While racial difference gains emphasis, then, the book offers its readers new grounds of identification. The focus is on Topsy's desire to play and her inner struggle—not her success.

The figure of Topsy, like that of Harry, asks a reader to identify with a child's point of view. Gillian Brown suggests that "Stowe takes us only as far with Topsy as sympathy will go."[40] But the "us" in this formulation refers to sophisticated, even professional, adult readers of the twentieth or twenty-first century. White antebellum children may well have gone further with Topsy, understanding her wish to have fun, experiencing her isolation, and taking seriously her efforts to be good.

Diverse scholars have argued that *Uncle Tom's Cabin* established sentiment as a widely shared interpretive convention for consuming the story of slavery. One of the hallmarks of sentiment, whether as generic norm or mode of response, is its capacity to reinforce the distance between one who is offering sympathy and one who is receiving it.[41] Although the tears of character and reader may "blur the distinction between them," as Karen Sanchez-Eppler suggests, a novel-reader can extend sympathy to a fictional character while maintaining his or her sense of difference and superiority. As Tavia Nyong'o argues, the image of a frightened slave child may alert the "protective instincts" of an adult or older child: "but protection is not the same as, perhaps is even the opposite of, identification."[42] Identification during reading creates a more complete (though still temporary) collapse of the distance between self and other, via the recognition of traits or feelings experienced as one's own. Insofar as young white readers accepted the reality and the subjectivity of Harry and Topsy, they may have felt that African American children were in some ways like themselves.

TOPSY BRINGING FLOWERS TO EVA.

"Oh mother dear, let Topsy stay,"
Says Eva in her gentle mood,
"She brought such pretty flowers to-day,
Indeed she's trying to be good."

11. Topsy bringing flowers to Eva. From Harriet Beecher Stowe, Pictures and Stories from Uncle Tom's Cabin. *Boston: John P. Jewett, 1853. Collection of The New-York Historical Society. Negative #83654d.*

Pictures and Stories invites a reader to enter a fictional world by sharing the perspective of a racially unmarked figure. The book encourages the reader to identify with that figure, and then, by showing how conventional practices make Harry (and subsequently Topsy) suffer, it challenges the naturalness of racialized norms. In this sense one might say that the book mobilizes the reading experience to "denormaliz[e] . . . whiteness"—much as Nella Larsen does in the opening scene of *Passing,* or as Octavia Butler does in *Kindred.* In *Pictures and Stories* the issue of race is subordinated to a drama rooted in common childhood concerns.[43] The meaning and impact of racialization emerge slowly.

The idea of Topsy as a human subject and ground of identification may seem far-fetched. Her lack of education, resistance to behavioral norms, and her intense black color all mark her as radically unlike the white children who read the tale: "No home, no school, no Bible she had seen, / How bless'd besides poor Topsy we have been!" (24). Yet many a middle-class child has imagined him- or herself as a foundling, and white antebellum children surely knew something about misbehavior, anger, and resentment. By presenting Topsy's experience as something to share, *Pictures and Stories,* more than *Uncle Tom's Cabin,* suggests that the white child reader may be "just like" the wayward Topsy, defiantly and playfully contemplating herself "at the looking glass" (24). Insofar as Topsy's story, like Harry's, models black children on the wishes and fears of white ones, it challenged antebellum reading conventions as much as Topsy defied the governing norms of proper white girl behavior.[44]

READING AND IMITATION: TEACHING BY EXAMPLE

In both *Uncle Tom's Cabin* and *Pictures and Stories* Topsy's dress-up episode raises questions about imitation as a dynamic process through which a child attempts to understand but also may challenge his or her position within a particular familial and social context. In 1850 imitation was also widely understood as a typical response to reading, especially for children. Stowe gave considerable thought to the function of imitation at both levels, so at this point it is useful to bring *Uncle Tom's Cabin* and other writings by Stowe back into the argument.

In *Uncle Tom's Cabin* as in *Pictures and Stories* Topsy's experience raises the question of whether African American children can develop and learn or whether they will never do more than imitate white practices. Homi Bhabha has sensitized us to the complex interplay of imitation and mimicry, especially in power relations such as those between master and slave.[45] Stowe was well aware of the way imitation always contains within itself the potential for parody, as her portraits of Adolph, Rosa—and Topsy—suggest.[46] All these characters imitate their masters, in one way or another. Although such imitation may imply a desire to be like master or mistress, these mimicries also critique their object, producing comic effects for Stowe's reader.

When Adolph and Rosa ape "genteel" manners, complete with such props as St. Clare's cast-off scented handkerchiefs or when Topsy dons Ophelia's clothes, the implication is that these characters aspire to something that is above them and that gaps between the knowledge (and privileges) of master and slave are unbridgeable. However, what looks like a grotesquely failed effort to imitate can also mock the source. When Topsy turns Ophelia's red shawl into a turban, she is not in fact imitating "Miss Feely"—who does not wear turbans and is not famous for her colorful wardrobe. Yet, as Elizabeth Young points out, "the scarlet shawl is Miss Ophelia's own, hidden away" in a closet.[47] Topsy thus embodies flamboyant possibilities that go beyond Ophelia's daily experience and that challenge the Northern woman's self-containment.

Dress-up play was limited when most clothing was preserved for future use, even in well-to-do families, and when amateur theatricals were still regarded with some hesitation. Dressing up is not among the recommended "domestic amusements" for children in Stowe and Catharine Beecher's *Principles of Domestic Science as Applied to the Duties and Pleasures of Home.* By the 1850s paper-dolls, including paper-dolls of *Uncle Tom's Cabin,* were popular; they provided a legitimate, limited, reality-bound opportunity to manipulate the clothing of a paper figure. As parlor entertainment, tableaux vivants encouraged imitation as a highly scripted opportunity for play. Topsy's unsanctioned use of Ophelia's "best" shawl is different. Her dramatic flourishes would in themselves have made her game appear transgressive. But even if Topsy had used the shawl to imitate Ophelia faithfully—draping the shawl on her shoulders with care as she might have expected Ophelia to do—Topsy's theft of the material for her game would have made it outrageous.

Imitation was a cornerstone of educational theory in the antebellum period. What William Alcott called the "universal principle of imitation" was understood to be a natural, indeed irresistible, impulse.[48] Parents were responsible for providing the first and most important models for their children to follow. Lydia

Maria Child begins her *Mother's Book* by citing Mrs. Barbauld: "Do you ask, then, what will educate your son? Your example will educate him; your conversation; the business he sees you transact; the likings and dislikings you express—these will educate him."[49] Numerous stories written for children were shaped by the idea that readers, especially young readers, imitate what they read.

Children's literature was to produce judicious and obedient boys and girls by providing good models to follow. But while imitation was widely considered a useful pedagogic tool, questions remained about how to impel and direct it. "Bad" examples were a special problem—they might be inadvertently imitated. "I do not approve of stories about naughty children," Lydia Maria Child wrote; "they suggest a thousand little tricks and deceptions, which would not otherwise be thought of."[50] Yet despite ongoing discussions about the negative force of "bad examples," in fiction (as in life), Topsy's disobedience was not a source of concern to antebellum readers and reviewers: the very extremity of her behavior (lies, resentment, mockery, and defiance) along with her status as an African American slave must have made many assume that no white child would take her as a model.

Like other commentators of the period, Stowe keenly felt that imitation had its dangers—for free white children as well as for slaves. From within *Uncle Tom's Cabin* the best exemplar of imitation gone wrong is Eva's little cousin, Henrique, who accurately reproduces his father's ideas and practices by brutally whipping his young slave Dodo (*UTC,* 388). Henrique is often left out of children's editions, and *Pictures and Stories* is no exception. Like *Uncle Tom's Cabin, Pictures and Stories* explicitly presents Eva as a model for Topsy ("Eva strove to make her good" [26]) and a model for the reader as well.[51] But the figures of Harry and Topsy offer reading pleasures that are less didactic than the norm, and less rooted in stereotypes. Some young white readers may well have longed to be as good (and as beloved) as Eva; but it would not be surprising if others had agreed with an antebellum commentator who asserts that "one Topsy is worth a dozen little Evas."[52] Topsy's violation of generic and pedagogic conventions goes beyond the limits that Stowe theoretically set for herself regarding the freedom that fiction could take with decorum in the interest of holding a reader's attention for higher moral and social goals.

Topsy's attempts at imitation are transgressive; Ophelia's efforts to teach Topsy via imitation are useless. As Gillian Brown points out, Topsy tries to make sense out of the catechism rather than repeating it by rote.[53] ("You'll have to give her a meaning or she'll make one," St. Clare says [*UTC,* 389]). Topsy can dress up as an imaginary Miss Feely (or comply and "confess" although she has committed no sin), but her behavior changes only as the result of an uneven process marked by desire, internal conflict, and resistance to external demands. Topsy's responses thus imply that African American children possess subjectivity; her changes of feeling and attitude also challenge the popular notion that efforts to educate African Americans would produce only grotesque imitations of white behavior, verging on parody. Thus Stowe complicates the "old-fashioned" theory of rote learning and punishment that informs Miss Ophelia's child-rearing practices, as Richard Brodhead and Sarah Robbins have argued. At the same time Stowe complicates a model of reading that still retained considerable force in the 1850s.

Like other antebellum writers, educators, and mothers, Stowe embraced the Lockean view that children are permanently marked by experience.[54] Listening to stories and reading—no less than actual events—were believed to produce indelible impressions. As Samuel Goodrich put it, "there is little difference as to the moral effect upon children between things real and things imaginary."[55] Stowe would have accepted this idea. Writing about the impact of reading on youth in 1842, she attacked Byron and Bulwer precisely because the language, appearance, and behavior of their fictional characters were so often imitated by young men who "tie their collars with black ribbon, . . . gaze with sullen gloom . . . drink gin and water, and write bad poetry [after reading Byron]." Abandoning irony, Stowe insists that Byron's "evil influence . . . on the minds of the young and sensitive is not to be lightly estimated." She also deems Bulwer "fatal to a young reader." The title of Stowe's piece—"Literary Epidemics" reinforces the notion of resistless influence, indeed contamination.[56] And if young drinkers of gin are helpless in the face of seductive impressions, what of small children?

Stowe's ideas were familiar and widely shared in antebellum pedagogic circles. Yet *Uncle Tom's Cabin* itself implies a conception of children's reading more capacious and flexible not only than the antebellum norm, but also than many of Stowe's own programmatic formulations. Although Stowe could expound the dangers of fiction-reading as late as 1870,[57] Harry's experience—in *Uncle Tom's Cabin* as well as *Pictures and Stories*—anticipates not only late nineteenth-century ideas about the value of narratives that engage a child's imagination, but also psychoanalytic assumptions regarding the emotional benefits of reading about danger and the extraordinary.[58] The image of Topsy violates antebellum educational theories about the risk of representing naughty behavior, and gives the white child reader more credit than Stowe's own didactic cautions. Both in *Pictures and Stories* and *Uncle Tom's Cabin* the figure of Topsy encourages young white readers to experience common ground with a child who has "black elbows" and no family, while expanding the imaginative bounds of domestic, sentimental, and abolitionist tales.

FROM IMITATION TO IDENTIFICATION

Antebellum pronouncements about the function of good and bad examples in children's books disclose considerable uncertainty about what children take away from stories, how they select objects of attention, and what makes didactic tales effective. Advice literature of the period often suggests that didactic elements should be unobtrusively woven into the texture of a story from the start, not tacked on at the end. Commentators note the pedagogical value of subtlety and "indirect means—silent, gentle and often unperceived."[59] Offering guidance about how to infiltrate the mind of a child, the author of *The Mother's Friend* suggests that "well chosen stories, *without any apparent reference to the child* may be related to him, displaying the good effects of courage as opposed to the folly and ill consequence of cowardice."[60] This strategy was widely accepted in principle; yet questions arose about the degree of indirectness, and the form it was to take. In this context, the use of animals as a stand-in for people was a matter of some disagreement. A closer look at this debate, and at the function of animal imagery in abolitionist tales, will clarify the difference between sympathy and identification in reading. It will also enable some concluding speculations about the functions that Harry and Topsy served for young white antebellum readers.

Some antebellum commentators thought that an animal story could exemplify desirable behavior for children, but only if children were to see themselves as the figures in the narrative without losing their hold on reality. In his widely distributed chapbooks for children, Lynn Cobb assured parents they would find no talking animals.[61] By contrast, the generally level-headed Lydia Maria Child recommended Aesop's fables, insisting that "children do not believe that dogs, foxes, and birds, talk to each other; nor do they think that the writer *intended* they should believe it; therefore it cannot be injurious to their love of truth" (92).

Yet the popular Samuel Goodrich, writing twenty-five years later, still emphasized the danger of fantastical images, such as talking animals. He reports his own "creeping horror" and his childhood fear of being devoured as a result of reading "Little Red Riding Hood."[62]

At issue here are doubts about how reading works. Nineteenth-century commentators did not relate the idea of "identification" to deeply unconscious processes; the unconscious was an unpopular concept in the United States even after Freud was well known.[63] But the questions that troubled Goodrich and others could be rephrased as follows: Do children always identify with the figure of a child in a story, even when that child has no "apparent reference" to the young reader of the tale? Do children identify with animals who behave wisely or foolishly only in situations familiar to the child? If a child can identify with a (wise or foolish) animal, can a boy identify with a girl? a white child with a black?[64] If children provisionally accept the reality of talking wolves, can this serve a moral purpose? Do readers of "Little Red Riding Hood" learn not to tarry on the way to grandmother's house, or do they only become wary of the neighbor's dog . . . ?

Suzanne Keen suggests that character identification can occur "even when the character and reader differ from each other in all sorts of practical and obvious ways"; she suggests that such "identification often invites empathy."[65] Antebellum moral tales regularly use animal imagery in this spirit, attempting to cultivate sympathy and kindness in children. A recurrent trope in abolitionist tales involves white children who liberate their pets, as Leslie Ginsberg points out. The image of the freed pet implies that all creatures love liberty, while outlining the white child's responsibility toward dependents and inferiors. While such stories propose that a young reader should empathize with a caged animal, they also reinforce the idea of a slave as a lesser being. In stories where white children either free their pets or resist the temptation to capture birds or butterflies, animals often serve as "explicit metaphor[s] for the master/slave relationship."[66] They thus position the white child reader not as similar to, but rather as quite different from, the pet: the child is the master/owner of the animal and the one who acts and chooses.[67] Both the child in the story and the child reader are encouraged to behave responsibly, to do the right thing. Neither child is encouraged to linger with the plight of the animal; rather, he or she is to embrace the obligations of benevolent authority and power.[68] While such animal imagery may encourage sympathy, it also reinforces distance and hierarchy: an animal is, precisely, not a human being. Some abolitionist tales, however, speak less to differences among children than to shared fears—of being abandoned, scorned, or mistreated. A brief look at one such story returns us to Stowe's rhetorical strategies for captivating children.

A tale by Sarah Grimke, published in the children's magazine *The Slave's Friend,* focuses on a slave child who is not imagined as a mistreated horse or captured butterfly but who expresses her fears in language. Grimke presents the tale as truth, an eyewitness retrospective account. "When I was a little girl," she explains, "I had a present. A little girl was bought out of a slave-ship, and given to me for my slave!"

> The poor little orphan child was frightened at the sight of white people. She would not eat, and was very thin and poor. I asked her why she did not eat and grow fat? She said she was afraid if she ate and grew fat, the white people would kill and eat her.
>
> When she saw the cook carving with his knife, she would tremble all over, thinking he was going to eat her. She told me her mother was a princess. . . .[69]

This story, with its echoes of Hansel and Gretel, the big bad wolf, and even Cinderella, is much stronger medicine than the allegory of the liberated pet. Grimke's account of an African girl, frightened, abandoned, and afraid of being eaten, evokes both culturally and developmentally typical fears in one image. According to slave narratives and historians, the fear of being eaten by whites was common among kidnapped Africans; according to psychologists the fear of being eaten is common among white middle-class children. It is a familiar feature of fairy tales.[70] Like Stowe's representation of Harry fleeing from the "ugly man" or of Topsy, playful and disobedient, Grimke's image of a frightened girl who says her mother was a princess blends reality and fantasy, encouraging a young white reader to wonder whether "this could be me," rather than to watch from afar, thinking: "poor little slave child—over there, not safe, *un*like me. . . ." None of these figures relies on sympathy to frame a perspective on otherness.

Pictures and Stories, like *Uncle Tom's Cabin,* presents Eva as a model of feeling and behavior for readers to imitate. Yet, at the same time, the option of identifying with Harry or Topsy offered children a welcome release from prescriptive norms, both social and literary. As we have noted, it was Topsy's blackness that enabled Stowe to dwell on her disruptive behavior with impunity (and humor). Because of Topsy's color and history, white children may have been able to discount the very feelings that drew them in (i.e., "Topsy is like me, but not really me"). Still, a certain blurring of subject position must have been part of this dynamic.

THE SENSE OF AN ENDING

Samuel Goodrich and other commentators who criticize frightening and fantastical stories for children stress that child readers often fail to make a distinction between fiction and reality. Many current psychologists and reading theorists would agree. As Peter Hunt has noted, "every statement about a book in relation to a child has to have the qualification 'It depends on the child.'"[71] Nevertheless, children often respond to stories with more immediacy and intensity than adults. They may enter more directly than adults not only into the subject position of a fictional character, but into alternative worlds created by their own imagination—and by reading.[72]

In its representation of race, *Pictures and Stories* is a more radical book than *Uncle Tom's Cabin* itself, but like *Pictures and Stories* the full-length *Uncle Tom's Cabin* captivated young readers by encouraging them to plunge deeply into a story of threatened children. This claim raises further questions about the reading experience: Were young antebellum readers more taken with little Harry's minstrel dance or with his flight and rescue? With Topsy's somersaults or her defiance? Her anger and pain, or her conversion? Such questions remind us that reader responses are individual and diverse, shaped both by personal history and by cultural context.

The difficulties of reconstructing the responses of antebellum children are formidable, so I want to end this chapter on a speculative and theoretical note. As reading theorists and historians of reading have taught us, fiction is never experienced in its entirety, as a complete whole, but rather selectively, according to the needs, desires, and interpretive habits of individual readers interacting with cultural norms. What is memorable to one reader may be forgotten by another. The well-known controversy about the ending of *Uncle Tom's Cabin* is a useful focal point for revisiting the unevenness of reader response and underscoring the selective attention that is always a factor in reading, especially among children. I propose that what happens in the course of a tale often leaves a more enduring impression than didactic messages or plot outcomes.[73]

The ending of *Uncle Tom's Cabin* has been much attacked; the removal of Eliza, George Harris, Harry, and Topsy to Africa at the end of the novel has been seen as a failure of Stowe's imagination and evidence of her racist assumptions.[74] It may also reflect her awareness of the "horizons of the publishable."[75] The resolution of *Uncle Tom's Cabin* was powerful enough to spark an ongoing discussion of racial ideology; but was it powerful enough to be memorable on other grounds? How memorable—how aesthetically or imaginatively effective—is the ending of *Uncle Tom's Cabin*? Do readers without a serious interest in what happens to freed slaves even remember the ending?

The psychologist and educator Arthur N. Applebee engages the question of whether and until what age children take stories as "real," with implications for the process of selective reading and the function of endings in a child's experience of stories. Drawing on experiments by the psychologists Evelyn Goodenough Pitcher and Ernst Prelinger, Applebee analyzes children's responses to questions about familiar stories in order to test the boundaries of reality and fiction.[76] His account shows not only how difficult it is to anticipate or understand what any particular child takes from a specific story, but also how easily children discount narrative endings, features often taken (by literary scholars) as important arbiters of meaning.[77] Children are likely to focus instead on what is compelling to them—which may be quite different from what a text prescribes, or what an adult responds to. As Walter Benjamin notes, "children['s] books, like everything else, can contain very different things from what adults see in them."[78] Caroline Hewins (born 1846 and an influential shaper of children's library services in the Progressive period) recalls having read *Uncle Tom's Cabin* "so many times," that when she later heard "Mrs. Stowe's son tell 'How Uncle Tom's Cabin was Built,'" she "could have helped him if his memory had failed and told many things that he omitted . . . could have described the cake that Aunt Chloe invited George to share, the difficulties thrown in the way of Haley starting in pursuit of Eliza, the scene at the senator's and in the Quaker family and just how Cassy and Emmeline's hiding place in Legree's garret was made and furnished."[79] It is not surprising that in a talk on "How Uncle Tom's Cabin was Built" Stowe's son did not provide a description of the cake that Aunt Chloe baked or the décor in Cassy and Emmeline's hiding place, elements that made a vivid impression on the young Hewins. As Peter Hunt remarks: "whatever is implied by the text, there is even less guarantee than . . . [with adults] that the reader will choose (or be able) to read in the way suggested."[80]

Applebee analyzes responses to a series of questions about Cinderella that Pitcher and Prelinger posed to children between the ages of six and nine. After asking each child where Cinderella lives (responses include "with her two ugly sisters. . . . in an old house"), the interviewer asked: "Could we go for a visit?" Some responses were variations of "No . . . cause they'll say Cinderella can't come she'll have to wash up the plates and all the dishes and wash the floor" (42). Such comments suggest that, as Applebee claims, "stories are astonishingly real even for six-year-olds who have had a year in a school environment where they hear stories at least daily" (42). But children who believe that Cinderella is still washing floors have forgotten the end of the story, along with the moral about good girls being rewarded.

Such responses reflect an idea of Cinderella frozen in time, perpetually scorned and mistreated by a wicked stepmother, as if she never went to the ball and was not saved by the prince. The early portion of the tale seems to have made so strong an impression on some of the children in Pitcher and Prelinger's sample that the happy ending was effectively upstaged. Enduring popularity is determined by select elements of a tale—but we cannot be sure which elements do the determining.[81]

A Book for "All Ages"

The popularity of *Uncle Tom's Cabin* as a children's book goes beyond, and helps explain, its attraction for adults. I have been suggesting that *Pictures and Stories* foregrounds neglected aspects of *Uncle Tom's Cabin* that contributed to the unprecedented impact of the full-length novel. The elements that made Harry and Topsy powerful figures for children are an integral part of *Uncle Tom's Cabin* and help account for its appeal.

A variety of scholars have argued that the adult capacity for being "lost in a book" is rooted in the childhood experience of reading.[82] As we have seen, antebellum readers often reported on the book's hold over them and their deep absorption in it.[83] But among adults such testimonies to the power of *Uncle Tom's Cabin* were generally accompanied by homage to the book's spiritual and political benefits—the good it would do. Reiterating the moral of the story in retrospective accounts, many readers distanced themselves from the more unsettling aspects of their own reading experience, and re-established their commitment to their customary selves.[84] The familiar emphasis on the moral and political importance of *Uncle Tom's Cabin* does not explain the power or attraction of Stowe's "story," what Frank Norris called the "page to page progress of the narrative."[85] I have addressed that issue here only to the extent of suggesting that while greatly absorbing narratives tend to draw on wishes and fears that are especially compelling at a particular historical moment, *Uncle Tom's Cabin* also has something in common with fables and legends that have endured for centuries. Legend, myth, and fairy tales are particularly appealing to children, especially when tales of the fabulous are scarce, as they were in the antebellum United States.

Exploring the child's construction of reality, Applebee notes that a story is a "powerful mode for extending the relatively limited experience of young children. The stories they hear help them to acquire expectations of what the world is like—its vocabulary and syntax as well as its people and places—without the distracting pressure of separating the real from the make-believe" (52). When adults offer fairy tales to children, the tales gain sanction, and the freedom they allow may be less fraught with anxiety than, say, Topsy's transgressive mimicry.[86] I have suggested that insofar as antebellum children saw aspects of their own experience reflected in the figures of Harry and Topsy, these figures challenged generic norms and expanded the experience available to young readers. Insofar as *Uncle Tom's Cabin* and *Pictures and Stories* drew children in and allowed them to imagine diverse subjectivities, some residue of feeling may even have remained to narrow the gap between their idea of themselves and their conception of slave "otherness."

When *Uncle Tom's Cabin* first appeared, it was widely seen as an asset to the abolitionist cause. Toward the end of the century many commentators gave the book credit for changes that led to emancipation. In 1896, the historian James Rhodes expressed a view that was widely shared by late nineteenth-century commentators. Rhodes suggested that the "youth of America," reading *Uncle Tom's Cabin* in the 1850s, acquired ideas and feelings that led directly to the Civil War ten years later.[87] Whether or not we accept this idea, attention to *Uncle Tom's Cabin* as a children's book helps us understand why so many people thought so.

5

Sentiment without Tears
Uncle Tom's Cabin *as History in the Wake of the Civil War*

> . . . now that slavery is only a historic thing, while peace and complete reunion assure the calmness needed for true criticism, we read *Uncle Tom's Cabin* with clearer eyes . . .
>
> —*J. H. Beadle, "Harriet Beecher Stowe" (1889)*

This chapter explores the renewed appeal of Stowe's novel for commentators, editors, and publishers toward the end of the century. It also sharpens my focus on two methodological questions that consistently inform this study: How can the paratextual material of individual editions (prefaces, introductions, illustrations) serve as a basis for general claims about the way a text was read and used at a particular historical moment? To what extent can we see the comments and editorial choices of literary professionals as evidence of culturally typical reading practices and as factors that shape the responses of others? These questions come to the fore in this chapter because *Uncle Tom's Cabin* became a different book by the 1890s. But while literary professionals agreed on new meanings for Stowe's tale, other readers demurred.

Editions are no direct proof of reading habits. In Roger Chartier's influential formulation, "readers use infinite . . . subterfuges to . . . read between the lines, and to subvert the lessons imposed on them."[1] Over the last twenty-five years scholars from a variety of disciplines (history, literature, sociology) have analyzed historically specific acts of reading and effectively explored some of the gaps between a text's manifest content and the diverse meanings that readers derive.[2] Readers may resist the didactic messages or protocol of reading inscribed in a text, along with interpretive guidelines offered by textual accompaniments. They may misunderstand, recast, or refuse explicit prescriptions formulated by teachers, reviewers, and writers of advice literature. Nonetheless, prescribed modes of reading are useful indicators of a cultural climate and, when set in diachronic perspective, they reflect shifts in social norms and interpretive conventions as well as developments in the literary marketplace. Responses by dissenting readers complicate the picture.

In the 1880s and '90s a consensus emerged (among professional white readers) about why and how *Uncle Tom's Cabin* should be read. This consensus had its roots in changing perceptions of slavery, race, the plantation South, and the reconstituted nation. Commentators began to give *Uncle Tom's Cabin* partial credit for emancipation and the Civil War when the dust had barely settled. In 1866, an article about Gamaliel Bailey, editor of the *National Era,* praises *Uncle Tom's Cabin* as part of the "advance-guard . . . of the armed boats who at last won the victory for humanity."[3] Stowe's novel was much celebrated in postbellum print culture. At the same time it was selectively reread as a gloss on the benign aspects of slavery, and as evidence for African American docility and loyalty. In the public sphere the book thus served the cause of reunion and tranquility on the one hand, segregation and racism on the other.

The reasons for praising *Uncle Tom's Cabin* in the 1880s and '90s were quite different from those proposed by commentators of the antebellum period. In 1852 *Uncle Tom's Cabin* was generally understood to be an evangelical abolitionist text that attacked slavery as a sin and enjoined white readers to look inward, to the state of their souls, as well as outward, to dangerous rifts in the nation's moral and social fabric. By contrast, late nineteenth-century commentators explained away or skirted both the political and religious agendas of the book. A sketch of Stowe, published in *Literature: A Weekly Magazine* in 1889, suggests that contemporary readers in the peaceful, reunified United States will find it difficult even to comprehend the tendentiousness of Stowe's work. Underscoring the distance between the antebellum and the postwar nation, the article notes that Stowe's "intellect reached its maturity in an age of most furious controversy. . . . Slavery and temperance, the divine Unity or Trinity, grace, free will and predestination, were debated with a heat and bitterness to which this generation is happily a stranger."[4] Many late nineteenth-century readers were unmoved by Stowe's evangelical fervor—or uncomfortable with it. A "Biographical Sketch" of Stowe, published in an edition of 1896 explains that the centrality of religion in the society of "Harriet Beecher's . . . girlhood . . . led to an introspection and analysis of motive which often passed into morbid self-consciousness."[5] Both the political and religious urgencies of *Uncle Tom's Cabin* had come to signify the retrograde, the narrow, and the divisive.

Amid mounting evidence that emancipation and the Civil War had created complex new social tensions, public pronouncements denied persistent sectarian divisions along with sectional ones. Affirmations of "one nation, indivisible," in the words of the Pledge of Allegiance (penned in 1892), also implied that racial conflict did not exist. As discrimination increased in the North and racial violence in the South, *Uncle Tom's Cabin* was invoked to support what Nina Silber calls the "romance of reunion."[6] But the reading public, like the nation, was less unified than many claimed. Divisions along the lines of age and race made for contradictory responses to *Uncle Tom's Cabin* after the Civil War.

READING STOWE IN THE 1870S: A GENERATION GAP

The sense of looking at *Uncle Tom's Cabin* over a great divide began shortly after Emancipation. As early as the 1860s, nostalgia informs discussions of the excitement created by Stowe's book. In 1867 one account explains that *Uncle Tom's Cabin* not only foretold the "triumph of the United States" but also gave rise to a unique reading experience: "It was read with passion," the commentator informs his readers (who presumably do not know this); "it was devoured; people sat up all night reading it; those who could, read it to those who could not. . . ."[7] A newspaper article of the following year explains the genesis of the novel and notes that "our older readers need not to be told with what avidity the weekly installments of this serial were caught up and devoured by the readers of the *National Era*." Situating the enthusiasm that greeted *Uncle Tom's Cabin* in the somewhat misty past of "older readers," the commentator frames the intensive reading of the novel as the relic of another time.[8]

Early in the 1870s Stowe gave a series of public readings. The Boston reading "was a great success," Annie Fields writes in *Authors and Friends:*

> [Stowe] was alive in every fibre of her being; she was to read portions of "Uncle Tom's Cabin" to men, women, and children, many of whom had taken no part in the crisis which inspired it, and she determined to effect the difficult task of making them feel as well as hear. With her presence and inspiration they could not fail to understand what her works had signified to the generation that had passed through the struggle of our war.[9]

Fields takes it for granted that making an audience of the 1870s "feel" in response to *Uncle Tom's Cabin* is a "difficult task." She assumes that those who took "no part in the crisis" will not understand what *Uncle Tom's Cabin* meant to the previous generation and that reading the book will not suffice to provide that "understanding." She implies that the presence and inspiration of the famous author are needed to do so.

Fields's account was published in 1893, when the idea of great authors as a national resource shaped not only testimonials and memoirs, but also schoolroom texts and practices; public interest in famous writers (as well as their families, houses, furniture, and clothing) reached new proportions in this period. People attended Stowe's reading, one commentator of the 1890s suggests, out of the "desire to . . . to come face to face with a celebrated woman."[10] *Authors and Friends* was designed to meet such desires, and Fields presents Stowe as an extremely important writer. But she also describes Stowe's reading as "the last leap of the flame which had burned out a great wrong" (221). The elegiac note is unmistakable, and the emphasis on Stowe's waning powers is still more prevalent in Fields's diary entries of 1872. She comments as follows on a reading that Stowe gave three days before the one described in *Authors and Friends:*

> [Stowe] was nervous, the night was warm and her reading was not altogether successful. People could not hear. She made a spot on the front of her pretty dress too at supper after our return for her obliviousness to all cares of this sort are wonderful and terrible. She takes everything offered to her at table and leaves quantities of bread and whatnot strewed about and her room is a tangle wherein nothing can be found—in spite of all this her talk is forever interesting and absorbing and her friendship a boon of heaven.[11]

This diary entry of September 25, 1872, expresses both disappointment and awe at Stowe's behavior and "obliviousness." Fields's unpublished remarks of 1872 reflect a painful sense of the ravages of time. Three days later, writing in her diary of Stowe's more successful second reading, Fields keeps the previous failure in mind: "this time [Stowe] delivered what she certainly had not done the first time." For Fields, Stowe's undisputed greatness offsets the older author's nervousness, distractedness, etc. Indeed these qualities are all the more poignant for Fields because she still perceives traces of Stowe's "awful power."[12] But in 1872 the generation that had not "passed through the struggle of our war" saw Stowe differently.

Alice Stone Blackwell of Boston kept a careful journal of her activities and her reading when she was fourteen to sixteen years old (1872–74). Blackwell was the only child of women's rights activist Lucy Stone and social reformer Henry Brown Blackwell. Her father had been Stowe's neighbor in Cincinnati during the volatile 1830s and '40s. Alice Blackwell went to hear Stowe speak on the same occasion that elicits Fields's wistful praise. Blackwell's comments about Stowe's reading on September 28 are sparser (and less ambivalent) than Fields's. "Saturday. Arithmetic and Grammar examination. Went into Boston and heard Mrs. Stowe read. She is a pleasant looking elderly lady, but her voice is hardly strong enough to be heard in a large hall. I changed a couple of books and went home."[13]

Fields's electrified sense of Stowe's performance is pointedly absent from Blackwell's remarks. Stowe was not "alive in every fibre of her being," for Blackwell; seeing and hearing Stowe did not inspire the girl either to think about the Civil War or to read *Uncle Tom's Cabin*. Yet Blackwell was an avid reader, and a devotee of fiction; her diary alludes to novels by Charles Dickens, George Eliot, Victor Hugo, Nathaniel Hawthorne, Elizabeth Stuart Phelps, and many others.[14]

In an "Introduction" to a new edition of 1879 Stowe recalls the anxiety she felt after she wrote the last installment of *Uncle Tom's Cabin*. "Would anybody read it? Would anybody listen?" Her "profound discouragement" persisted after "the last proof-sheet had been sent to the office [for book publication]. . . . It seemed to her that there was no hope, that nobody would hear, nobody would read, nobody would pity."[15] Stowe's anxiety about being read was more justified in 1879 than it had been in 1852. *Uncle Tom's Cabin* was internationally famous when the new edition with Stowe's "Introduction" appeared; a review praises the essay as "a literary history whose frankness and simplicity will appeal to everyone." Nevertheless, the reviewer adds that the "depth and force" with which the novel once moved anyone "with a mind to think and a heart to feel" is something that "none but those who remember slavery as an actuality can understand."[16] Other commentators agreed.

LOOKING BACKWARD: NEW MEANINGS FOR UNCLE TOM

Public interest in the plantation South and the Civil War declined sharply after the end of hostilities: the photographer Matthew Brady spent a decade trying to persuade Congress to purchase his photos of the battlefield.[17] By the 1880s however, as interest in the war and its images started to revive, collections of photographs were sold in a variety of formats, accompanied by a rhetoric of heroism, sacrifice, and national unity.[18] Unanswered questions about the future of race relations in the United States began to spark curiosity about the prewar past.[19]

Photographers, artists, and correspondents went South in the mid-eighties, seeking to capture an image of rural black culture before all traces of slavery had vanished.[20] Editors of pictorial weeklies and illustrated monthlies cultivated the desire to glimpse this foreign territory—a world that "amounted to terra incognita for most northern readers."[21] The institution of slavery had disappeared, but it had shaped Southern life and its vestiges could be recaptured in words and pictures. Writing in the *Century* in 1887, the Kentucky author James Lane Allen reported on his journey to a Southern "negro town." Allen stresses the importance of scanning this "landscape of the past. . . . before it grows remoter and is finally hidden by the mists of forgetfulness."[22]

Journalistic accounts such as Allen's often included visual accompaniments, in this case by E. W. Kemble, illustrator of *The Adventures of Huckleberry Finn* (1884) and later of *Uncle Tom's Cabin* (1891).[23] Kemble's illustrations perpetuated time-honored icons such as "the Mammy" and "the Cook" (figs. 12 and 13). His images of elderly black women tending white children, or a white woman at the bedside of a frail black one, graphically suggest the passing of a population characterized by devotion, represented as reciprocal. Like plantation fiction of the period, such accounts render a lost world, where African Americans "remain content with their inferiority" and have no higher ambitions.[24]

Allen's account of "the Southern negro" is entitled "Mrs. Stowe's 'Uncle Tom' at Home in Kentucky." Allen (or the editors) apparently assumed that this title would speak for itself, as if "Mrs. Stowe's 'Uncle Tom'" were an appropriate generic label for all African Americans. In relying on this reductive association, Allen—like other readers and writers of the 1880s and '90s—adapted Stowe's text to specific contemporary needs and transformed its cultural function. Tom became the epitome of the devoted servant—nothing

THE MAMMY.

12. "The Mammy." "Mrs. Stowe's 'Uncle Tom' at Home in Kentucky," From The Century
34 (October 1887). Collection of The New-York Historical Society. Negative #83664d.

THE COOK.

13. "The Cook." "Mrs. Stowe's 'Uncle Tom' at Home in Kentucky," From The Century 34
(October 1887). Collection of The New-York Historical Society. Negative #83665d.

more. Aunt Chloe was the "despot in the kitchen," Mrs. Shelby the exemplary mistress.[25] Such images not only idealized Southern ways but also radically flattened Stowe's text. Racialization now served new ends.

Like other journalistic accounts of the rural South, "Mrs. Stowe's 'Uncle Tom' at Home in Kentucky," was offered to the reading public as an objective description of a social phenomenon and a region in transition. The figure of "Uncle Tom" became a measure of social conditions located at a considerable distance from the novel that generated him. This was Phoebe Palmer's worst nightmare come true: the line between fiction and truth was elided; fiction had become an index to reality.[26] "Uncle Tom" became shorthand for the idea of black loyalty and subservience.[27] With the help of such commentary (and such illustrations, as we shall see in Chapter 6), *Uncle Tom's Cabin* gained new explanatory power regarding both the prewar era and African Americans in the contemporary United States. In the name of respect for the receding past, Stowe's imaginary figures were reworked to serve a story of race relations for the present and implicitly the future.

Insofar as Stowe's novel could be taken as a guide to the enduring simplicity, ready affection, and natural devotion of African Americans, it offered a reassuring story to anxious white readers in an increasingly charged racial landscape. This reading strategy dominated discussions and editions of *Uncle Tom's Cabin* in the 1880s and '90s. The appeal of Uncle Remus tales, romantic plantation novels, and even the conjure tales of Charles Chesnutt attests to growing fascination with the war and the antebellum South.[28] Read as the image of a gracious world, unfortunately lost, and framed as what one full-length edition called "a homely plantation story,"[29] new editions of *Uncle Tom's Cabin* (mostly published in the North) even attracted Southern readers.[30]

Reawakened attention to *Uncle Tom's Cabin* was nurtured and intensified by strategies for packaging, marketing, and illustrating the novel, geared primarily to the lucrative Northeastern and the growing Western market. Repackaging was essential, for while many elder statesmen, men of letters, and other readers fondly recalled the excitement with which they had first read *Uncle Tom's Cabin* in the 1850s, the book did not have a similar appeal for men and women born during and after the war. Editions of the 1890s often acknowledge that "the great emancipation question of a few decades ago" did not sustain "all the old interest" for contemporary readers.[31] Many discussions of Stowe included explanations designed to counter anticipated resistance—the feeling that Uncle

Tom had "outlived his usefulness, his day and generation."[32] The novel's politics, melodrama, and didacticism, like its evangelicalism, made "the most remarkable book of the age" seem anachronistic. But although white readers no longer devoured *Uncle Tom's Cabin* "with the intensity of other days,"[33] the novel gained growing attention in published commentaries and reprints. It continued to sell and circulate well into the new century; it appeared on lists of recommended reading, for children and adults.

GENERATING A PUBLIC CONSENSUS: *UNCLE TOM'S CABIN* AS A NATIONAL TREASURE

A revised "protocol of reading," inscribed in paratextual materials and commentaries, helped rekindle interest in *Uncle Tom's Cabin* by adapting it to the needs of an increasingly secular, white, primarily Northern, middle-class reading public that was learning to be suspicious of sentimental fiction, that was not as interested in social reform as it used to be, and that was plagued by racial anxieties.[34] As the emotional draw of the book receded, its virtues were publicly rehearsed. At the same time, its racist potential was maximized.

By the 1890s the idea of black racial inferiority drew increasing support from multiple sources—from evolutionary theory, from ethnographic journalism, and from widely shared anxiety among white citizens, North and South, about the implications of the freedom so recently gained by ex-slaves. After the war the idea of racial equality became more threatening than it had been when the institution of slavery kept African American desires and ambitions in check. With the demise of the colonization movement and the failure of Reconstruction, freed African Americans began leaving the South in search of work, new places to live, and education. White Northern anxiety increased in this context, but was allayed by a combination of factors. In the 1890s, as Rayford Logan notes, "Negroes in the North did not impinge upon the white population as much as they did in the South." In addition, scientific, political, and literary discourse suggested that African Americans were designed by nature for menial jobs and had neither intellectual nor political goals.[35] As Charles Chesnutt notes in a letter to George Washington Cable on June 5, 1890, African Americans in the "magazine press" are generally characterized by "dog-like fidelity to their old master."[36] Brander Matthews expresses widely shared assumptions about black people when he praises Twain's representation of Jim (in *Huckleberry Finn*) for displaying "the essential simplicity and kindliness and generosity of the Southern negro."[37] As we shall see in Chapters 6 and 7, illustrations and children's editions of *Uncle Tom's Cabin* adapt Stowe's text in this spirit. Introductions and visual images reinforce existing attitudes to essentialized racial difference, often turning Stowe's slave figures into caricatures. Editions of the nineties foreground the idea of black inferiority and promote the separation of races. The imaginative distance between white readers and Eliza or Tom (not to speak of Topsy) increased exponentially.

In 1893 Stowe's novel entered the public domain. In 1896 (the year of the court decision *Plessy vs. Ferguson*) Stowe's eighty-fifth birthday was widely publicized; her death soon followed. These events provided the impetus for retrospectives as well as new editions of her influential book. Assuming that a deluge of reprints would follow expiration of copyright, Stowe's publisher Houghton Mifflin issued new editions of its own, hoping to "fill as many market niches as possible" before the flood began.[38] Other publishers, also anticipating fresh opportunities for profit in *Uncle Tom's Cabin,* asked themselves how to make the novel attractive to a new generation of readers.

By 1890, the status of fiction as a genre had risen considerably in U.S. literary culture. As we have seen, antebellum advertisements and Northern reviews of *Uncle Tom's Cabin* had avoided the word "fiction" and often used religious terminology in praising the book's holy mission.[39] By contrast, *Uncle Tom's Cabin* was emphatically a secular fictional work in late nineteenth-century editions and commentaries. Stowe's well-known remarks about God having written *Uncle Tom's Cabin* were received in the 1850s and '60s with respect for the book as inspired—"called of God, by faith she went forth," according to a retrospective newspaper report of 1868.[40] But by the nineties, Annie Fields recounts Stowe's claim that "God wrote" the book only to add that the author was then an "old lady" whose "absent-mindedness grew upon her with increasing years."[41] Where Stowe's tale had once been advertised among sermons, it was now advertised with other novels.[42] At the end of the century *Uncle Tom's Cabin* was a "remarkable piece of fiction," one whose initial impact was proclaimed to be "almost beyond precedent in the history of fiction."[43] Fiction had become not only a respectable genre but one with a history—a past worthy of consideration. "Masterpiece" and "novel" were no longer contradictory terms. Indeed, *Uncle Tom's Cabin* had become a "great American classic."[44] The claim of literary greatness was inscribed in prefatory material for new editions, and in commemorative articles marking Stowe's eighty-fifth birthday, her death, the "semi-centennial of this remarkable book's publication,"[45] the centennial of Stowe's birth—and so on.

Nevertheless, even advocates of *Uncle Tom's Cabin* tended to assume a generic hierarchy in which fiction was positioned beneath older, more distinguished literary forms. As a genre, fiction continued to suffer from what Harold Bloom has called belatedness.[46] *Uncle Tom's Cabin* was now understood to have been popular in the 1850s precisely *because* it was fiction ("its power as a novel . . . carried it . . . through the land");[47] but its very popularity testified to its "lowly" origins. "*Uncle Tom's Cabin* ranks among the world's wonderful books," the introduction to one edition of the nineties proclaims. "Like *Robinson Crusoe* and the *Pilgrims Progress* it stands out among myriads of works of infinitely higher aim and ambition."[48] Terms like "wonderful" or "marvelous" identified *Uncle Tom's Cabin* as a fictional text characterized not by its elevated "aim and ambition"—the high seriousness deemed appropriate to works of art—but by its capacity to engage and divert a reader, often a woman or child.[49] By the 1890s *Uncle Tom's Cabin* (like *Robinson Crusoe* and the *Pilgrims Progress*) was widely read as a children's tale, and often republished as such.

In the antebellum period, as we have noted, children and adults frequently read the same books. The line between children's literature and "Literature" was not clear. By the turn of the century, however, that division had crystallized, at least for publishers, editors, and librarians.[50] Nevertheless, reviewers and commentators often took young people—especially girls—as a standard for the appropriateness (if not the ultimate value) of literature. As William Dean Howells famously put it, the novel in America was partly intended "for young girls to read."[51] The "young girl" often had as little relation to real girls of the period as prescriptions for reading had to real reading, but she was much discussed by educators and reviewers. Sometimes she was seen as the exemplary fiction-reader and a gauge of decorum; more often she was demonized as undiscriminating and foolish—in need of protection and control.[52] For good and ill she was an influential figure in literary culture well into the twentieth century. Advocates of "realism," launching a concerted attack on sentiment and romance, took the young girl not only as the prototypical novel-reader, but also as "the iron Madonna" whose taste was destroying American literature.[53]

Uncle Tom's Cabin with its domestic and relational emphasis, its piety and moral rigor, was well suited to meet the standard for entry into the white middle-class parlor, including the standard for acceptable girls' reading (especially if certain "inappropriate" matters were ignored). But while the identification of *Uncle Tom's Cabin* with children and young women bolstered the image of the book as wholesome reading and helped to keep it in the public eye, it also preserved the novel's inferior status.[54] Commentators sometimes proclaimed that *Uncle Tom's Cabin* defied categorization, and publishers reissued it in such well-respected frameworks as Appleton's series of "The World's Great Books,"[55] but efforts to propel Stowe's novel into the emerging canon of literary masterworks labored under a considerable handicap.

Proponents of Stowe's novel attempted to fortify their case by asserting the "timelessness" of *Uncle Tom's Cabin* and linking it to older literary forms as well as other acknowledged "classics." In 1896, Richard Burton, writing in the *Century,* referred to Stowe's novel as the *"epic* of the slave" (my emphasis).[56] The same year, Charles Dudley Warner linked Stowe with Homer, Cervantes, and Turgenev.[57] Yet the very designation "classic" risked reinforcing the novel's association with the ossified or the dead. "Soon I will become a classic," one writer tells another in an early Wharton story (1901): "Bound in sets and kept on the top shelf . . . brrr, doesn't that sound freezing?"[58] Classics occupied a paradoxical position in literary culture. In the words of one typical turn-of-the-century editorial: "Homer, Virgil, Dante, Shakespeare and Milton are shelved classics"—respected from a safe distance.[59]

At the end of the century, the most enthusiastic defenders of *Uncle Tom's Cabin* as important American literature were well-known figures who had consumed the book before the war. *Uncle Tom's Cabin* is a "very great novel . . . still perhaps our chief fiction," William Dean Howells declared in 1895.[60] A year later Charles Dudley Warner suggested that *Uncle Tom's Cabin* fulfilled "the one indispensable requisite of a great work of imaginative fiction." In Warner's definition the sine qua non of artistic greatness was "universality, [the] . . . appeal to universal human nature in all races and situations and climates."[61] For Warner and other distinguished "men of letters," *Uncle Tom's Cabin* fulfilled the central criterion for a great book; in the words of Walter Besant, it "appeals to every age and all ages."[62] Many commentators of the nineties shared this definition of serious art. As James Russell Lowell put it, great books "are not national, but human." It is "their universal and perennial application to our consciousness and our experience [that] accounts for their permanence."[63] Praising "the genius and not the moral" of Stowe's book, Lowell suggested that *Uncle Tom's Cabin* was a literary masterpiece despite Stowe's moral purpose, not because of it.[64]

But the mantle of literary greatness did not rest easily on *Uncle Tom's Cabin*. Some critics of the period asserted that it was not the "universality" but, on the contrary, the book's "purposiveness" that accounted for its importance. The idea of *Uncle Tom's Cabin* as a "purpose-novel" was at odds with the notion of its "universality," but contemporary literary and critical voices as varied as Charlotte Perkins Gilman, Frank Norris, and Grant Allen took ethical and social "purposiveness" as an important component of literary value.[65] In "Novels Without a Purpose," an article published in the *North American Review* and reprinted in *Current Literature* in 1896, Allen wrote: "All the most successful novels of the last half-century from *Uncle Tom's Cabin* to *Jude the Obscure*, have been novels with a purpose." Claiming that the three "great epics of the world," *The Aeneid, The Divine Comedy,* and *Paradise Lost*, must all "plead . . . guilty to purposiveness," Allen concludes that "the novel without a purpose stands condemned . . . to the second class, and the infancy of humanity."[66] "*Uncle Tom's Cabin,* like *Les Misérables,* and a few other novels will live, because written with a purpose," Sarah Knowles Bolton wrote in *The Lives of Girls Who Became Famous* (1886); "no work of fiction is permanent without some great underlying principle or object."[67]

Fiction with a "purpose" had many proponents in the last twenty years of the nineteenth century; it also had deep roots in U.S. literary culture. The idea of active and purposeful reading had long served as an antidote to anxieties about fiction-reading in particular as rooted in idleness; some commentators and educators still accused fiction of encouraging passivity, foolishness, and a distorted sense of reality.[68] Purposive reading was a gendered concept identified with manliness, seriousness, maturity, and success. The "novel with a purpose" was celebrated not only as a higher kind of fiction but also as an antidote to the vapidity of "Art for Art's Sake."[69] Still, the idea of Stowe's "purposiveness" was difficult to reconcile with the idea of *Uncle Tom's Cabin* as a masterpiece and a classic. To read it for "purposiveness" was to lay bare its political commitments and social critique. The novel's representation of past American conditions, and its alleged role in transforming those conditions, made the claim of universality impossible to sustain. Insofar as *Uncle Tom's Cabin* attacked specific social practices and had moral relevance to a particular historical period, the book did not rise above its own cultural moment. But the emerging canon of great American literature was heavily weighted toward the universal and the transcendent. As a "great book" *Uncle Tom's Cabin* remained an anomaly.

The idea of Stowe's "purpose" necessarily drew attention to the problem of race, a problem that seemed all the more intractable as the institution of slavery receded further into the past. Although racial issues loomed large in society, they were widely neglected in literary discourse of the period. As Richard Ohmann notes, popular turn-of-the-century journals avoided the subject of race altogether: "race was not exactly unmentionable, and black people were not literally invisible; but race—what was elsewhere called 'the Negro problem'—made no appearance as a constituted issue."[70] In keeping with this strategy, new editions of *Uncle Tom's Cabin* assiduously avoided implying any connection between the institution of slavery and the problem of race at the turn of the century. But the idea of *Uncle Tom's Cabin* as a "great purpose novel" made it especially difficult to keep the issue of race out of the field of vision.

Several tactics gradually emerged for promoting *Uncle Tom's Cabin* without raising the question of contemporary race relations. Stowe's "purpose" and even the novel's "outdatedness," could be turned to good account with a subtle shift of emphasis. If the thematic concerns of *Uncle Tom's Cabin* were effectively restricted to the American past, discussions of the novel could steer clear of volatile contemporary problems. As publishers and editors of the nineties sought additional grounds for claiming the cultural significance of Stowe's novel, they hit on the idea of history. An emphasis on the book's historical significance soon became the most popular strategy for promoting it. This strategy shaped the Stowe display at the World's Columbian Exposition (1893) as well as paratextual material for reprints of the period. Prefaces, introductions, and other commentaries present *Uncle Tom's Cabin* as a trigger of the Civil War and an agent of emancipation.

THE NOVEL AS HISTORICAL ARTIFACT: *UNCLE TOM'S CABIN* WITHOUT RACE

The idea that *Uncle Tom's Cabin* played an important role in the history of the United States provided a way around many of the problems posed by the novel's uneasy position in literary culture. Although Stowe was not included in the prestigious American Men of Letters series, Houghton Mifflin began reissuing *Uncle Tom's Cabin* in the 1880s and '90s;[71] paratextual material included in the book was designed to reflect its literary, scholarly, and especially its historical importance. The redefinition of Stowe's book as a historical document gave it new stature in the age of American realism and the "culture of professionalism." The alliance with history implied objectivity, truth, and professional authority. The book's "historical significance" also gave it new amplitude—it was no longer merely a "marvelous" "wonderful" fictional work, not even a "purposive" one. It was a major social force. Most important, it had completed its cultural work and deserved attention precisely for that reason: "Changes Wrought by One Book" one headline of 1911 proclaimed, marking the centenary of Stowe's birth.[72]

The historical importance of *Uncle Tom's Cabin* was already a theme in the prefatory materials of the 1879 edition, which included Stowe's discussion of the novel's genesis and impact. Introductions of the 1880s and '90s proclaimed the book "an event in American history."[73] The nature of that event was defined as a milestone in an irresistible march of American progress. *Uncle Tom's Cabin* was the book that "first brought the iniquity of slavery prominently before the people of the North. . . . one of the great forces that led to the Civil War."[74] It was a novel that helped "chang[e] the Constitution of the United States."[75] Abraham Lincoln's purported words upon meeting Harriet Beecher Stowe—"So you're the little lady who started this great war"—were widely quoted at the end of the century.[76] Some editions printed the Emancipation Proclamation as part of the prefatory matter.[77]

In one sense, framing *Uncle Tom's Cabin* as a work of the past effectively supported claims for the book's literary greatness: most late nineteenth-century commentators agreed that only a work tested by generations of readers could be a masterpiece. However, another aspect of the novel's historicity—like its "purpose"—opened it to a criticism often leveled against the realist fiction that flourished in the 1880s and '90s: the book too clearly evoked a time-bound era and locale to be seen as a work that rose above mere particulars. Like the designation "classic," the historical emphasis intensified the impression of *Uncle Tom's Cabin* as a book that belonged *only* to the past. But if claims for the universality, purposiveness, and historicity of *Uncle Tom's Cabin* clashed at one level, they were mutually supportive at another: all could be adjusted to maximize the distance between *Uncle Tom's Cabin* and racial anxieties of the present. The heightened consciousness of *Uncle Tom's Cabin* as a work of, for, and about the past could serve at least this function: it deflected attention from contemporary racial matters. Thus the historical emphasis neatly transformed the potential liability of datedness into an asset.

According to Michael Winship, *Uncle Tom's Cabin* had "steady popular appeal" in the 1880s and '90s.[78] When readers of *The Literary News* sent in their nominations for "the Ten Best Novels," *Uncle Tom's Cabin* and *The Scarlet Letter* were the only American books on the list.[79] *Uncle Tom's Cabin* was the only American novel on G. P. Putnam's "Suggestions for Household Libraries" in Lyman Abbott's *Hints for Home Reading.*[80] Stowe's novel appeared on "recommended reading" lists in many other contexts. But there is a difference between books read intensely, in private, and books celebrated in public. Even books bought, given as gifts, or borrowed from libraries are not necessarily read.[81] *Uncle Tom's Cabin* was much discussed in print and much reissued in these years. But readers no longer finished the book in three days, neglecting other duties or weeping and looking into their souls. Insofar as late nineteenth-century white readers consumed the book, it must have given them other satisfactions. *Uncle Tom's Cabin* had new cultural work to do at the turn of the twentieth century.

Discussions and editions of the novel in the 1890s unanimously proposed new guidelines for reading: readers were to approach the book as a historical artifact, an important reminder of the national past, but also as a historical agent, a book that had shaped significant events. These two emphases dovetailed with another: the injunction to consume Stowe's novel "without torture and tears."[82] "Feeling right" now referred neither to faith nor to sentiment. *Uncle Tom's Cabin* remained a "thrilling" tale,[83] but it no longer required religious contemplation, self-criticism, or action on the reader's part. In an introduction to the Appleton edition of 1898, Thomas Wentworth Higginson put the case emphatically but typically: "The time is past, fortunately, when 'Uncle Tom's Cabin' need be read in any sectional spirit or as anything but a thrilling delineation of a mighty wrong, whose responsibility was shared by a whole nation and for which the whole nation paid the bitter penalty."[84] Celebrating *Uncle Tom's Cabin* both as one of "the world's great books" (the series title) and as a powerful agent of social change, Higginson and others suggest that with the help of Stowe's novel the nation's problems have been solved. The preface to a children's edition of 1904 puts it this way: "'Uncle Tom's Cabin' is a sad story, but there are no slaves now who can be made to suffer like Uncle Tom and the other people in the book, so we need not be sad over it. We should rather be glad when we remember that this very story helped to make the poor slaves happy and free."[85] While the publication of *Uncle Tom's Cabin* had been "an event of national importance . . . slavery [was] only a historic thing" followed by "peace and complete reunion."[86] Positioned within such a script, the book became a rich ground for cultural self-congratulation. The framing of *Uncle Tom's Cabin* in the Stowe exhibit in the Woman's Building Library at the Columbian Exposition exemplifies this dynamic.

The year that *Uncle Tom's Cabin* entered the public domain (1893) was also the year of the Columbian Exposition in Chicago. The Harriet Beecher Stowe display was the centerpiece of the Connecticut Women's exhibit in the library of the Woman's Building. Describing the Stowe collection in a report on the work of Connecticut women at the fair, Kate Brannon Knight, president of the Board of Lady Managers, stressed "Mrs. Stowe's unique place in literature" and the importance of *Uncle Tom's Cabin*: "Since we were so fortunate as to be able to claim for our own State the writer of the most marvelous work ever written by a woman, we naturally gave Mrs. Stowe's Works and *Uncle Tom's Cabin* the most prominent place in our exhibit."[87] In the bookcase at the World's Fair, as in many other contexts throughout the 1890s, *Uncle Tom's Cabin* was employed to support an optimistic narrative of America's recent past and triumphant present. The exhibit reflects the growing consensus about how to read the book.

The strategies employed to showcase Stowe's novel as the jewel in the crown of the Connecticut women's exhibit were designed not only to reconfirm the book's value for long-time devotees, but also to restore the novel's broad appeal by countering the somewhat uncomfortable sense that "the stir which the book made at its birth" was not palpable to contemporary readers (24–25). Anxiety about a possible time-lag, a muted but recurrent refrain in Knight's account, was inscribed in the report on the fair and implicit in the exhibit itself.[88] As historical artifact and historical agent *Uncle Tom's Cabin* gained an important place in the master-narrative of the fair—a success story that positioned the United States on the top rung of the evolutionary ladder of nations.[89] Seen in this way, the potentially troubling time-lag made the book meaningful, rather than irrelevant. *Uncle Tom's Cabin* represented both America's literary coming-of-age,[90] and its moral, political, and cultural maturity. At the fair, as elsewhere, the idea of *Uncle Tom's Cabin* as intimately bound to history—both representing it and shaping it—won out over the idea of *Uncle Tom's Cabin* as a work of genius with universal appeal.[91]

The new protocol of reading which emerged had multiple advantages. For one thing, it averted questions of literary form. Downplaying the aesthetic issue was important because times had changed: sentiment was no longer attractive, at least to literary commentators.[92] The "technical" and "artistic" defects of *Uncle Tom's Cabin* were often noted.[93] The focus on history neutralized this issue, while framing Stowe's novel as a text that faithfully exposed the social fault lines of a bygone era, a time of injustice and discord. This history was worth recalling, but from a distance, with a sense of satisfaction. "Now the war is over," Knight wrote in her report on the exhibit, "slavery is a thing of the past; slave-pens, bloodhounds, whips, and slave coffles are only bad dreams of the night" (100). *Uncle Tom's Cabin* could now be read without pain; dismissed as a "bad dream of the night," slavery itself might never have existed.

The fact of emancipation took center stage in the narrative of progress featured by the Stowe exhibit and by the fair generally. Although the end of slavery was not represented in *Uncle Tom's Cabin* (written well before the Emancipation Proclamation) this development was regularly privileged in discussions of the novel. Abraham Lincoln's description of Stowe as "starting" the Civil War may be coy or apocryphal, but serious historians of the period made similar claims. In the 1880s and '90s, history books regularly argued that *Uncle Tom's Cabin* had had a significant effect on events.[94] What David Brion Davis has called "the emancipation moment" became a metonym for the important role of *Uncle Tom's Cabin* in U.S. culture.[95] At the Columbian Exposition as elsewhere, showcasing this moment concertedly ignored any actions taken by African Americans themselves and reinforced popular assumptions about the childlike dependence of black people. Within the Stowe exhibit the idea that *Uncle Tom's Cabin* had helped put an end to slavery was summed up visually by a "beautiful silver inkstand" representing "two slaves freed from their shackles" (93–94).[96] In this miniature sculpture, a white man breaks the shackles of a slave while the slave, on his knees with his head bowed, is immobilized in a posture of submission (fig. 14).[97]

The role of African Americans had been radically circumscribed at the fair itself. Despite "Colored People's Day," African Americans were denied the opportunity to frame exhibits of their own. As a result, Ida B. Wells raised

MRS. STOWE'S SILVER INKSTAND.

14. "Mrs. Stowe's Silver Inkstand." From Kate Brannon Knight, History of the Work of
Connecticut Women at the World's Columbian Exposition, *1898. General Research
Division. The New York Public Library. Astor, Lenox and Tilden Foundations.*

the money to publish a stinging commentary, *The Reason Why the Colored
American is Not in the Columbian Exposition;* Wells refused to participate in
the fair at all.[98] Frederick Douglass, for his part, gave a speech at the fair: "The
Race Problem in America." The tensions surrounding the question of African
American participation in the Exposition reflect the growing conflict about
African Americans' control over the shape of their own future. White
Americans still held the purse strings of black institutions. They dominated
the boards of trustees, established the curriculum, set the goals, and framed
the images that represented African American progress to both black and
white America. In this context it is unsurprising as well as ironic that the
Stowe exhibit should have been one of the few displays within the White City
to acknowledge the existence of African Americans.

But by framing *Uncle Tom's Cabin* as an agent in freeing the slaves, and
stopping the narrative there, the Stowe exhibit too elided black agency, along
with the problematic postwar history of the South and ongoing questions
about the future of African Americans. Stowe's narrative itself—plot, charac-

ters, dialogue, imagery—was nowhere in evidence at the fair. The Stowe display was a memorial to Harriet Beecher Stowe and her books, not a hands-on exhibit, not a library to be used. "The books unfortunately could not be handled," as Jeanne Madeline Weimann notes.[99] They were closed volumes, neatly arranged behind the doors of a mahogany bookcase, "with glass upon every side, and glass shelves, the whole about five feet in height."[100] Also on display was the *Key to Uncle Tom's Cabin,* which asserted the book's basis in historical reality, and a complete set of Stowe's collected works, specially printed and newly bound for the fair by Houghton Mifflin. An early portrait of the author and a marble bust of Stowe on a pedestal joined the silver inkstand as part of the exhibit as well. All of these artifacts (including the bookcase) asserted substantial achievements worthy of commemoration. But within this material tribute to the novel, the painful details of Stowe's plot remained invisible. The absence of the story served a revised interpretive convention that is (paradoxically) still more apparent in the paratextual materials of new editions.

Editors and other commentators encouraged readers not to cry or to question themselves when reading Stowe's novel, but rather to enjoy it, while experiencing a feeling of cultural pride. The intense, emotional, contemplative mode of reading prescribed by Stowe and embraced by many of her first readers was discredited. Urging sophisticated readers to maintain the decorum of historical objectivity, some commentators placed *Uncle Tom's Cabin* within the newly available generic frame of realism. Proponents of realism affirmed the elevated taste of the reader and rejected interpretive strategies identified with sentiment. Tears were no longer a sign of either literary or political right-mindedness. A typical formulation of the period appears in an introduction to the "Art Memorial Edition": "since it was written a new generation has grown up and the state of affairs to which it refers has long since passed away. . . . it can be read today with as deep enjoyment . . . as in the days when all the world went wild over the sorrows of Uncle Tom and wept at the death of the saint-like Eva."[101] Weeping over a novel in the 1890s marked the reader as lacking in critical judgment. Introductions and other commentaries drew less and less attention to brutalized or martyred slaves, to families separated, women raped, or children bought and sold. In general the "harassed, hunted fugitive" disappeared from sight and memory in the post–Civil War years.[102] The white reading public of the nineties was eager to forget the divisiveness of an underground railroad and the outrage of whips, shackles, and the auction block, along with the problem of race—the most enduring legacy of slavery. Perhaps partly for this reason many fiction readers at the turn of the century remained as indifferent to *Uncle Tom's Cabin* as Alice Stone Blackwell was in 1872.

White Readers: Indifferent or Amused

Many of Stowe's characters became household words within a year or two of the novel's appearance. But in the last quarter of the century Stowe's characters were wrenched out of their initial context and put to new uses. As Uncle Tom became the proverbial "loyal servant," so Topsy became the lively, naughty one. In periodicals of the 1880s she was no longer the brutalized child whose scarred back made Miss Ophelia's "heart . . . pitiful within her" (*UTC* 355) but rather "a middle-sized 'Topsy'" in a Southern sewing room, "pushing rudely forward, tossing her head"; a "coal-black specimen" of a baby nurse, "as veritable a Topsy as ever 'growed'"; a "handmaiden . . . as precious an imp as any Topsy ever was," full of tricks and lies, etc.[103] On stage during and after the Civil War, Topsy was often hypersexualized, flagrantly promiscuous.[104] Elsewhere in the 1870s, '80s, and '90s Topsy ceased to be human at all; the idea of having "just growed" like Topsy was applied indiscriminately to plants and trees, new towns, tiled roofs, musical instruments, the post office, the government of Chicago, the British Empire, modern battleships, and Thanksgiving Day.[105]

By the turn of the century, *Uncle Tom's Cabin* was better known than read. A small notebook, compiled at this time probably by a white girl or a young woman, reflects the marginal position of *Uncle Tom's Cabin* in the imagination of one anonymous but committed reader.[106] This painstakingly wrought "reading notebook," eight and a half by four and a half inches, with thirty-eight pages, is filled with lists of authors, poems, and novels. The names and titles are written in a careful, florid script, on both sides of each page, interspersed with small (sometimes tiny) newspaper photos of authors and titles as well as clippings announcing new books. This artifact, which opens like a stenographer's notebook, begins with a frontispiece of authors' faces and the phrase "Beautiful Books" (all cut out of newsprint). An article on "How to Read" ("Rules Cannot be Fixed as Each Man has His Own Standard") is pasted into the back cover.

The notebook is primarily focused on fiction. Page after page mingles contemporary popular fiction with classics (Defoe, Austen, Dickens, Cooper, Howells, and James but also Keats, Longfellow, Gibbon, Plutarch, Socrates). Sometimes single lines of newsprint ("Scott never grows old") are pasted alongside longer articles or handwritten lists. Although novels dominate the notebook, poets appear regularly as well. Other famous people are briefly mentioned and identified ("Beethoven [German] Grandest of musicians"; "Henry Ward Beecher, Presbyterian Minister"; "Edwin Forest, born American, A Celebrated Actor"; "Victoria born England, Queen of England, Died 1901"; "U.S. Grant born-America, President of U. States U S. Army Officer Federal Gen. in U.S. Army during Civil War 1861–1865)."

Mentions of Stowe are strikingly limited. Her name appears once in the compiler's handwriting, as "author of 'Uncle Tom's Cabin' and other Works," preceded by the name of Dante ("Italian poet") (fig. 15). She also appears in very small print in three advertisements: as one of the subjects in *Girls Who Became Famous* by Sarah K. Bolton (fig. 16); in "An Attractive Offer" for works by Robert L. Stevenson, Nathaniel Hawthorne, Richard H. Dana, Jr., Edgar Allan Poe, Harriet Beecher Stowe, and others (this advertisement includes a large picture of four volumes; *Uncle Tom's Cabin* is not among them [fig. 17]); and finally, in a puff for "Three Books by J. T. Trowbridge" which notes that "'Cudjo's Cave' undoubtedly ranks next to Mrs. Stowe's 'Uncle Tom's Cabin.'" But full pages are devoted to figures such as Scott and Bulwer-Lytton; Shakespeare dominates two separate pages. Pictures of varying sizes represent James Whitcomb Riley, Mark Twain, Benjamin Franklin, Abraham Lincoln, Maria Corelli, Rose N. Carey, and others. Authors from Shakespeare and Cooper through Bulwer-Lytton, Henry Ward Beecher, and Henry Harland occupy more space than Stowe.

The lack of attention to Stowe does not result from any shortage of available references or images. In making the notebook, the girl used advertisements and photographs that appeared in periodicals where Stowe was often represented. A biography of Stowe, written by her son, came out 1889. The press regularly commemorated Stowe's birthdays during the early nineties. Annie Fields, Elizabeth Stuart Phelps, Florine Thayer McCray, and others wrote chapters or books about Stowe that were published first in periodicals, then advertised and reviewed when issued in book form. Houghton Mifflin published a newly illustrated edition of *Uncle Tom's Cabin* in 1891, and a

15. "Uncle Tom's Cabin and Other Works." From anonymous reader's scrapbook/notebook, ca. 1900. Collection of Ellen Gruber Garvey.

16. "Girls Who Became Famous." From anonymous reader's scrapbook/notebook, ca. 1900. Collection of Ellen Gruber Garvey.

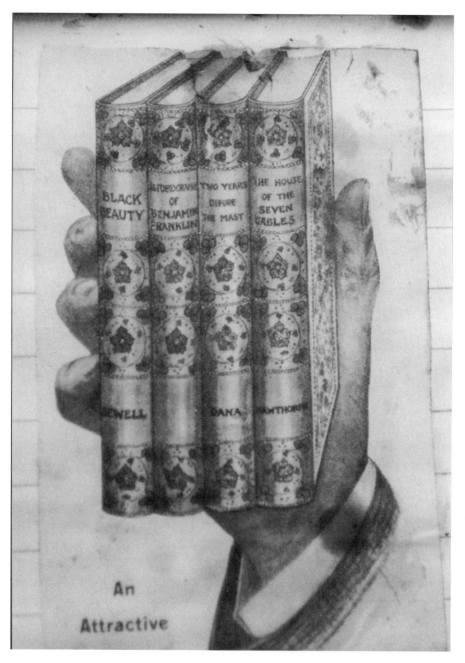

17. *"An Attractive Offer." From anonymous reader's scrapbook/notebook, ca. 1900. Collection of Ellen Gruber Garvey.*

multi-volume edition of Stowe's collected works in 1896. After Stowe's death, illustrated retrospectives appeared in newspapers and magazines all over the country.

Stowe is also a significant absence in an autobiographical account of childhood on "a Missouri prairie farm" at the turn of the century. Accounts of reading were a predictable part of early twentieth-century autobiography, and Mary Margaret McBride's *How Dear to My Heart* is no exception.[107] Born in 1899, McBride was not a "common" reader—she became a professional journalist and a radio host in the 1930s. Many of her comments are characteristic of the period, however; they also provide a useful contrast to antebellum concerns about absorption and undirected reading by the young. Although McBride mentions her difficulty "as a small child" telling "the difference between book people and real ones," this seems to have been a source of pleasure rather than anxiety: "I had absolutely no gauge except my own likes and dislikes," she declares (104, 105–6). McBride describes summers spent in the house of her Aunt Mary, where the sitting room was "lined with bookcases. . . . I read everything with beautiful impartiality—fiction, serials, articles on how to make wastebaskets out of tin cans, advice to young parents, social leaders and the lovelorn" (106). McBride discovers a set of Dickens's novels in her aunt's sitting room "and then came enchanted weeks with Oliver, Little Nell, David Copperfield and Pip" (106). For children in literate families of the 1890s and the first quarter of the twentieth century, absorption and "enchantment" by books was more than legitimate; it signified imagination and intellectual potential.[108] McBride recalls reading *Black Beauty, Little Women,* Grimms' fairy tales, *Five Little Peppers, Alice in Wonderland,* and other childhood classics, as well as some books read "without permission" (*Tempest and Sunshine* by Mary J. Holmes, *John Halifax, Gentleman*) (104–8, 114, 142, 146). She also mentions a local man, a "stranger-than-fiction character," who had been an "out-and-out abolitionist" when "everybody in our part of the state owned slaves and believed slavery was right" (113). She says nothing about *Uncle Tom's Cabin.*

It is not surprising that, despite her "beautiful impartiality" in choosing books, McBride does not mention Stowe's novel. Hostility to *Uncle Tom's Cabin* lingered in the South; the book excited "some of the same . . . antagonism that it did before the war," as one commentator wrote in 1886. Nevertheless, as the commentator also notes, the book was "having a larger sale from year to year in Southern homes, . . . many who, twenty years ago would not tolerate the mention of its name in their presence, now not only openly read it but praise it."[109] New ways of reading *Uncle Tom's Cabin* made it increasingly palatable in the "New South," as we have seen. This process continued well into the twentieth century. Perhaps McBride never encountered a copy of *Uncle Tom's Cabin,* or perhaps looking back at her own childhood from the perspective of the 1940s (a low point in Stowe's literary fortunes) she saw other reasons to avoid claiming familiarity with the book. Still, her omission—like her affirmation of indiscriminate childhood taste—reflects characteristic changes in reading practices more broadly. *Uncle Tom's Cabin* is a significant omission in many journals of the period. Charlotte Perkins Gilman, Alice Hamilton, Alice James, and others read widely in the last quarter of the century and recorded their responses to numerous novels. But one often looks in vain for a reference to *Uncle Tom's Cabin* in such sources.[110]

Stowe's novel does make fleeting appearances in many autobiographical and fictionalized accounts of postbellum childhood; but such references only confirm the idea that for many white readers of the period the book had lost its moral, political, and spiritual edge. As Topsy became a figure for growth, helter skelter, without any reference to slavery, so Eliza is put to new uses. The autobiography of Nebraska newspaper editor Walter Locke (born in West Virginia in 1875) describes growing up with only three books in the house (the Bible, Reverend Randall's book of travel in the Holy Land, and McGuffey's *Fifth Reader*).[111] Locke waxes poetic about the hard-won pleasures of reading: "a book, the while we are buried in it, is our world. It is our life, our self. In it we live and move and have our being."[112] An "omnivorous reader" all his life, as Joan Shelley Rubin notes,[113] Locke mentions *Uncle Tom's Cabin* only indirectly, using the image of Eliza slipping and sliding on the ice as a generalized figure for risk and human uncertainty.[114] In a romantic story published in the *Century* in 1893, Eliza appears at a still greater remove from her origins. During a conversation about the advantages of using a typewriter, one character demonstrates the proper mode of typing with the comment: "You did n't think that you were to go hesitatingly from letter to letter, with a little fearsome pause between each jump, like Eliza in 'Uncle Tom's Cabin,' escaping on the floating ice, did you?"[115] Such allusions reflect the assumption that "Eliza" will be familiar to the general reader, one way or another. But her moral, spiritual, and political meaning have drained away.

After the turn of the century, as segregation became entrenched ideology and policy, and as *Uncle Tom's Cabin* became a well-known "classic," white readers read it with diminishing affect. In *A Stepdaughter of the Prairie* (a series of sketches published in the *Atlantic* and then issued as a book in 1914) the narrator recounts her "simple and natural indulgence in reading" and notes in passing that having "just finished the Legree section of *Uncle Tom's Cabin* for the third time. . . . the last comfortable shiver had died away up [her] spine" when her sister approaches and distracts the narrator's attention. This girl consumes Stowe's novel for the "comfortable" pleasure of its predictably chilling effect. The book now provides transient and guilt-free delights; it has neither ethical nor social ramifications.[116] Eliza, Topsy, and Tom became debased common coin and the stuff of racialized banter.

In an autobiographical tale of a white boy growing up in Indiana, Jock Wilson (born 1898) relates leaving school in eighth grade to help his family by working in the mines with his father. The first chapter introduces Jock and his dog—Topsy—with "glossy hair, black as . . . lumps [of coal]."[117] By 1951, when the *Dark and the Damp* was published, Topsy was firmly ensconced in the American imaginary as a comic figure for blackness. While walking home from the mine after his first week there, Wilson falls through the ice of a creek and when he returns to the shaft a (white) fireman, covered with coal dirt, instructs the boy to take off his clothes, lays them out beside the boiler to dry, and tends to Wilson's bleeding heel.

> "I don't believe I know who you are," I said, removing my clothes. "You look like Uncle Tom."
>
> "Uncle Tom!" He repeated then he grinned. "Yeah, but I didn't fall in crossing the ice—"
>
> "Neither did Uncle Tom," I laughed. (95–96)

Like other contemporary allusions to "Uncle Tom" or "Eliza" this exchange suggests not only that key moments and characters of Stowe's book were widely familiar; but also that they were loosed from their moorings. Between the 1890s and the 1950s *Uncle Tom's Cabin* was stripped of its religious, ethical, or political gravity. White readers no longer devoured it with emotion or patriotic pride. But in the ongoing wake of the Civil War, unintended readers—especially African Americans—found new meaning in the book.[118]

UNINTENDED READERS

Uncle Tom's Cabin has often intrigued marginalized readers. Children were part of Stowe's audience from the beginning.[119] White antebellum women, Karen Sanchez-Eppler has argued, read the book out of identification with the weak, particularly with slave women.[120] In a small library of a British prison a woman "read and re-read 'Uncle Tom's Cabin,' 'till she must have known by heart every incident. . . ."[121] The servant girl Winifred Roley read the book avidly, after finding it in her mistress's attic.[122] *Uncle Tom's Cabin* drew a variety of postbellum American readers to a concern for disadvantaged groups. Helen Hunt Jackson adapts Stowe's tale for the cause of Native Americans. In a letter to Thomas Bailey Aldrich on May 4, 1883, she writes: "If I could write a story that would do for the Indian a thousandth part [of] what *Uncle Tom's Cabin* did for the Negro, I would be thankful for the rest of my life."[123] Upton Sinclair claimed in 1906 that *Uncle Tom's Cabin* was his model when writing *The Jungle.*[124] Like Frances Hodgson Burnett, Sinclair Lewis appreciates the "picturesque" aspects of slavery, but he is impelled by Stowe's book to take up the cause of the "wage slave."[125] *Uncle Tom's Cabin* inspired the Hungarian immigrant Edward Alfred Steiner with "a passion for the common people," as he recounts at some length in his autobiography *Against the Current: Simple Chapters from a Complex Life* (1910). The protagonist of Elias Tobenkin's novel *Witte Arrives* (1916) responds to *Uncle Tom's Cabin* in a similar way. He dreams of writing his own work of fiction. Taking Stowe's narrative—particularly her slave characters—as his model, he imagines making poor working people "so palpable that no one could mistake them, that once seen they could not be forgotten." "There was room for an Uncle Tom's Cabin of industry," he reflects. "He would paint the helplessness of the modern factory worker, the horror and despair of worklessness."[126]

There is a difference, however, between white readers, who were stimulated by *Uncle Tom's Cabin* to take up a social cause, and African Americans, who often read the book in a more intensely personal way.[127] We could say that Jackson, Lewis, Steiner, and Tobenkin were all marginalized in U.S. literary culture—Jackson as a woman who overcame significant obstacles before becoming a writer, Lewis as a poor boy with an alcoholic father, Steiner as a Jewish Hungarian immigrant, and Tobenkin as a Jewish immigrant from Russia.[128] *Uncle Tom's Cabin* may have helped these readers to experience solidarity with other outsiders, such as working men or Native Americans. Yet by acting upon their reformist impulses and pursuing their professional ambitions, such writers mitigated their own marginality. *Uncle Tom's Cabin* had a different kind of appeal for African American readers—a population that had grown significantly between the 1870s and the end of the century.[129] Bypassing the emphasis on historical distance—but not the emphasis on history—black Americans often read the book in an intensely personal way, especially in this period.

The narrator of James Weldon Johnson's fictionalized *Autobiography of an Ex-Colored Man* reads *Uncle Tom's Cabin* "with feverish intensity" as a child.[130] But Stowe's novel means something to the boy that it did not mean to white readers. He asserts that Stowe's book "opened my eyes as to who and what I was and what my country considered me" (29). As a free African American in the South after the Civil War, Johnson's narrator ignores Stowe's guidelines for how to read the story, absorbed by and absorbing it as an account of his own heritage and as a forceful comment on contemporary conditions that particularly affect black people. Like many late nineteenth-century white commentators, Johnson's narrator reads the book more as history than as fiction, but unlike white historians such as James Ford Rhodes, or literary spokesmen of the period such as William Dean Howells, Charles Dudley Warner, or Thomas Wentworth Higginson, Johnson's fictional character takes *Uncle Tom's Cabin* as the measure of an ongoing problem—not its solution. He experiences the problem as intimately his own. Real African Americans of the period shared this perspective.

Between the 1870s and 1903 William H. Dorsey, an African American from Philadelphia—artist, book collector, and son of an escaped slave— pasted newspaper clippings about "the Negro race" into three hundred and eighty-eight scrapbooks organized by subject. The subjects include Education, Crime, Religion, Africa, Black Migration and Emigration, Lynching, the World's Columbian Exposition, and many "personages" such as Booker T. Washington, Frederick Douglass, Alexander Dumas, Abraham Lincoln, and Ida B. Wells.[131] One of Dorsey's scrapbooks is devoted almost entirely to Harriet Beecher Stowe.[132] His selections allow us to glimpse an African American reader who devoted considerable time and energy to Stowe in the 1890s, as the book became a "classic," but as mainstream white readers either read it nostalgically or grew increasingly indifferent.

Dorsey's scrapbooks document African American experience of the period; they present a dense and richly textured picture of race relations. The scrapbook devoted to Booker T. Washington, for example, is far from a paean to his achievement. Angry letters from African American newspaper-readers about Washington's compromises appear alongside numerous accounts praising his achievements at Tuskegee, his acceptance of an honorary MA Degree at Harvard, his lecture tours, and pronouncements on "The Future of the Race," or "How to Advance the Negro."[133] Dorsey's scrapbook also contains newspaper reports of the controversy sparked by Washington's dinner with Theodore Roosevelt at the White House. As the scrapbook shows, Roosevelt's invitation to Washington triggered commentary that ranged from celebration of a landmark event through the outrage expressed by a confirmed segregationist senator, Benjamin Tillman of South Carolina. In Tillman's words: "The action of President Roosevelt in entertaining that nigger will necessitate our killing a thousand niggers in the South before they will learn their place again."[134] By including such disparate clippings in his scrapbook, Dorsey creates a complex historical contextualization of Washington.

The Harriet Beecher Stowe scrapbook focuses on the years 1895–98. Many of the articles that Dorsey clipped and pasted are taken from numerous pieces that appeared in the press on the occasion of Stowe's eighty-fourth birthday in 1895, and after her death in 1896. In some ways this artifact is similar to another scrapbook of newspaper clippings compiled in the same period by a member of the Beecher-Stowe clan, probably Stowe's son, Charles.[135] Many of the articles in Charles Stowe's scrapbook appear in Dorsey's as well.[136] Dorsey's clippings, like Charles Stowe's, include some celebratory articles such as "Mrs. Stowe's 84th Year."[137] Both scrapbooks accurately reflect the general tenor of obituaries in the press ("The Author of 'Uncle Tom's Cabin' Dies Peacefully at Hartford—Close of a Remarkable Life"[138]). Yet the differences are telling. Charles Stowe's scrapbook contains no trace of the initial controversy stirred by the novel. By contrast, a heading for one of Dorsey's clippings reads "Glad of Mrs. Stowe's Death"; "General Bradley J. Johnson Says She Wrote Much of the South that was False."[139] Later in the Dorsey scrapbook a letter to the editor of the *Philadelphia Bulletin* trashes *Uncle Tom's Cabin* as "absurd sentimental rot."[140]

Dorsey's scrapbook reflects an intense interest in the author of *Uncle Tom's Cabin* and perhaps a belief in her important contribution to the progress of "the Negro race." Yet it also implies a reading experience that diverges from the white consensus. Several articles in the Dorsey scrapbook are devoted to alleged prototypes for characters of *Uncle Tom's Cabin*. Charles Stowe's scrapbook includes only one article of this sort: "The Story of Eliza" recounts the appearance of the Rev. S. G. Rankin at the "Fourth Church" to relate "Incidents Which Formed the Basis of one of the Dramatic Incidents of 'Uncle Tom's Cabin.'"[141] Articles in Dorsey's scrapbook, by contrast, question the truth of Eliza's miraculous escape. In one of these, Norman Argo, who often claimed to be the source for Uncle Tom, alleges that "Eliza's escape was very prosaic." Another news item quotes Argo as saying that "the wonderful description of Eliza crossing the river on the floating ice is a myth." According to him, "she made the trip on a ferry boat."[142]

Several of Dorsey's clippings from 1897 include obituaries for "the most prominent figure in the novel." Announcing the "Funeral of Mrs. Stowe's Negro Hero," articles recount the death of this figure—Lewis G. Clark—"the 'George Harris' in 'Uncle Tom's Cabin.'"[143] The identification of George Harris as the novel's "hero" and its "most prominent figure" may come as a surprise to readers of this study. Academic discussions of *Uncle Tom's Cabin* tend to give George Harris less attention than Uncle Tom, Eliza, Eva, or even Ophelia and Topsy. In an essay devoted to Stowe's use of slave narratives as sources, Robert Stepto characteristically calls George Harris Stowe's "secondary hero."[144] Yet Dorsey's clippings about Lewis G. Clark not only make George Harris Stowe's "most prominent" character, they include pictures of Clark and give him considerable authority as the man "who gave Mrs. Stowe Information for her 'Uncle Tom's Cabin'."[145] One article notes, "For the first time in the history of Kentucky the body of a negro has lain in state here, and crowds gathered to see the remains of Lewis George Clark."[146] A clipping of an earlier article provides evidence for identifying Clark with George Harris and includes a large picture with the heading "'George Harris' Still Lives."[147] Dorsey's scrapbook thus underscores Clark's value and cultural importance.

It is impossible to tell whether or not Dorsey accepted the common view that (in the words of one Clark obituary) *Uncle Tom's Cabin* was "destined to bring about the emancipation of American slavery."[148] But the inclusion of multiple clippings identifying Clark with George Harris, and dubbing Harris a central figure in the book, suggest some of the ways in which Dorsey, reading—or reading about—*Uncle Tom's Cabin* in the 1890s, was drawn to elements that were not routinely highlighted by white readers of the period. The headings of several obituaries for Lewis George Clark fore-ground the significance of Clark as freedom fighter, resourceful fugitive, loyal husband and brother, self-made man. Dorsey's clippings on the subject of Clark/Harris are in harmony with the widespread strategy throughout late nineteenth-century print culture of reading *Uncle Tom's Cabin* as a his-torical document and often blurring the line between reality and fiction in doing so. Yet both the repetitions and omissions in Dorsey's scrapbook show how one African American reader gave *Uncle Tom's Cabin* a different sort of attention than white readers—many of whom thought of slavery now as an old story, when they thought of it at all. The death of Clark was reported in newspapers across the United States, but there is no record of it in Charles Stowe's scrapbook.[149]

For many white readers and commentators of the period, slavery belonged to the past and had no serious implications for the present. A 1901 cartoon published in *Puck* with the caption "Thinking of U.T.C."[150] graphically evokes the increasingly popular belief that, analogously, a new generation of African Americans took slavery as nothing more than an entertaining stage perfor-mance (fig. 18). However, for black readers Stowe's narrative—like slavery itself—remained intensely meaningful. One final example here will reinforce the point that black readers continued to rethink *Uncle Tom's Cabin* and, like Dorsey, often recast Stowe's plot and characters for their own ends.

In October 1894 the *American Missionary* published a very odd poem, "A Visit to Uncle Tom's Cabin," by J. W. Holloway of Turin, Georgia, a "Graduate of Class of 1894, Fisk University, Nashville, Tenn."[151] The *American Missionary* was fervid in its affirmations of black progress, but its perspective on "the Negro" in general and the figure of Uncle Tom in particular was often informed by the period's widely shared romantic racialism. As one typical article in the publication puts it, the strength "of the Negro character. . . . lies in his warmth, affection, ardent hope, vivid imagination and boundless faith. It is this that made an Uncle Tom possible under the deep shadow of slav-ery."[152] Or again: "Uncle Tom's boys are proving themselves worthy. . . . They are pious, moral, Christian."[153] As we have seen, white commentators of the 1880s and '90s regularly used the figure of "Uncle Tom" in this way.

"A Visit to Uncle Tom's Cabin" is different. Like James Lane Allen's "Uncle

AN EGOTIST is a man who, after he has been weighed in the balance and found wanting, declares that the machine must have been out of order.

THINKING OF U. T. C.   COPYRIGHT, 1901, BY KEPPLER & SCHWARZMANN

GRAN'MA.— Yes, honey, when I wuz a slave, I offen seen de po' runaways chased by de crool bloodhounds.

LITTLE 'RASTUS.— An' wuz dere two *Markses* an' *Little Evas* in de show den, like dere is now?

18. *"Thinking of U.T.C." From* Puck *48, issue 1248 (February 6, 1901). Collection of The New-York Historical Society. Negative #83663d.*

Tom at Home in Kentucky," "Uncle Tom" in this poem seems at first to be a generic figure for a romanticized African American, modeled on Stowe's "hero of renown" and "his old log cabin" (p 362). By the end of the second verse, however, the speaker indicates that he will be correcting the assumptions of a hypothetical reader who believes that he knows all about Uncle Tom ("'Ah!' Say you, 'I've heard the story / As it's told by Mrs. Stowe, / That old man is dead and buried, / Must be years and years ago'" [lines 13–16]). The poem proceeds to uncover a radically transformed Uncle Tom.

The speaker of the poem is a teacher; his pupils include Uncle Tom's children. Although Uncle Tom seems to welcome the visitor, his own ideas about education resemble neither Stowe's nor the speaker's. "[You m]ust be scorin' de child'en heavy," Uncle Tom remarks

> Kase dey're learnin' pow'ful fas
> I believe in edication
> When you teach it wid a pole;
> Den you make 'im wise but humble,
> Ruin his back but save his soul. (lines 51–56)

Although the speaker/teacher suggests that "Love will win where force will fail" (line 62), Uncle Tom cites the Bible to support his own theory ("Sho's you spare de rod you spile 'em, / Don't the Good Book tell you so" [lines 59–60]). By conviction and experience Uncle Tom is devoted to violence. "I was overseer in slave time," he explains, "And a mean un, so dey say / Strapped Ma' Ann so much, ha! ha! / She married me to get away" (lines 85–88).

The poem creates an uncertain perspective on Uncle Tom's pride in such doings. When he falls asleep after supper his "slumber is that of contentment, / Dreaming and smiling o'er memories fond" (lines 99–100)—is it his own whipping of his future wife that he "fondly" recalls? The poem offers a brutal untold story that attributes both sadism and cynicism to "Uncle Tom" ("Never ketch me trustin' people, / Do dey're deacons in de church" [lines 65–66]). One by one, the poem undoes the very qualities for which Stowe's hero became famous.

Given the subversive potential of a violent, suspicious Uncle Tom, it is hard to say why the editors of the *American Missionary* printed this poem. How did they understand it? The American Missionary Association was committed to abolition in the antebellum period; later it supported racial equality, but also "calm meliorism," affirming Christian education as the "best hope for racial progress."[154] Religious instruction was a crucial component of the program at black colleges such as Fisk. Chapel services, prayer meetings, and other religious observances were required; salvation was "the guiding purpose of education," the executive committee of the American Missionary Association stated in 1891.[155] The editors of the *American Missionary,* the Association's journal, would have been unlikely to endorse an attack on the idea of Uncle Tom's Christian faith. But perhaps this "Uncle Tom" is intended to suggest what Du Bois called "the debauchery of slavery"[156]—especially by way of contrast with a Fisk graduate who writes poetry. Uncle Tom's taste for whipping others and retrospectively chuckling about it could then be dismissed as the vestige of a "darker time."

The final verse of the poem invites such a reading by stressing understanding of the past and hope for the future. Yet the idea that Uncle Tom's "intent [must] be accounted for right" does not dispel the more disturbing implications of his past and present behavior.[157] Perhaps the editors of the *American Missionary* were so pleased to exhibit rhyming verses penned by a black college graduate that they read the piece selectively. The verses certainly display the fruits of education in the speaker—not only a sense of "duty" (line 109) but linguistic proficiency and a mastery of contemporary literary modes, including dialect and local color. Yet the poem implicitly asks whether the ideology and pedagogy at Fisk is fully adequate to the job at hand.

The speaker/teacher himself seems uncertain. He is ironic about his own methods: after dinner, while he gives what he wryly refers to as "a lecture broad and deep," "Uncle Tom" begins to snore (line 96). The teacher faces a formidable challenge, and Uncle Tom epitomizes the problem. The "dirty dozen [children]" who "whoop . . . and yell . . . like all possessed" around their father's chair would surely be a handful for this teacher. James McPherson notes that "the mission societies became increasingly concerned about . . . 'counteracting influences in [black] homes' that subverted the cleanliness, discipline and piety taught in the schools."[158] Nonetheless the *American Missionary,* like other publications of the mission movement, generally minimized such worries, projecting cautious optimism instead.[159] "A Visit to Uncle Tom's Cabin" violates this policy.

At the very least, the poem draws attention to after-shocks of slavery rarely noted in print culture of the period, except as romance or broad caricature. Stowe would have shuddered at this image of her hero.

I have been suggesting that *Uncle Tom's Cabin* was often employed by late nineteenth-century white commentators to imagine recent history as a benign narrative with a happy ending. This narrative had considerable appeal and helped to revive public interest in Stowe's novel. But crucial aspects of *Uncle Tom's Cabin* had to be displaced in order to suggest that slavery had many virtues, and that anyway the problems created by the peculiar institution were over. It was relatively easy to employ Stowe's novel as support for this script in contexts such as the Stowe exhibit, which kept the drama and the details of the story out of view. But eliding the tale from the reprints that proliferated in the course of the nineties presented a more difficult challenge. Editors and commentators who were eager to reissue, market, and celebrate the novel were fearful of reopening a Pandora's Box of painful memories (which might also limit sales). How could they blindside Stowe's narrative in editions presumably published to be read? After all, the story could not be dropped from the printed page. But introductions and other prefatory material could attempt to reshape it and, aided by the "pictorial turn" in literary culture, illustrations could upstage it.[160] In the next chapter I explore this dynamic. A hard look at two late nineteenth-century editions reveals the new protocol of reading that was inscribed in *Uncle Tom's Cabin,* and that remade Stowe's novel as a reassuring story about race for white readers of the 1890s.

Imagining the Past as the Future
Illustrating Uncle Tom's Cabin *for the 1890s*

> [*Uncle Tom's Cabin*] will always be famous . . . as the most vivid picture
> of an extinct evil system.
>
> —*George William Curtis*

The Stowe display in the Woman's Building Library at the Columbian
Exposition of 1893 included two American editions of *Uncle Tom's Cabin:* the
first edition, published by John P. Jewett in 1852, and the most recent edition
at the time of the fair, published by Houghton Mifflin in 1891. This chapter
examines the illustrations of these two editions, both issued by Stowe's publisher, in order to show how changes in visual imagery framed and interpreted
Uncle Tom's Cabin for readers separated by forty turbulent years of social
history.[1]

The "negro problem" intensified in the 1890s. Lynching increased in the
South and discrimination in the North as Southern blacks began to enter northeastern cities. In 1896, the Supreme Court handed down the influential decision
Plessy vs. Ferguson, establishing the legal grounds for separation of the races in
schools, buses, and other public areas.[2] In this context, *Uncle Tom's Cabin* was
illustrated for ends quite different from Stowe's initial purposes, and the new
pictures played a significant role in reshaping the meaning of the novel. The
1880s ushered in the golden age of American illustration. Newspapers, magazines, books, calendars, self-contained lithographs, and trade cards spread
images from coast to coast.[3] A rapidly expanding reading public became accustomed to seeing illustrations and eager for more. Illustrations helped "literary"
journals such as *Scribner's* or the *Century* to court new readers—and even "non-
readers, the 'illiterate,'" as Robert Scholnick suggests.[4]

Like the literary, historical, and material framing of the novel discussed in
Chapter 5, illustrations for new editions of the 1890s firmly situated *Uncle*

Tom's Cabin at a temporal remove from the contemporary United States—especially from its ongoing, unresolved racial problems. Although editors and commentators praised *Uncle Tom's Cabin* as a significant factor in emancipation, images such as those by the well-known illustrator E. W. Kemble idealized the Old South, endorsed the color line, and implied that African Americans should remain subservient to white authority. Rendering the antebellum South as colorful and picturesque, Kemble's images of field hands and domestic servants were informed by nostalgia. Yet Kemble's illustrations also reflect a generic transformation that made it possible to read *Uncle Tom's Cabin* as a kind of realism, an objective rendering of a former social reality. At the same time, his images of slaves had prescriptive implications for African Americans at the turn of the century.

This chapter begins by analyzing differences between Billings's illustrations of 1852 and Kemble's illustrations of 1891; it ends by considering the visual materials in another carefully produced, high-end edition, issued by Appleton in 1898 with an introduction by Thomas Wentworth Higginson. Higginson was exceptional among commentators of the period in suggesting that *Uncle Tom's Cabin* had begun—but not completed—the difficult task of eliminating racial injustice in the United States. However, in keeping with widely shared interpretive conventions, his introduction, like the illustrations that accompany this well-made full-length edition, tones down the disruptive potential of *Uncle Tom's Cabin* for turn-of-the-century America.

The two American editions of *Uncle Tom's Cabin* in the bookcase of the Woman's Building Library at the Columbian Exposition epitomized the cultural significance of Stowe's book for the United States. The Stowe display, as we have seen, celebrated *Uncle Tom's Cabin* for its contribution to America's coming of age, its role in the narrative of progress promoted by the fair.[5] However, a closer look at the illustrated American editions exhibited will help us see how Stowe's abolitionist text came to serve the cause of segregation and the ongoing subordination of African Americans.

UNCLE TOM'S CABIN WITHOUT BLACK LITERACY

Descriptions of the Stowe display in the Woman's Building Library repeatedly mention the two American editions of *Uncle Tom's Cabin* included in the collec-

Eliza comes to tell Uncle Tom that he is sold, and that she is running away to save her child. Page 62.

19. "Eliza comes to tell Uncle Tom that he is sold." From Harriet Beecher Stowe, Uncle Tom's Cabin. *Boston: John P. Jewett, 1852. Collection of The New-York Historical Society. Negative #83641d.*

THE FREEMAN'S DEFENCE. Page 254.

20. "The Freeman's Defense." From Harriet Beecher Stowe, Uncle Tom's Cabin. *Boston: John P. Jewett, 1852. Collection of The New-York Historical Society. Negative #83642d.*

tion: the first edition of the novel in "two little black-covered volumes," with engravings by the celebrated abolitionist artist Hammatt Billings; and "the latest reprint of Uncle Tom by Houghton, Mifflin & Co." issued in 1891.[6] The "latest reprint" was a two-volume edition with the new illustrations by E. W. Kemble. Each of the six illustrations in the first edition represents a key moment of Stowe's plot. Billings's illustrations were much reprinted and often imitated in the antebellum period. The scenes he singled out for visual representation—such moments as "Eliza comes to tell Uncle Tom that he is sold" (fig. 19), George Harris fighting for his freedom (fig. 20), "Eva Reading the Bible to Uncle Tom in the Arbor" (see fig. 5 in Chapter 2)—helped to shape the meaning of the novel for readers of the 1850s.

An illustrator is a very specialized and articulate kind of reader, one whose understanding of the written text is expressed in the images designed to accompany it. When illustrations "work," as Werner Sollors puts it, "they begin to affect our reading of texts, just as texts (including captions) affect our understanding of images." Sollors suggests that book illustrations only "work" when they "remain in intelligible relation to characters from the texts."[7] Yet illustrations shape our reading even when the relation between text and image is puzzling, or when text and image appear to be at odds. When story and illustration do not seem to agree, a power struggle begins. The attention of the reader and the meaning of the text are at stake in this struggle. As W. J. T. Mitchell argues, conflicts "between visual and verbal representations are inseparable from struggles in cultural politics and political culture."[8]

On October 30, 1851, Gamaliel Bailey, the editor of the *Era,* printed an enthusiastic reader's letter praising a recent episode of Stowe's narrative and suggesting that the scene in which Tom and Eva write to Chloe would make an effective painting.[9] The episode was subsequently much illustrated in antebellum editions of the novel. It made its way onto the cover of the book as well. "'Uncle Tom's Cabin,' improves as it progresses," the reader's letter begins: "Long life and prosperity to its author, say I. There is one scene in the last chapter which . . . would make a good subject for a painting. It is the one where Uncle Tom is . . . intently engaged over the slate, with Eva peeping over his shoulder. . . ." The letter goes on to suggest that such a painting would "doubtless receive the commendation of the public," and "might be engraved as a suitable embellishment" to *Uncle Tom's Cabin* "when it shall be published in book form."[10] An advertisement for Stowe's novel appears in another column on the same page of the *Era* as the

21. Eva and Tom writing to Chloe. From Harriet Beecher Stowe, Uncle Tom's Cabin. *Boston: John P. Jewett, 1853. Collection of The New-York Historical Society. Negative #83646d*

reader's letter. Although the serialized narrative was only half-completed at this time, the future of *Uncle Tom's Cabin* as an illustrated book was already assured. Hammatt Billings included the letter-writing scene in the holiday edition (fig. 21).

It is much to the point of my argument that the first publicly proposed illustration of *Uncle Tom's Cabin* engaged the issue of slave literacy. Billings's designs for the first edition, and even more so for the holiday edition, affirmed and elaborated Stowe's representation of reading, as we saw in Chapter 2. Billings was in a sense Stowe's "ideal" reader. Sympathetic to her abolitionist, evangelical message, he emphasized the humanity of Stowe's slave characters, especially their capacity for interpersonal relations, faith, and moral agency. Billings's illustrations (like Stowe's text) are open to charges of romantic racialism, but it is easy to forget that Stowe's narrative had a radical edge in 1852 that it lost in the course of the twentieth century.[11] When the novel first appeared, prohibitions on slave literacy added political urgency to Stowe's representation of reading. By rendering Tom, George, and other black characters not only as Christians but also as readers, Billings (like Stowe) questioned the validity of common assumptions about the spiritual, emotional, and intellectual capacities of African Americans.[12] When we turn from Billings's designs to Kemble's, scenes of reading disappear. In the 1890s, Stowe's emphasis on slave literacy lost its appeal. Kemble's illustrations, like Billings's, constitute readings of *Uncle Tom's Cabin* and imply radically different perspectives on African Americans as well as race relations. The interpretive grid created by Kemble reveals new functions served by Stowe's novel toward the turn of the century.[13]

When Kemble illustrated *Uncle Tom's Cabin* in 1891 he was already a familiar figure to readers of books and periodicals. Kemble became a steady contributor to *Life Magazine* from its inception in 1883; one of his early drawings for *Life* prompted Mark Twain to engage him as illustrator for *The Adventures of Huckleberry Finn* in 1885. Kemble had not been south at this point in his career (he used a white model for his images of Jim[14]). But he soon gained a reputation "as an illustrator of Southern themes and humour."[15] Between 1884 and 1891, as a staff member of the *Century Illustrated Magazine,* Kemble toured the South; subsequently he spoke of himself as "a delineator of the South, the Negro being my specialty."[16] He became well known for his images of African Americans. An article on book illustrators claims in 1894 that "Mr. Kemble is . . . closely associated in the public mind with negro sketches."[17]

Most often working in pen and ink, Kemble, like other illustrators of the period, benefited from technological advances in printing and paper-making and from photo-mechanical processes that enabled mass-market periodicals to reproduce images cheaply and easily. These developments allowed illustrators to increase their range of tone and nuance as well as speed, unconstrained by the limitations of earlier modes, such as wood-engraving (the prime medium for antebellum illustrators, including Billings).[18] In illustrating *Uncle Tom's Cabin* Kemble created many drawings of the kind already familiar to his public; in addition he prepared fourteen full-page "photogravures." The Houghton Mifflin edition was ambitious; in the words of one advertisement, "This is to be in every respect an entirely new edition of 'Uncle Tom's Cabin,' designed to be the best and most adequate presentation that has yet been made of this world-famous book."[19] Unlike Kemble's "negro sketches," or his illustrations for *The Adventures of Huckleberry Finn* (a book that had never been illustrated), his illustrations for

Uncle Tom's Cabin involved remaking images that were already familiar to the reading public.

Kemble's illustrations for *Uncle Tom's Cabin* prominently feature Stowe's slave characters. Many of these are depicted working in the field; others are represented as if posed for formal portraits (figs. 22 and 23). One reviewer praised "A Field Worker" as "the most striking of the photogravures."[20] Like the display of native peoples on the Midway Plaisance at the Columbian Exposition, Kemble's slaves were clearly marked as exotic.[21] With their naked feet and bare arms, baskets of cotton, kerchiefs, earrings, and provocatively plunging necklines, Kemble's images of African American men and women violated norms of appearance characteristic of the white middle class. Such figures also divert attention from Tom, Eva, and other characters whose images were dominant in antebellum editions. Kemble steers clear of Stowe and Billings's evangelical emphasis. He does not allude to black literacy.

In the 1890s African Americans were legally entitled to literacy, and had more access to books, at least in theory. But black education was a controversial issue. In the course of the nineteenth century the act of reading had become ever more strongly associated with autonomy, moral authority, and economic success. These associations of literacy made images of black readers symbolically still more potent at the turn of the century than they had been when the institution of slavery kept the more radical implications of such images in check.[22] Public celebrations of black achievement often masked segregationist, even white supremacist agendas.[23]

Conventions for representing African Americans had hardened into popular stereotypes by 1890. Kemble himself contributed to this process, producing hundreds of comical images, many of which make laziness, thievery, and appetite the primary characteristics of black men and children.[24] Some of these images were used in support of legalized segregation.[25] Robin Bernstein persuasively argues that Kemble's "Coon Alphabet" (1898) helped naturalize the idea of acceptable violence against African Americans.[26] This alphabet book, designed for white children, never suggests that black people might be readers.[27] At the turn of the century, white ambivalence about black literacy was widespread. An image of a black person with a book stirred anxiety.

The end of Reconstruction had held out promise for black education as well as free enterprise in the South; during the 1880s, many educators and politicians had suggested that under the right conditions, African Americans could be

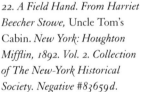

22. A Field Hand. From Harriet Beecher Stowe, Uncle Tom's Cabin. *New York: Houghton Mifflin, 1892. Vol. 2. Collection of The New-York Historical Society. Negative #83659d.*

morally and intellectually "uplifted," even transformed. Numerous aspects of African American life were implicated in the debate about schooling; questions about the nature and the limits of black education intensified in this period. The conflict between Booker T. Washington and W. E. B. Du Bois is only the most famous expression of the heated controversy over whether or not African Americans should be fully integrated into American culture and whether their intellectual potential was to be fostered or whether their education was to be confined to vocational tasks.[28]

While many educators and politicians of the 1880s and '90s hoped that literacy would help produce self-sufficient black carpenters and mechanics, the antebellum argument about the unforeseen results of Bible-reading among slaves reappeared in a new guise at this point, triggering fears that if former slaves gained access to higher forms of literacy they might set their sights beyond the vocations for which they were being trained at black colleges.[29]As Du Bois put it in *The Souls of Black Folk* (1903) many people were appalled at the notion of a

23. *"A Field Worker." From Harriet Beecher Stowe,* Uncle Tom's Cabin. *New York: Houghton Mifflin, 1892. Vol. 2. Collection of The New-York Historical Society. Negative #83662d.*

24. *Tom and St. Clare. From Harriet Beecher Stowe,* Uncle Tom's Cabin. *New York: Houghton Mifflin, 1892. Vol. 2. Collection of The New-York Historical Society. Negative #83660d.*

black boy with a French grammar book. Accordingly, the emphasis on Tom, George, and Topsy as readers was dropped from many illustrated editions of *Uncle Tom's Cabin.*[30] In the Houghton Mifflin edition of 1891 books are the exclusive possessions of white masters (fig. 24).

Kemble's illustrations consistently deflect attention from Stowe's representation of slave literacy. In Chapter X of *Uncle Tom's Cabin* ("The Property is Carried Off") Aunt Chloe cries, while "Tom sat by with his Testament open on his knee" (162); Kemble's accompanying illustration elides the book and shows "Tom and his Children." Kemble accompanies the important scene of Tom and Eva's letter-writing with an image of "The Youngest Urchin" in a large straw hat. In Chapter XXII "Tom read, in his only literary cabinet, of one who had, 'learned in whatsoever state he was, therewith to be content'" (378); Kemble's illustration represents "Tom Marketing."[31] Kemble may not have been directly involved in the positioning of his images, but he surely made choices regarding which scenes and figures to represent.[32] Adam Sonstegard suggests that the editors "often match Kemble's imagery exactly to Stowe's prose passages,"[33] and some illustrations in this edition do depict episodes taken from Stowe's narrative (e.g., Eliza and Harry arriving on the shore of the Ohio River, Ophelia and St. Clare watching Topsy and Eva, Tom listening to St. Clare play the piano). Yet many images pointedly depart from the story, always in the direction of proposing a sharp contrast between primitive peoples on the one hand, the realm of authors, illustrators, and consumers of print on the other.

This contrast was increasingly familiar in literary and political culture of the 1890s. At the Columbian Exposition, where "natives" of various kinds were exhibited on the Midway Plaisance, spatially separate from (and implicitly unfit for) the industrialized world associated with the "White City," tribal groups, wearing furs or skins, were displayed for the edification and entertainment of the fair-goers. The "ethnological villages" at the fair were designed to show the distance America had come from its own pre-industrial past.[34] At the same time, the exhibits offered graphic demonstrations of the functions that "primitive" peoples were expected to serve in the late nineteenth-century United States—especially service and entertainment. Kemble's illustrations for *Uncle Tom's Cabin,* like the displays on the Midway Plaisance, imply that while men and women of color were particularly suited by nature for physical labor and domestic service, white Americans had evolved to a superior stage of civilization.

DANGEROUS REPRESENTATIONS: VISUALIZING THE COLOR LINE IN *UNCLE TOM'S CABIN*

I now take a closer look at some characteristic illustrations by both Billings and Kemble, keeping three central criteria in mind: first, the principles of selection (which scenes deserve emphasis?); second, the representation of slave figures (how are they positioned on the page, in relation to white characters? in relation to each other?); third, the harmony (or discord) between the illustration and the words of the text. I proceed from the assumption that an illustration is at once an interpretation of a text, and a text that requires interpretation. Throughout this discussion, Billings's popular antebellum images

25. *"Recordare jesu pie." From Harriet Beecher Stowe,* Uncle Tom's Cabin. *New York: Houghton Mifflin, 1892. Vol. 2. Collection of The New-York Historical Society. Negative #83661d.*

provide a reference point for understanding the changed implications of Kemble's visual rhetoric. While Billings often represented Tom, George, and Topsy reading, writing, or holding a book, sometimes in a domestic space shared with white characters, Kemble's illustrations eliminate not only black literacy but also personal contact between black and white figures. In the Houghton Mifflin edition of 1891 black and white characters rarely appear in the same illustration. When they do, they are often separated by a sharp dividing line (fig. 25; see also fig. 24). The vertical line that separates Tom from St. Clare in such images contrasts sharply with the arch that encloses Eva and Tom in Billings's illustration of the letter-writing scene (fig. 21).

Kemble's illustrations readjust the focus of Stowe's text by avoiding the very events singled out for emphasis by early reviewers and illustrators. Scenes and characters which have looked increasingly saccharine and patronizing to readers since the 1970s were strong medicine in an earlier day; but their resonance can be felt only if they are thickly contextualized. When Billings's initial illustration of Eva and Tom reading the Bible was reprinted in the more elaborate gift edition of 1853, small changes in the design subtly deemphasized the intimacy between Eva and Tom. In the second version, Eva's feet are on the ground, rather than folded comfortably beneath her skirt on the bench.[35] Illustrations of Tom and Eva together were not as "harmless" in the nineteenth century as they seem today. In the literary and political climate of the 1890s, some of the best-loved antebellum illustrations became so highly charged that they were not reproduced at all. As Marcus Wood notes, the moment when Eva's love converts Topsy was one of "the most widely illustrated in all the [early] editions of *Uncle Tom's Cabin*" (fig. 26).[36] Yet when Kemble depicts St. Clare and Ophelia observing Eva and Topsy, his image displaces the interaction between the children themselves: he pictures two pale white adults, at a window frame (fig. 27). St. Clare and Ophelia, watching the drama between Eva and Topsy, are lightly outlined, barely adumbrated. They do not register the impact of the scene they observe. Indeed, it is as if, with regard to what they see, the less said the better. The illustration discourages the reader from visualizing Eva's hand on Topsy's shoulder.

Children's editions of the period often revised Stowe's text in similar ways, while shortening it for young readers. As we shall see in Chapter 7, *Young Folks Uncle Tom's Cabin* (1901) eliminates moments of interracial contact such as Eva hugging Mammy, as well as Topsy's conversion itself. But where children's editions often alter the words of the text, full-length editions rely on prefatory material and illustrations to create shifts of emphasis.

In *Picture Theory,* W. J. T. Mitchell explores the idea of the "paralyzing spectacle"—the image that is too "dangerous" for representation.[37] The idea of the "dangerous representation" can be usefully applied to a series of important moments in *Uncle Tom's Cabin* that Kemble's illustrations avoid. Kemble's elisions constitute a radical departure from Billings's perspective on black subjectivity and relationships across the color line. Such elisions constitute and shape interpretation. They reflect widespread anxiety about the place of African Americans in the United States and provide a reassuring subtext that added to the appeal of new editions. That subtext suggests that African Americans will always "know their place."

Kemble's illustrations for *Uncle Tom's Cabin* employed two distinct aesthetic modes. In addition to the kind of pen-and-ink work for which he was

26. Eva and Topsy. From Harriet Beecher Stowe, Uncle Tom's Cabin. *Boston: John P. Jewett, 1853. Collection of The New-York Historical Society. Negative #83647d.*

27. St. Clare and Miss Ophelia listen. From Harriet Beecher Stowe, Uncle Tom's Cabin. *New York: Houghton Mifflin, 1892. Vol. 2. Collection of The New-York Historical Society. Negative #83659d.*

already famous, Kemble created full-page slave portraits in a very different style. These images were reproduced by the new technology known as "photogravure." Unlike Kemble's familiar line drawings, these portraits have a realistic flavor. The word "photo" within the term "photogravure" (reiterated many times in the list of illustrations) may have intensified the sense of the "real" for readers and viewers newly encountering such images in the dawning age of illustration—and photography. "Photogravure" refers only to the process by which the image is reproduced and printed, but the word "photo" was widely associated with objectivity and scientific progress in 1891. This association added to the images' reality-effect.

In discussing Kemble's illustrations it is not my intention simply to identify stereotypes.[38] In fact, Kemble's full-page slave portraits complicate the view of Kemble as a reductive caricaturist. His small drawings for *Uncle Tom's Cabin,* such as "one black head," or "wooly heads and glistening eyes" (titles that appear in the list of illustrations) certainly prime the reader/viewer to see slaves as comic objects. Kemble's full-page illustrations, however, are rarely comic, and this makes their impact more subtle as well as troubling. Like his small drawings, his full-page images underscore and endorse the deep cultural divide between African American characters and the white reader, implying an unbridgeable distance between black and white experience. Portraits of an impassive "Field Worker" (fig. 23) or a beaming "Field Boy" (fig. 28) isolate these figures. They are not presented in meaningful intercourse with white characters, or even with each other. They are never pictured with books or other accoutrements associated with white privilege. Yet at the same time, some of these portraits are complex. The figures sometimes appear to be posing—whether for the white illustrator, or for others within their own world. "Adolph," for example, is dressed in his master's clothes (as Stowe too represents him) (fig. 29). "A Field Boy," smiling broadly, might be seen as more effectively masked. The brooding silence of other figures implies inaccessibility, perhaps resistance.

At least one anonymous reviewer disliked these images intensely. He or she felt the "photogravures lack finish" and were "quite out of keeping with the high mechanical excellence of other features of this work." Perhaps the reviewer read these illustrations as a disquieting challenge to social and generic expectations—strangely unlike Kemble's familiar drawings. The reviewer much prefers Kemble's "fascinating little negro girls and boys" and pronounces them

28. "A Field Boy." From Harriet Beecher Stowe, Uncle Tom's Cabin. *New York: Houghton Mifflin, 1892. Vol. 1. Collection of The New-York Historical Society. Negative #83655d.*

"easily the most effective."[39] Kemble's two distinct systems for representing slave bodies provide conflicting signals. Despite the stereotypical physiognomy that marks the full-page portraits as racial types, we might say that some of them—neither comedy nor caricature—offer a certain respect to adult slaves. Yet whether we read them as haunting, beautiful, or alien, they are always segregated—from each other, from white figures, and from Stowe's narrative. The contrast between Kemble and Billings remains sharp, and this contrast implies radically different readings of Stowe's text.

Billings's illustrations, unlike Kemble's, emphasize emotional, intellectual, and physical engagement across the color line.[40] We have seen that Billings repeatedly visualized Eva and Tom in close, casual, physical contact and verbal exchanges. In "The Freeman's Defense" George stands and fights, shoulder to shoulder with Quaker friends. These images suggest that, like free white people, African American slaves are capable of action, faith, literacy, and interracial give and take. Other illustrations by Billings extend Stowe's emphasis on the vitality of interpersonal relations among the slaves themselves. When Eliza pauses at her friends' cabin in the first precious moments of her flight, she does so not only for the purpose of getting a message to her husband, but also to warn Tom of his own impending doom; the sequence suggests that African Americans are capable not only of love, friendship, and family feeling, but also of deliberation and choice. Billings's images stress the fact that slaves take initiative and risks; they accept responsibility for themselves and others. Kemble's illustrations discount the domestic and the relational emphasis of Stowe's narrative, systematically representing black figures alone on the page, eliminating virtually all interactions among them. Intercourse between black adults is particularly rare. Although an occasional field hand may be comely or statuesque, these figures are nonetheless objects on display, like exhibits in the "ethnological villages" of the Midway Plaisance.

Paradoxically, the effect is still less that of dynamism or interplay when Kemble provides a "group portrait." Thus Kemble's full-page illustration "Slaves at Their Toil" (fig. 30) shows a line of nearly identical figures, choreographed and synchronized, frozen in their tracks. Like the well-known abolitionist image of the middle passage, "Description of a Slave Ship,"[41] Kemble's image of "slaves at their toil" creates a sense of passive entrapment; he pictures no exchanges of either words or gestures. The task at hand is all-important; its pace and goal is determined by the overseer whose face is the only fully visible one in the scene.

29. *"Adolph." From Harriet Beecher Stowe,* Uncle Tom's Cabin. *New York: Houghton Mifflin, 1892. Vol. 1. Collection of The New-York Historical Society. Negative #83657d.*

Turned away from the viewer, the slaves' faces are blurred and expressionless, inaccessible, de-individualized.[42]

WORDS AND IMAGES: RECASTING STOWE'S STORY

Book illustrations that accompany a novel are always embedded in or surrounded by language. But an illustrator has considerable freedom to adjust the relation between illustrations and the words of the text, between verbal and visual imagery. Kemble's designs are uncontaminated by writing. The absence of the written word helps assert the primacy of the image. Captions appear on pages of their own. The only word that appears in Kemble's illustrations is Kemble's own name—often prominently displayed in a corner. Language is the white illustrator's prerogative; silence the portion of slaves. These distinctions are reinforced by the objects that share the visual space of the picture with Kemble's figures: a basket of cotton or a hoe for African Americans; a piano or a Bible for white masters. "The 'differences' between images and language," Mitchell suggests, "are not merely formal matters—they are, in practice, linked to things like the difference between the (speaking) self and the (seen) other."[43]

Kemble denies his slave figures the use of language, and distances them from Stowe's words. By contrast, Billings not only represents Tom, George, and Topsy speaking, writing, reading, he sometimes includes words from Stowe's text within the frame of his illustrations. The close alliance of Billings's illustrations with Stowe's narrative is evident in the tight alignment of his illustrations with the events of her plot. His images collaborate with Stowe's. Eliza pausing to speak to Tom and Chloe before fleeing the plantation, Eva and Tom reading the Bible or writing a letter together, Tom reading his Bible to "Two Negro Women" after a brutal workday on Legree's plantation—these are moments with thematic implications, but they are also events in an ongoing story. Billings's images tell that story.

Kemble's illustrations, on the other hand, are often dissociated from the language of the text, placed on a separate page with a semi-transparent sheet of paper between text and illustration. These extra pages served a practical function: they were to prevent the ink of the illustration from rubbing off on the facing page of text. But the clouded page, blank except for a brief, objectifying,

30. "Slaves at Their Toil." From Harriet Beecher Stowe, Uncle Tom's Cabin. *New York: Houghton Mifflin, 1892. Vol. 1. Courtesy of the American Antiquarian Society.*

authoritative label, creates a hush, so to speak, that gives added importance to the image that follows; setting the image off from the rest of the text, and asserting its independent life. The distinction between text and image remains as absolute as the division between black and white. While the caption on the clouded page is sometimes a phrase taken from the novel, it is often a phrase wrenched out of context. Sometimes it is not taken from Stowe's text at all. Read in sequence, Kemble's full-page illustrations tell a separatist and thoroughly racialized story that is not easily recognizable as *Uncle Tom's Cabin*. Praised by one reviewer as "seizing the salient features of the negro face, bearing, and character,"[44] some of the full-page portraits seem to make a claim for serious, artistic representation; but in doing so they draw attention to themselves and upstage Stowe's story.

I have said that Kemble's illustration of "Slaves at Their Toil" shows a line of slaves at work, silent, humble, controlled by others, without initiative or autonomy. This image deserves additional consideration because it so flagrantly violates the very text it claims to illustrate. Kemble's full-page illustration "Slaves at Their Toil" diverts attention from one of the most extended scenes of reading in *Uncle Tom's Cabin*. In Chapter XIV, as Tom sits reading his Bible on the ship that is taking him south to be sold, Stowe devotes a long passage to the functions served by Tom's reading practices, as we saw in Chapter 2. An 1853 edition of the novel for youth—*A Peep into Uncle Tom's Cabin*—rearranges Stowe's plot to begin with the moment when Tom studies his Bible among the cotton bales; an unsigned illustration of "Tom Reading on the Cotton Bales" is the first one in the book (see fig. 6). Billings's illustration for this chapter, in Jewett's holiday edition of 1853, renders Tom, characteristically seated with the Bible on his lap, encountering Eva for the first time (fig. 31). Other passengers, in the background, pause and watch. The composition of the image suggests that the meeting between the black man, the white child, and the holy book repays consideration.

By contrast, Kemble illustrates a transient moment early in the episode, when Tom, seated on the cotton bales, catches a glimpse of the far-off "slaves at their toil" (*UTC,* 228). By elaborating this image, Kemble encourages his reader to hurry past Stowe's description of Tom's emotional struggle and engagement with the Biblical text. The reader is invited (unlike Tom) to read quickly, to turn the clouded page and uncover what it conceals. Stowe's representation of Tom is upstaged: his pain, faith, and experience of reading are

31. Eva and Tom meet on the ship. From Harriet Beecher Stowe, Uncle Tom's Cabin. *Boston: John P. Jewett, 1853. Collection of The New-York Historical Society. Negative #83648d.*

replaced by his fleeting glimpse of slaves in the distance. Stowe's text is rewritten for new ends: Tom's subjectivity and literacy are elided; anonymous slaves are objectified and exhibited. For readers of the novel Tom's glimpse of "slaves at their toil" might be understood as a foreshadowing of his future. But at this point in the text Stowe, unlike Kemble, lingers with Tom the contemplative, pious man—husband, father, and reader—not with the workers in the field.

Kemble accomplishes multiple ends by eliminating the imagery of books, words, and letters. By avoiding scenes of reading, he marginalizes the idea of African American initiative, ambition, or internality (once a slave, always a slave). By keeping written language out of his designs, he implies that his pictures speak for themselves, suppressing the notion of competing perspectives. When read as an autonomous sequence of pictures, Kemble's full-page illustrations seem to have a documentary or journalistic purpose, as if transparently representing an aspect of the world. As Neil Harris suggests, the new half-tone

technology of the period "immeasurably enhanced" the viewers' "illusion of seeing an actual scene or receiving an objective record of such a scene."[45] There is a
dramatic difference between images that draw attention to their nature as made-
things—compositions or designs—and images that suppress this aspect of their
being. Pictures with words within them have self-reflexive overtones. They raise
questions about the interplay of text and image and draw attention to complexi-
ties of reading and interpretation.[46] Kemble's photogravures not only displace
Stowe's text and naturalize the visual image, but also efface the illustrator's relation to his subject, as if it is one of unproblematic neutrality—the position aspired
to and idealized by turn-of-the-century curators, ethnographers, anthropolo-
gists, and writers of realist novels.

Where Stowe and Billings present the relation between the white and
black world as a difficult problem, demanding solution, Kemble situates slavery in a kind of timeless present which reifies the relation between white
master and black slave. Kemble's images systematically strip his slave figures
of "white" capabilities and possessions—no literacy, no domesticity, no human
relations. The suggestion of realistic portraiture in the full-page illustrations
reinforces the idea that the distance between races and the subordination of
African Americans is a natural, inevitable state of affairs. Kemble's images
express nostalgia for the Old South and an investment in the ongoing viability
of slave imagery and practices.

Uncle Tom's Cabin as Prescriptive Realism: A Protocol of Reading for the 1890s

Illustrated scenes of Bible-reading at mid-century not only suggested that
slaves could acquire many of the virtues associated with literacy, but also helped
legitimize novel-reading, as we have seen (Chapters 2 and 3). These functions
were extraneous in the nineties. In an expanded print culture, Scripture did
not carry the widespread authority it had claimed at mid-century, nor was it
generally presumed to promote docility in subordinates. Between the 1850s
and the 1890s, moreover, the novel acquired a new position in literary culture.
As fiction made its slow and uneven way toward the status of "literature," commentators promoted aesthetic discrimination and critical distance rather than
tears as the most appropriate responses to serious novels.

The rise of realism and the change in the status of the novel as a form had a direct bearing on illustrations of *Uncle Tom's Cabin*. While both Stowe and her most successful illustrators at mid-century repeatedly linked *Uncle Tom's Cabin* with the holy book, late nineteenth-century writers, editors, and illustrators adopted a different model of authority and value. In the "culture of professionalism" an alliance between fiction and history, journalism, or science was more advantageous than an attempted alliance with Scripture. As we have seen, publishers, editors, and illustrators, taking their cue from other professionals, now framed *Uncle Tom's Cabin* not as a political, spiritual, and religious text, but as a historical document—evidence of the moral conscience, political right-mindedness, and progress of America as a nation. Yet by lingering with and sometimes aestheticizing the details of slave labor, Kemble creates a backward drag that undermines or at least complicates the narrative of progress. As one commentator of the nineties put it, *Uncle Tom's Cabin* "will always be famous . . . as the most vivid picture of an extinct evil system."[47] The description of *Uncle Tom's Cabin* as a "vivid picture" of the slave system is especially telling in the present context. The historical purpose once served by the novel legitimized the desire to look back at slavery, not only as an "extinct evil," but also as a "vivid" and colorful one.

After the Civil War, slave narratives were rarely reprinted.[48] Instead, popular plantation novels of the period gave readers of the nineties access to a distant world, divertingly brought back to life.[49] So too *Uncle Tom's Cabin*—the very book that had helped "overthrow an evil system"—made that system vibrantly accessible on the printed page, especially when accompanied by illustrations that presented the plantation South as an intriguing foreign culture. If the realism of Dreiser, Wharton, Crane, and others gave middle-class readers a chance to tour lower- (and sometimes upper-) class terrains located beyond many a reader's accustomed horizon, new editions of *Uncle Tom's Cabin* offered a late nineteenth-century tour of a racial terrain which many Northern white readers knew even less about.

Kemble's graphic images of men and women working in the field purported to represent an "extinct" culture; but Kemble's skill also gave them embodied immediacy. Unlike language, pictures don't have a past tense. When represented visually, the sense of the past drops away, unless emphatically underscored as such through stylistic or thematic markers of an earlier period. The soft light, rural dress, and captions of such images as Kemble's "Slaves at Their

Toil" or "Field Hands Coming In" (fig. 32) presented the antebellum South in a nostalgic light that was particularly appealing when many white readers felt increasingly uncertain about race relations. Kemble's slave portraits could be read as a prescriptive comment on African Americans of the nineties.

In popular magazines of the period, picturesque elements of the Old South gained attention. As a subject for "art," images of slavery could be attractively packaged, providing a refuge from racial discord. In "Mrs. Stowe's 'Uncle Tom' at Home in Kentucky," James Lane Allen argues that "a volume of incidents might readily be gathered, the picturesqueness and beauty of which are due so largely, if not wholly, to the fact that the negroes were not free servants, but slaves."[50] In this context Uncle Tom's Cabin itself could be read as a kind of realism—especially where illustrations synthesize the idea of "art" with that of documentary photographs.

The photographic documentary—such as Jacob Riis's How the Other Half Lives—was a new form in 1890, one that purported to offer objective images of the world. Many readers of the period were already accustomed to browsing through magazines with illustrated features that brought the cultural monuments of Europe and the landscape of the South or the West into their parlors. At the same time, the emergence of "pictorial photography," as Alan Trachtenberg has shown, "came to mean misty atmospheres, fuzzy surfaces, exotic tableaus—or in its genre and city views, 'picturesque' effects." Trachtenberg suggests that toward the turn of the century Scribner's used photographs to turn "the city's discordant realities . . . into picturesque beauty."[51] Alfred Stieglitz's New York street pictures were "examples of the triumph of art, its transformation of 'low' subjects into picturesque images."[52] So too, Kemble's full-page photogravures contributed to readings of Stowe's novel as a picturesque text that, like local-color fiction, captures fading aspects of American society and implies regret for their disappearance.

Some commentators of the period praised Uncle Tom's Cabin for its positive image of the antebellum South. Through a selective citing of Stowe's novel, James Lane Allen emphasizes Stowe's rendering of "the mildest form of the system [which] is to be seen in the State of Kentucky," and explains that "the typical boy on a Kentucky farm was tenderly associated from infancy with the negroes of the household and the fields."[53] This "typical boy" has a particularly warm relationship with "Uncle Tom":

32. "Field Hands Coming In." From Harriet Beecher Stowe, Uncle Tom's Cabin. *New York: Houghton Mifflin, 1892. Vol. 1. Collection of The New-York Historical Society. Negative #83656d.*

How often has he straddled Uncle Tom's neck, or ridden behind him afield on a barebacked horse to the jingling music of the trace-chains! It is Uncle Tom who plaits his hempen whip and ties the cracker in a knot that will stay. . . . Many a time he slips out of the house to take his dinner or supper in the cabin with Uncle Tom. . . . Like the child who listens to 'Uncle Remus," he too hears songs and stories, and creeps back to the house with a wondering look in his eyes and a vague hush of spirit.[54]

Pressed into such service, Stowe's novel appears to celebrate the advantages of the slave system, and can be read as mourning its demise. Sometimes the same edition that stressed the role of *Uncle Tom's Cabin* in dealing "the whole [slave] system a deadly blow"[55] included illustrations that presented the Old South not only as the cradle of a quaint and simple mode of life, but as a society that was truer to the essential nature of African Americans.

Kemble's illustrations framed Stowe's work of fiction not only as a measure of the way things had once been, but also as a measure of the way they still were—and should be. Far from challenging the norms (and clichés) of slave culture, Kemble's images lovingly affirm the past. His African Americans are repeatedly pictured as patiently serving, or foolishly imitating white masters (e.g., Tom, figs. 24 and 25; Adolph, fig. 29). Such postures reflect enduring assumptions about black people as loyal but childish and benighted. In racial theory of the 1890s African Americans lagged well behind white ones on the evolutionary scale. Skeptics about African American education argued that the result would be only delusions of grandeur and ineffective imitation—at best mildly foolish or comic; at worst ridiculous and, when primitive "nature" reasserted itself, violent (as graphically dramatized in the work of Thomas Dixon). In Henry Wonham's words, Kemble's "coons" "fail at racial impersonation and uplift."[56]

Wonham also rightly notes that the "intersection of the realist and the caricatured image" complicates the familiar "linkage of realism and progressive social change."[57] That linkage was important not only to realist fiction but also to illustrated documentaries such as those by Riis, and later by Marguerite Bourke-White or James Agee and Walker Evans. Kemble's illustrations are a complex blend of elements shared by caricature, realism, and photography. Kemble claimed to distrust photography. " 'The camera habit,' he said, 'is a dangerous one. You get to trusting the camera instead of your own eyes.' "[58] But it was partly by adapting conventions newly appropriate to photo-journalism and pictorial photography toward the turn of the century that Kemble departed so sharply from interpretive norms for reading *Uncle Tom's Cabin* in the antebellum period. Late nineteenth-century reporters—like photographers, ethnographers, and writers of realist novels—often presented foreign populations and "low" subjects to the white American middle class. As Michael Elliott has shown, scientific ethnography and literary realism—both committed to the project of documenting culture, especially cultural difference—shared a range of discursive strategies.[59] These discursive strategies claimed cultural authority; they also implied that white middle-class Americans were now in a position to study more "primitive" social and racial types. If, like the display of "native peoples" on the Midway Plaisance at the Columbian Exposition, the representation of otherness sometimes verged on caricature, that is hardly surprising.

I turn now to the Appleton edition of 1898, and the interpretive framework provided there by illustrations and by an "Introduction" written for the volume by Thomas Wentworth Higginson—former abolitionist, commander of a black unit in the Civil War, and a committed social activist. The paratextual materials of the Appleton edition do not rework Stowe's text as thoroughly as Kemble's illustrations, but they too deflect attention from Stowe's plot. New visual accompaniments provide a focus of attention that has nothing to do with Stowe's tale of abuse, suffering, and heroism. Like Kemble's images, those of the Appleton edition avoid Stowe's emphasis on black literacy and human relations across the color line. Like other commentators of the 1890s, Higginson locates the cultural work of Stowe's novel in a distant era: "the time is past fortunately, when 'Uncle Tom's Cabin' need be read in any sectional spirit or as anything but a thrilling delineation of a mighty wrong, whose responsibility was shared by a whole nation and for which the whole nation paid the bitter penalty."[60] Like many editions of the period, the Appleton edition effaces the unresolved racial tensions in the turn-of-the-century United States.

SERVING NOSTALGIA AT THE TURN OF THE CENTURY

In the Appleton edition of 1898 paratextual materials frame *Uncle Tom's Cabin* as a reassuring tale of race for white readers of the period. Higginson's "Critical and Biographical Introduction" to that edition includes a closing caveat which touches on the continuing struggle of "a greatly injured race," and "the brave effort that is being made by that race to raise itself" (xiv). As we have seen, this emphasis on unfinished business was exceptional in white commentary about *Uncle Tom's Cabin*. Nevertheless, the Appleton edition as a whole framed Stowe's novel in a characteristic way: as a work that had completed its service to a great cause and redeemed American society. Illustrations and their captions provide a scholarly and historical aura for the book and play a significant role in this framing. The Appleton edition foregrounds a selection of "Famous and Unique Manuscript and Book Illustrations: A series of facsimiles, showing the development of manuscript and book illustration during four thousand years."[61] This definition of the visual accompaniments to *Uncle Tom's Cabin* offers a diachronic perspective and places Stowe's book in an evolving literary and pictorial tradition that becomes a national heritage.

The Appleton edition sold for seven dollars—a very expensive book at the time, perhaps partly intended to appeal to book collectors. The historical, even scholarly, emphasis of both the introduction and the illustrations was characteristic of the series ("The World's Great Books"), which included works by Aeschylus, Plato, Cervantes, and Heine as well as Stowe, Poe, and Richard Henry Dana.[62] The first image is a portrait of Stowe, followed by a color plate of "Anne of Brittany and her Patron Saints," a "miniature for a book of 'Hours,' painted toward the end of the fifteenth century." This illustration renders Anne of Brittany, her hands pressed together in prayer, over what appears to be an open book. Two of the three patron saints in the background seem to be contemplating the volume as well (fig. 33). Although Anne of Brittany seems an odd choice for an accompanying illustration to *Uncle Tom's Cabin,* we might say that the image foregrounds both piety and literacy through the "book of 'Hours' " thus linking Stowe's novel to holy purposes generally. Engaging some of the text's central themes in this way also recalls antebellum marketing strategies which, as we have seen, often stressed the book's religious goals and the author's divine inspiration.[63] However, the "system of theology" and the "strong religious opinions which prevailed in the circle in which [Stowe] lived" as a child, required almost as much explanation to new readers of the 1890s as the peculiar institution itself.[64] As we have noted, Stowe's evangelicalism, like her politics, seemed irrelevant to many contemporary readers. The religious emphasis typical of antebellum advertisements and reviews is absent in commentary and advertisements of the 1890s. Religious fiction such as the "wholesome, uplifting" work of Harold

33. *"Anne of Brittany and her Patron Saints. Miniature from a book of 'Hours,' painted toward the end of the fifteenth century."* Frontispiece from Harriet Beecher Stowe, Uncle Tom's Cabin. *Appleton, 1898. General Research Division. The New York Public Library. Astor, Lenox and Tilden Foundations.*

Bell Wright was enormously popular at the turn of the century, but Wright's reassuring, optimistic, complacent Christianity was a far cry from Stowe's, even if he preached a "sermon in every sentence."[65] Stowe's preface to the first edition with its urgent call for sympathy and its warnings about judgment day is framed as a historical curiosity in new editions, when it is included at all.

Insofar as the image of Anne of Brittany and her book of "Hours" draws attention to the religious function of literacy, it places the act of reading at a considerable remove from U.S. culture, and still farther from the theme of black literacy. The Appleton edition represents reading and writing as privilege, the prerogative of queens, saints, authors, and editors—not African Americans. The image of Anne of Brittany is aligned not with Stowe's thematics of reading and the American social context, but rather with "four thousand years . . . of manuscript and book illustration" (iii). This emphasis foregrounds the value of both literary tradition and technology. It introduces *Uncle Tom's Cabin* not as a narrative about slavery, but as an archive of publishing history. Through its focus on changing modes of book illustration the Appleton edition (like the Stowe display at the World's Fair or Kemble's illustrations of 1891) presents *Uncle Tom's Cabin* as a historical artifact in an upbeat narrative of cultural advance.

The next illustration in the Appleton volume reproduces an illustration by Billings, an image we have already discussed: Eliza stopping at Uncle Tom's cabin before fleeing the Shelby plantation. As reproduced in 1898, however, this image subordinates a dramatic moment of Stowe's plot to an emphasis on the way *Uncle Tom's Cabin* contributed to the development of a literary mode. Here the initial caption "Eliza comes to tell Uncle Tom that he is sold" (fig. 19) is only the prelude to a further explanation: "Photogravure for a drawing in the first illustrated edition of 'Uncle Tom's Cabin,' showing the style of book illustration in 1852."[66] Hammatt Billings, the most popular early American illustrator of *Uncle Tom's Cabin,* thus becomes (like Stowe) the focus of a retrospective narrative. The last visual image in the book is a portrait of "Josiah Henson—the original 'Uncle Tom' Photogravure from a drawing made for this work."[67] The case for Henson as "the original" Uncle Tom is somewhat shaky,[68] but his image—offered here in part as testimony to the historical "truth" of Stowe's novel—is a perfectly typical device for framing *Uncle Tom's Cabin* in this period.[69] The death of Lewis George Clark, alleged model for George Harris, was widely reported in the press in 1897, as we saw in Chapter 5; obituaries of Norman Argo (another claimant for the title of Uncle Tom) appeared in 1903.[70] Such news items, reprinted across the country, bolstered claims for Stowe's representation of the "real," while intensifying the memorial aspect of attention to the book.

However, the caption for Henson's portrait, like the caption for "Eliza tells Uncle Tom He is Sold," also highlights changes in the art of book illustration—not only since the early modern period when a book of hours was a hand-painted artifact, but over the preceding fifty years. Technological and aesthetic "progress" was another characteristic focus in editions of the 1890s. According to the introduction for the "Art Memorial Edition" of 1897, "When 'Uncle Tom's Cabin' was originally published, the modern method of illustration was unknown, and only crude and old-fashioned woodcuts were available. . . . it is to [the] developed tastes [of the new generation] that the publishers have catered."[71] Reprints of the period were regularly justified, then, not only by the story of moral and political improvements in American society, but also by an emphasis on evolution in aesthetic taste of the reading public and the technology of printing and book design.

The Appleton edition is shaped by a concept of the past designed to foreground the achievements of the present, but this concept has strong nostalgic undercurrents. Images of "The Levee at Baton Rouge" or "The Planter's Home" do not evoke specific characters or events in *Uncle Tom's Cabin*.[72] Rather, they frame the "Old South" as a geographical space that deserves the attention of contemporary readers rightly curious about the national past. Three additional illustrations—an image of "The House in Brunswick Maine Where 'Uncle Tom's Cabin' Was Written," and two portraits of Harriet Beecher Stowe—commemorate the author and the book. But as in other framings of the nineties, Stowe's story itself disappears in visual accompaniments that direct attention away from plot and characters. The image of Stowe's house in Maine follows the page which relates the conversation between the Senator and his wife, prior to Eliza's appearance after crossing the icy river (90); a photograph of Stowe follows the page which relates the scene of Tom's death (470); an additional portrait faces the title page of the volume. If we look only at the illustrations and their captions, we encounter neither racial tensions nor sentiment. Emotional responses, like racial or political divisions, are deflected.

Four images in the Appleton edition are labeled as engravings based on photographs. The reference to photography in the captions ("Photogravure from a photograph") asserts the reality of the represented subject or object. As we have noted, photography was increasingly identified with objectivity as well as technological expertise toward the end of the century. Roland Barthes suggests that photographs are often "taken as the pure and simple denotation of reality," as if reading photographs requires no interpretive code, even in the twentieth century.[73] Scholars of the last half century have developed a heightened awareness of photographs as texts that frame and interpret their materials. But when photographic practices were at an early stage of development, excitement about the new art derived partly from its claim to scientific accuracy, a way of transcending the merely personal vision. Attacking literary realism in 1894, W. R. Thayer took the identification of photography with scientific objectivity for granted: "The Realist was impartial," Thayer wrote; "he eliminated the personal equation; he would make his mind as unprejudiced as a photographic plate."[74] The inclusion of photographs in editions of *Uncle Tom's Cabin* lent the authority of technology, science, and reality to the novel that Henry James had called Stowe's "wonderful leaping fish."[75] Taken together, the illustrations in the Appleton edition present *Uncle Tom's Cabin* not as a gripping tale, a text inspired by God, or a narrative with relevance to contemporary social issues, but rather as a book that provides a reliably documented historical perspective on a famous author, on an influential literary work, on the antebellum South, and on the technology of book illustration. The emphasis on history, technology, and progress also serves to mask the nostalgia implicit in such images as the "Levee at Baton Rouge" or "The Planter's Home"—mementos of a receding past.

Like the Houghton Mifflin edition of 1891 and the Appleton edition of 1898, other editions of the nineties often avoid representing black and white characters in close physical proximity and minimize the representation of black readers. When illustrators of the period do allude to black literacy, the illustration often strikes a comic note, stressing the incongruity of a slave with a book or a slate. "Not that way, Uncle Tom!" are the words of one caption for an image of Tom writing under George Shelby's tutelage. The frontispiece for one children's edition of 1901 shows Tom scratching his head and looking absolutely stymied by the difference between a "g" and a "q."[76] Although Tom's difficulty learning his letters is taken from Stowe's text, the emphasis on his comic incapacity increases dramatically in the postwar period.

Editions at the turn of the century feature images of slaves that deliver reassuring messages of continuity and stability to white readers unsettled by a changing racial landscape. Images that stress African Americans' inability to learn, or

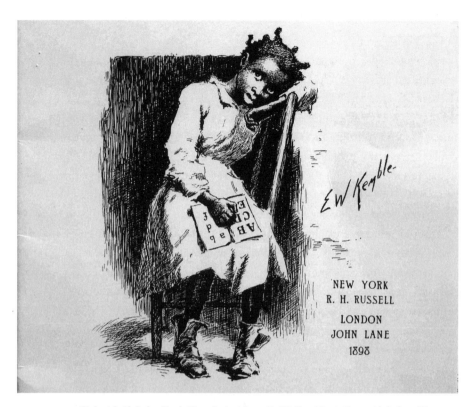

34. *Girl with Alphabet Book. Frontispiece from E. W. Kemble,* A Coon Alphabet. *New York: John Lane, 1898. Courtesy of the Cotsen Children's Library. Department of Rare Books and Special Collections. Princeton University Library.*

that radically constrict the matter to be mastered, imply that African Americans will constitute neither threat nor competition within a stable status quo. One typical illustration by Kemble—this one from the title page of *A Coon Alphabet* (1898)—shows a little girl holding an alphabet book but looking as if the letters are unfriendly alien objects, if not an occasion for despair (fig. 34). The "Art Memorial Edition of *Uncle Tom's Cabin*" (1897) includes an illustration entitled "Ophelia Shows Topsy How to Make a Bed" (fig. 35). This moment in Stowe's novel, never illustrated in the 1850s, suggests that a black American girl will make a "fine little maid," as another edition puts it.[77] The image foregrounds docility, subordination, and service, as if these qualities were the only ones appropriate to African Americans.

In editions of the 1890s many illustrations of *Uncle Tom's Cabin* implied that black people could never acquire the skills that seemed the birthright of white

35. *"Miss Ophelia shows Topsy how to make a bed."* From Harriet Beecher Stowe, Uncle Tom's Cabin. *Art Memorial Edition. Chicago: Thompson and Thomas, 1897. Rare Book and Manuscript Library. Columbia University.*

U.S. citizens. On the one hand, paratextual materials present Stowe's novel as having already accomplished its political goals. On the other hand, introductions and illustrations speak to the practical concerns and racial anxieties of white readers by assuring them of African Americans' continuing obedience, gratitude, and loyalty to white authority. As we shall see in the following chapter, children's editions took this strategy further. Children's literature as a genre had long depended heavily on illustrations. Like the editions just examined, children's editions from the 1890s onward benefited from the new ease with which images could be reproduced. Unlike full-length editions designed for adults, however, children's adaptations assumed that Stowe's narrative itself—plot and characters—would appeal to the target audience, especially if the story were retooled for the needs of contemporary boys and girls. Children's editions did not rely on illustrations to tell the story—they remade the story itself. In *Uncle Tom's Cabin* for "young folks" at the turn of the century the racialization of the characters becomes the dominant feature of the tale. The reassuring subtext of illustrations that project the illiteracy and subservience of African Americans into an unending future is especially visible in children's editions of the period. The goals and strategies of one such edition deserve a separate chapter.

7

Sparing the White Child

The Lessons of Uncle Tom's Cabin *for Children
in an Age of Segregation*

> No one could tell the sacrifice the stern Vermont housekeeper was making when she
> allowed the wild little black girl to touch her bed.
>
> —*Young Folks Uncle Tom's Cabin, 1901*

Harriet Beecher Stowe died in 1896, the year that the court decision *Plessy vs. Ferguson* made segregation a legal and widespread social practice in the United States. After her death publishers found it both timely and profitable to reissue *Uncle Tom's Cabin,* often with fresh introductions and visual accompaniments.[1] Adaptations for children and youth also proliferated in this period. By the turn of the century Stowe's book had become a "classic" and was widely recommended to juvenile readers.[2]

Children's editions of a classic always retell a well-known story, but they alter the text, recasting a familiar plot and characters with a young audience in mind. Always shorter than the original, such editions require choices about what to include or omit. These choices reflect an interpretation of the source along with assumptions about what children's books are or should be.

This chapter examines the direction of change in *Young Folks Uncle Tom's Cabin,* a turn-of-the-century children's edition by Grace Duffie Boylan with black and white illustrations by Ike Morgan. First published in 1901, the book was reissued by a variety of publishers until as late as 1956.[3] *Young Folks Uncle Tom's Cabin* was a radically different book from the one that adults wept over and children eagerly devoured when Stowe's novel first appeared.[4]

Antebellum children's editions, like Stowe's text itself, featured children, spoke to children, and positioned both children and books as important grounds of value in the family. As we have seen, *Pictures and Stories from Uncle Tom's Cabin* (1853) and *A Peep into Uncle Tom's Cabin* (1853) were faithful to Stowe's text in many ways.[5] Like *Uncle Tom's Cabin* itself, these editions stressed white social responsibility, religious faith, black literacy, and spiritual equality between the races. By contrast, children's editions of the Jim Crow period virtually eliminate Stowe's moral, social, and religious concerns. They also flatten compelling elements of her tale such as the drama of Harry's danger and rescue; Eva's social awareness and moral autonomy; Topsy's history, anger, ambivalence, and development.[6] More than either *Uncle Tom's Cabin* or antebellum children's editions, *Young Folks Uncle Tom's Cabin* posits sharp differences between the moral and intellectual capacities of its black and white characters. As a result of such revisions this much-reprinted book transforms the experience of reading Stowe's tale. *Young Folks Uncle Tom's Cabin* offers clear prescriptions for the continued subordination of African Americans in U.S. culture and pointed lessons in white middle-class complacency. It also reflects contemporary anxieties about what little white boys and girls are made of.

Stowe's "romantic racialism" and even racism has been much discussed. However, in looking back at Stowe from what we take to be our own enlightened perspective we sometimes inordinately privilege hindsight and neglect significant changes in the functions of a book. Reprints of the 1890s turned Stowe's racialism into full-blown racism, as we have seen. But while full-length editions rely on new introductions and illustrations to create shifts of emphasis, children's versions freely edit Stowe's text, shortening the book and making substantial changes.[7] Children's editions at the turn of the century intensify the racist implications that *Uncle Tom's Cabin* had already acquired in other contexts.

Young Folks Uncle Tom's Cabin goes much further than either *Uncle Tom's Cabin* or antebellum children's editions in restricting African American characters to a small and static number of subject positions and social roles. Tom and Chloe lack spiritual depth along with the capacity for individual initiative; they exemplify loyalty and service. In Ike Morgan's illustrations they are like the merry and foolish black figures that populate turn-of-the-century cartoons and food advertisements.[8] Topsy is no longer Stowe's abused, conflicted child, but merely the comic entertainer that she became in late nineteenth-century theatrical productions.[9] Illustrations of Topsy belong to the iconographic tradition in which African Americans appear to be members of a separate species—as in E. W. Kemble's images for *A Coon Alphabet* (1898) or in political cartoons of the period that represent Filipinos as grotesque little savages.[10]

In *Young Folks Uncle Tom's Cabin* white children are positioned at a secure

moral distance from the African Americans who divert them by telling stories and performing tricks.[11] A changed conception of the book's intended
readers is implicit in these revisions. The role offered to white children (especially girls) is thoughtless and passive. They are to be amused by the antics of
others (especially African Americans). White children pay a price when they
take their cues from such a text; but the message for African American children who might have encountered the book is still more disturbing.[12] The
textual changes designed to adapt *Uncle Tom's Cabin* for "young folks" at the
turn of the century imply a series of cultural transformations. Not only changing conceptions of race, but also the consolidation of class divisions, and new
theories of child development are writ large in *Young Folks Uncle Tom's Cabin*.
Amid widespread anxiety about social change, white Americans increasingly
affirmed the inevitability and naturalness of social hierarchies and binary
oppositions. This process, shaping the ideology and the policies that enabled
racial segregation, also reshaped the goals of children's literature.

In the antebellum *Pictures and Stories from Uncle Tom's Cabin* "Eva had
long yellow curls, and a fair, pretty face" but, "better than that, she had the
fear of God and the love of all goodness in her heart" (19). In *Young Folks
Uncle Tom's Cabin* Eva is a "little golden-haired girl [who] flitted about the
decks of the Mississippi steamer like a fairy" (79). Fairies, unlike angels, are
magical and pagan. The revamped little Eva exemplifies sweetness, good
cheer, and playfulness, not spiritual faith or moral seriousness.[13] Alterations in
the image of Uncle Tom and Topsy intensify racist elements that are implicit
in Stowe's original text but are qualified there by other emphases.

Throughout *Uncle Tom's Cabin* Stowe argues that slavery corrupts the master while destroying the slave. Black and white characters are knit together in
reciprocal relations shaped by slavery. Insofar as this reciprocity affects children, it is richly encapsulated in the figure of St. Clare's nephew Henrique,
whose potential for brutality is maximized by his prerogatives as a little master.
When Henrique whips his young slave Dodo, the moral damage to both boys
is evident. This episode is not included in either antebellum or post–Civil War
children's editions of *Uncle Tom's Cabin,* which always elide the text's more
extreme violence, along with sexuality, adult doubt, and vulgar or complex
language. But *Young Folks Uncle Tom's Cabin* goes well beyond children's editions of the antebellum period, not only by evading such themes but also by
dulling the imaginative edge of Stowe's tale. In *Young Folks Uncle Tom's Cabin*

children (whether black or white) rarely experience fear, pain, anger, or inner conflict, not to speak of religious faith or ethical awareness.[14] Eva, Topsy, and even little Harry are significantly reduced in complexity. These changes imply assumptions about real children—assumptions that are racially inflected and intertwined both with new ideas about the function of children's reading and with new doubts about children's imaginative, moral, and instinctual life. In what follows I examine the ways *Young Folks Uncle Tom's Cabin* recast Stowe's narrative for a new generation of readers. I suggest that specific shifts of focus reflect ongoing changes in attitudes toward race, reading, and children.

Children and Books at the Turn of the Century

When books for young children began to proliferate in the United States during the 1830s and '40s, amusing tales that would sustain a child's interest gained legitimacy, but didactic fiction continued to emphasize piety, duty, obedience, and self-denial. Moral tales for young readers stressed personal responsibility and often kept the future pain of life in view.[15] From the 1850s onward what G. Stanley Hall later called "the mysterious play-instinct" received growing attention as a valuable part of child development.[16] As Gillian Brown, Karen Sanchez-Eppler, and others have shown, amusement gradually came to be seen as a legitimate component of children's experience, appropriate to a stage of life marked off from the pain and obligations of adulthood. In the second half of the century, children's literature, reflecting this shift, became both more secular and more fanciful.[17]

The notion of childhood as a separate sphere was well established by the 1890s and helped to make children's literature a significant source of income for publishers as well as an important feature of public libraries.[18] After the Civil War, improved technologies for reproducing texts and illustrations, better transportation, and more efficient marketing made the sale of books for children big business. In the course of the nineteenth century, the middle class, consolidating its economic and social position, had enthusiastically embraced the "ideology of literacy": editors, educators, and other cultural commentators promoted "the reading habit" as both a moral value and a key to upward mobility.[19] By the turn of the century, a family's possession and consumption of books—including children's books—pointed clearly to cultural status. As Gail Schmunck Murray puts this, the "child-centered middle class" became convinced "that books should fill the child's life."[20]

At the end of the century, books written for children affirmed childhood as a benign and carefree realm. White children who did not work, and whose childhood years were prolonged within the home, constituted a visible sign of middle-class prosperity and self-regard.[21] The religious and didactic function typical of antebellum children's literature all but disappeared in this context. Indeed, overtly moral tales elicited considerable hostility. In the words of one poem for children in 1906: "I don't want a goody-goody tale."[22] The "supernaturally angelic" Eva tried the patience of some reviewers.[23] Anglo-American children's books of the 1890s were more often designed to entertain than to teach. Fantasy and whimsy, frowned upon by educators in the antebellum United States, grew increasingly popular. Palmer Cox's widely circulated primers were full of little elf-like "brownies." *The Wizard of Oz* (1900) evokes an imaginative realm located at a considerable distance from the normative and the familiar. Children's tales of the period rarely foreground social responsibility.

After the Civil War, as both race relations and labor relations grew increasingly charged, even violent, middle-class reformers turned much of their attention to less controversial causes, such as children's welfare.[24] The nuclear family, secure and self-enclosed, epitomized middle-class success and became a model held up to immigrants and the working class. Central to this image of the family was the privileged child in its midst—protected, nurtured, encouraged to play, encouraged to be patriotic (in a general way), but discouraged from seeing him- or herself as touched by wider social currents, especially problematic ones.

Turn-of-the-century children's books participate in this series of cultural shifts—from the morally responsible to the indulged child, from the white middle-class family as an integral part of society to the family as self-enclosed unit; from a reformist concern with race relations as a problem, to a growing sense of racial separation and social hierarchy as a solution; from a belief in children's literature as food for reflection and moral action to a celebration of books as consumer objects, designed to amuse. But the price of the new premium on literacy as pleasure was a certain infantilization of the child. The emphasis on childhood as a separate sphere—inscribed with increasingly rigid divisions of both race and gender—subverted the autonomy and moral agency of young people.[25]

GROWING LIKE TOPSY: RACIST ASSUMPTIONS IN *YOUNG FOLKS UNCLE TOM'S CABIN*

All children's editions of *Uncle Tom's Cabin* rework the structure of the story, putting children (Little Harry, Eva, and Topsy) at the center. However, antebellum children's editions not only retain Stowe's moral and didactic emphases, they sometimes give more space to Harry's fairy tale of rescue than to Eva's role in the narrative;[26] they foreground Topsy's mistreatment and struggle to be good. As we saw in Chapter 4, that struggle must have been of special interest to white antebellum children who were regularly urged to restrain their impulses and obey authority without hesitation.[27] Children's editions at the turn of the century had a different agenda.

Like the children's adaptations published in the antebellum period, *Young Folks Uncle Tom's Cabin* reprinted large portions of Stowe's original text verbatim. Additions, omissions, and other revisions are especially revealing in the context of numerous passages that are included just as they initially appeared. One of the most striking changes in *Young Folks Uncle Tom's Cabin* is its removal of all detail pertaining to Topsy's past: Topsy's experience as a brutalized child disappears from the book.

Stowe had embraced widely shared Lockean ideas about the malleability of the young;[28] *Uncle Tom's Cabin* ascribes Topsy's indifference and unruliness to the cruel treatment she has endured as a young slave. "It is your system makes such children," Ophelia tells St. Clare (*UTC*, 364). Stowe clearly suggests that white children, too, are shaped by their experience: Henrique is a violent child because of the inordinate power he can wield over others; Eva's death is a symbolic consequence of the painful scenes she has witnessed. Antebellum children's editions retained Stowe's emphasis on the shaping force of experience. In *Pictures and Stories from Uncle Tom's Cabin,* Topsy's history of mistreatment and neglect accounts for her "naughty ways." She is "a child whom bad men from her mother sold / Whom a harsh mistress used to cuff and scold, / Whom no one taught or cared for" (*P&S*, 22).[29] In *Young Folks Uncle Tom's Cabin,* by contrast, Topsy's character is an essentialized function of race. Her past is only indirectly noted. Topsy is introduced with a brief reference to her "cruel owners," and she appears at one point "clothed for the first time in her life in a decent dress" (*YFUT*, 90, 91); but no details of her history are included to explain her actions or feelings.[30] Race explains her inability to behave and confines her future to a life of domestic service. In the *Young Folks* edition, Ophelia tells Topsy: "we shall make a fine little maid of you I am sure" (94). This opportunity is represented as a generous gift of white benevolence. In a significant addition to Stowe's text the narrator comments: "No one could tell the sacrifice the stern Vermont housekeeper was making when she allowed the wild little black girl to touch her bed" (93).

Young Folks Uncle Tom's Cabin eliminates Topsy's potential for moral, intellectual, and spiritual growth along with her history. Where the antebellum *Pictures and Stories* represents Topsy's inner conflict and her "trying to be good" against great odds (*P&S,* 25, 26), *Young Folks Uncle Tom's Cabin* accentuates Topsy's inability to learn, intensifies her dialect, increases her grammatical errors, and highlights her dancing, singing, and acrobatic tricks. Topsy's main function here is comic—she is designed to amuse both little Eva and the reader. Without Topsy's history, Stowe's social criticism disappears and racism comes to the fore: Topsy's misbehavior, unexplained, appears to be a "natural" trait; but since mischief is not presented as "natural" in white children (least of all in little girls), Topsy's unruliness is implicitly attributed to her racial inheritance.[31]

In the antebellum *Pictures and Stories,* as we have seen, the figure of Topsy provides a rare opportunity for white children to imagine mischief and wildness from a sympathetic perspective, contemplating otherness while entertaining the possibility of being themselves "just like Topsy" (24). In *Young Folks Uncle Tom's Cabin* the reader—like little Eva—is invited to watch Topsy's performances from a distance, rather than imagining herself in Topsy's bare feet (fig. 36). Everything about the figure of Topsy (her appearance, her speech, her behavior) works against ascribing interiority to her. The image of Topsy as performer is reinforced by illustrations (a shoeless, dancing Topsy with spikey hair appears on the cover of one 1901 edition). Topsy barely appears to be human—certainly nothing like a proper white girl.

Topsy violates the image of the child so precious to middle-class adults of the period. As Gillian Brown, Carolyn Steedman, and others have argued, one of the most endearing aspects of childhood for nineteenth- and early twentieth-century educators and parents was the child's capacity for unself-

" I dunno, missis," said Topsy, and then in a moment she was down on the floor walking on her hands, with her black feet in the air. She made the circle once around, before her astonished and horrified mistress caught breath enough to exclaim:

"Get up, Topsy, you wretched child, and tell me—Do you know who made you?"

"No, mom. Nobuddy neber made me. I 'spect I growed. Nobuddy done tuk de trouble ter make me, as I knows."

Miss Ophelia felt that she was not making much progress.

"Do you know how to sew?" she asked.

"No, mom. I dunno how ter sew."

"What did you do for your master and mistress?"

"Nuffin dat I could help."

"Were they good to you?"

"Yessum. Dey licked me free er four times er day ter make me good, but I ain't good yit."

Topsy's black eyes glittered with mischief as she struck up in a shrill voice:

" O I'se a mis'ble sinneh, yes I is;
O I'se a mis'ble sinneh,
An I kaint hab no dinneh,
Yes I is!"

She kept time to this with her feet and hands, knocking

Walking on her hands, with her black
feet in the air

36. *Topsy walks on her hands. From Grace Duffie Boylan,* Young Folks Uncle Tom's Cabin. *Chicago: Albert Whitman, 1942. Author's copy.*

conscious absorption, a capacity which many adults looked back on nostalgically.[32] Unlike performance, absorption implies both innocent spontaneity and inner depth. But the Topsy of *Young Folks* is all externalization and exhibitionism; her speech and her acrobatics are geared to an audience, as if she were in a minstrel show. She thus contradicts the ideal script of childhood and fulfills the racial stereotype.

Like the figure of Topsy, the image of Tom is reduced to a racial cliché in *Young Folks Uncle Tom's Cabin*. An early scene establishes Tom's entertainment value, while stripping him of moral stature. "You taught me most everything I know," young George Shelby tells Tom, "to swim and ride and everything—and you make me dandier kites than anyone" (9–10). Tom here is a playmate, even a plaything, for white children. In Stowe's text, as in early children's editions, Tom is a father in his own right, a man with considerable (indeed increasing) moral authority not only within his own family, and among other slaves, but also with George Shelby and Eva, St. Clare, and Ophelia. In *Young Folks Uncle Tom's Cabin,* by contrast, although little George Shelby claims that Tom has taught him "everything [he] knows," that "everything" is confined to fun and games. Uncle Tom entertains little Eva as well, making toys, telling amusing stories. In one particularly suggestive textual change, Tom and Eva do not ponder the Bible together as their acquaintance develops: instead, Tom amuses Eva with tales of "Br'er Rabbit and Missy Cottontail" (82). The image of Uncle Tom fades into that of Uncle Remus.[33]

Guidelines for reading cannot tell us how texts were actually read; there is always a difference between the overt themes of a children's book and the meanings that specific children take. But through Eva and Topsy's stark polarities of speech, appearance, and behavior, *Young Folks Uncle Tom's Cabin* proposes a rigid dividing line that militates against empathy or even sympathy with Topsy. The book offers its readers prescriptive subject positions and discourages conflicting identifications.[34] Cross-racial identification looks preposterous.

ROLE MODELS FOR CAREFREE WHITE CHILDREN

As a counterpart to its servile and comic black figures, *Young Folks Uncle Tom's Cabin* projects an image of indulged and carefree white children. As little George Shelby celebrates the fun provided by Uncle Tom, so Eva is comfortable with the privileges she enjoys; her awareness of slave suffering is minimal.[35] Stowe makes slavery responsible for Eva's death; in *Young Folks Uncle Tom's Cabin* her illness is minimized and its cause is obscure. Now Eva's primary function is to play and consume—good preparation for her projected future as a twentieth-century woman of leisure.[36]

In *Uncle Tom's Cabin,* as in children's editions of the 1850s, Eva's moral understanding shapes her wish to purchase Tom (19). Eva's aim is to make *Tom* happy—"You will have good times," she tells him (*UTC,* 233). In the antebellum *Pictures and Stories* Eva directly expresses the hope that she will convince her father "to set [Tom] free" (19). But in *Young Folks Uncle Tom's Cabin,* when Eva persuades St. Clare to buy Tom, it is because she wants to own him, so that he can divert and serve her. "You will be my Uncle Tom," she says (*YFUT,* 80). In *Young Folks Uncle Tom's Cabin* Tom and Eva's friendship has little to do with Eva's desire to make Tom happy—still less to free him. He is to be a delightful new possession. "You will buy him for me, won't you papa?" she pleads, looking at her father, "confidently" (81). St. Clare answers: "Yes, little one, if you wish to have him" (81). Accordingly, while Eva is an unconflicted little mistress, Tom displays all the qualities required to fulfill the role of a loyal servant, indeed, the perfect slave.[37] From the start he is inordinately ready to die for his master(s) (10, 23, 62, 65, 100), though Stowe barely alludes to this point.[38]

An image of the intended child reader is implicit in these textual alterations, especially in the figures of Eva and Topsy. This point will be clearer if we consider changes in an episode that was repeatedly illustrated in editions of the 1850s and much discussed by twentieth-century scholars. I refer to the scene which foreshadows Eva's death. When Eva and Tom read the Bible together at Lake Pontchartrain, Eva points to the sky and tells Uncle Tom that "before long" she will be "going there." In Stowe's text this scene foregrounds both the relationship and the analogy between Eva and Tom—their mutual responsiveness, awe in the face of death, and equality in the eye of God.[39]

Young Folks Uncle Tom's Cabin consistently downplays spirituality as a quality of character and Bible-reading as a practice or a trope.[40] The scene at the lake includes more substantial revisions; it adds Topsy to the episode. Topsy interrupts Tom and Eva's colloquy, creating comic relief and deflecting attention from both the spiritual and political issues implicit in the image of Eva and Tom exchanging reflections on the holy book. A hymn which Eva and

Tom sing together is replaced with a comic song about a blackbird, sung by
Topsy. Topsy's "weird melody" subverts the solemnity of the moment (101). As
the chapter continues, Topsy's naughtiness intensifies. The girl cuts Ophelia's
bonnet trimming "all to pieces to make dolls' jackets" (103) (fig. 37). Although
this incident is taken from the full-length *Uncle Tom's Cabin,* it belongs to a
different chapter there (*UTC,* 407). *Young Folks Uncle Tom's Cabin* reshuffles
Stowe's sequence of events to transform a contemplative, even somber scene
between Eva and Tom into a Topsy spectacle. In addition, Topsy's disobedience
continues well after Eva's death.[41] The implication is that black children do not
mature and cannot learn. As for little white readers, on the one hand they are
encouraged to feel superior; on the other, they are asked not to expect a book
to challenge their emotions, their intellect, or their imagination.

Antebellum children's books were intended to help mold a young reader's
character. Promoting obedience, diligence, and regular habits was central to
this project, as was the assumption that children irresistibly imitate what they
read, especially when good models are offered. The question of whether children's books should include "bad" examples was much debated, as we saw in
Chapter 4. Antebellum educators and commentators feared the wrong model
might be imitated; Lydia Maria Child disliked "stories about naughty children," for that reason.[42] In the antebellum consensus, naughty children, if
represented at all, were to be rendered as unattractive as possible, and swiftly
punished by the plot. Nevertheless, Child, Stowe, and other writers and educators sought to promote thoughtful imaginative engagement with a narrative. Antebellum children's books aimed to convey information about the
world, to cultivate moral awareness, a sense of responsibility, and (often) a
social conscience. *Young Folks Uncle Tom's Cabin* reflects a different conception of children's reading, which in turn implies a changed understanding of
what children are, want, or need.

THEORIES OF CHILDHOOD AND THE
LURE OF THE BLAND CHILD

Late nineteenth-century developments in theories of childhood help explain
some of the changes in juvenile editions of *Uncle Tom's Cabin:* not only the
flattening of Eva and the unmitigated distinctions between Eva and Topsy,

our sore, black hearts and make them well and clean!
Come, little missy, the evenin' dew is fallin'.   Come in."

They went toward the house just in time to see Miss
Ophelia drag Topsy into the drawing-room.

"Come here, now," she said, "I will tell your master."

Topsy took refuge, as usual, behind Mr. St. Clare's
chair.   He was always more amused than angry at her

"* * * cut it all to pieces to make dolls' jackets."

antics.   Miss Marie, as Mrs. St. Clare was called by her
servants, was far more severe in her treatment.

"What's the case now?" asked Augustine.

"The case is, that I cannot be plagued with this child
any longer!   It's past all bearing; flesh and blood cannot
endure it!   Here, I locked her up, and gave her a hymn

37. Topsy makes doll jackets. From Grace Duffie Boylan, Young Folks Uncle Tom's Cabin.
Chicago: Albert Whitman, 1942. Author's copy.

but also the difference between the two girls, on the one hand, and little George Shelby on the other.

Up to a point, late nineteenth-century theorists of child development, child-rearing, and education provided support for the increasingly popular idea of childhood as a separate, playful realm; educators and commentators agreed that children should have their own spaces (both in the house and in the neighborhood), their age-appropriate toys and games, their protection from toil and trouble.[43] Yet late nineteenth-century theories of childhood also included elements that pulled away from the idea of innocence and that therefore made images of the naïve, benign white child in fiction (and elsewhere) even more appealing.

The assumption of childhood depravity as the inheritance of original sin was long gone by the end of the century; but in the 1890s the work of G. Stanley Hall, James Mark Baldwin, Sigmund Freud, and others reintroduced harsher elements of childhood—not on doctrinal religious grounds but as developmental inevitabilities. Drawing on evolutionary theory, these writers generated a model of child development that was largely inner-driven. Children, they suggested—like the nation-state and the human race as a whole—go through stages of development that are influenced but not determined by impressions from without. As W. B. Drummond put this, "every child in the course of his growth . . . passes through stages which correspond to stages in his ancestral history."[44]

This idea of childhood provided grounds for optimism about child-rearing in general, with implications for the function of parents. "I am an optimist root and core," Hall insisted, " . . . because an evolutionist must hold that the best and not the worst will survive and prevail."[45] In the antebellum period educational theories had imagined the child as a blank slate or wax tablet and warned that impressions received during childhood would be critical. It was up to parents to regulate what a child would see and hear. In *Uncle Tom's Cabin*, Eva becomes faint after hearing Prue's story (327), and St. Clare soon regrets that he "ever let [her] hear such stories" (403). But it is too late: these impressions have already had an irreversible impact. "They sink into my heart," as Eva famously reiterates.[46]

New theories of childhood toward the end of the century lessened the burden of parental responsibility for forming an offspring's character; parents were encouraged to be confident that good traits would triumph in the course of a natural process, as long as the child was nurtured and given freedom to develop. Indeed, the challenge now was not to interfere with the process—not to pressure the developing child prematurely.

The theories that informed and emerged from "child study" were disseminated to educated middle-class readers via the periodical press. Discussions by well-respected psychologists and educators appeared not only in the elite *North American Review* or the *Century* but also in the more moderately priced *Scribner's* and the even less expensive *Ladies' Home Journal*.[47] These widely circulated ideas were also published in learned journals and book form. Addressing professional readers but also the general reading public, psychologists and educators as well as popular writers for boys and girls such as Kate Wiggin and Frances Hodgson Burnett promoted the careful observation of children. James Baldwin enjoined fathers to participate actively in child-rearing; Hall suggested that important insights were available to any patient observer.[48]

In a piece titled "The Imitative Functions" published in the *Century,* Josiah Royce invites parents, teachers—or any reader—to help him along with his research by writing to him with examples they have seen of children imitating either familiar or imaginary figures. The complex dynamic of imitation gained new attention in the 1890s. "Nothing less than the child's personality is at stake in the method and manner of its imitations," Baldwin writes.[49] On the one hand, as before, imitation was understood to be a "deep-seated" natural tendency, central in the early stages of child development and a factor much later as well.[50] Yet increasing uncertainty about what children imitate and why complicated the model. Baldwin suggests that "the ethical life itself, the boy's, the girl's conscience, is born in the stress of the conflicts of suggestion—born right out of his imitative hesitations."[51]

The idea of "imitative hesitations" leaves room for a child's independent exercise of the will in choosing objects to imitate.[52] Royce stresses the interplay of imitation and originality in child development. Baldwin, Royce, Drummond, and others agreed that a child participates actively in self-fashioning, despite the traits and constraints he or she inevitably inherits from both the family and "the race." While the emphasis on "hesitations" opened the way to uncertainty (what and how does the child decide to imitate?) the evolutionary paradigm with its focus on passing stages and good outcomes was reassuring, especially for white middle-class parents who assumed that their own prosperity and social position already certified their place on the "higher" rungs of the evolutionary ladder.

The image of childhood that Baldwin, Hall, and other psychologists of the period produced implied that much disruptive behavior should be tolerated precisely because it was natural—and temporary.[53] Frances Hodgson Burnett's autobiographical account of her childhood, published in installments in *Scribner's* magazine in 1893, neatly exemplifies the way a certain amount of surprising or unruly child behavior (even for girls) could be contained by the notion of developmental phases. It also returns us directly to the question of *Uncle Tom's Cabin* for children.

In "The One I Knew Best of All" Burnett explains that her childhood reading of Stowe's novel marked "an era in [her] existence." As we have already seen, Burnett describes enacting scenes from *Uncle Tom's Cabin*. Using a favorite doll, she keeps Eva "actively employed slowly fading away and dying." Burnett herself, however, was far more "actively employed" than Eva: her mother was horrified one day to see her small daughter red in the face, "apparently furious with insensate rage, muttering to herself" as she "brutally lashed" a doll she had tied to the candelabra stand.[54]

Burnett's account of violently recreating Stowe's narrative would have been unpublishable in the antebellum period, when it was generally assumed that little girls who read the book would take the virtuous Eva as a model. In the 1890s, by contrast, psychologists and educators suggested that children could imaginatively enter many roles, that it was good for them to do so, and that they would eventually settle on the appropriate ones. Thus it was possible in 1893—as it would not have been in 1852—for adult readers to find charm in Burnett's account of whipping her doll. The conviction that children outgrow such behavior gained welcome support from the fact that the girl who "brutally lashed" her doll had grown up to be a writer of such children's books as *The Secret Garden* and *Little Lord Fauntleroy*. Nonetheless, adults may also have been disquieted by the growing attention lavished on aggressive, impulsive, even savage aspects of early childhood. Drummond suggests that that children's "often ungovernable passions" and "destructive impulses" are "instinctive"; G. Stanley Hall emphasizes the "widespread animism if not fetishism of children and savages"; Freud suggests that there is such a thing as infantile sexuality.[55] Psychologists and educators insisted that reason, conscience, and social consciousness emerged only at puberty.

The popular Kate Wiggin and her sister Nora Archibald Smith reinforced the claims of psychologists and educators such as Hall by asserting that the moral sense in children develops late. Where antebellum texts for and about children could assume the presence of reason and moral consciousness in a three-year-old, educators of the 1890s criticized the morally precocious child.[56] In this context it is not surprising that the Eva of *Young Folks Uncle Tom's Cabin* bears no trace of the weighty moral and spiritual preoccupations that made her a teacher of adults as well as a sacrificial lamb in the antebellum period. According to Hall, "reason, true morality, religion, sympathy, love and esthetic enjoyment are but very slightly developed [in the years between 8 and 12]"—not to speak of earlier.[57] The Eva of *Young Folks Uncle Tom's Cabin* bears little relation to the figure Stowe created.

Children's books at the turn of the century are crowded with charming and affectionate white children who exemplify sweetness and goodness. Perhaps the representation of innocence in books designed for children and the general avoidance of complex and unpleasant childhood realities served as a kind of counterweight—for adults—to a growing uncertainty regarding what motivates children and how they should be educated, including what they should read. Overtly didactic models were no longer popular, but whether encouraging imitation or providing reassurance, many turn-of-the-century fictions for children share with *Young Folks Uncle Tom's Cabin* an image of white boys and girls effectively purged of all but the most fleeting negative or unruly impulses. The "savagery" so clearly set out by psychologists of the 1890s is rarely represented in children's books of the period.[58] Even the precious quality of absorption disappears—indeed, the opaque, thoughtful, sensitive child has become something to worry about—gestured at in such fiction for adults as "The Turn of the Screw," but rare in children's books. As Anne Macleod puts it, "reviewers warmed to cheerful unsophisticated fictional children without secrets."[59]

One additional aspect of turn-of-the-century child study deserves attention here: the assumption (shared by Freud, Hall, Baldwin, and Burnett, as well as by little Eva and Tom's other young master, George Shelby) that "everyone" has servants. This assumption shapes the young Burnett's delight when she hears the news that her family may be going to America ("The land of *Uncle Tom's Cabin*! Perhaps to see plantations and magnolias. To be attended by Aunt Chloe and Topsy!" [655]) as well as the caution, often expressed by commentators in passing, that many a child will pick up low habits from his or her "foreign nurse."[60] Concern with what and how children imitate, consistently central to theories of childhood, reinforced the anxiety about otherness that was heightened at the turn of the century both by racial tensions and by the rising tide of immigration that would lead to strict new entry quotas by the 1920s. The need to protect the white child from foreign influence repeatedly appears in the margins of child study.

The idea of the child, then, continued to be as much a source of anxiety as of hope. While the question of what children inherit, how they grow, and what this implied for pedagogy was debated in both popular and scientific contexts, books written for children, as MacLeod, Avery, Lurie, and others have emphasized, became ever milder and more careful to steer clear of conflicts and the dark side. In keeping with the lingering fear that a child might inexplicably imitate the wrong fictional model, children's books carefully framed mildly unacceptable behavior as temporary, and radically unacceptable behavior as beyond the pale. Both the insipid, complacent Eva and the incorrigible Topsy make sense in this context.

GENDER REALIGNMENTS: LITTLE GEORGE SHELBY IN THE SPOTLIGHT

In *Young Folks Uncle Tom's Cabin* the binary opposition suggested by Eva and Topsy is sharper than ever, their differences reinforced by racial theories that placed African Americans at an earlier stage of evolution than white children.[61] This narrative conveniently bolsters the notion that an African American child such as Topsy would not only retain traces of the primitive, but also would naturally want and need to sing and dance for others rather than feel and think for herself. Because Topsy was a girl, her antics were a particularly flagrant violation of white middle-class norms of behavior. Her ways were accounted for by her race and reinforced by her gender.

Gender binaries, like racial oppositions and age-marked categories, were increasingly rigid in children's books of this period, even as (or partly because) the "new woman" was emerging.[62] Unlike the antebellum *Pictures and Stories, Young Folks Uncle Tom's Cabin* begins with a focus on little George Shelby. He is presented as a smart and playful boy who undertakes the difficult task of teaching Uncle Tom to write (the difficulty is re-emphasized in the caption of the frontispiece: Tom scratches his head and stares, as if stymied by the marks on George's slate [fig. 38]. The caption reads, "That makes a 'q,' don't you know?"). George also runs the prayer meeting in Uncle Tom's Cabin, early in the story. This episode, taken from Stowe's novel, gains pride of place near the start of *Young Folks Uncle Tom's Cabin;* in its revised form it gives George Shelby far more authority than he has in either *Pictures and Stories* or in *Uncle Tom's Cabin* where, as Dawn Coleman has noted, Tom gains considerable moral weight as a lay preacher.[63]

George Shelby plays a minor role in antebellum children's editions. After the scene in which he parts from Uncle Tom, he is mostly forgotten until he appears, fully grown, toward the end of the story at Legree's plantation, just in time to bury Tom; he also makes a brief appearance at the end of the story as the "liberator" who frees the slaves on his old Kentucky home. But little George does not gain much sustained attention early in *Uncle Tom's Cabin,* and his role is still smaller in the antebellum *Pictures and Stories* where the primary emphasis is on little Harry, Eva, and Topsy, who provide action, pathos, and inner drama.

By contrast, *Young Folks Uncle Tom's Cabin* ends as well as begins with George Shelby and, in a unique addition to the text, little George gains additional attention in the middle of the book where he pens a letter to Uncle Tom which is given in full. This letter (which replaces the familiar and much illustrated antebellum episode in which Tom and Eva write to Chloe) elaborates the image of George, suggesting that he is at once boyish—unschooled in the ways of the world—and charmingly self-important, as well as loyal and noble. George is the ideal role model offered by the book, and the antithesis of the popular "bad" boys in fiction of the period. He is as much a figure without nuance as Eva, whose main qualities—she is pretty, good, and ill—ensure that she will take center stage only in death.[64]

George gains additional importance toward the end of *Young Folks Uncle Tom's Cabin* when he arrives at the Legree plantation in time to purchase Tom before he dies. The new finale, which brings Tom back to Kentucky alive, participates in the growing tendency to end children's books on the upbeat.[65] But this textual change also reflects the popular trend by which historical romances of the period emphasize the generous deeds of white masters and the gratefulness of slaves. A concluding chapter in which Ophelia, Topsy, and

"That makes a 'q,' don't you know?"

38. "That makes a 'q,' don't you know?" Frontispiece from Grace Duffie Boylan, Young Folks Uncle Tom's Cabin. *Chicago: Albert Whitman, 1942. Author's copy.*

the Harris family visit the Shelby plantation after the war emphasizes reconciliation between North and South. This chapter became a fixed feature of
Young Folks Uncle Tom's Cabin after 1901.[66]

YOUNG FOLKS UNCLE TOM'S CABIN
AS LIBERAL HUMANISM

I have been suggesting that in the Jim Crow period, Stowe's text was adapted
to support a secular, hierarchical, and racist status quo. *Young Folks Uncle
Tom's Cabin* offers a simplistic vision of white children and displaces the
unruly and "weird" onto Topsy. Still, when we compare this edition to other
children's books of the period, a somewhat more complex picture emerges.
Turn-of-the-century children's literature rarely included black characters.
Two notable exceptions, Uncle Remus and Little Black Sambo, only confirm
the idea of African Americans as comic figures, designed to amuse (and in
some sense produce) little white readers.[67] Seen in this context, *Young Folks
Uncle Tom's Cabin* performed some additional cultural work: even in its
watered down form it brought slavery to the attention of children who might
otherwise have known little about it—beyond the idea that an enlightened
America did away with it.[68] Although *Young Folks Uncle Tom's Cabin* does not
dwell on the pain of slavery, problematic aspects of the "peculiar institution"
are visible: the Fugitive Slave Law is specifically discussed (45); separated
families and endangered children remain central to the plot. Though neither
transaction is much elaborated, Harry is sold, Topsy bought.

   One final point is worth pausing over. From the early publication history
of *Uncle Tom's Cabin,* as is well known, the novel's ending was attacked, especially by black readers. Stowe's narrative does not project a future for freed
slaves within the United States. The black characters who survive at the end
of *Uncle Tom's Cabin*—Topsy, Eliza, George Harris—become missionaries
and leave for Africa. In Robert Stepto's words, Stowe "sends them packing."[69]
Young Folks Uncle Tom's Cabin makes a noteworthy textual change here:
Topsy and the freed slaves of the Shelby plantation (including, in this version,
Uncle Tom) remain in the United States. They remain as hired laborers or
domestic servants, but they are no longer slaves and their presence in America
appears as a matter of course.

In the final chapter, moreover, the narrator explains that George Harris, who has settled with his family in Canada, "occupied a position of trust and importance with a banking firm, and Harry had just been graduated with honors from Amherstburg, and had excellent prospects for a successful business career" (159).[70] George Harris asserts his love of liberty, recounts his escape in detail, exhibits his fighting spirit, and justifies his decision to use force in order to gain liberty. This material does not neutralize the image of Uncle Tom and Topsy as racial stereotypes, but it does draw attention to a wider range of black intellectual and moral experience than *Uncle Tom's Cabin* itself. Editorial changes, then, point in several directions.

Despite the racist details that pervade *Young Folks Uncle Tom's Cabin,* perhaps its frequent republication during the first five decades of the twentieth century reflects an incipient desire in the United States to address the role of slavery in the national past. Grace Duffie Boylan, author of *Young Folks Uncle Tom's Cabin,* also wrote other texts for children, many of them about distant or foreign "kids of many colors": Eskimos, Puerto Ricans, Cubans, and Filipinos.[71] The analogy between children and savages or "primitives," so prominent in the work of turn-of-the-century psychologists, pervaded political debates about annexation of the Philippines. In this context, the compound image of savage and child affirms the need for adult white governance. Boylan's tales remove this element. *Kids of Many Colors* projects a vision of sweet and innocent children from diverse parts of the world, emphasizing not only customs that are different from those of American children, but also potential common ground—food, fun, parental care.[72] It would be easy to trash this book for its Orientalism, its image of a South Africa without Africans, or its romanticizing of "North American Indians." But as a final point about *Kids of Many Colors* I want to note instead the book's inclusion of a black child in the illustration for the section on the "United States."[73] Three white and one black little boy appear lined up beneath a set of verses entitled "The Awkward Squad." The boys wear oddly assorted hats, carry broomsticks, and follow the lead of "brave lieutenant Teddy." The features of the boys, as well as their clothing, suggest ethnic origins, but all four are included in the game (fig. 39).

Liberal goals sometimes bear fruit despite inconsistent or fitful expression and imperfect action. To recognize these contradictions is to recognize the unevenness of social change.[74] When *Young Folks Uncle Tom's Cabin* was first

Now shoulder arms! Don't be so slow,
Just when I speak begin it.
Now Billee Stumbleheels, you pick
Your rifle up, this minute!

"Present arms, now, I guess that's next.
Right shoulder shift and carry!"
"I think we'll take the prize for drill,"
Said Color-sergeant Harry.

Then Teddy gave a fearful frown,
And raised his voice up higher,
And all the soldiers shook to hear:
"Now ready! aim, and fire!"

147

39. *"The Awkward Squad." From Grace Duffie Boylan,* Kids of Many Colors. *Chicago: Jamieson-Higgins, 1901. Author's copy.*

published, race relations were at a low point in the United States; lynching was common and segregation had become the law of the land. The book is a curious blend of racist assumptions and liberal ideals. Since the 1960s, adaptations of *Uncle Tom's Cabin* for children and serious children's books about slavery have proliferated.[75] Gauging the distance between *Uncle Tom's Cabin* and *Young Folks Uncle Tom's Cabin* can help us understand what Stowe's novel achieved in its own time. Gauging the distance between *Young Folks Uncle Tom's Cabin* and children's books about race in the United States today creates some perspective on race relations of the twentieth century—two steps forward, one and half steps back.

ADDENDA: CHILDREN READING

The "Editor's Preface" to the antebellum children's edition, *A Peep into Uncle Tom's Cabin,* suggests that "in its present form [the story] . . . cannot be placed into the hands of children."[76] Yet Stowe's own prefatory remarks to this edition ("Address from the Author . . . to the Children of England and America," positioned in the book before the Editor's "Preface") includes a version of her much-repeated claim that "Long before it was ever written down at all, it was told to a circle of children, and then, as fast as it was told to them, it was written down; and there was a great deal of laughing and crying among these children, you may be sure, and a great deal of hurrying that it might be got through with. So you see the story belongs to children very properly."[77]

By the beginning of the twentieth century, as we have noted, many people thought of *Uncle Tom's Cabin* as a children's book. In 1883, Caroline M. Hewins, influential head of the Hartford library and one of the first children's librarians in the United States, included the book on her relatively short list of recommended fiction for children.[78] By the 1890s Stowe was a widely revered icon, and one closely identified with children in the public mind.

A newspaper item of 1894 reports that "the members of Mrs. Myers' Wednesday 'current events' class" had a "genuine surprise" one day when Harriet Beecher Stowe was the topic under discussion: every child in the room received a card autographed by the author. The reporter notes with satisfaction the excitement that ensued when these cards were distributed.[79] Although the article does not cite any children directly, autographed cards may well have been exciting to boys and girls who had been primed to value Stowe. Two years later, on the occasion of Stowe's eighty-fifth birthday, a news article appeared with the headline: "85TH BIRTHDAY / Letters and Gifts to Mrs. Stowe / Many Were From Children."[80] This article reports the "noticeable fact" that Stowe received a "great number of letters . . . from children throughout the country. Each epistle told of the affection and esteem in which Mrs. Stowe is held by the little ones." The teacher of "Grammar School no. 40 in New York city" enclosed a letter about the "great affection" that the schoolchildren had for Stowe, and "appended to the letter were the signatures of fifty-nine of the little pupils." Writing to famous people was a popular practice in elementary education of the period.[81] But letters by children were also penned individually, and sometimes included a gift—such as a seashell with the inscription: "Harriet Beecher Stowe, 1811–1896" from a fourteen-year-old in Atlantic City, New Jersey. A letter from Tekomah, Nebraska, by another teenager, included the following "wonderful sentiment for a child of that age. . . : 'Jesus made such a civilization possible, The United States of America made such a woman as Harriett [*sic*] Beecher Stowe possible, and Harriett Beecher Stowe made such a work as "Uncle Tom's Cabin" possible.' "[82] Parents surely had a hand in framing many of the "wonderful sentiments" sent to Stowe by individual children. Yet the misspellings and the inscribed seashell suggest that some children took an active part in honoring the author.

The reading pleasure of children is particularly difficult to document and interpret; guidelines for reading are even less binding on children than on adults. But the idea of the child reader deserves attention despite the need to rely on intuition, inference, and other indirect interpretive tactics. Evidence of children's reading usefully deepens our sense of the gap between a "protocol of reading," and any particular reading experience. Children's responses are a healthy reminder that the only way to make valid generalizations about the impact of a book is to come at it from multiple angles.

It is possible and productive to speculate about why children found *Uncle Tom's Cabin* appealing because from the beginning children have been among the book's most enthusiastic readers. Children's editions tell us less about real children than about what adults want to convey to children, but they contain cultural information about the changing goals of children's literature and about new meanings that accrue to a book over time. Reissued by half a dozen publishers in Chicago, Philadelphia, Boston, and New York until 1956, *Young*

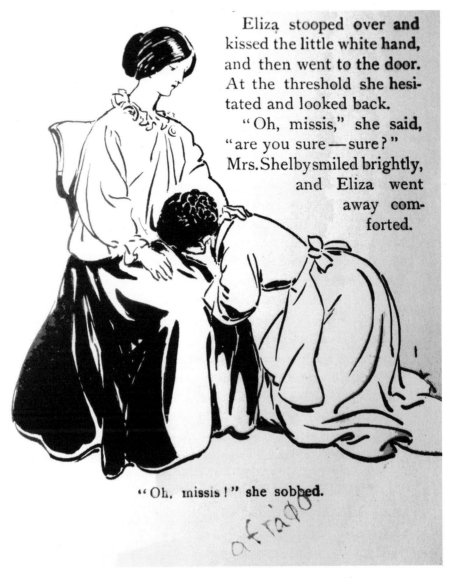

Eliza stooped over and kissed the little white hand, and then went to the door. At the threshold she hesitated and looked back.

"Oh, missis," she said, "are you sure — sure?" Mrs. Shelby smiled brightly, and Eliza went away comforted.

"Oh, missis!" she sobbed.

40. "afraid." Inscription in Grace Duffie Boylan, Young Folks Uncle Tom's Cabin. *Chicago: Albert Whitman, 1942. Author's copy.*

Folks Uncle Tom's Cabin was purchased for schools and public libraries across the United States—in the South and West as well as the Northeast.[83] It was inscribed by siblings to one another and by parents to children. It was much used—for math homework, penmanship practice, and just plain scribbles as well as for reading. A copy printed in 1942 was at one stage the property of

Macedonia High School in Texarkana, Texas. One man (Mr. P. B. Johnson) and two women (Lydia Agrava, Mrs. Vernia Agravia) of Dallas signed their names in the book. At least one child seems to have used it to practice addition, subtraction, and long division on the inside covers. The pages of this copy are mostly free of marks, but when Legree orders his slaves to whip Tom and adds that he would "take fifty dollars for his black carcass now," the words "fifty dollars" are underlined.[84] And beneath an illustration of Eliza weeping at the possibility of Harry being sold, someone has written "afraid"—and seems to have struggled with the spelling of the word (21) (fig. 40).

These traces of reading—or not reading—do not help us much in evaluating the impact of an edition. We cannot even know whether the child who used the covers to practice arithmetic was the one who stopped reading to underline the sum of money Legree would have taken for Tom; or whether it was that child who paused over Eliza's plight and wrote "afraid" in the margin. But the multiple well-worn copies of *Young Folks Uncle Tom's Cabin* still circulating in the United States, available on Ebay and elsewhere, suggest that many children continued to find Stowe's narrative compelling in the first half of the twentieth century, even in its revised form. Marginalia cannot tell us exactly what drew such readers to the tale, but it shows that a book was much used, and often used in ways not mandated by its "protocol." In my Epilogue I reflect upon traces of reading left by black readers between the 1890s and the middle of the twentieth century—the age of legalized segregation in the United States. Many black readers commented on *Uncle Tom's Cabin* in this period. These comments—long and short—reflect a particularly intense experience of Stowe's novel, a book that black readers often encountered in childhood and youth.

Devouring *Uncle Tom's Cabin*

Black Readers between Plessy vs. Ferguson *and* Brown vs. Board of Education

"There was something about that book. I couldn't understand it.
He just read it over and over and over again."

—*Emma Berdis Jones Baldwin (mother of James Baldwin)*

Throughout this study we have seen the complex interplay of personal and cultural history in shaping reader response, the pitfalls of taking readers' testimony at face value, the highly charged politics of literacy, and the frequent gaps between the public consensus and individual experiences of reading. I want to end this book by pursuing the unique meaning of *Uncle Tom's Cabin* for African Americans as the ongoing repercussions of the Civil War and the failure of Reconstruction were intensified by legalized segregation.

Over the last twenty years, with the burgeoning of reception studies, reading studies, and the history of the book, scholars have devoted serious attention to the way "underrepresented" and "understudied" groups have used books, newspapers, and periodicals to gain cultural competence and to understand their own position in society.[1] As this multifaceted project proceeds, historians of reading have become increasingly sensitive to the difficulties of finding evidence for "so elusive a practice as reading,"[2] and to the challenge of contextualizing and interpreting that evidence, especially when it is skimpy, eclectic, or outside the framework of published reviews and other institutional practices (e.g., schools, libraries, or book clubs). Elizabeth McHenry suggests that "new ways of looking at the multiple uses of literature" in African American communities will help us gain "a more accurate and historically informed understanding of a complex and differentiated population."[3] In this chapter I draw on the work of McHenry, Karla F. C. Holloway, and other historians of reading to disclose and clarify neglected aspects of the African

American reading experience—and changes in the meaning of *Uncle Tom's Cabin*.

Uncle Tom's Cabin was an extremely important book for African American readers in the years between the court decision *Plessy vs. Ferguson* (1896), which made segregation legal, and *Brown vs. Board of Education* (1954), which reversed that decision. In the intervening years, when many young African Americans were the children or grandchildren of ex-slaves, information about slavery was paradoxically scarce. In the public sphere, slave narratives "virtually disappeared from American cultural memory for over a century," as W. J. T. Mitchell notes.[4] Ex-slaves themselves, eager to move on, were reluctant to hand down stories of their experience to their children. In this context *Uncle Tom's Cabin* was an eye-opener for young black readers who were hungry for information about their family's past and about slavery in general. In 1944 when the Federal Writers' Project gave scholars access to ten thousand pages of interviews with former slaves, slave narratives started to be published again.[5] Soon the Civil Rights movement began. At this point the meaning and function of *Uncle Tom's Cabin* changed radically once more, at least for professional readers. James Baldwin's famous critique of Stowe, "Everybody's Protest Novel," published in *Partisan Review* in 1949, ushered in an era during which *Uncle Tom's Cabin* was either attacked or neglected. When (white) feminist scholars gave the book a new lease on life a generation later, Baldwin's attack remained a touchstone for black anger at Stowe, as if his critical understanding of her novel summed up the African American response. Yet other black readers, from the 1890s well into the 1940s, read *Uncle Tom's Cabin* differently. In fact, Baldwin's essay does not fully represent his own experience of reading Stowe's novel. As a child Baldwin read it "obsessively" and "compulsively" by his own account.[6] As an adult he revisited the book several times.

USING FICTION: *UNCLE TOM'S CABIN* ON THE BLACK READING LIST

From Frederick Douglass through Henry Louis Gates, African American writers have overwhelmingly affirmed the ideology of literacy; their autobiographies often become a space to foreground "faith in reading" among their credentials as full-fledged participants in the racialized literary culture of the

United States.[7] As Holloway has shown, black writers have regularly avoided "lengthy lists of black books" in autobiographical accounts of what they read.[8] Conversely, "white" classics play an important role in narratives that are often designed to demonstrate a black reader's discernment and sophistication. Although *Uncle Tom's Cabin* was widely regarded as a classic by the 1890s, it was a problematic choice for an African American booklist.

In the course of the nineteenth century, African Americans who celebrated higher literacy accepted and even intensified the governing cultural ambivalence about fiction in general. In the antebellum period, as McHenry shows, the black press consistently emphasized the "difference between a program of 'solid' reading and the informal, relaxed reading implied by the nature of fiction and other 'fanciful and imaginative' texts."[9] At least as far back as Frederick Douglass's *Narrative,* African American stories of reading tend to affirm the author's consumption of books for practical and intellectual rewards, not idle pleasures. Late nineteenth-century (white) commentators prioritized literary study, useful reading, and European classics; the African American community, plagued by the need to counter widely shared racialized assumptions about black laziness and intellectual inferiority, was particularly hesitant about legitimizing the imaginative pleasures and diversion offered by fiction. Although some black literary societies of the 1890s defended novel reading, provided that novels were chosen selectively and read discriminately, others insisted that literature was to be read for "refinement" rather than "amusement" or endorsed literature "that would help prepare African Americans to more fully address their racially and socially defined concerns" (McHenry, 169, 172–73, 229–38). Booker T. Washington makes a characteristic bid for both cultural superiority and social relevance when he claims, in *Up from Slavery* (1901), that he prefers newspapers or biography—i.e., "reality"—to fiction.[10] Kathryn Johnson, a black itinerant bookseller of the 1920s, included no fiction on her "two foot shelf." "My buyers don't want fiction," she explained in an interview with Mary White Ovington: "they look at such a book and say 'it's only a story,' and put it down. They want to spend their hard earnings for reality."[11]

Despite (and because of) the novel's growing popularity, resistance to fiction persisted among many educators, librarians, and other cultural arbiters. Nevertheless, by the last quarter of the nineteenth century, readers across the United States benefited from the increasing availability of fiction and its ongoing if uneven rise in cultural status.[12] African Americans participated in this process. Ida B. Wells assigns fiction an important role in her adolescent reading, as if a refuge from reality could be as significant as "refinement" or useful knowledge. "I could forget my troubles in no other way," she writes of the "long winter evenings" when, as a lonely teenager with a teaching job in Memphis, she read Dickens, Louisa May Alcott, Charlotte Bronte, and Oliver Optic.[13] From Wells through Marita Golden, black writers have read "white" fiction for diversion and escape. Growing up in Washington, D.C., in the 1950s, Golden found "comfort and salvation" in *Vanity Fair, Tom Jones, Oliver Twist,* Jane Austen, and Charlotte Bronte. "Books simply saved me," she writes.[14] For Golden, British fiction (like the private attic space in which she read it) provided a refuge from "the perplexities and strains of her family," as Holloway notes (*Bookmarks,* 22). But long novels about other times and places also offered Golden some escape from encroaching awareness of racial tensions in Washington ("scarred by Jim Crow laws") and perhaps from her father's "bitter, frightening tales of slavery" handed down via his "great-grandparents, from memories that refused to be mute."[15] Golden's book is dedicated to her father "who told me the stories that matter" and her "mother who taught me to remember them." At times, Fielding, Scott, Thackeray, and Dickens must have been a welcome alternative to those more pressing tales.

For a black writer to include *Uncle Tom's Cabin* on an autobiographical "booklist" was (and is) quite different not only from including canonized dramatists and poets such as Shakespeare, Dante, or Goethe but also from including novelists such as Fielding, Scott, or Dickens—not to speak of Sinclair Lewis or Theodore Dreiser.[16] A black writer citing *Uncle Tom's Cabin* between the 1890s and the 1950s was in an especially difficult position. For one thing, Stowe's status in literary culture declined as sentiment gave way to realism, then to modernism. For another, in Darryl Pinckney's words, "people wanted to put the years of strife behind them."[17] In addition, a black writer's affirmation of *Uncle Tom's Cabin* could be interpreted as a kind of toadying—paying homage to the "little lady who started the great war" while overlooking her racialized stereotypes. Still, *Uncle Tom's Cabin* appears on the booklists of many well-known African Americans in this period. It appears more than once in journals, autobiographies, and other writing by James Weldon Johnson, Ida B. Wells, Mary Church Terrell, James Baldwin, and others. Both the novel and a biography of Stowe, written by her son Charles, also appear on lists of books the black press recommends to "students of the Negro Problem and general readers. Your library will be incomplete without a selection from this up-to-date list."[18] Stowe is well represented in the book collection of William Carl Bolivar, African American bibliophile and community historian in Philadelphia who, until his death in 1914, devoted himself to documenting African American social and cultural history through acquisition of books, newspapers, and other printed materials.[19] In 1952 Dodd, Mead, and Company published an edition of *Uncle Tom's Cabin* with introductory remarks and captions by Langston Hughes.[20]

Many black readers were powerfully drawn to *Uncle Tom's Cabin* in the first half of the twentieth century. When Marion Wilson Starling wrote a Ph.D. thesis on "The Slave Narrative" at New York University in 1946, the topic of slavery was woefully neglected by scholars. For Starling, *Uncle Tom's Cabin* was a model of both literary value and social impact, inextricably intertwined with the history of slavery. Starling's dissertation, a project of historical reconstruction, was published in 1981 as *The Slave Narrative: Its Place in American History.* In an "Author's Prologue" she explains that her parents were upset by her work. Like angry black readers who wrote to Toni Morrison after *Song of Solomon* appeared, asking why she wrote about magic, incest, violence, and other matters that had nothing to do with them,[21] Starling's parents were embarrassed by the material she was bringing to light. Starling knew that her parents were uncomfortable with her research into the slave past and so she "kept her work from publication [for many years], though with an aching heart," out of "deference to [her] family."[22]

Starling's parents were also embarrassed by her grandfather, a former slave and living reminder of the world he came from. In her "Prologue" Starling emphasizes her respect for this grandfather and her fascination with the very stories that her parents did not want to hear. She recalls her grandfather's description of "the day when 'Master' had brought all the slaves together in the 'Big House,' and had told them that they were 'free.' In the pandemonium that followed, the little ten-year-old boy was pushed aside, and he was soon standing alone, not understanding what was going on. When he suddenly realized that the slave-holder was walking toward him yelling, 'You are FREE, I told you!' my grandfather jumped back in fright, and crashed into the large hall mirror behind him" (xxiii). This tiny narrative—so different from official homages to emancipation—dramatically captures some of the confusion, and incomprehension that accompanied the end of the slave era. Starling's research was designed precisely to peer beneath historical accounts that focus on the triumph of abolition and the "emancipation moment."[23] For Starling, *Uncle Tom's Cabin* has both historical and aesthetic significance. The figure of Stowe is a looming presence through her study. "A crusade is again in progress," she writes by way of conclusion, "this time for the purpose of emancipating humankind from the neurosis of racial prejudice. A Mrs. Stowe is again needed to fuse the Negro's story and the imaginings of wishful thinkers" (310).

In 1946, when Starling completed her Ph.D. thesis, segregation was a powerfully entrenched legal practice; its demise was difficult to imagine. The court decision *Brown vs. Board of Education* was eight years away and would be only the first significant sign of slow changes to come. Perhaps as a graduate student, Starling was under some pressure to celebrate Stowe. Yet Stowe's standing in U.S. print culture was particularly low in the 1940s. Jonathan Arac claims that the forties were the only time that *Uncle Tom's Cabin* was out of print.[24] Starling herself is often critical of Stowe. Discussing an article of 1849, written by the Reverend Ephraim Peabody ("probably the best essay that has been written on the 'Narratives of Fugitive Slaves'"), Starling adds: "Mrs. Stowe's guardian angel should have looked to the destruction of all copies of this [article] . . . upon the death of that gifted lady, for it is quite evident from her perfect silence concerning Peabody in her elaborate and 'complete' *Key to Uncle Tom's Cabin* that she intended to keep the secret of the influence of that article upon her" (Starling, 238). However, both Starling's criticism and her praise of Stowe reflect her belief in *Uncle Tom's Cabin* as an extremely important book. Other black readers of the period agreed.

Stowe's novel served important functions for young African Americans from approximately the 1890s into the 1950s—the very years when, as we have seen, young white readers grew indifferent. *Uncle Tom's Cabin* stirred intense mixed feelings in black readers in the age of segregation. The comments of African American readers of *Uncle Tom's Cabin* should not be taken as evidence of a monolithic "African American reading experience," but certain remarks recur often enough to suggest some typicality. Although most of the comments I analyze below are by writers and intellectuals, these readers possessed varying levels of education and sophistication when they first read the novel. Many were raised in working-class families. Starling's grandfather was a janitor; her father was organist of a tabernacle in Zion, Illinois. Her mother "dreamed" that her daughter would become a high school English teacher and "never forgave [her] for accepting a position on the faculty of Spelman College, the women's college of Atlanta University" (xxiii). James Weldon Johnson's father was a waiter; his mother a schoolteacher. James Baldwin's Harlem family was poor; his stepfather was a preacher. Starling, Johnson, Baldwin and others encountered Stowe's book well before becoming professionals, sometimes as far back as childhood. The tension between "high" and "low," as well as past and present, which informs the retrospective accounts I discuss, helps to clarify changes in the meaning of *Uncle Tom's Cabin* for black readers over time.

Readers' comments always trail behind the reading experience—they are produced when reading stops, as we have noted before. A gap between the time of reading and the time of reporting on it is inevitable in all written responses. When adults depict childhood reading, the gap is substantial and may well be a source of distortion. Yet by taking the contexts of reading and of writing into account we can learn a great deal from such comments—especially when diverse responses confirm one another, as they do in the case of the African American reader/writers in this chapter.

PERSONAL MOTIVATIONS: *UNCLE TOM'S CABIN* EXPLAINS THE PAST

There is good reason to suggest that many African Americans between the 1890s and the 1950s read *Uncle Tom's Cabin* with "feverish intensity," as did the narrator of James Weldon Johnson's 1912 fictionalized *Autobiography of an Ex-Colored Man.*[25] But in trying to understand what Stowe's novel meant to black readers in the wake of slavery and the Civil War we need to distinguish between two distinct grounds of Stowe's appeal. For some the book was a model to emulate, out of the desire to have an impact on social conditions. Black readers of this sort include Charles Chesnutt who found both professional inspiration and social relevance in *Uncle Tom's Cabin*. "Why could not a colored man . . . write a far better book about the South than Judge Tourgee or Mrs. Stowe has written?" Chesnutt asks in 1880, in a much cited passage of his journal.[26] Ida B. Wells praised Stowe's sense of mission in 1885 and accepted the idea, so popular among white commentators of the period, that *Uncle Tom's Cabin* was "one of the causes of the abolition of slavery."[27] Mary Church Terrell determined to write a novel that, like *Uncle Tom's Cabin,* would influence contemporary conditions.[28] But Stowe's novel often had a more personal meaning for African Americans as well. It provided a range of characters, events, and images that black readers could use to imagine black experience of the past and to clarify their own racialized position in the segregated United States. Some African Americans read Stowe's fiction for "reality" with a vengeance, absorbing it for knowledge of historical facts and attitudes that continued to affect the reader personally but that were not much discussed in public—or even in private.

Both Wells and Terrell were the children of ex-slaves who would not talk about the slave experience. Terrell's mother "never referred to that fact."[29] Wells's father rarely did either. "The only thing [Wells] remember[ed] about [her] father's reference to slave days" dates from one exceptional occasion when the subject triggered a sharp exchange between her father and grandmother. Hearing her father speak bitterly about whipping, starvation, and forgiveness, the young Wells "was burning to ask what he meant, but children were seen and not heard in those days. They didn't dare break into old folks' conversation."[30] As adults both Wells and Terrell affirmed the value of *Uncle Tom's Cabin.* Much earlier, however, an experience of engaged, often painful, and always deeply personal reading informed their understanding of Stowe's novel.

If Terrell's mother, like Wells's father, avoided talking about slavery in front of the children, this reticence was only one of many factors that prevented the young Terrell and Wells from learning about slavery as they grew up. In the last quarter of the nineteenth century black reluctance to dwell on the past privately joined white reluctance to do so publicly, creating a powerful wall of silence. By the time Wells got her first teaching job she had read Louisa May Alcott and Oliver Optic, as well as Shakespeare and the Bible, but she "had never read a Negro book or anything about Negroes."[31] The importance of this lack, shared by readers from Wells and Terrell to Malcolm X, cannot be overestimated.[32] *Uncle Tom's Cabin* sometimes helped black readers break a pattern of avoidance that was exacerbated by the fact that former slaves, like most whites in the dominant culture, were eager to separate themselves from the past.

Terrell's beloved grandmother on her mother's side "could tell the most thrilling stories imaginable," Terrell writes in her autobiography, "and I listened to her by the hour. I wish I had inherited her gift."[33] Sometimes Terrell's grandmother (unlike her parents) told stories about slave experience, "tales of brutality perpetrated upon slaves who belonged to cruel masters" (11). As a child, Terrell tried hard not to cry during such tellings because she knew that if she did her grandmother would stop talking. Nevertheless, the stories often "affected her and me so deeply she was rarely able to finish what she began. I tried to keep the tears back and the sobs suppressed, so that grandmother would carry the story to the bitter end, but I seldom succeeded. Then she would stop abruptly and refuse to go on, promising to finish it another time" (11). *Uncle Tom's Cabin* was no direct substitute for the repeatedly deferred story that Terrell's grandmother failed to complete. However, Stowe's novel makes many appearances in Terrell's work. Terrell was a particularly enthusiastic black reader of *Uncle Tom's Cabin;* she claims that "No author has ever done more with the pen for the cause of human liberty than [Stowe] did" (*Colored Woman,* 282). At the same time, Terrell's autobiography, written over fifty years after her childhood, repeatedly circles around the obliquely glimpsed, yet inaccessible story of slavery.

One of Terrell's chapters dwells on Stowe at length. As the centenary of Stowe's birth approached in 1911, Terrell "wrote a short *Appreciation of Harriet Beecher Stowe,* so that it might be available to as many as possible. It pained and shocked me to see how few, comparatively speaking, especially among young people, knew anything about the great service which has been rendered by Mrs. Stowe" (*Colored Woman,* 280). Terrell's *Appreciation,* a small pamphlet of 23 pages, draws on familiar sources of information about Stowe's life and her composition of *Uncle Tom's Cabin* (Stowe's introduction of 1879, Charles Stowe's biography of his mother [1889], Annie Fields's *Life and Letters of Harriet Beecher Stowe* [1897], etc.). These and other discussions of Stowe's life and work circulated widely through the United States at the turn of the century, in books, newspaper articles, magazines, and prefatory material for new editions of the novel.[34] Terrell's discussion includes several well-known vignettes: how the scene of Uncle Tom's death initially came to Stowe in a vision as she sat in church, how Stowe read the scene aloud to her boys, how Lincoln allegedly greeted her at the White House, and so on. However, in sharp contrast to other contemporary accounts, Terrell's *Appreciation* not only stresses the novel's historical significance, but also foregrounds the painful details of slavery.

By recalling the representation of "inhuman cruelty and legalized crime" in *Uncle Tom's Cabin,* Terrell challenges the dominant early twentieth-century interpretive convention that we have traced by which editors, illustrators, and commentators celebrated Stowe's achievement while diverting attention from the outrages of slavery.[35] Defying this unwritten norm, Terrell begins by detailing the genesis of *Uncle Tom's Cabin* in "the delicate woman['s] . . . horror . . . when she thought . . . [that] thousands of helpless men and women were even then being lashed and tortured and murdered under the very eyes of the church" (3). Terrell's pamphlet graphically suggests how intensely she herself read Stowe's novel. *Uncle Tom's Cabin* seems to have come as something of a revelation, approximating the story her grandmother could not or would not provide. "Who has not wept as he has stood at the deathbed of old Uncle Tom," Terrell writes:

> . . . How we have looked with horror upon the lifeless form of poor old Prue, who had been whipped to death, and . . . put down in the cellar, where the flies had got her. But, stand with Mrs. Stowe at the auction block, witness the agony of the mother torn from her child, see the despair of the wife, as she casts the last, long, lingering look upon the husband she will see no more on earth, hear the cries that are wrung from broken hearts crushed by the master hand without one pang of remorse, if you would feel this woman's power and *learn what slavery was.* (*Harriet Beecher Stowe,* 12–13; my emphasis)

Terrell's rehearsal of details from *Uncle Tom's Cabin* continues at some length ("how we blush with shame . . . when the beautiful, virtuous Emmeline is sold to the loathsome Legree, to be made a slave of the passions of this fiend in human form. With what a sigh of relief do we see the waters of the river close over the form of Lucy, whose husband had been sold and whose only child stolen, so that life was too bitter for her to bear . . ." [13]). Precisely such examples were routinely subject to cultural repression in the 1890s and the teens of the twentieth century. No wonder that, as Terrell explains in her autobiography, her pamphlet "did not sell enough . . . to pay for the expense of printing it." Terrell speculates that this failure was due to her "inexperience . . . in 'salesmanship' " (*Colored Woman,* 280). But the failure was also due to a deep cultural need—for amnesia and denial—shared (for different reasons) by black and white adults.

SLAVERY FROM A DISTANCE: INSIGHT BY ANALOGY

The theme of witnessing appears often in Terrell's writing. She figures the reading of *Uncle Tom's Cabin* itself as a kind of witnessing ("Who has not wept . . . at the deathbed of old Uncle Tom. . . . How we have looked with horror upon the lifeless form of poor old Prue. . . . witness the agony of the mother torn from her child. . ." etc.[12–13]). The act of witnessing is also central to an "important event" that, in Terrell's account, "changed the whole course of Harriet Beecher's life" as a young woman in Cincinnati (*Harriet Beecher Stowe*, 5). Terrell explains that when Stowe crossed "the river into Kentucky to make a visit on an estate . . . she caught the first glimpse of slavery, and became acquainted with the hardships of the slave" (*Harriet Beecher Stowe*, 5). Direct glimpses of slavery were denied to Terrell—as to all African Americans in the post–Civil War period. For first-generation free blacks, such as Terrell and Wells, or the children of free blacks who had not been slaves, such as Chesnutt or Johnson, the sense of slavery as so far and yet so near seems to have been especially harrowing. Perhaps partly for this reason Terrell accepts a familiar account of Stowe's motivation that has been much criticized by scholars who object to sentiment for demeaning and coercing its objects.

Terrell's *Appreciation* of Stowe cites a well-known story about the genesis of *Uncle Tom's Cabin* which suggests that at the "dying bed and . . . grave" of Stowe's baby she "learned what a poor slave mother may feel, when her child is torn away from her" (*Harriet Beecher Stowe*, 7).[36] Like Stowe's account of reading *Uncle Tom's Cabin* to her young sons (they cried and condemned slavery), her comments about the novel's origin exemplify the way benevolent reformers believed empathy could work, enabling one person to grasp the pain of another, even someone in a radically different cultural position.[37] Since the Stowe revival of the 1970s and '80s scholars have criticized *Uncle Tom's Cabin* for its attempt to depict the inaccessible experiences of American slaves. The novel is often charged with eliciting emotions that are self-indulgent, rather than politically effective. But Terrell accepts Stowe's model of insight by analogy and takes tears as a natural and legitimate response to *Uncle Tom's Cabin*.

Like Stowe and many of her white readers Terrell herself could learn about slavery only indirectly—through the medium of stories, by extrapolation from her parents' behavior and silences, and by analogy. When Terrell was four years old, a cat caught her mother's canary bird.

> A woman who worked for us decided to punish the animal, called some of her friends together for that purpose, and with their assistance beat it to death. I remember well how I fought and scratched and cried, trying to save the cat's life. When I found I could not do so I fled from the awful scene before it succumbed.
>
> As I look back upon that shocking exhibition of cruelty to animals, I can easily understand why those ignorant women were guilty of it. They had all been slaves and had undoubtedly seen men, women, and children unmercifully beaten by overseers for offenses of various kinds, and they were simply practicing upon an animal which had done wrong from their point of view the cruelty which had been perpetrated upon human beings over and over again. (*Colored Woman,* 13–14)

Writing of this scene as an adult, Terrell interprets the women's brutal behavior as a form of displacement. At the same time, this scene is among many directly witnessed by Terrell that came to constitute her understanding—by analogy—of "what slavery was" (*Harriet Beecher Stowe,* 13).

For Terrell the story of slavery is the story her grandmother could not/ would not tell, as well as the story she herself would have liked to tell. Terrell not only wished she had "inherited her [grandmother's] gift" for telling stories in general (*Colored Woman,* 10); she also had something specific in mind: she wanted to write an updated version of *Uncle Tom's Cabin,* "a novel showing the shackles by which colored people are bound today, though nominally free, as the original *Uncle Tom's Cabin* bared the cruelties perpetrated upon them, when they were legally enslaved." When she asked Ray Stannard Baker, one of the editors of the *American Magazine,* "if he thought that his or any other publication would accept a modern version of *Uncle Tom's Cabin,*" the answer was no (*Colored Woman,* 233). Terrell "discovered that there are few things more difficult than inducing an editor of the average magazine to publish an article on the Race Problem, unless it sets forth the point of view which is popularly and generally accepted" (*Colored Woman,* 224). Between the 1880s and the early years of the twentieth century, as we have seen, the figure of Uncle Tom was often adapted to romanticized and nostalgic evocations of black loyalty and devotion, images that deflected rather than represented the realities of race relations in the United States.[38] *Uncle Tom's Cabin* was rarely invoked or revised to expose ongoing injustice or black humiliation in this period.

Terrell was "bitter[ly] disappoint[ed] . . . that [she] did not succeed as a story writer." Unstinting in her praise of *Uncle Tom's Cabin,* she was convinced that "the Race Problem could be solved more swiftly and more surely through the instrumentality of the short story or novel than in any other way" (*Colored Woman,* 234). Stowe was the subject of one of Terrell's first public lectures, which "was truly a labor of love," as she writes in her autobiography; "I poured out my soul when I delivered it" (*Colored Woman,* 162). Terrell lectured about Stowe, wrote about her, appeared as the figure of Stowe in a historical pageant organized by W. E. B. Du Bois in 1913[39] and, drawing on her keen sense that black children lacked information about the past, planned to write a "Child's Life of Mrs. Stowe" (*Colored Woman,* 280). Like Charles Chesnutt at age nine in 1875, noting in his journal that he has read *Uncle Tom's Cabin* (but not for the first time), Terrell often returned to Stowe's book.[40]

Personal Motivations: *Uncle Tom's Cabin* Explains the Present

In his fictive *Autobiography of an Ex-Colored Man,* which was published a year after Terrell's *Appreciation* of Stowe, James Weldon Johnson includes an episode that centers on his reading of *Uncle Tom's Cabin:* Johnson's narrator/protagonist is drawn to, shattered, and "enlightened" by the book. Though *Autobiography of an Ex-Colored Man* is not a "real" autobiography, it deserves a place in my analysis for several reasons. The story of the "Ex-Colored Man" was first published anonymously and, while the identity of the author "gradually leaked out and spread," as Johnson explains in his own autobiography, his novel was authoritatively revealed to be fiction only when reissued in 1927 with Johnson as its avowed author. Both of Johnson's ploys—anonymity and fictionality—served important functions: they prevented the narrative from being read as a record of his own life. This double generic protection allowed Johnson to address highly controversial results of racialization—such as the desire to "pass"—without suggesting that his protagonist's despair, or solution, was his own.[41] The generic norms of fiction also enabled Johnson to stage an elaborate scene of reading *Uncle Tom's Cabin* within the story of a boy's coming-of-age, without presenting this incident as his personal experience.

The childhood and youth of Johnson's "ex-colored man" is shaped by the absence of a usable past. The son of a black Southern "sewing girl," seduced by her employer's son, Johnson's narrator grows up with no awareness of being different from white people—he learns that he is not "white" only when the principal visits his class and asks the white pupils to stand. When the boy gets up, the teacher quietly asks him to "sit down for the present" (11). The boy leaves school that day "in a kind of stupor" (11). Returning home he buries his face in his mother's lap, then looks up and blurts out, "Mother, mother, tell me, am I a nigger?" With tears in her eyes "she hid her face in my hair and said with difficulty: 'No, my darling you are not a nigger. . . .You are as good as anybody; if anyone calls you a nigger don't notice them.' But the more she talked the less was I reassured" (12). Only later—by reading *Uncle Tom's Cabin*—does the boy begin to understand his own and his mother's "position, and what was our exact relation to the world in general" (28). Neither history books nor newspapers give him "real information" or explain his own experience to him: "But one day I drew from the circulating library a book that cleared the whole mystery, a book that I read with the same feverish intensity with which I had read the old Bible stories, a book that gave me my first perspective of the life I was entering; that book was *Uncle Tom's Cabin*" (28).

Johnson's own early history was quite different from that of his narrator. Born in 1871, the son of two legally free, married African Americans, Johnson grew up in Florida. As an adult he was a racial activist and general secretary of the NAACP. While writing his novel, he was serving as U.S. consul to Venezuela. But in his autobiography, *Along This Way,* Johnson writes that "neither my father nor mother had taught me directly anything about race." Like other parents who felt one could not be far enough removed from slave origins, Johnson's father did not discuss the past: "I never heard him speak of his childhood and what lay back of and beyond it," Johnson recalls. Like his fictional protagonist Johnson himself took time to grasp the implications of being "black." It took "some years" beyond childhood before he understood "the brutal impact of race" and "how race prejudice permeated the whole American organism."[42] Johnson's representation of a young man's reading in

Autobiography of an Ex-Colored Man does not match his own experience with regard to biographical detail. Yet both the emotional tone and political implications of the fictional episode accord with and clarify the experience of reading *Uncle Tom's Cabin* for other (real) black Americans of the period. An editorial that Johnson published in the *New York Age* in 1915 suggests that he read *Uncle Tom's Cabin* in much the same spirit as the character in his novel.[43] In *Along This Way* Johnson equates *Uncle Tom's Cabin* with *The Souls of Black Folk* for its "effect upon and within the Negro race."[44]

In *Autobiography of an Ex-Colored Man* the adult narrator is well aware of the "unfavorable criticism" often leveled at Stowe (29), and he speculates as to whether or not Stowe's book can be taken as "truthful." But this question is not significant for him. "However that may be," he says, the book "opened my eyes as to who and what I was and what my country considered me" (29).[45] *Uncle Tom's Cabin* enables the boy to gain perspective on the formative realities of his situation. "One of the greatest benefits I derived from reading the book was that I could afterwards talk frankly with my mother on all the questions which had been vaguely troubling my mind. As a result, she was entirely freed from reserve" (29). She begins to explain "things directly touching her life and mine and . . . things which had come down to her through the 'old folks.' What she told me interested and even fascinated me . . ." (29–30). *Uncle Tom's Cabin* provides a language, concepts, images of the past and the present—"it gave me my bearing" (29). The boy's reading of Stowe's novel is a turning point in his life and helps him clarify his experience. His relation to race shifts again and again in the course of his narrative, but the insight he gains from reading Stowe remains a foundational moment and ultimately leads him to abandon his "race" altogether, passing into whiteness, and anonymity.

African American children were drawn to Stowe's novel by questions and doubts that were not urgent for white ones. Many white children read *Uncle Tom's Cabin* eagerly, after the war as in the antebellum years, but in both periods the source of their interest in the book was often different from that of black children.[46] In *A Mid-Century Child and Her Books* (1926) the (white) pioneer children's librarian Caroline Hewins singles out the look of Chloe's freshly baked cake, and the feel of Cassy's garret hiding place among her most important childhood memories. Hewins repeatedly includes Stowe's novel on her influential lists of recommended children's books, though she cautions that while the book is "always interesting to children, . . . [it] is sometimes too exciting for those of sensitive nerves."[47] Although Hewins worried about the impact of *Uncle Tom's Cabin* on "sensitive" (white) children, she probably could not have imagined the impact of Stowe's novel on such a child as Johnson's young narrator, or on Mary Terrell, who at the age of five was bewildered when a train conductor tried to send her to a "dirty" railway car even though, as she later explained to her mother, "my hands were clean and so was my face," and she was behaving "like a little lady." Later, although she "plied [her] father with questions" she could get "no satisfaction" from him: "he refused to talk about the affair and forbade me to do so" (*Colored Woman,* 16).

A brief autobiographical narrative written in the late 1920s or early 1930s by a young African American woman, probably born in the first decade of the century, forcefully exemplifies the function of *Uncle Tom's Cabin* for black readers during the era of widespread legal segregation in the United States. Everett Stonequist's *The Marginal Man* (1937) includes the "life history document" of a "negro girl" in a chapter-section titled "Racial Minorities: the United States."[48] According to this narrative, the girl was "born in New York" and raised in a Catholic orphanage by "loving sisters" among "fifty kids [of] all races except the Jew" (171–72). Like the narrator of Johnson's "ex-colored man" the girl had no racial consciousness as a child. "The word negro was never used by the father nor the sisters," she explains. "We were all children in their care. . . . Two years later a Southern white child was placed in our home by her divorced parents. This girl would call all the dark-skinned children 'niggers.' She was placed on bread and water several times for this act. She soon was broken of it. I never had any feelings when she said negro. Negro to me was only a word used by angry children" (172). However, when the girl finished grammar school she was sent to a Southern College for Negroes: "This is where my sorrows began" (172). At the college she was subjected to "speakers [who] would come and tell how different negroes were from whites" (172). In response, the girl begins to read "all the books I could get on negro life"—among them *Uncle Tom's Cabin* (173). "The more I read the more I brooded over just what was fit for the negro to do," she notes. With the help of her reading she forms clear and radical opinions about her obligations to herself and her race: "the negro must rise up and fight for his own. Pleading, begging and arguing will not solve the problem, only war can and must" (173). Her comments conclude with an expression of anger at the status quo and at the hypocritical ideology of the period: "If America is such a melting pot," she writes, "why can't she consider the negro as one of her finest products. The negro is not a by-product but a true product produced and raised on American soil" (173).

The girl's comments provide no details about her responses to *Uncle Tom's Cabin;* but Stowe's novel is among eight works she "brood[s] over." These works span a considerable gamut of approaches to race. They include *Hazel*—one of the earliest chapter books written for African American children, much advertised in W. E. B. Du Bois's paper, *The Crisis; Fire and Flint* (1924) and *Flight* (1926)—two tales of passing and racial violence by African American writer and activist Walter White; and *The Leopard's Spots* (1902)—Thomas Dixon's white-supremacist response to *Uncle Tom's Cabin*.[49] Placed in this company, Stowe's novel becomes part of the girl's personal experience and self-fashioning. It is one of the books that helps answer her question: "just what was fit for the negro to do."[50] This is exactly the question early black readers of Stowe's novel—such as Frederick Douglass and Martin Delany—asked themselves and argued about.[51]

African Americans rarely report crying over *Uncle Tom's Cabin,* but the book elicited reactions in some black readers that were as intense as the antebellum responses we have discussed.[52] In his well-known 1949 essay "Everybody's Protest Novel," Baldwin attacks Stowe—as a writer of sentiment, melodrama, and polemics. According to Henry Louis Gates, the terms of this critique suggest that in his account of Stowe Baldwin is really "talking about himself *as a novelist* speaking to his own deepest fears that *as a novelist* he was guilty of the same thing he disdained in Stowe" (my emphases).[53] *Uncle Tom's Cabin* has been a source of deep ambivalence for black readers; African American writers of the twentieth century have often indicted the book and tried to free themselves from its influence. As Hortense Spillers puts this: "Stowe, the writer, casts a long shadow, becomes an implacable act of precursor poetics that the latter-day black writer would both outdistance *and* 'forget.'"[54] However, before black authors can engage Stowe in dialogue by their writing, they have already done so in their reading. As Octavia Butler often notes, you cannot be a writer without being a reader first.[55]

Well before influentially pronouncing *Uncle Tom's Cabin* a "very bad novel,"[56] Baldwin read *Uncle Tom's Cabin* "over and over" as a child, immersed in it deeply enough to shut out the noise of young siblings for whom he was babysitting and who, as a result "probably suffered."[57] He first mentions his childhood reading of Stowe in the Preface to *Notes of a Native Son* (1955), six years after publication of the much-reprinted "Everybody's Protest Novel." Twenty years later, in *The Devil Finds Work*, Baldwin elaborates this account of his own childhood reading. Baldwin was not the child of ex-slaves (though his stepfather's mother had been one); nor was he long deprived of information about his racial past as were Ida B. Wells, James Weldon Johnson, or Stonequist's "negro girl." But the young Baldwin found himself repeatedly impelled to reread Stowe's tale. As his mother recalls in an interview, her son

> lived in books. He'd sit at a table with a child in one arm and a book in the other. The first book he ever read through was *Uncle Tom's Cabin*. I think it came to us from a friend. Jimmy was about eight. There was something about that book. I couldn't understand it. He just read it over and over and over again. I even hid it away up in a closet. But he rambled around and found it again. And, after that, I stopped hiding it.[58]

Baldwin's often-cited critique of *Uncle Tom's Cabin* had a powerful, negative impact on Stowe's standing in literary culture of the late 1940s and '50s. But in his own words, Baldwin had "lived with the people of *Uncle Tom's Cabin*" for a long time before attacking the book.[59]

In *The Devil Finds Work* Baldwin speaks of having "lived with the *people* of *Uncle Tom's Cabin*" (my emphasis)—not about living with its "characters." This sentence appears in a discussion of movies that Baldwin saw as a child; but in discussing movies he refers to the characters as "actors."[60] His point is, precisely, that when he was a child the characters of certain books were real to him, far more real than those of the big screen. "Intrigued, but not misled, by . . . Tom's forbearance before Simon Legree," Baldwin writes; ". . . I . . . believed in their situation, which I suspected, dreadfully, to have something to do with my own" (11). He says he had "no idea . . . what *Uncle Tom's Cabin* was really about, which was why I . . . [read it] so obsessively." But like James Weldon Johnson's "ex-colored man," or Stonequist's "negro girl," Baldwin knew the book "had something to tell me. [Reading it] was this particular child's way of circling around the question of what it meant to be a nigger" (10–11). Baldwin reemphasizes: "I had read *Uncle Tom's Cabin* compulsively. . . . I was trying to find out something, sensing something in the book of some immense import for me: which, however, I knew I did not really understand" (14). Tom "was not a hero for me," Baldwin writes, because "he would not take vengeance into his own hands" (18). Yet even as a child Baldwin understood that Tom was not the abjectly complicit slave he became in popular memory ("Tom allowed himself to be murdered for refusing to disclose the road taken by a runaway slave" [18]). Baldwin's experience of reading Stowe's novel was complex. He did not praise the novel but, like Mary Terrell, he repeatedly wrote about it. His 1949 critique gave a long-lasting impetus to the case against sentiment; but he was intensely aware that a book which could captivate him so powerfully in childhood would not be laid to rest with one essay.

READING READERS

If the gap between published testimony and the reading experience tells us anything, it is that many acts of reading remain unrecorded, or are revised in the telling. We must read between the lines. In her 1942 autobiography, *Dust Tracks on a Road,* Zora Neale Hurston describes a box of books sent to her by two "very white" ladies who visited her village school and were impressed by her reading aloud of the myth of Persephone in class. Hurston has something to say about books she did not like. "There were . . . thin books about this and that sweet and gentle little girl who gave up her heart to Christ and good works. Almost always they died from it, preaching as they passed. I was utterly indifferent to their deaths. . . . I didn't care how soon they rolled up their big, soulful, blue eyes and kicked the bucket."[61] *Uncle Tom's Cabin* was no "thin book," but Hurston's description of "this and that sweet and gentle little girl" who dies with Christ in mind fits little Eva to a T. It doesn't tell us how Hurston felt about Eva, but it gives us a pretty good idea of how she would have felt if she had read Stowe's novel as a child. (Hurston's letters confirm that she regarded the book with considerable anger; though it is not clear when she first encountered it.[62])

It has been my aim, throughout this study, to contextualize individual, sometimes fleeting, responses to *Uncle Tom's Cabin* so as to understand their wider cultural resonance. At the same time, I have tried not to flatten particular instances of reading by absorbing them too hastily into a master narrative of shared contexts and practices. Reader response is always intertwined with personal as well as cultural history, inflected by race, age, and other aspects of a reader's position in family, community, society at large. A delicate balance between analyzing individual and cultural experience is indispensable to a history of reading and one of the hardest things to get right. To understand reading as "creative appropriation" and individual agency can sometimes be to minimize the constraints on reading as a cultural practice within a social infrastructure. Yet to overemphasize the social leaves out not only the idiosyncratic or resisting reader but also the most private aspects of the reading experience.

More work is needed to add nuance to the narrative of reading in the nineteenth- and twentieth-century United States, especially among marginalized groups where evidence is particularly scarce. As we try to recover what the experience of reading has been for individuals as well as communities, insiders and outsiders, men, women, and children, upbeat narratives about the social benefits of literacy are tempting. Like many teachers and scholars of literature I certainly bought into that narrative as a child—and it has served me well, personally and professionally. But reading takes many forms and has many results, not all of them benign. Reading studies make the important move of introducing "the reader" into the narrative of how books matter in culture. But while this "reader" (unlike the implied or ideal reader) is a "real" historically specific figure, he or she by now tends to play a predictable role in a familiar script—making meaning and actively appropriating texts for personal, often transformational, ends. In this story, reading is always beneficial.

A comprehensive history of reading with concrete specificity as well as cultural validity requires careful attention to failed and quirky reading experiences as well as those that result in successful self-fashioning. "Creative appropriation" has become a byword of reading studies—but also its Achilles' heel. Comments about books that readers have hated can be especially revealing. A combination of interpretive strategies is indispensable to this project. We must listen to—and contextualize—not only diverse readers, but also the texts that they have read. The history of reading requires close textual analysis of everything that we count as evidence of the reading experience. My focus on multiple ways of responding to one book over time has been an attempt to add range, depth, and concreteness to the effort of historicizing reading.

In a 1962 essay that anticipated the return of *Uncle Tom's Cabin* to critical consciousness, Edmund Wilson reflects upon its steadily waning literary fortunes after the Civil War. Wilson claims that after the war the novel was available only as a used book until the Modern Library issued a new edition in 1948.[63] In fact, as we have seen, *Uncle Tom's Cabin* was available during the 1890s in both cheap reprints and expensive new editions, sometimes with freshly commissioned illustrations. But although *Uncle Tom's Cabin* remained in print during the postbellum period, changes in society and in literary culture transformed white adult responses to the novel. As Darryl Pinckney suggests, *Uncle Tom's Cabin* became "a book that . . . few read without good reason."[64] In the first half of the twentieth century, white readers no longer picked up the novel expecting to be absorbed and moved—emotionally, morally, or politically. However, in the age of segregation an increasingly literate portion of the reading public had plenty of "good reason" to read *Uncle Tom's Cabin*. Many African Americans did so, intensely, for more than a good cry.

In the first half of the twentieth century disempowered readers, especially young African Americans, most nearly fit the profile of Stowe's initial "intended readers"—readers with moral consciousness, gripped by social and racial concerns. During these years, *Uncle Tom's Cabin* spoke with peculiar force to a growing population of literate black Americans, keenly aware of their racialized place in society and seeking, often in vain, for information about the slave past of their own parents and grandparents.[65] By contrast, white readers of the period did not often read the book with either a personal or social sense of urgency—or with empathy. As June Howard writes, "empathy and sympathy have different politics at different moments, and at any given moment are likely to have mixed and complicated politics; they constitute specific, historical relationships."[66] By the start of the twentieth century *Uncle Tom's Cabin* left many white adults cold. But as the century wore on, a variety of new, unintended readers, particularly African Americans, "devoured" Stowe's novel with "feverish intensity," like James Weldon Johnson—or "over and over and over again," like the young James Baldwin at the kitchen table.

Notes

Introduction: The Afterlife of a Book

1. Harriet Beecher Stowe, *Uncle Tom's Cabin* (Penguin, 1987), 234–35. Further references to this edition are included in the text. This influential edition remains widely available.

2. Harriet Beecher Stowe, "Preface to the First Edition," lxxxiv. There is a vast literature on *Uncle Tom's Cabin,* sympathy, and sentimental conventions. The important accounts that revived interest in Stowe are Douglas, *The Feminization of American Culture,* and Tompkins, *Sensational Designs.* June Howard suggested in 2001 that it has been notoriously difficult to get beyond the influential terms of the Douglas-Tompkins debate regarding the valuable or damaging moral and cultural effects of sentiment (Howard, *Publishing the Family,* 215–16). Despite useful contributions to the discussion, the problem remains. Seminal analyses include Fisher, *Hard Facts;* Samuels, ed., *The Culture of Sentiment;* Dobson, "Reclaiming Sentimental Literature." Sentiment has been much critiqued as coercive of its objects, "a tool for the control of others" in the words of Laura Wexler, "Tender Violence: Literary Eavesdropping, Domestic Fiction, and Educational Reform" (15). See also Sanchez-Eppler, "Bodily Bonds: The Intersecting Rhetorics of Feminism and Abolition," in *Touching Liberty;* Hartman, *Scenes of Subjection.* For Lauren Berlant sentiment, like "compassionate liberalism is, at best, a kind of sandpaper on the surface of the racist monument whose structural and economic solidarity endures" (*The Female Complaint,* 6). A significant exception is Marianne Noble who, despite her critique, suggests that "the dangers of sympathy pale before the dangers of a lack of sympathy" (*The Masochistic Pleasures of Sentimental Literature,* 223, n. 11). For other complications of the idea that sentiment colonizes its objects, see Hendler, *Public Sentiments,* esp. 7–10; and Weinstein, *Family, Kinship, and Sympathy in Nineteenth-Century America.*

3. On the Southern response see Gossett, *Uncle Tom's Cabin and American Culture;* Starling, *The Slave Narrative,* 304–7; Weinstein, "*Uncle Tom's Cabin* and the South,"

39–57. On anti-Tom fiction see Lake, *Whitewashing Uncle Tom's Cabin.* For a sample of abolitionist responses see Wendell Phillips, *Speeches, Lectures and Letters,* 131–32; "The Literature of Slavery" (Unsigned), 591–92; Lydia Maria Child, *Lydia Maria Child: Selected Letters,* 264.

4. See Parfait, *A Publishing History of Uncle Tom's Cabin,* chap. 6; Winship, "The Greatest Book of Its Kind."

5. McPherson, *The Abolitionist Legacy,* 107–20. See also Fredrickson, *The Black Image in the White Mind;* Blight, *Civil War in American Memory;* Silber, *Romance of Reunion.*

6. See for example, Annie Fields, *Authors and Friends,* 181; "Days with Mrs. Stowe," 148; Williams, "Reminiscences of the Life of Harriet Beecher Stowe and Her Family," 128.

7. Silber, *The Romance of Reunion.*

8. Logan, *Betrayal of the Negro,* 62. On race relations in the 1890s see also Fredrickson, *The Black Image in the White Mind;* Woodward, *The Strange Career of Jim Crow;* McPherson, *The Abolitionist Legacy.*

9. All the pages in this book are blank on one side. This may have been because of the size of the woodblock illustrations, which would have bled through to the wrong side of the page if printed in the traditional way. (I am grateful to Georgia B. Barnhill, Director of the Center for Historic American Visual Culture at the American Antiquarian Society for this clarification!) The inscribed pages of *Little Eva: Flower of the South* are the backs of pages 3 and 4.

10. Frow, "Afterlife: Texts as Usage," 15. Efforts to reconstruct the reading experience of children include psychoanalytic approaches such as Bettleheim's classic account of fairy-tales, *The Uses of Enchantment;* Spitz's *Inside Picture Books* and *The Brightening Glance.* See also the work of other psychologists and educators (e.g., Applebee, *The Child's Concept of Story* [1978]; Bartlett, *Remembering: A Study in Experimental and Social Psychology* [1932]; Blackford, *Out of This World: Why Literature Matters to Girls* [2004]; Pitcher and Prelinger, *Children Tell Stories: An Analysis of Fantasy* [1963]) and retrospectives in the form of what Seth Lerer calls "Biblio-autobiography," such as Spufford's *The Child That Books Built* (2003) or Dorris and Buchwald's *The Most Wonderful Books: Writers on Discovering the Pleasures of Reading* (Lerer, "Epilogue: Falling Asleep Over the History of the Book," 230). Cobb's *The Ecology of Childhood* includes a bibliography of biographies and autobiographies focused on childhood. Historians and literary scholars of American culture have also drawn attention to children as readers and writers; see Crain, "Spectral Literacy: The Child in the Margin"; Sanchez-Eppler, "Doors onto Childhood." See also Sanchez-Eppler's account of children's diary writing, especially their appropriation of and resistance to interpretive conventions and expectations in *Dependent States,* chap. 1.

11. Walter Ong offers useful remarks on the "addressee" of a diary in Ong, "The Writer's Audience Is Always a Fiction."

12. See Sanchez-Eppler, *Dependent States,* 30; Zboray and Zboray, *Everyday Ideas,* 5–16.

13. Frow, "Afterlife: Texts as Usage," 15.

14. See Benjamin, "The Task of the Translator."

15. For exceptions, see Brown, "Reading and Children"; Robbins, *Managing Literacy, Mothering America;* Gail Smith, "Reading with the Other."

16. As Barbara Sicherman, Janice Radway, and others have shown, many people continued to read "intensively" at the end of the nineteenth century and beyond. On "women's intense engagement with books" in the Progressive era, see Sicherman, "Sense and Sensibility: A Case Study of Women's Reading in Late-Victorian America," 202 and passim; on twentieth-century romance-readers, see Radway, *Reading the Romance.* As we shall see, some readers read *Uncle Tom's Cabin* intensively well after the Civil War—though others did not.

    On the idea of a "reading revolution" see Darnton, "First Steps toward a History of Reading"; Hall, "Uses of Literacy in New England: 1600–1850"; Gilmore, *Reading Becomes a Necessity of Life;* Wittmann, "Was There a Reading Revolution at the End of the Eighteenth Century?"; Casper, "Antebellum Reading Prescribed and Described"; Gross, "Reading for an Extensive Republic"; Zboray, *A Fictive People.*

17. On the publishing history and reception of *Uncle Tom's Cabin* see Gossett, *Uncle Tom's Cabin and American Culture;* Parfait, *The Publishing History of Uncle Tom's Cabin, 1852–2002;* Winship, "'The Greatest Book of Its Kind': A Publishing History of 'Uncle Tom's Cabin.'"

18. Among many influential efforts to put "the reader" at the theoretical center of interpretation see Holland, *Nine Readers Reading;* Iser, *The Act of Reading;* Iser, *The Implied Reader;* Poulet, "Criticism and the Experience of Interiority." Useful collections of reader-response theory include Suleiman and Crosman, eds., *The Reader in the Text,* and Tompkins, ed., *Reader-Response Criticism.* In *The Return of the Reader,* Elizabeth Freund provides a concise rundown of theories that emerged in the 1970s and '80s. In the '90s "the reader" was gradually rescued from the position of an abstract textual function and repositioned in historical context. See Davidson, *Reading in America;* Harris, *Nineteenth-Century American Women's Novels;* Machor, ed., *Readers in History;* Raven, Small, and Tadmor, eds., *The Practice and Representation of Reading in England.* Recent efforts to conceptualize the reader take an increasing number of complications into account—race, class, gender, and region. See Kelley, *Learning to Stand and Speak;* Sicherman, "Reading *Little Women*"; Ryan and Thomas, eds., *Reading Acts,* 137–60; Pawley, *Reading on the Middle Border;* Schweickart and Flynn, eds., *Reading Sites;* Badia and Phegley, eds., *Reading Women;* Rubin, *Songs of Ourselves.* For a range of interdisciplinary approaches, see Goldstein and Machor, *New Directions in American Reception Study.*

19. Mailloux, "Misreading as a Historical Act," 4. On reader roles inscribed in the text see Iser, *The Implied Reader,* and Ong, "The Writer's Audience Is Always a Fiction." On "the horizon of expectations"—generic norms that shape readers' responses—see Jauss, *Toward an Aesthetic of Reception.*

20. While interest in the "common" reader has quickened, the term itself has fallen out of favor because it suggests condescension. Jonathan Rose uses the term "non-professional" reader for "readers who did not read or write for a living" (Rose, "Rereading the English Common Reader," 51). Discussions of the 1970s and '80s that pay attention

to individual readers are generally concerned with live contemporary readers—not readers of the past. See for example Holland, *Nine Readers Reading;* Radway, *Reading the Romance;* Steig, *Stories of Reading.*

21. Jameson, *The Political Unconscious,* 9.

22. The 2007 National Endowment for the Arts report on American reading habits triggered numerous responses, including a nation-wide drive to increase reading in schools. As Leah Price notes, the NEA report "identifies who reads as the best predictor of who exercises, plays sports, volunteers, votes and stays out of jail" ("You Are What You Read," 19). In 2008, an article with the headline "Using Video Games as Bait to Hook Readers" appeared on the front page of the *New York Times* (Rich, "Using Video Games"). The article explores whether video games "stimulate reading," or put an end to it. The piece is the second in a series on "The Future of Reading" which "look[s] at how the Internet and other technological and social forces are changing the way people read" (A 19). Such questions are at issue in the NEA report as well as responses to it in the press. For an analysis of surveys that attempt to assess changes in reading as a leisure activity, see Salter and Brook, "Are We Becoming an Aliterate Society?"

23. Buell, "The Rise and 'Fall' of the Great American Novel." Cathy Davidson and Nina Baym suggest that the novel was a well-established genre at mid-century. See Davidson, *Revolution and the Word;* Baym, *Novels, Readers, and Reviewers,* especially chap. 2 ("The Triumph of the Novel"). As I argue below, however, the novel continued to suffer from what Harold Bloom calls "belatedness," even in the first half of the twentieth century. On the ongoing resistance to fiction see Radway, *A Feeling for Books;* Dee Garrison notes that "there were still locked-away collections" in public libraries as late as 1922, despite "a widespread acceptance of mass reading demands" (*Apostles of Culture,* 100, 271 n. 66). Other useful accounts of the novel in the American context include Brodhead, *Cultures of Letters;* Rubin, *The Making of Middlebrow Culture.* See also Barbara Hochman, "Readers and Reading Groups."

24. Darnton, *The Kiss of Lamourette,* 159.

25. On the problem of interpreting such "watersheds," see chaps. 1 and 2 in Kaestle, *Literacy in the United States,* especially pp. 7, 47–54.

26. See De Certeau, *The Practice of Everyday Life,* chap. XII, "Reading as Poaching."

27. Chartier, "Texts, Printings, Readings," 156.

28. Warner, "Uncle Tom's Cabin Half a Century Later," 487.

29. Goethe's "The Sorrows of Young Werther" (1774) and Rousseau's *La Nouvelle Heloise* (1767) are possible analogues.

30. Many complete editions can be accessed online at Stephen Railton's website "Uncle Tom's Cabin and American Culture," www.iath.virginia.edu/utc/

31. Chartier, "Texts, Printings, Readings," 162–63; Darnton, *Kiss of Lamourette* 181.

32. Rhodes, *History of the United States,* 278–79.

33. "Never but once before," Rhodes claims, "had a novel produced such an excitement. One cannot fail to be struck with the likeness between the impression occasioned by Rousseau's story [*Nouvelle Heloise*] and that made by 'Uncle Tom'" (282). "The bright

boys of France, who in their youth read the 'Nouvelle Heloise' and 'Emile' became revolutionists in 1789, and the youth of America whose first ideas on slavery were formed by reading 'Uncle Tom's Cabin' were ready to vote with the party whose existence was based on opposition to an extension of the great evil" (*History of the United States*, 285).

34. Darnton, *The Great Cat Massacre and Other Episodes in French Cultural History*, chap. 6.

35. On Delany's response to Stowe and his conflict on the subject with Frederick Douglass see Levine, *Martin Delany, Frederick Douglass, and the Politics of Representative Identity;* McHenry, *Forgotten Readers*, 127–28.

36. Parfait, *The Publishing History of Uncle Tom's Cabin*, 184.

37. I borrow the phrase "unintended readers" from Laura Wexler, "Tender Violence." On marginalized readers see especially Chapter 5 and Chapter 8.

38. Stowe's description appears in her Introduction to the 1879 edition of the novel (Houghton), reprinted by Houghton Mifflin several times (Houghton Mifflin, 1896, xxxv). Later versions include Charles E Stowe, *The Life of Harriet Beecher Stowe Compiled from Her Letters and Journals*, 148–49; Sarah K. Bolton, *Lives of Girls Who Became Famous*, 11; Thomas Wentworth Higginson's "Introduction" to an edition of *Uncle Tom's Cabin* (Appleton, 1898), iv. More recent discussions of Stowe sometimes mention the vignette as well. See for example Roth, "The Mind of a Child," 99. E. Bruce Kirkham examines the contradictions among several versions of the story in *The Building of Uncle Tom's Cabin*, 72–75.

39. In one well-publicized incident, a man who allegedly hears sobbing behind a hotel-room wall bangs on the partition and asks whether someone is ill or "reading *Uncle Tom's Cabin*." Cited in Noble, *The Masochistic Pleasures of Sentimental Literature*, 143. Noble cites other weeping and agitated male readers of *Uncle Tom's Cabin* as well. See also Gossett, *Uncle Tom's Cabin and American Culture*, 165–67. On the *Uncle Tom's Cabin* handkerchief see Bernstein, *Racial Innocence*.

40. Elizabeth Stuart Phelps's account of her girlhood classmate appears in the chapter on "Mrs Stowe" in Phelps's collection *Chapters from a Life*, 135. It was reprinted in *McClure's Magazine*, 4. Evangelical abolitionists often referred to slavery as "accursed"; the term appears as well in another much-cited vignette about the Stowe family and the genesis of *Uncle Tom's Cabin*. Stowe's sister-in-law reportedly wrote to Stowe, "If I could use a pen as you can . . . I would write something that would make this whole nation feel what an accursed thing slavery is"; when Stowe came to this passage she "rose from her chair, crushing the letter in her hand, and with an expression on her face that stamped itself on the mind of her child, said: 'I will write something. I will if I live'" ("Biographical Sketch," *Uncle Tom's Cabin* [Houghton, Mifflin, 1896], xxii). See also Hedrick, *Harriet Beecher Stowe: A Life*, 207.

41. On the book's appeal for children and young people see also Chapters 4 and 7.

42. "I thought I was a thorough-going Abolitionist before," Stowe's friend Georgiana May writes after finishing the book late one night, "but . . . I seem never to have had *any* feeling on this subject till now." An introduction that Stowe wrote for a new edition of

Uncle Tom's Cabin in 1879 printed May's letter alongside comments by more famous readers (e.g., Lord Carlisle, Charles Kingsley, Jenny Lind, George Sand) who make "feeling" the handmaiden of abolitionist convictions, moral or spiritual benefits, and action. ("Introduction" to *Uncle Tom's Cabin* [Boston: Houghton Mifflin, 1893; c. 1879] xxxviii). May's letter has often been cited. See Noble, *Masochistic Pleasures of Sentimental Literature,* 141; Gossett, *Uncle Tom's Cabin and American Culture,* 167.

Stowe's introduction, reprinted for decades, understandably showcases letters that endorse her political and moral messages. By contrast, antebellum advertisements, reviews, and some readers note the thrilling and humorous aspects of the book as well. "Much of [*Uncle Tom's Cabin*] . . . is very amusing," Sarah Barker Tufts Wheaton writes in a letter to Francis Henshaw Dewey, May 3, 1852 (Dewey-Bliss Family Papers Box 2, Folder 8; American Antiquarian Society). Charles Cobb, a New England farm worker, read *Uncle Tom's Cabin* along with "The Pirate," *Don Quixote,* and other novels that happened to come to hand (Zboray and Zboray, *Everyday Ideas,* 185).

43. Joan Hedrick begins her biography of Stowe by citing Abraham Lincoln's alleged words on meeting "the little lady" (Hedrick, *Harriet Beecher Stowe,* vii). Noble describes *Uncle Tom's Cabin* as "an undisputably important political novel" (*The Masochistic Pleasures of Sentimental Literature,* 126). According to Tompkins, "*Uncle Tom's Cabin* convinced a nation to go to war and free its slaves" (*Sensational Designs,* 41).

44. Zboray and Zboray, *Everyday Ideas,* 249.

45. Stowe, "Introduction" to *Uncle Tom's Cabin* (xxxviii).

46. Gillian Brown, "Reading and Children," 77–78. Georgiana May acknowledges a disjunction between the "storm of feeling" she experienced while reading, and any political action she might take. "What can we do?" she writes, echoing Stowe's well-known "Concluding Remarks." "Alas! Alas! What can we do?" (141). As George Ticknor put it in 1852, "It deepens the horror of servitude but it does not affect a single vote" (cited in Rhodes, *History of the United States,* 284). Scholars who question the link between tears and political action include Douglas, *Feminization of American Culture;* Fisher, *Hard Facts;* Trubey, "'Success Is Sympathy': *Uncle Tom's Cabin* and the Woman Reader."

47. Berlant, *Female Complaint,* 40–41.

48. See for example Harriet Beecher Stowe, "Literary Epidemics," 1 and 2; Harriet Beecher Stowe, *House and Home Papers,* 326–27. Catharine E. Beecher and Harriet Beecher Stowe. *Principles of Domestic Science,* 255.

49. Hendler, *Public Sentiments,* 2. Discussing the purpose of sentiment for Hannah More, Gillian Silverman writes: "it elicits and reinforces self-control while simultaneously creating benevolence and community" (Silverman, "Sympathy and Its Vicissitudes," 9).

50. Since the Stowe revival of the 1970s and '80s, discussions of Stowe's imperative to "feel right" have emphasized the first word in the phrase—emotion, sentiment, sympathy. These words have taken on connotations of free-floating and excessive emotion, connotations that were not central to their meaning in 1852. As June Howard notes, the (official) goal of reading in the eighteenth and early nineteenth century was the cultivation of "improving, morally legitimizing emotions" (*Publishing the Family,* 225). In Glenn

Hendler's terms, for Stowe to "feel right" was to have *proper* sentiments, an *appropriate* response to the scenes of suffering and redemption that the reader . . . witnesse[s]" (*Public Sentiments* 3; my emphases). Silverman suggests that the "perfect 'union' in which there is no differentiation between subjects constitutes the threat of sympathy for Stowe. . . . Eva's death [can be seen in part as] a cautionary lesson on the dangers of feeling too much, or of overidentification" ("Sympathy and Its Vicissitudes," 19). But while Stowe surely embraced the idea of properly measured and appropriate responses, her novel elicited emotions that were constrained by propriety only up to a point. A text may *ask* readers to respond in a certain way; it cannot ensure that they do so.

51. On antebellum readers see especially Chapter 3 and Chapter 4. On Southern readers see also Jordan-Lake, *Whitewashing Uncle Tom's Cabin;* Weinstein, "Uncle Tom's Cabin and the South."

52. Antebellum readers who experienced discomfort with the depth of their absorption in *Uncle Tom's Cabin* often wrote about it afterwards, thus distancing themselves from the emotional upheaval caused by reading. In letters and diaries they confess their self-indulgence and neglect of mature responsibility, draw properly moral conclusions, and come back to "reality." Psychoanalyst Leon Balter analyzes "the aesthetic illusion" in a way that helps explain this dynamic. Balter argues that the "aesthetic illusion" produced when a reader becomes engrossed in a narrative can be understood as "a particular form of day dreaming" which involves a certain "abrogation of reality testing. However, as with all aspects of daydreaming, it must take place in a voluntary, controlled, circumscribed and reversible manner, in accordance with the ultimate goals and aims of mature, reality-oriented ego functioning. Else, there will be no aesthetic illusion—indeed, no aesthetic experience at all—and instead an involuntary, massive, regressive overthrow of mature ego functioning, corresponding to the involuntary mental regressions that occur in dreaming, in some group or religious phenomena, and in severe psychopathological states" ("On the Aesthetic Illusion," 1320). While the absorption in someone else's "daydream" yields "emotional-instinctual gratification" (1329), the reader "must be able to conclude, if and when it is necessary to do so, 'This is not *my* daydream! It is the *artist's*!'" (1320). In Balter's account, the "aesthetic process" has two stages: "one concerns the initiation of the . . . process; the other its completion." "One is pleasure-oriented; the other is defensive" (1330). For antebellum readers, unaccustomed to giving themselves over to fiction, the retrospective recasting of the reading experience in moral terms was indispensable for averting excessive guilt about the pleasure and excitement stirred by reading *Uncle Tom's Cabin.* See Chapter 3.

53. Cited in Zboray and Zboray, *Everyday Ideas,* 249.

54. Letter from Maria Woodbury to Miss Lucy Marshall of Holden, Mass., probably June 4, 1852. Marshall Family Papers; American Antiquarian Society. Maria Woodbury was a cousin of Lucy Marshall, living in Westfield, N.Y., at the time of this letter.

55. Wheaton, *The Diary of Ellen Birdseye Wheaton.*

56. On the isolated fiction-reader see also Hunter, "The Loneliness of the Long-Distance Reader"; Watt, *The Rise of the Novel,* 88–92; Iser, *Act of Reading,* 140. Recent correctives to the idea of the "solitary" reader emphasize the social contexts of reading. See

Chartier on the "sociability of reading [as a] fundamental counterpoint to the privatization of the act of reading" ("Texts, Printings, Readings," 158); Long on the "social infrastructure of reading" ("Textual Interpretation as Collective Action," 191); Sicherman on the Victorian "culture of reading" ("Reading and Middle-Class Identity in Victorian America," 206 and passim); Schweickart and Flynn, *Reading Sites*. Zboray and Zboray emphasize the social context and function of reading throughout *Everyday Ideas*.

57. Walter Benjamin, "The Storyteller," 100.

58. Catharine E. Beecher and Harriet Beecher Stowe, *Principles of Domestic Science,* 255.

59. This imagery has persisted and been put to multiple uses both in the academy and the popular press. Berlant indicts "the pleasure of being morally elevated by consumption. . . . the moral work of entertainment culture is to encounter the scene of national trauma and to have the right feelings about what is wrong in it, so that the light, frothy remains of the violent history can be consumed as a meringue, a dessert made of air and sugar and just a few broken eggs" (*Female Complaint,* 54). For a critique of the metaphor as used to discount popular literature, see Radway, "Reading Is Not Eating." David M. Stewart analyzes the function of the metaphor in relation to nineteenth-century crime fiction as well as the reading and eating habits of antebellum working men ("Consuming George Thompson."). On the trope of reading as eating in relation to emerging views of adolescence in late nineteenth-century America, see Mailloux, "The Rhetorical Use and Abuse of Fiction"; Glazener, *Reading for Realism,* esp. chap. 3. On the use of this trope by librarians in the 1870s and '80s see Ross, "Metaphors of Reading," 149.

60. In one typical formulation, William Alcott urges young men not "merely [to] devour books—swallow them whole—[but to]. . . 'read, mark, learn and digest'" (*Familiar Letters to Young Men,* 76). Zboray and Zboray emphasize antebellum concerns about "reading with attention"—with "time to read and reread, if necessary, 'digest' and ponder" (*Everyday Ideas,* 170, 178). In 1880 A. K. Fiske typically called the popularity of British and French fiction an "appetite—taste it cannot be called—which craves a stimulant for passion" in his article "Profligacy in Fiction: Zola's 'Nana.' Ouida's 'Moths,'" cited in Ouida, *Moths,* 554. On the educational values associated with reading in the antebellum period, see Casper, "Antebellum Reading Prescribed and Described"; Robbins, *Managing Literacy, Mothering America,* 116–56; Stewart, "Cultural Work, City Crime, Reading, Pleasure," esp. 687, 691–92. On the disciplinary discourse of reading later in the nineteenth century see Mailloux, "Rhetorical Uses."

61. As Gossett notes. "Southern reviewers often complained that it was unjust to expect them to . . . comment on incidents which had not really happened. . . . William Gilmore Simms, himself a novelist, . . . extensively developed the argument that it was unfair to use a novel as a vehicle of social criticism" (*Uncle Tom's Cabin and American Culture,* 195).

62. Woodbury letter, Marshall Family Papers, (probably June 4, 1852). Readers often echo reviews and ads as well as the novel itself. One review (or puff) of *Uncle Tom's Cabin*

in the *National Era* on April 15, 1852, notes that "The paper mills are constantly at work, manufacturing the paper, and three power presses are working twenty-four hours a day, in printing it . . . still it has been impossible as yet to supply the demand . . ." (62). In her letter to Francis Henshaw Dewey I, May 3, 1852, Sarah Wheaton reproduces the widely circulated image of the printing press and paper mills unable to meet the demand (Dewey-Bliss Family Papers). This image is repeated as well in the review "Literature of Slavery." Taking one's cue from an ad or other commentary and citing an image directly is somewhat different, however, from transmuting Stowe's imagery for other ends—i.e., readers imagining themselves as "bound captives" or Stowe's book as a dying child, etc. The first kind of citing simply echoes the point and uses it with the same emphasis as the original; the second kind recasts the initial image and suggests a more thorough imaginative or emotional reworking.

63. Phillips, *Speeches, Lectures and Letters,* 131. Further references to Phillips are included in the text.

64. Phillips compares the success of *Uncle Tom's Cabin* with the relative failure of Richard Hildreth's *Archy Moore* (a "book of eminent ability" but "a work born out of due time"). *Archie Moore* gained recognition only when revised and reissued, after the success of *Uncle Tom's Cabin.* As Sarah Meer notes, *The Narrative of the Life of Frederick Douglass* took five years of promotion to sell 30,000 copies in the 1840s (*Uncle Tom Mania,* 4). On *Archy Moore* see Chapter 2.

65. See especially Berlant, *Female Complaint;* Douglas, *Feminization of American Culture;* Sanchez-Eppler, *Touching Liberty;* Samuels, "Identity of Slavery"; Wexler, "Tender Violence"; Keen, *Empathy and the Novel.*

66. Fisher, *Hard Facts,* 104–7; Ryan, *Grammar of Good Intentions,* 150.

67. Keen, *Empathy,* 4, 11.

68. As Keen notes, "significant components of what psychologists today call empathy appear under the label of sympathy in the works of eighteenth-century philosophers David Hume and Adam Smith" (xxii).

69. See Kohut, "Introspection, Empathy and Psychoanalysis." I am grateful to Leon Balter for his help in clarifying these distinctions.

70. For Berlant both the "great promise" and the "radical threat" of sentiment—the "affective aesthetic"—is precisely "the possibility that through the identification with alterity you will never be the same" (*Female Complaint,* 47). However, Berlant minimizes the threat of destabilization that I want to stress.

71. Ryan, *The Grammar of Good Intentions,* 19. Hendler, *Public Sentiments,* 5, 7.

72. On Harper and Stowe see Hendler, *Public Sentiments,* 7–8. On "the insufficiency of sympathy" and the "disruption of sympathy" in Harper's poem, see also Dana Luciano, *Arranging Grief: Sacred Time and the Body in Nineteenth-Century America,* 188, 192. On Delany's objections to Stowe, see Levine, *Politics of Representative Identity.*

73. "All through my duties this morning it haunts me," May writes. Cited in Stowe, "Introduction" to *Uncle Tom's Cabin* (Houghton Mifflin, 1896), xxxviii.

74. One of the earliest attacks on Stowe's colonizationist sentiments toward the end of the novel appears in a review published in Garrison's *Liberator* on March 26, 1852. For

another early assertion that *Uncle Tom's Cabin* is "distinctively a Colonization book" see "Literature of Slavery," 594.

75. Risman, "Strategies for Interviewing Kids about Inequality." See also Bonilla-Silva, *Racism without Racists.*

76. The classic account of "romantic racialism" is Fredrickson, *The Black Image in the White Mind.*

77. See ibid.; Levander, *Cradle of Liberty;* Riss, "Racial Essentialism and Family Values in *Uncle Tom's Cabin*"; Tawil, *The Making of Racial Sentiment.*

78. For Stowe's letter to Bailey outlining her plan see Parfait, *A Publishing History of Uncle Tom's Cabin* (20). On Stowe's negotiation with Bailey in the course of serialization see Parfait, *Publishing History of Uncle Tom's Cabin,* 21–31. For other aspects of *Uncle Tom's Cabin* as a serial see Susan Belasco Smith, "Serialization and the Nature of *Uncle Tom's Cabin.*" Margaret Beetham addresses the dynamic of reading a novel in serial form in "Toward a Theory of the Periodical as a Publishing Genre." See also Chapter 1.

79. As one introduction of the period puts this: *Uncle Tom's Cabin* "can be read today with as deep enjoyment of its thrilling story and as absorbing interest in its exciting subject, as in the days when all the world went wild over the sorrows of Uncle Tom and wept at the death of the saint-like Eva" (Harriet Beecher Stowe, *Uncle Tom's Cabin: Art Memorial Edition*), 10.

80. "Introduction," Harriet Beecher Stowe, *Uncle Tom's Cabin* (Eaton and Mains, 1897), xvii.

81. Knight, *Connecticut Women at the World's Columbian Exposition,* 24–25, 100. See also McCray, *The Life-Work of the Author of Uncle Tom's Cabin,* 100, 118. On turn-of-the-century guidelines for reading see Chapters 5, 6, and 7.

82. Fredrickson, *Black Image in the White Mind,* 273.

83. On *Plessy vs. Ferguson,* see Logan, *Betrayal of the Negro;* Painter, *Standing at Armageddon;* Woodward, *The Strange Career of Jim Crow.*

84. On intensified racism in stage representations of Topsy at the end of the nineteenth century, see Gossett, *Uncle Tom's Cabin and American Culture,* 380; Lott, *Love and Theft,* 221. In an edition of 1952, issued by Dodd, Mead and Company, Langston Hughes makes the following point: "In the book Topsy is humorous, but human, and was played so by Caroline Fox Howard, wife of the drama's first producer. But gradually the stage character degenerated into a comedy 'wench' typified by New York's Topsy, Queenie Smith, in the Players' Club's 1944 production with Otis Skinner as Uncle Tom" (144).

85. I discuss these changes in detail in Chapters 6 and 7.

86. James Lane Allen, "Mrs. Stowe's 'Uncle Tom' at Home in Kentucky," 866.

87. "Introduction," Stowe, *Uncle Tom's Cabin* (Eaton and Mains, 1897), vii.

88. Frances Hodgson Burnett, "The One I Knew Best of All: A Memory of the Mind of a Child," *Scribner's* 13.1 (January 1893): 76. Retrospective accounts often remake the initial experience, but memories of reading are personally significant and published statements such as Burnett's also reflect interpretive norms at the time of writing:

"One wept all through 'Uncle Tom's Cabin' because [the slaves] had not their freedom, and were sold away from their wives and children, and beaten and hunted with bloodhounds, but the swarms of them singing and speaking negro dialect on the plantations, were such a picturesque and lovable feature of the story . . ." ("The One I Knew Best of All: A Memory of the Mind of a Child" *Scribner's* 13.4 [April 1893]: 653). On Burnett and her doll see also Chapter 7 and Bernstein, *Racial Innocence*.

89. Frank Norris, "The Novel with a Purpose," 92. In 1853, John Ross Dix, a British commentator, made a similar point: "it is a live book, and it talks to its readers as if it were alive. It . . . creates such an interest in the story it is telling that they cannot let it drop until the whole story is told. And this is done not because it is a tale of slavery but in spite of it" (*Transatlantic Tracings*, 75).

90. James Lane Allen, "Mrs. Stowe's 'Uncle Tom' at Home in Kentucky," 861.

91. Belasco Smith, "Serialization and the Nature of *Uncle Tom's Cabin*," 69. Jane Tompkins agrees: *Uncle Tom's Cabin* "has come to be thought more fit for children than for adults" (*Sensational Designs*, xii). Ask educated middle-aged adults all over the world today whether they have read *Uncle Tom's Cabin*, and you are very likely to hear they read the book as children.

92. Cited in Brodhead, *Cultures of Letters*, 106.

93. Cited in Gossett, *Uncle Tom's Cabin and American Culture*, 345.

94. This is not to say that every child is more susceptible to fantasy than every adult; but generally speaking there are dramatic differences between what children and adults take away from a story. On the propensity of young children to enter a fictional world more readily than adults, often blurring the line between reality and fiction, see especially Applebee, *The Child's Concept of Story;* Bettleheim, *The Uses of Enchantment;* Blackford, *Out of this World;* Kris, *Psychoanalytic Explorations in Art;* Spitz, *Inside Picture Books;* Spufford, *The Child That Books Built.* See also Chapter 4.

95. Writing about developments in the field of translation, Andre A. Lefevre notes that the "source text" is no longer given a privileged status, above the "target text" and that the translated text "belongs primarily to the target rather than the source culture." As Lefevre notes, the study of translation has come to include the "historically undeniable role of translations in the development of cultures" (*Encyclopedia of Literary Translation,* 1416). See also Benjamin, "The Task of the Translator."

96. According to the reception aesthetics of Hans Robert Jauss, a popular success is created when a work fulfills—rather than disturbs—generic expectations. Since Jauss seeks a way to differentiate major from minor works, popularity is at odds with "greatness." The great work disrupts convention, while the popular one merely fulfills it; I argue that *Uncle Tom's Cabin* both fulfilled and disrupted interpretive norms.

97. See Lott, *Love and Theft;* Meer, *Uncle Tom Mania;* Morgan, *Uncle Tom's Cabin as Visual Culture;* Reid, "Racial Profiling"; Williams, *Playing the Race Card;* Wood, *Blind Memory.*

98. See especially Berlant, *Female Complaint;* Lott, *Love and Theft;* Meer, *Uncle Tom Mania;* Williams, *Playing the Race Card.*

99. Sonstegard, "Artistic Liberty and Slave Imagery," 507.

100. Michael T. Gilmore notes that Stowe renders Eliza's escape on the ice in "a single paragraph" ("*Uncle Tom's Cabin* and the American Renaissance," 62); but he goes on to analyze Stowe's language and writes, "Brief as it is, the moment is indelible. . . . Stowe's contemporaries . . . so relished the episode that they insisted on seeing it regularly reproduced on stage for the next half century" (63). It was Stowe's text that first mesmerized readers—something that readers in an electronic age often find hard to fathom.

101. James's inimitably dense prose seems to have obscured the fact that he did indeed read the book (*before* seeing the play) and that his comments are all about the reading experience. The whole passage is well worth unpacking, but it is enough here to cite the following, with a few cuts in the interest of brevity: "We lived and moved at that time, with great intensity, in Mrs. Stowe's novel, which—. . . I should perhaps substitute for *The Initials* earlier mentioned here, as my first experiment with grown-up fiction. There was . . . for that triumphant work no classified condition; it was for no sort of reader as distinct from any other sort, save indeed for Northern as differing from Southern. . . ." The "leaping fish" formulation comes a bit later, but the comment that "for an immense number of people [*Uncle Tom's Cabin*] was less a book than a state of vision, of feeling and consciousness" is precisely James's tribute to the impact of Stowe's novel as a printed object which transports readers into another mode of seeing and being (James, *A Small Boy and Others*, 167–68).

1. *Uncle Tom's Cabin* in the *National Era*

1. For discussions that address the serialization of *Uncle Tom's Cabin* see Kirkham, *The Building of Uncle Tom's Cabin*, 61–149; Belasco Smith, "Serialization and the Nature of *Uncle Tom's Cabin*"; Winship, "The Greatest Book of Its Kind"; Parfait, *The Publishing History of Uncle Tom's Cabin*.

2. See especially Ryan, *The Grammar of Good Intentions*, 17, 19; Hendler, *Public Sentiments*, 5.

3. Cited in Reynolds, *Uncle Tom's Cabin and Mid-Nineteenth-Century United States*, 76.

4. Victor Shklovsky, "Art as Technique." The term "defamiliarization" is commonly used in English to represent Shklovsky's Russian expression. It appears in Lemon and Reis, *Russian Formalist Criticism*.

5. Andrews, *To Tell a Free Story*, 184.

6. A review of *Uncle Tom's Cabin* in the London *Times* praises Stowe for "not preach[ing such] a sermon" (Stowe, *Uncle Tom's Cabin*, ed. Elizabeth Ammons, 478). In Stowe's "Introductory Essay" to her brother's narrative *The Incarnation*, she addresses the problem of those who "are desirous of reading the Bible" for spiritual inspiration but who fail to take fire from the too-familiar words and "rise from [the attempt] sighing and discouraged" (Stowe, "Introductory Essay," iv). See also Hochman, "Introduction" to Harriet Beecher Stowe's "Introductory Essay" for Charles Beecher's *The Incarnation*.

7. Even works of fiction that are "written for mere amusement" can be harmful for some people, especially those "with quick and active imaginations," Stowe and her sister write in *The American Woman's Home,*" (p. 218). Throughout the 1840s, Stowe considered the pros and cons of fictional modes from Bulwer to Dickens. See especially Harriet Beecher Stowe, "Literary Epidemics," 1 and 2. "Works of the imagination," Catharine Beecher writes in her "Preface" to Stowe's *The Mayflower or Sketches of Scenes and Characters Among the Descendents of the Pilgrims, "might* be made the most powerful of all human agencies in promoting virtue and religion and yet, through perversion they are often the channel for purveying the most pernicious poisons. And the most dangerous part of these evils is their insidious and unmarked operation. The havoc they often make in tastes, feelings, principles and habits is ordinarily as unnoticed as the invisible miasma, whose presence is never realized until pale cheeks and decaying forms tell of its fatal power." Beecher's "Preface" to *The Mayflower* echoes some of her remarks about novel-reading from her popular domestic manual *A Treatise on Domestic Economy for the Use of Young Ladies at Home and at School* (1841). She and Stowe repeat these remarks, often verbatim, in a variety of forms including, almost thirty years later, in *The American Woman's Home*. Stowe endorses them as well in her *House and Home Papers*, first published serially in the *Atlantic Monthly* under the pseudonym Christopher Crowfield.

8. Charles E. Stowe, *The Life of Harriet Beecher Stowe Compiled From Her Letters and Journals,* 9; Isabella Beecher Hooker, *A Brief Sketch of the Life of Harriet Beecher Stowe By Her Sister,* 9. Annie Fields cites Stowe directly: "Such a thing as a novel was not to be found in our house. And I well recollect the despairing and hungry glances with which I used to search through father's library, meeting only the same grim sentinels. . . . Then there was a side-closet full of documents, a weltering ocean of pamphlets, in which I dug and toiled for hours to be repaid by disinterring a delicious morsel of a 'Don Quixote' that had once been a book. . . ." Fields, ed., *Life and Letters of Mrs. Stowe,* 36–37. See also Hedrick, *Harriet Beecher Stowe,* 18.

9. On Norcross see my Introduction, and Chapter 3.

10. Hedrick, *Harriet Beecher Stowe,* 14–16.

11. Charles E. Stowe, *The Life of Harriet Beecher Stowe,* 8.

12. Buell, "Harriet Beecher Stowe and the Dream of the Great American Novel," 190.

13. Cited in Camfield, "The Moral Aesthetics of Sentimentality," 330. See also Charles E. Stowe, *The Life of Harriet Beecher Stowe,* 44.

14. Hedrick, *Harriet Beecher Stowe,* 19, 20.

15. "I am reading Scott's historic novels in their order. To-night I finish the 'Abbot;' shall begin 'Kenilworth' next week; yet I am constantly pursued and haunted by the idea that I don't do anything," Stowe wrote in a letter to her sister-in-law, on Dec. 17, 1850 (cited in Charles Stowe, *The Life of Harriet Beecher Stowe,* 139). See also Hedrick, *Harriet Beecher Stowe,* 198.

16. Harriet Beecher Stowe, "Literary Epidemics 1," 235.

17. Harriet Beecher Stowe, "Introductory Essay" for Charles Beecher, *The Incarnation* (iv, viii). Further references to this edition are included in the text.

18. Beecher, "The Strange Woman," 180. Further references to this edition are included in the text.

19. Indeed Beecher knew the *Mysteries of Paris* well enough to offer a detailed analysis of its characters—Madame Lucenay's "unblushing adultery," "the diabolical voluptuousness of Cecily," the "assignations of the *pure* Madame D'Harville," and the lies of Rodolphe ("The best character in the far-famed Mysteries of Paris") (214). As David Stewart points out: "Beecher's ability to spellbind audiences with violent accounts of vice and crime made him one of the most sought after reformers of his day" ("Cultural Work, City Crime, Reading, Pleasure," 691). Hedrick notes that Stowe had heard Byron read in her childhood (20) and contemplated writing a "condemnatory article" devoted to Sue (165). For Stowe on Byron and Bulwer see also "Literary Epidemics 1&2."

20. Buell, "Harriet Beecher Stowe and the Dream of the Great American Novel," 191.

21. In a letter to Dickens in 1852 Stowe writes that "there is a moral bearing" in Dickens's work "that far outweighs the amusement of a passing hour" and expresses the hope that she may "do only something like the same" (Stowe, "Introduction," *Uncle Tom's Cabin* [1896], xli). In 1870 she still suggests that works "which are written for mere amusement" even when they have no "bad moral influence" will be dangerous for some readers. She proposes that "some men should keep a supervision of the current literature of the day, as guardians to warn others of danger." But these men are to "use every precaution to prevent injury to themselves; having as little to do with pernicious exposure as a benevolent regard to others will allow.... There is much danger, in taking this course, that men will seek the excitement of the imagination for the mere pleasure it affords, under the plea of preparing to serve the public. . . ." Beecher and Stowe, *Principles of Domestic Science,* 255.

22. David Reynolds explores the balance between subversive and conventional elements in *Uncle Tom's Cabin.* Reynolds's emphasis on the "dark" undercurrents in Stowe's novel has been overshadowed by the critical preoccupation with sentiment. See *Beneath the American Renaissance.* On some of the "transgressive pleasures" of reading *Uncle Tom's Cabin* see Noble, *The Masochistic Pleasures of Sentimental Literature,* 141–43. See also Chapters 3 and 4.

23. Stowe uses the phrase "new eyes" in her pamphlet *Earthly Care: A Heavenly Discipline* in order to emphasize the difficulty of both perceiving and representing God's involvement in everyday life (p. 14).

24. On the balance of fiction and news in antebellum newspapers, see Zboray, *A Fictive People,* 126–29. On the penny press see Mott, *American Journalism,* and Schudson, *Discovering the News,* 12–60. For a succinct discussion of the difference between the "story papers" and the "penny press" see Denning, *Mechanic Accents,* 10–11. Ann Douglass argues that in the 1840s and '50s the religious press tried to compete with popular women's magazines by a judicious use of fiction "designed to precipitate religious sensibility" (*The Feminization of American Culture,* 234). On the role of periodicals in antebellum literary culture see Lehuu, *Carnival on the Page,* and the "Introduction" to Belasco Smith and Price, *Periodical Literature in Nineteenth-Century America.*

25. The closest thing to an exception in the year before *Uncle Tom's Cabin* began is Stowe's

own "The Freeman's Dream," which appeared in the *Era* on August 1, 1850, 121. This brief "parable" engages the problem of fugitive slaves in a fictionalized form. But its brevity, combined with the dream-motif and "parable" aspect, makes it quite different from *Uncle Tom's Cabin*. E.D.E.N. Southworth's *Retribution,* serialized in 1849, attempted to address the subject of slavery but, as Lyde Cullen Sizer notes, Southworth represented slaves "only marginally" (as well as reductively). See *The Political Work of Northern American Women Writers and the Civil War,* 52–54.

26. Gamaliel Bailey, "Our Annual Letter," loose sheet inserted into the *National Era,* November 13, 1851.

27. As Gillian Brown suggests, *Uncle Tom's Cabin* represents the family not as a refuge from but as an index to contemporary economic and political issues. See "Domestic Politics in *Uncle Tom's Cabin*" in Brown, *Domestic Individualism,* 13–37.

28. "The Poor Boy," an exhortatory piece, presents the typical moral found in fiction about "the poor": "Don't be ashamed, my lad, if you have a patch on your elbow. It's no mark of disgrace. . . . No good boy will shun you, because you cannot dress as well as your companion; and if a bad boy sometimes laughs at your appearance say nothing, my lad, but walk on. . . . Be good my boy; and if you are poor you will be respected a great deal more than if you were the son of a rich man and were addicted to bad habits" (151).

29. In "Ill-Starred" by Patty Lee, for example, a well-matched pair of good-for-nothings die in poverty and disgrace. "Ill-starred" was serialized in the *Era* between July 17 and October 9, 1851. Lee was a frequent contributor to the *Era*. See also "Be Patient" by Mary Irving, 205.

30. The only example I have found of a fleeting reference to slavery in the fiction that shared the pages of the *Era* with *Uncle Tom's Cabin* is in the following lines from "Ill-starred": "Mrs. Bates said she . . . had come to say something that would have been very much to Mr. Claverel's advantage, and that she would rather be to the advantage of a black slave than to the disadvantage, but that if he was not of a mind to have an advantage. . . ." (Sept. 25, 1851, 153).

31. H. B. Stowe, "Earthly Care: A Heavenly Discipline," 60. Stowe's pamphlet was frequently reprinted over the next 19 years.

32. Mary Irving, "Be Patient," 205.

33. Obituary of Mary Osgood (*Era,* 1851), 110; obituary of Isabella Rose (*Era,* 1851), 123. "Death loves a shining mark" says the narrator of "Light and Shade," by Patty Lee, which appeared on the same page as installment six of *Uncle Tom's Cabin* (July 10, 1851) 109.

34. "Guard Thy Trust," a poem by "Meta" (137); Kavenaugh, "The Lost Child," 98. As a typical poem puts it: "Oh she was choicer, sweeter far / My lovely fragrant rose / More beautiful, beyond compare / Than thy broad garden knows" ("Meta," "Guard Thy Trust," 137).

35. Kavenaugh, "The Lost Child," 98 (cf. the "smitten bud" in "Thoughts at a Grave" a poem by "Constance," 153). Alice Carey, "Annie Clayville," 94. In "Bessie" by Phoebe Carey, she is "hushed away from mortal pain" (183).

36. On the shifting norms of mourning in antebellum America see Douglas, *Feminization;* Halttunen, *Confidence Men and Painted Women,* 125–52; Kete, *Sentimental Collaboration;* Luciano, *Arranging Grief.* On middle-class mourning as a bastion of the home see Sanchez-Eppler, *Dependent States,* 107.

37. As one characteristic poem puts it, "[i]mmortal youth crowns him who 'died young'" (Caroline Chesebro, "Finis," 141); or, in the final stanza of another, "Oh! many a blossom, blighted / Drooping on Earth's cold sod, / Transplanted blooms in beauteous life, / In the Paradise of God" (Kavenaugh, "The Lost Child," 98). Cf. "She blooms in brighter bowers" ("Constance," "Thoughts at a Grave," 153).

38. Children's obituaries provide additional emphasis, as do multiple ads for products that claim to cure bronchitis, consumption, and other "diseases of the lungs." Such ads, which sometimes appeared in the same column as obituaries, often included testimonials from patients, "statistics" stating (for example) that "one sixth of the whole population die annually of consumption" or reminders of the danger in neglecting even "a slight cough" (advertisement for "Wistar's Balsam of Wild Cherry," [June 5, 1851], 91; advertisement for "Wistar's Balsam of Wild Cherry," [Jan. 31, 1851], 123). A large, two-sided advertisement, inserted into the pages of *The Liberator* (Feb. 1, 1850) provides "Evidences Showing the Cures Effected in a Great Variety of Cases and in almost every form of Pulminary Disease by the use of Ayer's Cherry Pectoral" (n.p.). News items on the subject were common as well. See for example "New Cure for Consumption," 188.

39. Douglas, Fisher, and others have argued that Eva's death achieves nothing, but at the level of the plot her death has a profound effect on Ophelia, who sets Topsy free as a result. Eva's death also begins to work spiritual changes with practical implications in St. Clare.

40. On reading conventions typical of antebellum fiction-readers see Baym, *Novels, Readers, and Reviewers;* Machor, "Fiction and Informed Reading in Early Nineteenth-Century America." For an influential theoretical discussion of interpretive communities see Fish, *Is There a Text in This Class?: The Authority of Interpretive Communities,* especially the title essay, "Is There a Text in This Class?" (303–21).

41. Fisher, *Hard Facts,* 103, 106–7; Brodhead, *Cultures of Letters,* 35; Vrettos, *Somatic Fictions,* 99–101. Stowe gives Eva the symptoms of consumption as well of course— persistent cough, hectic flush, misleading remissions. But this "realistic" motivation does not make the symbolic implications less emphatic.

42. When her infant Charley died of cholera in July 1849, Stowe wrote to her husband as follows: "Many an anxious night have I held him to my bosom and felt the sorrow and loneliness pass out of me with the touch of his little warm hands. Yet I have just seen him in his death agony, looked on his imploring face when I could not help nor soothe nor do one thing, not one, to mitigate his cruel suffering, do nothing but pray in my anguish that he might die soon" (cited in Hedrick, *Harriet Beecher* Stowe, 191).

43. The notion of children's impressibility—susceptibility to impressions that literally "sink into" the heart—became central to educational theory early in the nineteenth century. See Cott, *The Bonds of Womanhood,* 46, 84–87; Halttunen, *Confidence Men and Painted Women,* 3–4, 40, 49–50; Crain, *The Story of A,* 57–60, 128. See also Chapter 4.

44. Grace Greenwood, "Dora's Children," 93. Typically the sentimental child is "meek and gentle and patient"—unlike her "wayward and petulant and fretful" sister, rival, or stepparent ("Light and Shade" by Patty Lee, 109).

45. Chapter XXVI of the book is numbered as Chapter XXV in the *Era*. Such discrepancies occurred sometimes because of an error, sometimes because installments contained more, or less, than a single chapter. Corrections and occasional changes by Stowe were made before the serial was published in book form.

46. Phoebe Carey, "Bessy," appeared on Nov. 13, 1851 (183). The same number of the *Era* included the famous scene of *Uncle Tom's Cabin*, in which Eva, reading the Bible with Tom beside Lake Pontchartrain, tells Tom of her approaching death (installment 22).

47. Patty Lee, "James McCary and His Boy," 193. In the episode of *Uncle Tom's Cabin* that was published on Jan. 1, 1852, St. Clare himself dies saying "Mother"; but, characteristically, Stowe's text soon shifts attention to the chaos St. Clare leaves behind.

48. Cited in Douglas, *Feminization,* 129.

49. The reason for the missed deadline is unknown. On Dec. 18, Bailey printed the following announcement: "We regret as much as any of our readers can regret, that Mrs. Stowe has no chapter in this week's *Era*. It is not our fault for up to this hour we have nothing from her. As she is generally so punctual we fear that sickness may have prevented. We feel constrained to make this apology, so profound is the interest taken in her story by nearly all our readers" (203). The episode that appeared in the following number of the *Era*—on Christmas Day—includes a conversation about Christian martyrdom between St. Clare and Ophelia which directly precedes St. Clare's death. Only three times after the serial began did the *Era* appear without an installment of *Uncle Tom* (Aug. 21, 1851; Oct. 30, 1851; Dec. 18, 1851). See also Parfait, *The Publishing History of Uncle Tom's Cabin,* Appendix I (207–9).

50. The following announcement appeared instead: "Chapter XII of *Uncle Tom's Cabin* reached us at too late an hour for insertion this week and Mrs. Stowe having requested that it should not be divided our readers may look for the entire chapter in the next *Era* (Aug. 21, 1851) 134.

51. Patty Lee, "Ill-starred," 133.

52. Billings had designed the masthead for William Lloyd Garrison's abolitionist newspaper *The Liberator,* and in 1849 he illustrated a volume of poetry with many verses on the subject of slavery by John Greenleaf Whittier (*Poems* [Boston: Benjamin B Mussey, 1849]). On Billings's career see O'Gorman, *Accomplished in All Departments of Art.*

53. From sentimental fiction through the dime novel, popular white heroines conformed to norms of gentility while others offered alternatives. Henry Nash Smith discusses the figure of the Indian girl who can ride and shoot as an alternative to the heroine as "passive sexual object" (*Virgin Land: The American West as Symbol and Myth*). In temperance fiction, non-genteel women characters demonstrate violent behavior, but like the mildly erring heroines of the *Era,* they are always punished or converted at the end. Another alternative to the genteel heroine is the figure of the prostitute—"the erotically deviant body." On this recurrent image in nineteenth-century fiction see Brooks,

Reading for the Plot, 154. On the conventions of representing the female body in the United States in this period see Sanchez-Eppler, *Touching Liberty,* 14–49, and Kasson, "Narratives of the Female Body: The Greek Slave," 172–90.

54. On Cushing, Woodbury, and other antebellum readers, see my Introduction and Chapter 3.

55. See Marcus Wood's fine analysis of the visual semiotics for representing fugitives in *Blind Memory: Visual Representations of Slavery in England and America, 1780–1865.* Wood notes but does not pursue the difference between Stowe's text and the visual images that often deformed her initial emphases (143).

56. See, for example, discussions of the "Christiana Case" or "Christiana Tragedy," which ran intermittently from Oct. 2, 1851 through Jan. 1, 1852.

57. In the antebellum period most people got their political information from newspapers. In the decades before the Civil War, the development of the telegraph and wire services helped stimulate the interest in "hard" news. As Menahem Blondheim puts this, the public "developed a taste for ever more and ever faster news. . . . It was the telegraphic columns the public craved, bought the newspaper for, read first, if not exclusively" ("Public Sentiment Is Everything: The Union's Public Communications Strategy and the Bogus Proclamation of 1864," 875). The function of the abolitionist weeklies was different from that of the mass-circulation dailies in many respects. The abolitionist press printed proportionately more editorial commentary, more correspondence, more "literature." Yet, as Stowe seems to have perceived, the growing availability of "facts," in the *Era* as elsewhere, left other readerly desires unfulfilled.

58. "Philadelphia Correspondence: The Christiana Tragedy," 158–59; "Commitment for Treason," 158.

59. Many scholars have taken this view. See Introduction, n. 2.

60. "The Buffalo Fugitive," 139.

61. "The Buffalo Outrage," 140. Further references to this article are included in the text.

62. William Lloyd Garrison's *Liberator* was more innovative than the *National Era* in using "attention-getting visuals, such as capital letters, bold face, and italics" for emphasis. On *The Liberator's* typographical strategies see Rohrbach, "'Truth Stronger and Stranger than Fiction': Reexamining William Lloyd Garrison's *Liberator,*" 739. Nonetheless, the norms of representing fugitives in *The Liberator* do not differ significantly from those of the *Era*. For characteristic examples, see the report of the "Case of Henry Long," 10; or "A Remarkable Decision in the Supreme Court," 17.

63. The official seal of the Society for the Abolition of the Slave Trade in London (1787) represented a "kneeling enchained male African beneath the question 'Am I not a man and brother?'" This image "was reproduced as the heading to a great number of anti-slavery publications appearing as stationery, in books, prints, oil paintings, newspaper headings, and as a ceramic figurine" (Wood, *Blind Memory,* 22). As Marion Wilson Starling notes, "The figure of the fugitive slave, panting in a swamp, with the slave holder brandishing a whip and surrounded by bloodhounds . . . became so popular as a symbol [after 1835] that dinner plates were made with the scene for a center

motif; the handles of silverware were embossed with the story. . . . and the fad even extended to the embellishment of transparent window blinds." *The Slave Narrative: Its Place in American History,* 29.

64. On self-control as indispensable in marking slaves as deserving of white sympathy see Castiglia, "Abolition's Racial Interiors and the Making of White Civic Depth," 37, 45–49.

65. "Liberty Ode," 188. See for example "Reform Verses" by Charles J. Smith, 20. This poem envisages "a better time for all," and stresses the speaker's "feeling for my fellow / In his most degraded state / Whom his Father in the heavens / In his image did create, / Whom his earthly brother visits / With so devilish a hate." But the poem does not refer to slavery directly.

   Frederick Douglass's Paper and *The Liberator* more regularly addressed slave issues in poetry that attacked the Fugitive Law, stressing the ironic contrast between a nation once committed to liberty but now a "land of vile oppression" ("M," "The Fugitive Slave Law," 4); the freedom of mind and soul even when the body is enslaved; the importance of extending sympathy to victims of slavery, seen as a persecuted group. Only toward the end of 1851 and the beginning of 1852 did *The Liberator* begin to publish poetry that attempted to capture the slave's point of view. Perhaps *Uncle Tom's Cabin* played a role in this shift of emphasis.

66. "The Fall of Hungary," 132. See also Belasco Smith, "Serialization and the Nature of *Uncle Tom's Cabin,*" 79–80, and Reynolds, *European Revolutions and the American Literary Renaissance,* 52–53.

67. In a much-cited description of George pursued by the slave catchers, Stowe writes: "If it had been only a Hungarian youth, now bravely defending in some mountain fastness the retreat of fugitives escaping from Austria into America, this would have been sublime heroism; but as it was a youth of African descent, defending the retreat of fugitives through America into Canada, of course we are too well instructed and patriotic to see any heroism in it . . ." (299).

68. For some exceptions see Mary Irving, "To Daniel Webster," 55. John Greenleaf Whittier, "On the Portrait of a Celebrated Magazine Publisher who has Lately Saved the Union and Lost a Contributor," 54; George W. Putnam, "To the Workingmen of America," 61.

69. Putnam, "The Northern Tournament," 52.

70. John Greenleaf Whittier, "A Sabbath Scene," 102.

71. S. H. Lloyd "The Slave—A Tableau," 9.

72. For other poetic attempts by the *Era* to give speech to slave women, see "The Slave Mother to Her Child," where a mother uses familiar sentimental terms to express satisfaction in the death of her child ("Thou art sleeping calmly dearest") but departs from the typical emphasis in child-death poetry by stressing that she can bear her own pain now: "For the dregs of slavery's chalice / *Thou* wilt never drink" (12). Another example is "The Free Negro Girl's Message," 13. Purportedly told in the voice of the "Free Negro Girl" herself, this poem tries to establish a link between the emotions familiar to a "gentle lady" who has loved someone with her "whole soul" and the love

of this girl for a man who has been "torn from [her] and sold! / Sold to the land of whips and chains / *For gold! For paltry gold!*" A strategy that had been used by Margaret Fuller, Lydia Maria Child, and other abolitionists is evident here: humanizing the black woman and elevating her moral and emotional standing by making it similar, if not superior, to that of white women. Its dramatic effect is lessened, however, by the speaker's high literary style, which undercuts the naturalness if not the credibility of the "Free Negro Girl's" speech. The drama is attenuated as well by the fact that the first half of the poem does not mention the slave issue and relies on a lengthy, generalized, and conventional narrative of lovers who love and are parted.

73. M. Hempstead, "The Wanderer," 68. I have been unable to establish the identity of this poet. A "Martha Hempstead" contributed a poem called "Liberty Bells" to *The Liberty Bell* of 1851; "Who is Free?" by "M. Hempstead" appeared on the fourth page of *Frederick Douglass' Paper* on Jan. 14, 1853.

74. See Winship, "Greatest Book of Its Kind," 312.

75. Harold Stanley suggests that Bailey was surprised at the unexpected stir created by *Uncle Tom's Cabin.* Not having expected or "contracted for such a long story," he had not advertised it in advance and in fact "he did not initially share the interest of his readers in the story." But once he realized what was happening, and signed Stowe as a "regular contributor" to the *Era,* there was "a precipitous rise in the *Era*'s circulation" (*Gamaliel Bailey and Anti-slavery Union,* 143). See also Parfait, "The Nineteenth-Century Serial as a Collective Enterprise: Harriet Beecher Stowe's *Uncle Tom's Cabin* and Eugene Sue's *Les Mystères de Paris,*" 127–52.

76. Sanchez-Eppler, *Touching Liberty,* 6–7; Wood, *Blind Memory,* 188–89. David Morgan traces the recurrent motif of "benevolent conduct" in antebellum school-books ("For Christ and the Republic: Protestant Illustration and the History of Literacy in Nineteenth-Century America," 52–57). See also Ryan, *The Grammar of Good Intentions.*

2. Imagining Black Literacy

1. *The Narrative of the Life of Frederick Douglass, an American Slave,* in Henry Louis Gates, Jr., ed., *The Classic Slave Narratives,* 274. Further references to this edition are included in the text.

2. The formulation is from Ishmael Reed's fictional slave narrative *Flight to Canada* (1976); cited in Henry Louis Gates, Jr., "Introduction" to *The Classic Slave Narratives,* ix. Gates emphasizes the "inextricable link in the Afro-American Tradition between literacy and freedom" (ix). He suggests that the black author's initiation into literacy was "a necessary principle of structure of virtually all of the slave narratives published between 1789 and 1865" (*The Signifying Monkey,* 147–48).

3. Castiglia and Stern, "Introduction" to *Interiority in Early American Literature,* 1.

4. On the legalities of slave literacy see Cornelius, *"When I Can Read My Title Clear";* Monaghan, "Reading for the Enslaved, Writing for the Free: Reflections on Liberty and Literacy," 309–41; Williams, *Self-Taught: African American Education in Slavery and Freedom,* especially Appendix, "African Americans, Literacy, and the Law in the

Antebellum South," 203–13. On the separation of writing and reading in theory and practice, see Hall, "The Uses of Literacy in New England: 1600–1850," 58–59; Monaghan, "Literacy Instruction and Gender in Colonial New England," in Davidson, ed., *Reading in America,* 53–80.

5. Billings designed the masthead for William Lloyd Garrison's *Liberator.* On Billings see O'Gorman, *Accomplished in All Departments of Art.* See also Chapter 6.

6. For a rundown of "reader figures" ("ideal reader," "informed reader," "implied reader," etc.) see Iser, *The Act of Reading,* 30–34; Freund, *The Return of the Reader.*

7. For discussions of *Uncle Tom's Cabin* that emphasize the coercive authority of altruistic abolitionist teachers see Sanchez-Eppler, *Touching Liberty,* 6–7; Wood, *Blind Memory,* 189.

8. Wood, *Blind Memory,* 186.

9. It seems that Jewett, not Stowe, chose Billings to illustrate her book. See O'Gorman, *Accomplished in All Departments of Art,* 47–48. Jo Ann Morgan suggests that "Stowe must have found his work acceptable, for she used him again for later books" (*Uncle Tom's Cabin as Visual Culture,* 24).

10. On the "ideology of literacy" see Soltow and Stevens, *The Rise of Literacy and the Common School in the United States,* 58–88; Graff, *The Literacy Myth.* On racial implications of literacy see Salvino, "The Word in Black and White." Sarah Robbins explores the way Stowe' represents reading for didactic purposes, and contextualizes such scenes within what Robbins calls the ideal of "domestic literacy management" (*Managing Literacy, Mothering America,* chap. 4).

11. Dawn Coleman suggests that Stowe's appropriation of preacherly authority in *Uncle Tom's Cabin* enabled her to reach thousands of people as no individual preacher could do ("The Unsentimental Woman Preacher of *Uncle Tom's Cabin,*" 285–86). Gail Smith explores the relation between Stowe's familiarity with Biblical hermeneutics and her representation of reading. See Smith, "The Sentimental Novel: The Example of Harriet Beecher Stowe," and "Reading with the Other: Hermeneutics and the Politics of Difference in Stowe's *Dred.*"

12. Elizabeth McHenry writes: "leaders in the free black community believed [literacy] would open doors of American society to black people"(*Forgotten Readers,* 86).

13. Salvino, "The Word in Black and White," 147. Further references to this essay are included in the text.

14. Tawil, *The Making of Racial Sentiment,* 151. On the "dangerous savagery" of Nat Turner as depicted by Thomas Gray in the *Confessions of Nat Turner* (1831) see Hedin, "Probable Readers, Possible Stories."

15. Lapsansky, "Graphic Discord: Abolitionist and Antiabolitionist Images," 213. As Jennifer Monaghan notes, David Walker's "Appeal" had an "electric" effect on the Southern states: "Two years after publication of David Walker's tract . . . reading and writing instruction were totally banned by a state for the first time in U.S. history" ("Reading for Enslaved," 331, 333). Richard Brodhead's discussion of "disciplinary intimacy" emphasizes the preoccupation with averting violence in educational rhetoric of the period (*Cultures of Letters,* chap. 1).

16. "Extract from a Speech," 99. In an earlier report on this speech, which was given in England, William Wells Brown expresses his outrage: "Professor Stowe, as you might expect, was looked upon as the lion of the speakers; but his speech disappointed all, except those of us who knew enough of American divines not to anticipate much from them on the subject of slavery. . . . He evidently wishes for no agitation on the subject, and said it would do no good as long as England purchased America's cotton. I look upon this cotton question as nothing more than to divert the public from the main subject itself" ("Letter from William Wells Brown," 97).

17. Bentley, "White Slaves: The Mulatto Hero in Antebellum Fiction," 501.

18. See especially Tompkins, *Sensational Designs,* 145; Fisher, *Hard Facts,* 111–14.

19. Harriet Beecher Stowe, *A Key to Uncle Tom's Cabin,* 111.

20. Ibid., 110–11. This passage seems to imply that that all slaves—not merely those with "white" ancestors—may be educated and transformed from their current condition.

21. On the origins and demise of *The Slave's Friend* see Kelly, ed, *Children's Periodicals of the United States;* Geist, "The *Slave's Friend:* An Abolitionist Magazine for Children"; McCulloch, *Children's Books of the Nineteenth Century;* Samuels, "The Identity of Slavery," 163–65.

22. Kelly, *Children's Periodicals,* 409. Sarah Roth notes: "Middle-class women like Harriet Beecher Stowe typically enjoyed far more frequent exposure to plantation novels and juvenile fiction that dealt with slavery than they did to minstrel shows, scientific discourse, or the most radical abolitionist tracts. It is impossible to know exactly which of these texts individual writers of the 1850s had encountered over the course of their lives. Anecdotal evidence suggests, however, that connections did exist between early children's literature and women who later composed slavery-related fiction" ("The Mind of a Child," 96–97).

23. "St. Thomas and Antigua," 9–10.

24. "About the Slave Trade" explains that "The slaves at first were stolen from Africa— they were brought across the ocean in ships. . . . Because the traders wanted to bring in as many, and get as much money as they could, they crowded men and women and little children, as thick as they could sit, in a dark place called the *hold,* where a child could hardly stand up straight. And then, if they were at sea a long time, there would not be bread and water enough. Then the wicked men would throw part of the slaves into the sea." See also "Zamor and Hinda." The details here, including children with names, are especially striking in the light of what Marcus Wood calls the "idealizing and abstracting tendencies" in descriptions of the middle passage. Wood argues that even abolitionist representation of the middle passage "conforms, to a frightening extent, to [Henry Louis] Gates' description of [black cultural] erasure" (*Blind Memory,* 22). While *The Slave's Friend* conforms to such practices up to a point, it sometimes appeals to elemental feelings in white children, asking them to enter directly into the carefully delineated and highly threatening position of black ones.

25. Among many examples see "Selling Slaves by the Pound" (4); "How Children Become Slaves" (5–7). "Three Little Abolitionists" provides a report on an auction "of human

flesh" in Washington: "How much for the mother and child? . . . do not forget there is a little boy in the bargain. Here the auctioneer was interrupted by a man who said, 'as for the child it is good for nothing; it is not worth a day's food, and if I buy the mother I will give away the child very quick'" (2–3); "The Burman Slave Girl" describes a girl beaten by "her cruel master" and shut up "in a secret room" so that her cries would not be heard (5).

26. *The Mother's Friend*, 120.

27. The impact of financial turmoil on both black and white abolitionists is explored by Stauffer, *The Black Hearts of Men*, esp. 102–10. The American Anti-Slavery Society disbanded in 1870.

28. The serialized version of 1851 addressed children directly in a sequence that was cut when *Uncle Tom's Cabin* appeared in book form. But many early reviews stressed the book's suitability for children. See also Introduction and Chapter 4.

29. In his popular advice manual, *The Mother at Home, or Principles of Maternal Duty*, John S. C. Abbott asserts that obedience is "absolutely essential to proper family government." Abbott offers several principles and many examples for what he takes to be the most important task of education: how to "teach a child obedience" (27, 31, and passim). Although painful punishments (much advocated by Abbott) were no longer popular in child-rearing at mid-century, obedience remained a central goal. In Francis Wayland's "Early Training of Children" (1854), "the first principle of education to instill into the mind of a child, is that of *unhesitating obedience*" (60–61). On generic norms for antebellum children's books see MacLeod, *A Moral Tale*; Avery, *Behold the Child*, and Chapter 4.

30. See Robbins, *Managing Literacy, Mothering America*, 129–31, 149.

31. The power of example was a bedrock of antebellum educational theory. See Chapter 4 and Chapter 7.

32. "To a Young Lady Who refused to give her name as a member of a Benevolent Society, because she thought her influence too small to be of any service," 13.

33. "What Can We Do?" 8–9; "The Burman Slave Girl," 8–9; "Juvenile Association," 14–16.

34. "To Juvenile Anti-slavery Societies," 11. See also "Act as Well as Feel," 3–4.

35. "Butternut Sugar," 9–10.

36. "Colored Infant Schools," 13.

37. "Murder of Lovejoy," 4–5.

38. "The Deaf, Dumb, and Blind," 4.

39. Sanchez-Eppler, *Touching Liberty*, 44. In the words of one abolitionist text for children: "Children you are free and happy. . . . When you become men and women you will have full liberty, to go, to come, to seek pleasure or profit in any way that you may choose, so long as you do not meddle with the rights of other people" (cited in Sanchez-Eppler, 44).

40. See Maingot, "Haiti and the Terrified Consciousness of the Caribbean," 53–80.

41. On the "revolution that resulted in a complete metamorphosis in the political, intellectual, and economic life of the colony," see Knight, "The Haitian Revolution," 105. For

a sample of approaches see also Gaspar and Geggus, eds., *A Turbulent Time;* Langley, *The Americas in the Age of Revolution;* Lynch, *The Spanish American Revolutions;* Maingot, "Haiti and the Terrified Consciousness of the Caribbean."

42. On the insurrection in Barbados, see Geggus, "Slavery, War and Revolution in the Greater Caribbean."

43. "Barbadoes" [*sic*], 14.

44. "Colored Infant Schools," 12.

45. "Barbadoes," 13.

46. "Barbadoes," 14.

47. "Children's Letters," 13.

48. "St. Thomas and Antigua," 11.

49. *The Liberator* was founded in 1831; the American Anti-Slavery Society in 1833 (nationalizing the "Anti-Slavery Society" of 1831). Theodore Weld's *Slavery as it Is: Testimony of a Thousand Witnesses* was published in 1839. This important publication meant to shock, and it did. As one commentator wrote in 1852, "With the spirit of such a book as that is, we have no sympathy. It is compiled and digested for the purpose of showing the darkest side of slavery, and nothing else; and it is therefore as unlike as possible to the representation of southern life given by Mrs. Stowe" ("The Literature of Slavery," 597). After Lydia Maria Child published *An Appeal in Favor of That Class Of Americans Called Africans* (1833) she lost many subscribers to the children's periodical she edited, the *Juvenile Miscellany.* On Child see Karcher, *First Woman in the Republic.*

50. "The *Slaves' Friend* is printed for children. The editor . . . has tried to write this little book so that very young children can understand it. It is hoped that all the little boys and girls in the land may read it" (Back cover, *Slave's Friend* I, no. 2 [1836]).

51. Before the appearance of *Uncle Tom's Cabin* only about a dozen full-length works of fiction had engaged the issue of slavery; none of these books was widely read. Stowe made "the peculiar institution" central to a literary genre that had largely ignored it.

52. Hildreth, *Archie Moore: The White Slave, or Memoirs of a Fugitive,* xxi. Unless otherwise noted, further references to *Archie Moore* are from this edition and are included in the text. In his introduction to the 1855 edition, Hildreth attributes revived interest in his book to "the publication and great success of Uncle Tom's Cabin [which] gave a new impulse to anti-slavery literature." Regarding the changes made for the new edition Hildreth writes: "To satisfy the scruples of the . . . publisher, some of the slaveholder's oaths were curtailed or struck out,—and contrary to the author's preference—and to give it the air of an entirely new work, the division into volumes was omitted, and a new title was bestowed upon it—that of the *White Slave,* under which it now appears" (xxi). As Bentley points out, the changes and additions were more substantial.

53. Darryl Pinckney writes that "it was thought at first to be a slave narrative" ("Introduction" to *Uncle Tom's Cabin* [Signet, 1998], xix). The first advertisement for the 1836 edition refers to it as "memoirs" (x). Charles Nichols suggests that the first edition was "regarded by the public as a genuine slave autobiography" ("The Origins of *Uncle Tom's Cabin,*" 330). Marion Starling notes "it is still to be found listed in bibli-

ographies and special studies as autobiography [although] *The Liberator* recognized the *Memoirs of Archy Moore* as fiction as early as January 14, 1837" (*The Slave Narrative*, 228). Early reviews that take the book as a fiction often emphasized its "truth" of incident and human relations (Hildreth, "Introduction," xiv, xix).

54. Bentley, "White Slaves: The Mulatto Hero in Antebellum Fiction," 509.

55. Hildreth provides his own brief publication history in the introduction to the new edition (ix–xxi). Initially, he explains, he could find no publisher "and so complete was the reign of terror, that printers were almost afraid to set up the types" (ix). He published the first edition anonymously, at his own expense (ix). It sparked praise as well as outrage but was not widely reviewed. In 1852, in a review of "The Literature of Slavery" that included a discussion of both *Uncle Tom's Cabin* and the newly reissued *White Slave, or Memoirs of a Fugitive,* the reviewer notes that "we had never seen" this book "commonly understood to be [by] Mr. Hildreth, the historian" (607). The reviewer claims that "to this book many of the criticisms preferred against Uncle Tom's Cabin, are justly applicable" (607).

56. See especially Charles Nichols, "The Origins of *Uncle Tom's Cabin*." Bentley notes in passing that the 1836 version of Hildreth's novel influenced Stowe ("White Slaves: The Mulatto Hero in Antebellum Fiction," n. 17; p. 521). Stowe's familiarity with *The Slave* is especially interesting in the light of her own reservations about fiction-reading in the years before writing *Uncle Tom's Cabin*. On this issue see my Introduction, Chapter 1, and Chapter 3.

57. On George as "a composite portrait" of Douglass and Henry Bibb, among others, see Stepto, "Sharing the Thunder," 140–42. Marion Wilson Starling takes George as a composite of Douglass and William Wells Brown (*The Slave Narrative*, 301). Starling's analysis of Stowe's sources includes Ephraim Peabody's "Narratives of Fugitive Slaves," which Stowe does not mention in the *Key*. Starling's discussion of Peabody's influence on Stowe is fascinating and unduly neglected.

58. Stepto, "Sharing the Thunder," 140–42. Some took George as the foremost black figure in the book. See Chapter 5.

59. The fact that George (like Archy and Douglass) is a mulatto may suggest that intellectual and moral superiority derives from "white" racial inheritance. But making George and Eliza light-skinned may also reflect Stowe's shrewd awareness of the beliefs and the sympathies of her reading public. In addition, of course, it was a plot device that enabled these characters to "pass" more easily en route to Canada.

60. Stepto, "Sharing the Thunder," 142.

61. Weld was convinced that sentiment was a useless strategy for exploring the outrages of slavery and suggests that "tender feelings" may coexist with "a hard heart." He exemplifies: "I remember a young lady who . . . was very ready to weep over any fictitious tale of suffering. I was present when one of her slaves lay on the floor in a high fever, and we feared she might not recover. I saw that young lady stamp upon her with her feet; and the only remark her mother made was, 'I am afraid Evelina is too much prejudiced against poor Mary'" (*Slavery as it Is,* 128, 127).

62. Useful discussions of Douglass and literacy include Andrews, *To Tell a Free Story,* 13;

Daneen, "While I am Writing," 649–60; Salvino, "The Word in Black and White," 150–52; Eric J. Sundquist, "Introduction," *Frederick Douglass: New Literary and Historical Essays,* 8–12.

63. William Lloyd Garrison, "Preface" to Douglass's *Narrative,* in Gates, ed., *The Classic Slave Narratives,* 249; Gates, "Introduction," *Classic Slave Narratives,* xii. On the function of white abolitionist prefaces to black slave narratives, see McCoy, "Race and the (Para)Textual Condition," 156–69.

64. Stauffer, *Radical Abolitionists and the Transformation of Race,* 28, 54–56, 59. Stauffer aptly notes that in *My Bondage and My Freedom* Garrison's flowery preface is replaced by an introduction written by James McCune Smith, black physician, abolitionist, and advocate of violence (56). See also Andrews, *To Tell a Free Story* (217–18).

65. See "Letter From Wendell Phillips Esq," prefatory to Douglass, *Narrative* in Gates, ed., *The Classic Slave Narratives,* 252.

66. Salvino, "The Word in Black and White," 153.

67. Andrews explores some of the reasons for what he sees as unjustified neglect of the other versions (*To Tell a Free Story,* 266–67).

68. Leverenz, *Manhood and the American Renaissance,* 128. See also Sundquist, "Introduction" *Frederick Douglass: New Literary and Historical Essays,* 8.

69. Dobson, "Reclaiming Sentimental Literature," 267–68. Noble, *The Masochistic Pleasures of Sentimental Literature,* 131.

70. Robbins, *Managing Literacy, Mothering America* (passim).

71. On October 30, 1851 the *National Era* published a letter from a reader who suggested that a scene in a recent installment would make a fine "embellishment" for the novel, when it is published as a book. The reader refers to the scene in which Eva helps Tom write a letter to Chloe. As Claire Parfait notes, the scene was not illustrated in Jewett's edition of 1852 (27, n. 91). But in the United States an image of the scene appeared in the 1853 edition and on the cover of the 1879 edition. It also appeared in the following: London: Nathaniel Cooke (1853) 199; London: George Routledge, (1853) 258; (New York: Hurst and Co., 187– (frontispiece); New York: Houghton Mifflin, 1888 (cover). A representation of Tom reading the Bible to two slave women on Legree's plantation was employed as the frontispiece of the much-reprinted British edition of 1853 with illustrations by Phiz, Gilbert, and Harvey.

72. Illustrated scenes of reading often disappeared from illustrated editions and children's editions of the 1890s. See Chapters 6 and 7.

73. Mitchell, *Picture Theory,* 49.

74. See Williams, *Playing the Race Card,* 50; Railton, "*Uncle Tom's Cabin and American Culture*"; O'Gorman, *Accomplished in All Departments of Art,* 53.

75. Wood, *Blind Memory,* 190. Jo Ann Morgan notes the "there was no visual precedent for a grown black man in the prime of life cozied up with a tiny white girl, alone within a natural setting" (*Uncle Tom's Cabin as Visual Culture,* 25.)

76. See Chapters 6 and 7.

77. David Paul Nord has shown that the American Tract Society shared with other religious publishing houses an "understanding of how reading should work. In numerous

essays on the nature of reading and the power of the printed word, writers for the religious publishing societies argued that reading, even cursory reading, could have powerful, direct, instantaneous, almost magical effects on the reader . . . at the same time, they believed that to be fully effective, reading must be slow, deliberate, repetitive and reflectively studious" (Nord, "Religious Reading and Readers in Antebellum America," 245). "It is better to read one book and understand it perfectly than to read a dozen and understand them imperfectly," Lydia Maria Child notes in her popular *Mother's Book* (96). This was just the kind of reading Stowe's text encouraged as well. On "intensive reading" see also Darnton, *Kiss of Lamourette,* Hall, "The Uses of Literacy in New England," and my Introduction.

78. Wood, *Blind Memory,* 188. Robbins suggests that white middle-class women in particular may have associated Tom with the familial figure of "the motherly teacher," thus seeing him as both feminized and benign (*Managing Literacy, Mothering America,* 129).

79. Graff, *The Literacy Myth,* xvi. Although Graff, Salvino, Pierre Bourdieu, and others have raised questions about the high expectations attached to literacy, literacy remains the cornerstone of primary education, presumed indispensable for "economic and social development, . . . individual advancement, and so on" (Graff, xvi). Surveys such as the National Endowment for the Arts report on reading habits suggest that anxiety about the decline of literacy in an electronic age serves to reaffirm the value and the promise of literacy. See my Introduction, n. 22. Further references to Graff are included in the text.

80. Monaghan, "Literacy Instruction and Gender in Colonial New England," 58–61.

81. Gates, *Signifying Monkey,* 132.

82. Salvino, "The Word in Black and White," 144.

83. Fliegelman, *Declaring Independence,* 62.

84. See Brodhead, *Cultures of Letters;* Robbins, *Managing Literacy, Mothering America;* Brown, "Reading and Children"; Sanchez-Eppler, *Dependent States,* especially chaps. 1 and 2; Stevenson, *The American Homefront.*

85. On nineteenth-century readers and the material book see Davidson, *Revolution and the Word,* 75–79; Moylan and Stiles, ed., *Reading Books: Essays on the Material Text and Literature in America;* Zboray and Zboray, "Books, Reading, and the World of Goods in Antebellum New England," 588 and passim. Zboray and Zboray, *Everyday Ideas,* esp. chap. 11.

86. Gates suggests that Gronniosaw's *Narrative* inaugurates "the genre of the slave narrative, from its 'I was born' opening sentence to the use of literacy training as a repeated figure that functions to unify the structure of his tale" (*Signifying Monkey,* 133). The first American edition of Gronniosaw's *Narrative* appeared in 1774, though earlier editions appeared in England. See also Andrews, *To Tell a Free Story,* 35–46; Starling, *The Slave Narrative,* 59–66.

87. On reading as a dynamic transaction in which the book is perceived as an 'other' see Bleich, *Subjective Criticism;* Poulet, "Criticism and the Experience of Interiority"; Rosenblatt, *The Reader, the Text, the Poem;* Steig, *Stories of Reading.*

88. Gillian Brown is one of the few scholars to analyze Topsy's reading as an element in Stowe's representation of a human child ("Reading and Children"). See also Chapter 4.

89. Stephen Railton notes that "Stowe herself wrote a new introduction for the book and clearly approved its republication in the United States, but very little has been learned about how that was arranged" (*Uncle Tom's Cabin and American Culture*, www.iath. virginia.edu/utc/childrn/peephp.html). The author of *A Peep* appears only as "Aunt Mary." In a "Bibliographical Account" included in the 1879 Houghton Mifflin edition of *Uncle Tom's Cabin,* the British librarian George Bullen identifies "Aunt Mary" as the daughter of Samson Low, Stowe's British publisher (lxix).

3. LEGITIMIZING FICTION

1. Novel-reading retained the lingering aura of a forbidden practice for many families of the 1850s. Davidson discusses resistance to fiction in the early republic (*Revolution and the Word,* 42–49); see also Kerber, " 'We Own that Ladies Sometimes Read': Women's Reading in the Early Republic." On the anti-fiction position in antebellum advice literature see Casper, "Antebellum Reading Prescribed and Described," esp. 137, 139. Cf. 145–46. Although novel-reading was emphatically gendered "feminine" by cultural arbiters, men also read novels in the antebellum period. See Zboray, *Fictive People,* chap. 11. On crime fiction and working-class men see Looby, "George Thompson's 'Romance of the Real': Transgression and Taboo in American Sensation Fiction"; Stewart, "Consuming George Thompson," 233–63.

2. "From general trends (realism, sensationalism, sentimentality) to specific types (moral tract, dime novel) genre became the principal way books were marketed and consumed. . . . [G]enre helped readers negotiate an expanding cultural marketplace and . . . publishers manage the risks of growing capital investment" (Stewart, "Review," *A History of the Book in America,* 323).

3. Gossett, *Uncle Tom's Cabin and American Culture,* 195.

4. By the end of the nineteenth century, patrons of public libraries "borrowed novels more than any other kind of reading, and did so at a rate that far exceeded the percentage of fiction held by collections" (Augst, "Faith in Reading: Public Libraries, Liberalism, and the Civil Religion," 176). However, most advice books and guides to reading still recommended history or biography far more readily than novels—especially American novels.

5. On diverse forms of popular fiction in antebellum print culture see Denning, *Mechanic Accents;* Lehuu, *Carnival on the Page;* Reynolds, *The Subversive Imagination in the Age of Emerson and Melville;* Streeby, *American Sensations.*

6. Beecher, "The Strange Woman"; Casper, "Antebellum Reading," 145–46.

7. Advice books address topics ranging from the choice of books to library "décor." See for example, Abbott, *Hints for Home Reading;* Abbott et al., ed., *The House and Home: A Practical Book.* Charles Norton's "Five Foot Shelf of Books" was designed in 1909 to "furnish a liberal education to anyone willing to devote fifteen minutes per day to reading" (Rubin, *The Making of Middlebrow Culture,* 27–28). The "novel-reading habit" long remained a prime culprit in the story of morally destructive reading prac-

tices. For an overview of lingering concerns about the dangers of fiction see Hochman, "Readers and Reading Groups."

8. Beecher, "The Strange Woman," 210–11. French novels were a particular target of attack for religious organizations and publishers, such as the American Tract Society. See Nord, "Religious Reading and Readers in Antebellum America," 248. French fiction was all but synonymous with transgression throughout the century (and beyond). On the transgressive potential of reform fiction, see Reynolds, *The Subversive Imagination,* and Looby, "George Thompson's 'Romance of the Real.'" Sanchez-Eppler examines the representation of violent as well as "more secret" forms of abuse in temperance fiction (*Dependent States,* 70–71, and chap. 2, passim).

9. Beecher, "The Strange Woman," 173. See Stowe, "Literary Epidemics."

10. See Chapters 1 and 2.

11. Gossett, *Uncle Tom's Cabin and American Culture,* 174–75. Tappan's personal scrapbook includes an anonymous letter from "a fugtive slave" praising Stowe's "genius and talent." The scrapbook is in the collection of the American Antiquarian Society. With thanks to Ellen Gruber Garvey for alerting me to this source.

12. "There is a tradition in the family, that the father in his lifetime read one whole novel and the half of another. In his efforts to fathom the Jesuits he dipped into Eugene Sue's 'Wandering Jew,' but recoiled from the greater part of it. 'Uncle Tom's Cabin' impressed him deeply and satisfied all his cravings for light reading" (Buel, "The Author of 'The Lady or the Tiger,'" 406).

13. A section on George Alfred Townsend, in Hart's *A Manual of American Literature: A Textbook for Schools and Colleges* notes that "*Uncle Tom's Cabin* was the only novel ever admitted to his father's house" (422). According to Amy Cruse, "The book was one of the very few secular stories that Edmund Gosse was permitted to read in his sternly repressed childhood" (*The Victorians and Their Books,* 253). James Ford Rhodes writes that "Lord Palmerston, who had not read a novel for thirty years, read 'Uncle Tom's Cabin' three times . . ." (*History of the United States,* 282).

14. Hallowell, ed., *James and Lucretia Mott: Life and Letters,* 377.

15. Ibid., 304.

16. Unsigned, "Uncle Tom's Cabin, the Story of the Story."

17. Thurman, *"O Sisters Ain't You Happy,"* 148.

18. Zboray and Zboray, "Books, Reading, and the World of Goods in Antebellum America," 587. Paul C. Gutjahr writes: "as early as 1817 one writer bemoaned the fact that the 'prodigious multiplication of books' in the United States had already 'jostled the Bible from its place'" (*An American Bible,* 2–3). This anxiety persisted in the religious press. In 1851 the *New York Evangelist* reprinted a paragraph from George Gilfillan's *Bards of the Bible* under the heading "The Best Book." On religious resistance to the novel see also Nord, "Religious Reading and Readers in Antebellum America," 245, 254.

19. Anna Quincy Thaxter Cushing Diary (April 1852–July 1853).

20. Cited in Zboray and Zboray, *Everyday Ideas,* 249–50.

21. Alcott, *Familiar Letters to Young Men on Various Subjects*, 76–77. David Stewart, "Sensationalism." On the dangers of novel-reading for young men see also William Eliot, *Lectures to Young Men*, 72–75; Beecher, "The Strange Woman," 170–214. Further page references are to this edition and are included in parenthesis in the text.

22. "Harriet Beecher Stowe Dead," 3. According to this article Beecher had refused to read the book as a serial. In an image that reflects anticipatory anxiety he prepared to "take it all at one dose." In Beecher's own account of the experience he describes sending his wife to bed because he "didn't want anybody down there. I soon began to cry. Then I went and shut all the doors for I did not want any one to see me. Then I sat down to it and finished it that night" (Henry Ward Beecher, "Tribute to Harriet Beecher Stowe," 52).

23. Cited in Zboray and Zboray, *Everyday Ideas*, 258. Mary Pierce Poor, a social reformer, was daughter of the Rev. John Pierce, for fifty years the minister of the First Church of Brookline, Mass. She was the wife of Henry Varnum Poor, a railroad journalist and economist. The Poor family papers are in the Schlesinger Library, Radcliffe.

24. Cushing Diary (April 13, 1852); letter from Maria Woodbury to Miss Lucy Marshall of Holden, Mass. (probably June 4, 1852).

25. In "The Aesthetic Illusion" psychoanalyst Leon Balter stresses the importance of a reader's return to customary ego functioning when immersion in a fiction is complete. See also "Introduction," n. 52.

26. Rosalie Roos, Letter dated May 4, 1853. *North American Women's Letters and Diaries.*

27. Cited in Starling, *The Slave Narrative*, 305.

28. Chesnut, *A Diary from Dixie* 114, 142, 184. The cited phrases are from Sept. 2, 1861; March 13, 1862; and June 12, 1862. Judging from her first reference to *Uncle Tom's Cabin,* Chesnut clearly read the book prior to 1861.

29. Excerpts from Charles William Holbrook's diary appear in Hall, "A Yankee Tutor in the Old South," 82–91. A note explains that "the diaries, one for each year [1850–1852] are of a standard pocket diary format. They are in private possession" (82). The article includes many excerpts from the diary. These excerpts contain only fleeting mention of reading matter; eight entries devoted to *Uncle Tom's Cabin* are an exception. A few comments about reading appear elsewhere in the excerpts—perhaps there are others in the diary itself, but the reading experience is not Hall's main concern. He writes that "for the historian the diary has three subjects of interest: Charles's reasons for taking the position, the manner in which he as a New Englander saw ante-bellum southern life, and his general observations of the South" (82–83). The entries about *Uncle Tom's Cabin* are of interest to Hall for the "reactions of the planter and his wife," not for Charles's responses to the book (84). Precisely because the excerpts have not been selected to exemplify reading, their implications are of interest here. Each excerpted entry on *Uncle Tom's Cabin* is complete. Further references to Charles Holbrook's diary are from this essay and are included in the text.

30. This event occasions "great distress" on the plantation, and in fact "Mr G" subsequently decides "not to let Henderson go away" (90).

31. Child, *Selected Letters,* 264.

32. Cited in White, *The Beauty of Holiness*, 152. Palmer met Catharine Beecher and Stowe in 1845 when she participated in an effort to promote women's education on the frontier (White, 61, 152). She later became a vehement critic of the Beechers (White, 152). She accused Stowe and Henry Ward Beecher of "aiding the kingdom of Satan amazingly" (cited in Raser, *Phoebe Palmer: Her Life and Thought*, 221).

33. Cited in French and Royce, eds., *Portraits of a Nineteenth-Century Family*, 64.

34. Smith, "The Sentimental Novel: The Example of Harriet Beecher Stowe," 222.

35. In his *Lectures to Young Men* William Eliot advises readers to "add to [their] reading one book which by many is thought old-fashioned, but which is not yet, thank God, out of print. . . . It is *the book*, the Bible" (81).

36. *Uncle Tom's Cabin* was eminently affordable. Available first as newspaper installments, the text circulated widely throughout antebellum print culture. Multiple readers often read a single issue of the *Era*. Forrest Wilson notes that copies were "passed from family to family to until they were quite worn out" (*Crusader in Crinoline*, 272). When the novel appeared in book form it was available not only in well-made illustrated editions but also in an inexpensive edition "For the Millions." Printed on cheap paper, in two columns of print, without illustrations, this edition cost 37 1/2 cents. See Parfait, *A Publishing History of Uncle Tom's Cabin*, 76–81.

37. Halttunen, *Confidence Men and Painted Women*, 53. Dobson, "Reclaiming Sentimental Literature, 268.

38. On Stowe and the Scottish common sense tradition see Camfield, "The Moral Aesthetics of Sentimentality"; Noble, *The Masochistic Pleasure of Sentimental Literature*.

39. As Cathy Davidson points out, early American novelists regularly included such disclaimers in their fiction (*Revolution and the Word*, 40). Later, writers of realism often critiqued popular reading and mass entertainment in order to affirm their own truthfulness and sophistication by contrast. See for example the mockery of sentimental fiction in *The Rise of Silas Lapham* or melodrama in *Maggie: A Girl of the Streets* and *Sister Carrie*. Early television episodes of *The Sopranos* repeatedly cite the film *The Godfather* for similar ends: promoting the "reality" of the host text. On this aspect of American realism see also Glazener, *Reading for Realism*, and Hochman, "Readers and Reading Groups."

40. Gustafson, *Eloquence Is Power*, 48, 278; Fliegelman, *Declaring Independence, 38*.

41. Gossett, *Uncle Tom's Cabin and American Culture*, 192.

42. Discussing DeForest's nomination of *Uncle Tom's Cabin* as the first "great American novel," Lawrence Buell suggests that "the documentary yardstick Stowe imposed on herself in *A Key*" was "inadequate" ("The Dream of the Great American Novel," 192). Indeed, Stowe clearly understood the difference between the *Key* and *Uncle Tom's Cabin*. She was as surprised as everyone else at the storm she had created with her novel. It is almost as if, in writing the *Key*, she attempted to put the genii back in the bottle.

43. Stowe, "Introductory Essay," iii–iv. See also Chapter 1.

44. George Sand valued St. Clare highly: "What hand has ever drawn a type more fasci-

nating and admirable?" she asks (*Uncle Tom's Cabin* [Norton, 1994] 461). Dickens praised the "great power and originality" in Stowe's conception of St. Clare (Belasco Smith, "Serialization and the Nature of *Uncle Tom's Cabin,* 86). Thomas Wentworth Higginson called St. Clare "the best drawn of the serious characters in the book" (*Uncle Tom's Cabin* [Appleton, 1898], xi).

45. Stowe, "Introductory Essay" to the *Incarnation* (viii).

46. Beecher and Stowe, *Principles of Domestic Science,* 254–55.

47. Gossett notes that *Uncle Tom's Cabin* sold 300,000 copies in the first year of book publication, a number then "unprecedented . . . for any book except the Bible, in so short a period of time." There was even "a movement in northern churches to make the novel a textbook for Sunday school classes" (*Uncle Tom's Cabin and American Culture,* 164). An "immense edition" of *Uncle Tom's Cabin* for Sunday schools was published in England in 1853. See Rhodes, *History of the United States,* 280, n. 1.

48. See Gutjahr, "Pictures," 83.

49. Stowe's comment was much repeated as evidence of both her inspiration and her humility, even late in the century, though by then it was sometimes seen as a sign of her failing mental powers (Annie Fields, *Life and Letters of Harriet Beecher Stowe,* 377). Frank Luther Mott's *Golden Multitudes: The Story of Best Sellers in the United States* begins by recounting the story as a way into the question of popularity. In his version a man, passing by the famous writer's garden in her old age, asked to shake her hand. " 'God wrote it,' said the old lady simply; 'I merely wrote his dictation.' " Mott adds that if the book "had sold only a few hundred copies, God would never have been credited with an assist" (1).

50. George Sand, "Review of *Uncle Tom's Cabin,*" 461.

51. Sherman, "Introductory Remarks," to *Uncle Tom's Cabin,* xviii.

52. Cited in Jewett's advertisement for *Uncle Tom's Cabin.* Reprinted in Parfait, *A Publishing History of Uncle Tom's Cabin* (55).

53. Carson, "Africana Constellations: African American Studies and *Uncle Tom's Cabin,*" 163.

54. Kirkham cites and reprints similar announcements and ads, referring to *Uncle Tom's Cabin* not as fiction, but as "The Story of the Age," a "Great American Tale" (146), "The Greatest Book of the Age" (147, 191). When *Uncle Tom's Cabin* was first published in book form by John P. Jewett and Co. (1852), Jewett's list of publications included anti-slavery and religious works, but few works of fiction or belles-lettres (Winship, "The Greatest Book of Its Kind," 318). In 1845 Jewett had published Henry Ward Beecher's *Lectures to Young Men.* As we have seen, Beecher's lecture "The Strange Woman," included in that volume, rails against the evils of fiction and other "heathen" literature in terms very like those repeatedly used by Stowe.

55. In the 1850s, *Uncle Tom's Cabin* was advertised primarily among sermons and other serious, weighty works; such advertisements were sometimes bound into the volume itself. In the nineties, it was advertised with other novels. See also Chapters 5 and 6.

56. Sherman, "Introductory Remarks," xiii.

57. See Jewett's full-page ad, bound into the novel.

58. Bailey's annual letter, encouraging subscribers to renew, was a loose sheet inserted into the paper toward the end of the year.

59. Stepto, "Sharing the Thunder," 137. See also Levine, "*Uncle Tom's Cabin* in *Frederick Douglass' Paper*," 536–38; McHenry, *Forgotten Readers,* 127–28.

60. "The Press," 4.

61. Swisshelm, "Letter to Country Girls," 4.

62. In "The Fear of Being an Old Maid," novels are responsible for persuading young women to marry out of fear rather than love (Hall, 4).

63. Mackay, "The Story Tellers," 4.

64. "Dialogue," 4.

65. "To the Author of 'Uncle Tom's Cabin,'" 4. Such recycling of published material was a common nineteenth-century practice. See McGill, *American Literature and the Culture of Reprinting.*

66. See, for example, ads for *Caste,* "A powerful Anti-Slavery Novel," and *The Rag Picker or Bound and Free* (Nov. 23, 1855); *Dred* (Oct. 3, 1856). An extract from *The Rag Picker* ("the new and thrilling work") appears on Oct. 12, 1855. Fiction not concerned with slavery also begins to appear; see, e.g., an excerpt from a temperance tale, "Cone Cut Corners" (Sept. 14, 1855).

67. McGill, *American Literature and the Culture of Reprinting,* 272–76.

68. Christopher Crowfield, pseud., Harriet Beecher Stowe, *House and Home Papers,* 326.

69. De Forest, "The Great American Novel," 28. On De Forest and Stowe see also Buell, "The Rise and 'Fall' of the Great American Novel"; Buell, "Harriet Beecher Stowe and the Dream of the Great American Novel"; Moers, *Harriet Beecher Stowe and American Literature,* 11.

70. Harriet Beecher Stowe, "Introduction" to *A Library of Famous Fiction: Embracing the 9 Standard Masterpieces,* vi.

71. See for example, Lubbock, *The Choice of Books;* Brander Matthews (Arthur Penn pseud.), *The Home Library;* Porter, *Books and Reading;* Abbott, ed., *Hints for Home Reading.*

72. Lowell, "The Five Indispensable Authors," 223–24.

73. Barrett, *A Literary History of America,* 354; Morris, "The Story of the Book and A Key to the Characters," 10, 29. See also Chapter 5.

74. Radway, *A Feeling for Books,* esp. chap. 4.

75. Moers, *Harriet Beecher Stowe and American Literature;* Tompkins, *Sensational Designs,* and Arac, *Huckleberry Finn as Idol and Target,* address the way changes in interpretive conventions have influenced the shifting status of *Uncle Tom's Cabin* in the academy. See also Chapter 5.

76. Dorothy Richardson calls *Uncle Tom's Cabin* a "precious childhood favorite" in 1905. Cited in Brodhead, *Cultures of Letters,* 106. See Introduction.

4. Beyond Piety and Social Conscience

1. Cited in Smith, "Serialization and the Nature of *Uncle Tom's Cabin,*" 70. Dawn

Coleman suggests that Stowe's parting words to children were a retreat from the more authoritative voice she assumed throughout much of the novel, but there is good reason to take seriously Stowe's claim of speaking to children as well as adults ("The Unsentimental Preacher of *Uncle Tom's Cabin*").

2. On Stowe's attention to children and child-rearing see Tompkins, *Sensational Designs,* 143; Brodhead, *Cultures of Letters,* 35–42; Fisher, *Hard Facts,* 125; Brown, "Reading and Children"; Robbins, *Managing Literacy, Mothering America,* 116–56.

3. Review-excerpt from the *Religious Recorder,* Syracuse, cited in an advertisement for *Uncle Tom's Cabin* placed by Jewett. Another excerpt claims that "50,000 families are alternately crying and laughing [over the book]" (*Unitarian Monthly Magazine*). Jewett's ad, published in *Norton's Literary Gazette* in 1852 and often reprinted, is reproduced in Parfait, *A Publishing History of Uncle Tom's Cabin,* 55.

4. Mary B. Kinney, *Putnam's Monthly Magazine,* 709.

5. Wheaton's children "devoured" the full-length novel—the only edition available at the time. "We know that the original *Uncle Tom's Cabin* was read aloud to many children by their parents," Stephen Railton notes ("*Uncle Tom's Cabin* and American Culture"). A sharp division between books for adults and for children emerged only toward the end of the century. According to Anne Scott MacLeod, specialists in children's reading dropped adult books from the lists of recommended reading toward the turn of the century because they were "too long or too complex for this or that child reader." From this point on there was a marked increase in books "written for children and a slow but steady decline of adult titles" (*American Childhood,* 124).

6. On Dreiser see Hakutani, *Young Dreiser,* 206, n. 33. On Burnett see "The One I Knew Best of All." On Reppelier see Gossett, *Uncle Tom's Cabin and American Culture,* 357. James's famous account of his "first experiment in grown-up fiction" appears in *A Small Boy and Others,* 167–68; see my Introduction, n. 101. In Johnson's fictionalized *Autobiography of an Ex-Colored Man* the narrator notes the "feverish intensity" with which he consumed the book as a child (28). Baldwin mentions reading *Uncle Tom's Cabin* "over and over again" in the course of his childhood in *Notes of a Native Son,* 11. On Johnson and Baldwin, see also my Epilogue.

7. Gail Schmunck Murray notes that the book "did not sell well," but gives no additional information (*American Children's Literature and the Construction of Childhood,* 124). Jewett's archive appears to be lost. The Hope Park fire destroyed the pre-twentieth-century Nelson records. Not many copies of *Pictures and Stories* survive, but it was a fragile volume with a soft cover, so it may have been read to death; alternatively, publishers of the 1850s may have overestimated the need for a separate edition. *Pictures and Stories* and *A Peep into Uncle Tom's Cabin* were the only children's editions published in the antebellum United States with the exception of a pro-slavery version, *Little Eva: A Flower of the South.* (See Introduction.) In the U.K. a tiny paper edition, *Uncle Tom's Cabin for Children,* was published in London by Groombridge and Sons (n.d., ca. 1850?) with engravings by E. Whimpers. In his "Bibliographical Account" (lxviii), George Bullen lists two books for children published in London in 1853: *All About Little Eva, from Uncle Tom's Cabin* and *All About Little Topsy from Uncle Tom's Cabin*

(no publishers noted). An adaptation by "Mrs. Crowe, Author of 'Pippies's Warning,' Etc." also appeared in London in 1853. This volume, for "juvenile readers," is almost as long as *Uncle Tom's Cabin* itself and is edited mostly to tone down brutal and sexual scenes. Certain sections and emphases were regularly omitted when Stowe's tale was adapted for juvenile readers. Religious doubt as well as violence, sex, adult conflict, and lengthy conversations were removed. In the 1850s, as later, inappropriate language (vulgarity but also irony and bad grammar) was deleted or recast. Children's editions proliferated in the 1890s, especially after the expiration of copyright (1893) and Stowe's death (1896). See Chapter 7.

8. For a discussion of "the volume and persistence of retold stories as part of the domain of children's literature" see Stephens and McCallum, *Retelling Stories, Framing Culture,* ix. Stephens and McCallum are primarily interested in modern retellings of traditional tales, especially retellings that challenge or modify the conservative "Western metaethic" (x). But they usefully emphasize the way "any particular retelling. . . . discloses . . . the attitudes and ideologies pertaining at the cultural moment in which the retelling is produced" (ix).

9. *Pictures and Stories* (Boston: Jewett & Co., 1853), "Editor's note," np. Gail Shmunk Murray writes that "Stowe . . . crafted a child's edition of the novel, *Pictures and Stories* . . . , with a simplified text" (*American Children's Literature and the Construction of Childhood,* 124). In a 1967 collection of Stowe's poems, John Michael Moran includes all the verses from *Pictures and Stories* in a section titled "Poems on Slavery." John Greenleaf Whittier's poem "Little Eva Song" is included in this section as well, which suggests that Moran did not unduly press the issue of authorship. Whittier's name does appear under the title of the reprinted poem, however. Claire Parfait accepts the idea that Stowe wrote the verses for *Pictures and Stories* (*Publishing History of Uncle Tom's Cabin,* 108–9). According to Stephen Railton's web archive "Uncle Tom's Cabin and American Culture," "the poems and the whole book are certainly the work of someone besides Stowe, although that person remains identified only as the 'authoress.' " Further references to *Pictures and Stories* are included in the text.

10. An editorial note explains that the verses were written with "the capacity of the youngest readers" in mind. "The prose parts of the book . . . are well suited for being read aloud in the family circle . . . and it is presumed that in these our younger friends will claim the assistance of their older brothers or sisters, or appeal to the ready aid of their mamma" (*Pictures and Stories,* np).

11. On the importance of books and reading in antebellum domestic life see Brodhead, *Cultures of Letters;* Brown, "Reading Children," Robbins, *Managing Literacy,* Sanchez-Eppler, *Dependent States.* On social concerns in educating antebellum children see Coontz, *The Social Origins of Private Life,* chap. 5.

12. Schweickart, Review of *Reading Women,* 733.

13. Samuel Goodrich, Dickens, and others critiqued violence in children's tales and nursery rhymes. See Goodrich, *Recollections of a Lifetime,* 172; Dickens, "A Witch in the Nursery," 245–52. For earlier examples that warn parents against 'Everything likely to excite sudden alarm or to terrify the imagination" see the anonymous *Mother's*

Friend or Familiar Directions for Forming the Mental and Moral Habits of Young Children, 120. In the popular *The Mother at Home, or Principles of Maternal Duty,* John Abbott emphasizes the "ruinous" result of "endeavor[ing] to amuse by relating [ghost] ... stories" or exciting fears in order "to govern" a child (107). On the opposition to folk and fairy tales in the United States during much of the nineteenth century see Avery, *Behold the Child,* 2–4, 56, 61–69; 72, 123–24, 129. Of course prescriptions for reading only partially reflect what is available in print culture, or how it is read.

14. Eighteenth-century novels, as William Warner notes, regularly cautioned adult readers against against the "dangers of mindless emulation" ("Staging Readers Reading"). In the antebellum consensus, good models were indispensable for children's literature; negative behavior, if included, was to be rendered unappealing and swiftly punished. The choice between good and bad had to appear "clear and unambiguous" (Wishy, *The Child and the Republic,* 61). On behavioral and pedagogic norms in nineteenth-century children's literature see Avery, *Behold the Child;* MacCleod, *A Moral Tale;* Morgan, "For Christ and the Republic"; Rogers, "Socializing Children," 356–57.

15. On the nineteenth-century child as a figure for human interiority see Steedman, *Strange Dislocations,* xi, 158–59, 172, passim. On antebellum interiority as "white" see Samuels, "Identity of Slavery," 160. On the abolitionist construction of interiority as white privilege see Castiglia, "Abolition's Racial Interiors."

16. Donnarae MacCann, by contrast, includes Stowe when she critiques the "stultifying sameness" in abolitionist children's books (*White Supremacy in Children's Literature,* 3, 26). MacCann suggests that as a children's book *Uncle Tom's Cabin* "was in line with the many [stories] about child 'Christ figures' who . . . convert irreverent adults"; for her, "'Uncle Tom' is of course the central figure" (18). Read in this way, with a brief nod to Topsy ("another minstrel figure—a kleptomaniac whose thievery is presented stereotypically" [20]), *Uncle Tom's Cabin* easily fits the pattern by which abolitionist tales for children support the myth of white supremacy (18–19).

17. See Harriet Beecher Stowe, *A Key,* 22.

18. Steedman, *Strange Dislocations,* 145. Stowe probably read *Wuthering Heights* (we know she read *Jane Eyre*) and was surely familiar with Goethe's Mignon, via Scott if not in the original. *Wilhelm Meister* was translated by Thomas Carlyle in 1839 and read all over the English-speaking world; Scott appropriated the figure of Mignon for *A Legend of Montrose* and *Peveril of the Peak* (Steedman, 145). Stowe was a great fan of Scott's novels and, as we have noted, she was rereading them "in order" just before writing *Uncle Tom's Cabin* (Hedrick, *Harriet Beecher Stowe,* 198).

Similarities between Mignon and Topsy are multiple and striking: Not only is Mignon, like Topsy, bought by a young man and abruptly inserted into a strange family, unable to say where she comes from or behave as expected, but Mignon is also a performer—an acrobat—who has suffered from abuse and continues to experience inner turmoil. She may well be a source that Stowe drew on for Topsy. Mignon shares qualities with Eva as well. Both characters die from physical causes (heart issues, tuberculosis) associated with larger spiritual or emotional traumas. We might say that the figure of Mignon splits into Eva and Topsy: Eva receives Mignon's depth of feeling and early death; Topsy receives her mysterious origins, lack of speech, anger, acrobatics, and inability to conform.

19. On the threat of being kidnapped and sold into slavery—among white children as well as black—see Levander, *Cradle of Liberty,* chap. 1.

20. Fuss, *Identification Papers,* 2, 12. For Fuss the end-product of this "detour" is "defin[ition] of a self" (2). Recent discussions leave more space for the play of the self in reading and challenge the notion of "a unified reading subject" (Schweickart and Flynn, *Reading Sites,* 8). I assume that the act of reading enables a transient play of subject positions—such as those posited by Cora Kaplan in *"The Thorn Birds:* Fiction, Fantasy, Femininity," 117–46; or by film scholar Carol J. Clover discussing adolescent boys watching horror movies (*Men, Women, and Chain Saws: Gender in the Modern Horror Film,* 5, 18–19, 62). Film theorists have paid special attention to identification as integral to the dynamic of spectatorship. See also Silverman, *Male Subjectivity at the Margins.*

21. Benjamin, "Children's Literature," 256.

22. In *Empathy and the Novel* Suzanne Keen addresses the extravagant claims made for empathy by philosophers, psychologists, writers of fiction, and other commentators, especially those who seek to promote novel-reading as a form of moral nourishment. Examining approaches to empathy from the eighteenth century onward, Keen affirms the value of empathy, while questioning the link between "experiences of narrative empathy" and moral action in real life (xiv). Recent work on empathy (whether aroused by observation of others or by reading) highlights its moral and social importance. See especially the work of M. L. Hoffman. On empathy, sympathy, and identification see also my Introduction.

23. Fuss, *Identification Papers,*141. Fuss emphasizes "the historical and social conditions of identification" (165).

24. On "the Negro [as] a phobogenic object, a stimulus to anxiety," see Frantz Fanon's influential *Black Skin, White Masks,* 151, 167–70, and Christopher Lane's collection, *The Psychoanalysis of Race.*

25. Sanchez-Eppler, *Touching Liberty,* 134.

26. From Lydia Maria Child to Henry Ward Beecher and Stowe herself, commentators stressed the dangers of extending sympathy to undesirable characters. See Child, *The Mother's Book,* 90–91. As we have noted, benevolent reformers often discouraged a "too-thorough identification between helper and helped" for fear of the "social leveling" that might result (Ryan, *The Grammar of Good Intentions,* 17, 19). In a different tone, reading theorists have suggested that the experience of fiction-reading can create a temporary breakdown of the boundaries between self and other. Theorists who make this claim include Poulet, "Phenomenology of Reading"; Rosenblatt, *The Reader, the Text, the Poem;* Steig, *Stories of Reading.* See also Schweickart and Flynn, *Reading Sites.*

27. Ellen Handler Spitz emphasizes [twentieth-century] children's pleasure in books where "transformational possibilities stay fluid" (*Inside Picture Books,* 150).

28. For an analysis of Harry's "uncanny ability to imitate" as evidence of Stowe's racialism,

see Tawil, *The Making of Racial Sentiment,* 164. Tawil takes the novel's "emphasis on the 'negro's' mimetic nature" as the "linchpin of [Stowe's] racial theory" (154).

29. For readings of Eva and Topsy in these terms see Levander, *Cradle of Liberty;* Sanchez-Eppler, *Touching Liberty,* 174, n.2.

30. Keating, "Reading 'Whiteness,' Unreading 'Race': (De)Racialized Reading Tactics in the Classroom," 323, 315. On the significance of racial markers in reading fictional characters, see also Butler, *Bodies That Matter,* 170–71; Holloway, *Bookmarks,* 144–46, 164–65.

31. Sam and Andy's delaying tactics are noted in *Pictures and Stories;* they laugh "until their sides ache" as soon as they are out of sight while "the trader . . . stood cursing and swearing, like a wicked man as he was" (8). But the comic, minstrel effects of this sequence are absent. *Pictures and Stories* also downplays not only Eliza's race and color but even her slave status. Mrs. Bird wonders "who or what she is" but no one asks whether she is a slave (as Mr. Bird does in *Uncle Tom's Cabin*).

32. On black visual imagery of the period see Wood, *Blind Memory;* Lacey, "Visual Images of Blacks," 137–80; Boime, *The Art of Exclusion.*

33. Samuels, "Identity of Slavery," 171.

34. See Richard Brodhead's influential account of "disciplinary intimacy" in *Cultures of Letters.*

35. Children's editions of the 1890s and the turn of the century often made significant changes to Stowe's text. In *Young Folks Uncle Tom's Cabin* (1901) Topsy's history all but disappears. See Chapter 7.

36. On animal imagery see MacCann, *White Supremacy in Children's Literature;* Ginsberg, "Of Babies, Beasts, and Bondage." *Uncle Tom's Cabin* includes animal imagery for Topsy. St. Clare is amused by her as by the "tricks of a parrot or pointer" (369). "Come here, Tops you monkey," he calls (407). She whistles, dances, and mimics. Late nineteenth-century editions maximize such character traits and imagery. See Chapter 7.

37. *Pictures and Stories* radically simplifies Topsy's story and renders it entirely in verse, reprinting none of Stowe's words about Topsy verbatim, and eliminating all the harshest details about Topsy's abuse. But, like *Uncle Tom's Cabin,* it makes Topsy's history responsible for her inability to behave.

38. Many abolitionist tales suggest that freed slaves quickly embrace middle-class norms: "The kind lady . . . is teaching [Joggy and Lorina] to speak as we do, to sew and to do housework. She says they are neat, learn fast, sing and run about quite merrily" ("Stolen Children," 2).

39. The distinction between absorption and performance is important in conceptualizing childhood. See Steedman, *Strange Dislocations;* Brown, "Child's Play," 13–39. See also Chapter 7.

40. Brown, "Reading and Children," 85.

41. See especially Fisher, *Hard Facts;* Ryan, *The Grammar of Good Intensions;* Sanchez-Eppler, *Touching Liberty,* and Wexler, "Tender Violence."

42. Nyong'o, "Racial Kitsch and Black Performance," 386.

43. One need not accept totalizing generalizations about "human" experience to accept

the idea that children of different races and cultures are generally more uncertain than adults about the line between fiction and fact, and more vulnerable than adults to fantasies and fears.

44. The burden of being "good" in U.S. children's literature has fallen heavily on little girls. For the antebellum context see Dawson "The Miniaturizing of Girlhood," 63–84. On analogous gender differences in twentieth-century children's picture books see Spitz, *Inside Picture Books*, 48, 148, 160–61. Sarah Meer explores Topsy's function as "blackface subversion for girls" (*Uncle Tom Mania*, 39). Elizabeth Young explores the complex interplay of black and white identifications created by the use of black-face by the white actress Caroline Howard playing Topsy on stage (*Disarming the Nation*, Chapter 1).

45. See Bhabha, *The Location of Culture*, especially chap. 4.

46. In discussing the neglected figure of Adolph, Michael Borgstrom analyzes Adolph's habit of imitating St. Clare: "In aspiring to become (or at least mimic) his master, Adolph blurs antebellum culture's discrete borders of identity, embracing an in-betweenness that violates the social hierarchies Dinah [and other slaves] observe. . . . By refusing to act like an authentic black male slave, Adolph implies that it is possible to reject such taxonomic classifications. . . . While the text ultimately disallows Adolph's innovative representation of identity, his character nevertheless indicates ways in which hybrid identities may challenge hegemonic categorization ("Passing Over: Setting the Record Straight in *Uncle Tom's Cabin*," 1295). See also Meer on "Topsy and the Endman: Blackface in *Uncle Tom's Cabin*" (*Uncle Tom Mania*, chap. 1).

47. Young's analysis of this scene does not address the implicit child-reader, but her emphasis on the "forms of disorder" implied by the scene of Topsy's theft and impersonation is cogent to my reading (*Disarming the Nation*, 42). Ophelia's "very best scarlet India Canton crape shawl" appears in the full-length *Uncle Tom's Cabin* (366).

48. William Alcott, *The Young Wife*, 266. Further references are included in the text.

49. Lydia Maria Child, *The Mother's Book*, title page. On the importance of "a mother's influence" see also John Abbott, *The Mother at Home*, dedication, 15, and passim. "Mother, be careful to teach by your own example," Lydia Sigourney writes, "that rest from worldly occupation and discourse, which the consecrated day prescribes, and by your heightened and serene cheerfulness, awaken a desire of imitation" ("Mothers as Christian Teachers," 2). Imitation gained renewed critical attention in educational and psychological theory at the end of the nineteenth century. See Chapter 7.

50. Lydia Maria Child, *The Mother's Book*, 91. Further references are included in the text.

51. *Pictures and Stories* explicitly proposes to "foster in the . . . hearts [of the youngest readers] a generous sympathy for the wronged negro race of America" (1). *A Peep into Uncle Tom's Cabin* includes a preface by Stowe which alerts the reader to the value of Eva as "the picture of a *Christian child*. Learn of her, dear children, to be as thoughtful, as kind to every creature, however poor and lowly, as she was . . . and try to do all the little good that lies in a child's power" (iv). Such instructions could not legislate response, however.

52. John Ross Dix, *Transatlantic Tracings,* 78. Of course, a reader may enter into multiple aspects of character and situation. As Barbara Sicherman notes, "identification with one character is far too restrictive an approach to an experience as complex as reading" ("Sense and Sensibility," 212).

53. See Brown, "Reading and Children" 80–81.

54. Exploring the "Forces of Early Impressions" in 1856, Goodrich asserts that "often a single incident, one momentary impression is indelibly stamped [upon a child's mind] as upon a die of steel" (*Recollections,* 46). Locke's influence on child-rearing practices in the antebellum United States was formative. See Brown, *The Consent of the Governed;* Crain, *The Story of A;* Reinier, *From Virtue to Character.*

55. Goodrich, *Recollections,* 170. In another typical formulation: "The sentiments and principles of many children are formed almost as much by reading, as by intercourse with the world" (*Christian Examiner* 5 [Sept.–Oct. 1828]; cited in Roth, "The Mind of a Child," 107).

56. Mrs. H. E. Beecher Stowe, "Literary Epidemics No. 1," 235.

57. Stowe and Catharine Beecher justify novel-reading but also warn of its potential dangers for youth in *Principles of Domestic Science as Applied to the Duties and Pleasures of Home,* 254–56.

58. The classic psychoanalytic defense of violence in fairy tales is Bruno Bettleheim, *The Uses of Enchantment;* see also Spitz, *Inside Picture Books.*

59. Alcott, *The Young Wife,* (24). John Abbott's widely read *The Mother at Home* stressed the "unobtrusive . . . secret and silent" but also "powerful and extensive: influence of a mother on her child" (9–10).

60. Anonymous, *Mother's Friend,* 123.

61. Lynn Cobb, *Cobb's Toys.* "This series of toys contains a more extensive and minute description of animals, birds, fishes, articles of manufacture, &c. than was given in the first series. . . . In this as well as the other series nothing has been permitted to find a place which is false, unnatural, or unphilosophical, or any details of conversations among animals which never did and which never can take place" ("Preface," 2). According to the American Antiquarian Society catalogue the *Cobb's Toys* series was issued until 1844. I am grateful to Laura E. Wasowicz for this reference.

62. Goodrich, *Recollections,* 170, 167.

63. On Freud's reception in America see Hale, *Freud and the Americans;* Hoffman, "The Spread of Freud's Theory," esp. chap. 2; Masse, "Constructing the Psychoanalytic Child."

64. On the crossing of gender lines by child readers see Segal, "As the Twig Is Bent . . . ," 175–77. Spitz recommends "cross-gendered reading" for children on the assumption that fluid identifications are possible (*Inside Picture Books,* 25). In *Childhood and Society* Erik Erikson outlines the destructive consequences for a black child of identifying with a white hero (217–18). Jacque Roethier explores the negative impact on black children of illustrated books designed for white children ("Reading in Color: Children's Book Illustrations and Identity Formation for Black Children in the Unites States"). The pitfalls of cross-racial identification for African American children have gained

scientific as well as imaginative life in Kenneth Clark's famous doll experiment as in Toni Morrison's *The Bluest Eye*. Yet scholars have raised questions about Clark's conclusions regarding racial preference and self-esteem. See most recently Bergner, "Black Children, White Preference" and Bernstein, *Racial Innocence*. Bernstein argues that books and material objects can invite or prompt (but not legislate) response; she engages the "script" of racialized reading, but also resistance to it, especially among children. Recent work on reading and identification emphasizes that although we all read according to our cultural location, a reader's flexible construction of meaning enables readers to expand their sense of self and social options. See Abel, "Black Writing, White Reading: Race and the Politics of Feminist Interpretation"; Sicherman, "Sense and Sensibility," 201–25.

65. Keen, *Empathy and the Novel,* 70.

66. Ginsberg, "Of Babies, Beasts, and Bondage," 87, 89.

67. The animals portrayed in nineteenth-century moral and abolitionist tales are a far cry from those of popular twentieth-century children's books such as Arnold Lobel's stories of "Frog and Toad," or Russell Hoban's "Frances" (the badger) books, or even the "Berenstain Bears." Animals in abolitionist and moral tales are like children insofar as some emotions or desires are attributed to them, but they are animals, first and foremost. By contrast, "Frog and Toad" et al. are intended to stand in for people and—like people—they wear clothes, live in houses, have families, voices, toys, sibling rivalries, etc. Moreover, the children for whom they are written—unlike nineteenth-century children—are presumed already to have had considerable experience with the interpretive convention of reading animals as human (via Disney cartoons, *Sesame Street,* and other texts).

   In an essay that brings J. J. Grandville's series of lithographs *Les Metamorphoses du jour* (1828–29) together with Art Spiegelman's *Maus*, Judith L. Goldstein raises questions about "the kind of identification . . . created with people who are portrayed as animals." She stresses the importance of "situation" and "relations among the figures" in making animals legible as human" ("Realism without a Human Face," 68, 78). In "Why Look at Animals" John Berger distinguishes between animals used as "moral metaphors" (lion as courage, cat as stealth) and animals used to suggest human forms of imprisonment (13–18). Spitz engages some implications of characters in "nonhuman form," especially in order to access children's inaccessible feelings (*Inside Picture Books,* 74).

68. Pro-slavery apologists also employed animal imagery to characterize African Americans (either as beast-like and requiring control; or as docile, affectionate, naturally dependent). Like abolitionist tales, pro-slavery adaptations of the animal trope emphasize the white child's moral consciousness or sense of obligation; they rarely elaborate the feelings of the animal/slave.

   In abolitionist tales, the pet bird or pursued butterfly narrative ends with the act of liberation. The next turn of the plot is unspecified. Winged creatures, once freed, will presumably disappear; they will return to nature and thrive there. The transition will be unproblematic. Not surprisingly, this story has a different ending in pro-slavery versions. There dog, cat, or domesticated bird either meets with destruction in the wild or simply refuses to go—out of fear, self-interest, or love for the master who offers to protect the animal. Such stories typically reinforce the divide between white children on the one hand, enslaved creatures on the other.

69. Sarah Grimke, "Juvenile Anti-Slavery Meeting in Boston," 12.

70. On African fears see "The Life of Olaudah Equiano" in *The Classic Slave Narratives*, 41–42; Davis, *Inhuman Bondage*. The fear of being eaten is inscribed in many of Grimms' fairy tales. For Bruno Bettleheim the appeal of "Hansel and Gretel" has everything to do with its representation of the "destructive aspects of orality" (*The Uses of Enchantment*, 162). Dorothy Bloch explores being eaten as a common (white, middle-class) childhood fear in *'So the Witch Won't Eat Me'*.

71. Hunt, "Narrative Theory and Children's Literature," 193.

72. For a psychoanalyst such as D. W. Winnicott it is axiomatic "that the child of two, three, and four is in two worlds at once"—the real world and an imagined one; for this child, unlike the "ordinary healthy" adult the distinction between "the realness of the world" and "the realness of what is imaginative and personal" is unclear (*The Child, the Family and the Outside World*, 70, 69). Drawing on interviews with contemporary girls (aged eight to sixteen), Holly Virginia Blackford concludes that, rather than identifying with any particular figure, these readers "experience a welcome diffusion of identity" by losing themselves in a "good story" (*Out of this World*, 9, 6). See also Bettleheim, *Uses of Enchantment*; Spitz, *Inside Picture Books*.

73. Lydia Maria Child and other nineteenth-century commentators often made this point. "Many readers and writers too," Child writes, "think that any book is proper for young people, which has a good moral at the end; but . . . some books with a long and excellent moral, have the worst possible effect on a young audience. . . . [Vicious] characters excite [the juvenile readers'] admiration, their love, their deepest pity; and then they are told that these heroes and heroines are very naughty. . . . What is the result? The generous bosom of youth pities the sinners, and thinks the world . . . cruel . . . to despise . . . them" (90–91). Some writers used a similar argument to denounce the representation of fantastical or violent events. *The Mother's Friend* condemns the practice of introducing "strange, terrific, or perhaps ghost-like appearances, to be in the sequel explained away. . . . The alarming image and nervous impression may continue, whilst the subsequent explanation and practical inference will most likely be forgotten" (123–24).

74. Sanchez-Eppler, *Touching Liberty*, 48; Stepto, "Sharing the Thunder," 142; Tawil, *The Making of Racial Sentiment*, 180.

75. The phrase is Rachel Malik's. See her "Horizons of the Publishable." Stowe had trouble finding a book publisher for *Uncle Tom's Cabin*. A long novel about slavery was not expected to sell (see Parfait, *Publishing History*, 33–34). As Darryl Pinckney notes "Stowe was not unmindful of Northern anxieties about having freedmen as competitors and neighbors" ("Introduction" to *Uncle Tom's Cabin*, xi). Stowe knew her reading public and the literary marketplace well enough to avoid the risks of a more radical ending.

76. Pitcher and Prelinger, *Children Tell Stories*. See also Applebee's summary of these experiments (*The Child's Concept of Story*, 41–47 and Appendix 1). Further references to Applebee are included in the text.

77. Influential accounts that assume the importance of endings and analyze the dynamic of reading from this point of view include F. R. Leavis, *The Sense of an Ending;* Peter Brooks, *Reading for the Plot*. Meir Sternberg discusses "primacy effect," "recency effect," and other "models of control" in *Expositional Modes and Temporal Ordering in Fiction*, 93–99, 151 and passim. Linearity does not always govern reading, however.

78. Benjamin, "Children's Literature," 250. Psychoanalytic accounts of children's responses to fairy tales and picture books provide some evidence of the gap between the way adults and children understand the same story. See Bettleheim, *The Uses of Enchantment*, 16–17; Spitz, *Inside Picture Books*, 7, 149. For a similar emphasis from a different theoretical perspective see Hunt, "Narrative Theory and Children's Literature."

79. Hewins, *A Mid-Century Child and Her Books*, 78–79. I am grateful to Courtney Weikle-Mills for alerting me to this passage.

80. Hunt, "Narrative Theory and Children's Literature," 191.

81. Suzanne Keen emphasizes the hold on readers of unresolved and conflictual elements in a narrative: "Empathy with situations tends to zero in on episodes, circumstances, or states of relationship at points of irresolution. That is, empathy with plot situation gravitates toward *middles* of plots, when problems and enigmas have not yet been solved or brought to closure" (*Empathy*, 79).

82. Victor Nell suggests that "vestigial" elements of childhood reading lurk "within every elite [adult] reader" but that adult readers always maintain some "reality orientation" while reading, even when deeply immersed (*Lost in a Book*, 5, 211). For psychoanalytic theorists such as Ernst Kris or Leon Balter, "aesthetic illusion" relies on the temporary regression of an adult reader to earlier developmental stage where imaginary characters and events may be taken as real; yet the reader never quite forgets that he or she will be able to return to adult "reality" and customary ego control when the reading experience is over (see Balter, "Aesthetic Illusion"). Kris takes a child's experience of play as the origin of an adult capacity for aesthetic experience: "Reality testing . . . establishes the confines of the actual and its distinction from the possible. The world of make-believe is at first thinly separated from the real world, but the distinction becomes ever more durable. The mechanism of denial can operate; a firm belief in the 'reality of play' can coexist with a certainty that it is play only. Here lie the roots of aesthetic illusion" (*Psychoanalytic Explorations in Art*, 42).

83. See Introduction and Chapter 3.

84. See also Chapter 3.

85. Frank Norris, *The Literary Criticism of Frank Norris*, 92.

86. According to Ernst Kris, "In play and fantasy the child's wishes live on, adapted to but still unhampered by reality, and in this very world a further step is made which carries the child in the direction in which it may later find pleasure in art. Instead of his own fantasies the child is ready to accept, and at certain points of his development prefers to accept, fantasies of others, the stories and fairy tales offered to him. . . . The fairy-tale

theme . . . [is often] chosen by the child as less dangerous and less forbidden [than some of his own fantasies]; it [is] . . . not a product of his own imagination, but a pattern for his emotional reaction offered to him with the consent of the adults" (*Psychoanalytic Explorations,* 42). For Winnicott too, fairy tales, provided by and approved by adults, allow toddlers to explore magical ideas, such as flying people—in a way that is acceptable to the child and others (*The Child, the Family, and the Outside World,* 70–71). Writing of adult readers, Keen notes that when we are aware that something is a fiction it allows "us to experience our full emotional registers in risk-free, no obligations mental stimulation" (n. 30, 176). See also Balter, "Aesthetic Illusion."

87. James Ford Rhodes, *History of the United States,* 285.

5. Sentiment without Tears

1. Chartier, *The Order of Books,* viii.

2. See for example, Ginzberg, *The Cheese and the Worms;* Radway, *Reading the Romance;* Long, "Textual Interpretation as Collective Action"; Sicherman, "Reading *Little Women:* The Many Lives of a Book."

3. "A Pioneer Editor," 743–44.

4. Beadle, "Harriet Beecher Stowe," 285.

5. "Biographical Sketch," in Harriet Beecher Stowe, *Uncle Tom's Cabin* (Boston: Houghton Mifflin, 1896), xi.

6. According to a newspaper article of 1911 "it never occurred to [Harriet Beecher Stowe] . . . that there was anything about 'Uncle Tom's Cabin' to precipitate a war" ("Friendly Plan Is Claimed for 'Uncle Tom': "New Life Story of 'Little Woman' Asserts Friendship for the South"; "Meant No Offence"). Beecher-Stowe scrapbook clipping. See also "Introduction."

7. Parton, "International Copyright," 431.

8. "Uncle Tom's Cabin, the Story of the Story," 1. The newspaper was published in Atchison, Kansas; the writer recalls reading *Uncle Tom's Cabin* as a child in Maine.

9. A. B. Fields, *Authors and Friends,* 220–21. Fields dates Stowe's Boston reading as 1872, as do Hedrick (*Harriet Beecher Stowe,* 383–84) and Alice Stone Blackwell (*Growing Up in Boston's Gilded Age,* 111).

10. Unsigned "Biographical Sketch," *Uncle Tom's Cabin,* xxviii. As Daniel Borus points out, "a flourishing cottage industry" catered to the reading public's interest in the private lives of authors (*Writing Realism: Howells, James, and Norris in the Mass Market,* 124). On the reverence for poets in late nineteenth-century schoolrooms see Sorby, *The Schoolroom Poets.* Horace Scudder reasons the importance of acquainting children with American authors in *Methods of Teaching.*

11. "Wed. 25" [Sept]. Annie Adams Fields Papers Reel 2. Massachusetts Historical Society. Diary #42, begun August 1872. I am grateful to Susan K. Harris for alerting me to these entries, sharing her notes and her thoughts. On Annie Fields see Harris, *The Cultural Work of the Late Nineteenth-Century Hostess.*

12. "Saturday" [28 Sept]. Annie Adams Fields Papers Reel 2.

13. Alice Stone Blackwell, *Growing Up in Boston's Gilded Age,* 111. According to a note in the edited journal, Blackwell had heard about Stowe from her father. She "attended [Stowe's] reading at Tremont Temple, where Stowe was introduced to the large audience by William Lloyd Garrison" (111, n. 13). I have silently omitted an editorial footnote in the citations.

14. Appendix 1, "Books and Periodicals Referred to in the Journal," lists numerous titles (249–53).

15. Harriet Beecher Stowe, "Introduction," *Uncle Tom's Cabin* (Boston: Houghton Mifflin, 1896; c. 1879), xxxvii. Further references to this "Introduction" are included in the text.

16. "Recent Literature: H. B. Stowe's Uncle Tom's Cabin," 407. Further references to this edition are included in the text.

17. Trachtenberg, *Reading American Photographs: Images as History,* 77.

18. Trachtenberg notes that reawakened interest in the war "culminated in 1911 in a tenvolume *Photographic History of the Civil War,* assembled by Francis Trevelyn Miller, editor of the *Journal of American History,* on the fiftieth anniversary of the firing on Fort Sumter" (*Reading American Photographs,* 78–79). The year 1911 was the hundredth anniversary of Stowe's birth and occasioned another wave of attention to her and her influential novel.

19. See Michaels, *Our America: Nativism, Modernism, and Pluralism;* Riggio, "Uncle Tom Reconstructed," 56–70; Silber, *The Romance of Reunion;* Sundquist, *To Wake the Nations.*

20. Brown, *Beyond the Lines,* 115.

21. Ibid.

22. Allen, "Mrs. Stowe's 'Uncle Tom' at Home in Kentucky," 854.

23. Some of Kemble's illustrations for Allen's text were reprinted as illustrations to *Uncle Tom's Cabin* when Houghton Mifflin brought out its 1891 edition. See Chapter 6.

24. Allen, "Mrs. Stowe's 'Uncle Tom' at Home in Kentucky," 867.

25. Ibid., 862, 861.

26. For Palmer's concerns about *Uncle Tom's Cabin* see Chapter 3.

27. Cf. Hill, "Uncle Tom Without a Cabin," 859–65.

28. The subversive content of Chesnutt's conjure tales has been a recurrent focus of analysis in recent years; but as "local color" tales, published in the prestigious *Atlantic,* they were probably read at the time as evoking the ravaged "old plantation," the charming and lovable loyal servant, and the colorful primitive, superstitious slaves. On Chesnutt see Brodhead, *Cultures of Letters;* Sundquist, *To Wake the Nations,* chap. 4. On plantation romances see Silber, *Romance of Reunion;* Sundquist, *To Wake the Nations,* 230–31. On the "Old South" imagined in the 1890s as a kind of restored aristocratic region and a white enclave see Michaels's discussion of Nelson Page and Thomas Dixon in *Our America,* 16–23.

29. Harriet Beecher Stowe, *Uncle Tom's Cabin* (New York: Eaton and Mains, 1897), vii.

30. James Weldon Johnson ironically renders this process in describing a theatrical production of *Uncle Tom's Cabin* that was made palatable for a Southern audience of 1915 ("Uncle Tom's Cabin and the Clansman," 612–13). See also my Epilogue, n. 43.

31. *Uncle Tom's Cabin* (Eaton and Mains), xvii.

32. "The Passing of Uncle Tom," from *The Argus,* Albany, N.Y., Sept. 17, 1905 (found in an envelope with other clippings about *Uncle Tom's Cabin* in an 1888 Houghton Mifflin edition of the novel [NYPL]). A bookplate in the front cover of this edition states: "Gansevoort-Lansing Collection given to the New York Public Library . . . by Victor Hugo Paltsits under the terms of the last will and testament of Catherine Gansevoort Lansing granddaughter of general Peter Gansevoort, junior and Widow of the Honorable Abraham Lansing, Albany, New York." The article is concerned with the Tom plays: "Poor old Uncle Tom!" it begins. "For the past 40 years he has traveled the country, up and down, as a great moral lesson, as a dramatic spectacle, and finally as a reminder of other days. But his usefulness is outlived, and there are rumors in the air that Uncle Tom, Little Eva, Topsy, the bloodhounds Eliza and the cakes of ice, Miss Ophelia, Legree and all, are passing away." This emphasis on the demise of Uncle Tom in the theater is closely linked to a growing sense that the novel itself is dated.

33. Knight, *History of the Work of the Connecticut Women at the World's Columbian Exposition Chicago 1893,* 24, 22.

34. Despite heightened concern with such issues as children's welfare, social reform of the 1880s and '90s tended to prioritize issues that served the newly consolidated, increasingly nuclear middle-class family, especially the white family. See Coontz, *The Social Origins of Private Life,* especially chap. 7 ("The Apex of Private Spheres, 1870–1890"). While the public library movement emphasized making books available to the urban poor, African Americans were rarely encouraged to visit the library in this period. On the library movement see Garrison, *Apostles of Culture;* Augst and Carpenter, *Institutions of Reading.*

35. Logan, *The Betrayal of the Negro,* 216. See also Fredrickson, *Black Image in the White Mind;* Silber, *The Romance of Reunion;* Blight, *Race and Reunion.*

36. Cited in Brodhead, *Cultures of Letters,* 206.

37. Mark Twain, *Adventures of Huckleberry Finn,* 294.

38. Winship, "The Greatest Book of Its Kind," 330. See also Parfait, *A Publishing History of Uncle Tom's Cabin,* chap. 6.

39. See especially Chapter 3.

40. Unsigned, "Uncle Tom's Cabin, the Story of the Story," 1.

41. Annie Fields, ed. *Life and Letters of Harriet Beecher Stowe,* 377–78.

42. A Houghton Mifflin edition of 1888 includes ten pages of advertisements for "Works of Fiction Published by Houghton Mifflin." American authors include James Fenimore Cooper, Francis Marion Crawford, Bret Harte, Nathaniel Hawthorne, William Dean Howells, Henry James, Sarah Orne Jewett, Elizabeth Stuart Phelps, and S. Weir Mitchell.

43. *Uncle Tom's Cabin* (Eaton Mains), ix.

44. "In every State of the American Union, one very rarely finds an adult who has not read the work; it has become a great American classic" (J. H. Beadle, "Harriet Beecher Stowe," 286). Wendell, *A Literary History of America,* 354; *Uncle Tom's Cabin* "has brought tears to more eyes and laughter to more lips than any other book ever written

and . . . has become a classic wherever the English Language is spoken" (*Uncle Tom's Cabin: Art Memorial Edition*, 10, 29). Jay Martin notes that "following the decline of instruction in Latin and Greek, Dickens, Cooper, Scott and their peers came to be known as 'classics' " (*Harvests of Change*, 19). See also Hart, *The Popular Book*, 183.

45. "Introductory Note" to a children's version (*The Story of Little Eva*).

46. On "cultural belatedness" as an aspect of the "literary situation" see Bloom, *The Anxiety of Influence*, xxv.

47. *Uncle Tom's Cabin* (Art Memorial edition), 29.

48. *Uncle Tom's Cabin* (Eaton Mains), xvii. In a similarly backhanded compliment another edition claims that *Uncle Tom's Cabin* was "more than a work of fiction" (Art Memorial Edition, 32).

49. Knight, *History of the Work of Connecticut Women*, 22, 26, 94. Florine Thayer McCray refers to Stowe's novel as a "wonderful story" while acknowledging its precariousness as a "work of art" (*Life Work of the Author of Uncle Tom's Cabin*, 98). See also Charles Edward Stowe, *Life of Harriet Beecher Stowe*, 156.

50. See MacLeod, *American Childhood*, 124. Dee Garrison notes that "the development of library service to children was the most important new form of public library activity in the Progressive period" (*Apostles of Culture*, 207). On the rise of children's librarianship as a profession see also Lundin, "Little Pilgrims Progress: Literary Horizons for Children's Literature"; Eddy, *Bookwomen: Creating an Empire in Children's Book Publishing, 1919–1939*.

51. William Dean Howells, *Criticism and Fiction*, 149–50. On anxiety about girls and the "new woman" see Smith-Rosenberg, *Disorderly Conduct*, 218–45 and Garvey, *The Adman in the Parlor*, esp. chap. 4.

52. On concerns about young women's reading in this period see Hochman, "The Good, the Bad and the Literary: Edith Wharton's *Bunner Sisters* and the Social Contexts of Reading"; Hochman, "The Reading Habit and 'The Yellow Wallpaper' "; Phegley, "I Should No More Think of Dictating," 105–28; Sicherman, "Reading and Middle-Class Identity."

53. Hjalmar Hjorth Boyeson, "Why We Have No Great Novelists," 615.

54. On the concern with wholesome reading matter in this period see Erin A. Smith, "Melodrama, Popular Religion, and Literary Value"; Garrison, *Apostles of Culture;* Radway, *A Feeling for Books.*

55. *Uncle Tom's Cabin* was published as part of this series in 1898. See Chapter 6.

56. Richard Burton, "The Author of 'Uncle Tom's Cabin,' " 699. *Uncle Tom's Cabin* is described as Stowe's "great slave epic" in a newspaper clipping marking Stowe's eighty-fifth birthday. Charles Stowe's scrapbook (Beecher-Stowe Collection).

57. Charles Dudley Warner, "*Uncle Tom's Cabin* Half a Century Later," 484, 487.

58. Edith Wharton, "Copy: A Dialogue," 113.

59. "Editor's Study," 152.

60. William Dean Howells, *My Literary Passions*, 50.

61. Warner, "*Uncle Tom's Cabin* Half a Century Later," 483, 487. Warner's essay was published simultaneously as an introduction to a Houghton Mifflin, Riverside Press

edition of the novel; *The Writings of Harriet Beecher Stowe: With Biographical Introductions, Portraits and other Illustrations* (1896) appeared in sixteen volumes.

62. Cited in Knight, *History of the Work of Connecticut Women,* 26.

63. Lowell, "The Five Indispensable Authors," 224.

64. Cited in Burton, "The Author of 'Uncle Tom's Cabin.'" 699.

65. Grant Allen, "Novels Without a Purpose," 408; Gilman, *The Living of Charlotte Perkins Gilman,* 121; Frank Norris, "The Novel With a 'Purpose,'" 92–93.

66. Allen, "Novels Without a Purpose," 408.

67. Sarah Knowles Bolton, *Lives of Girls Who Became Famous,* 16.

68. Late nineteenth-century advice literature regularly recommends purposiveness in reading. As Charles Richardson puts it, "Every book that we take up without a purpose . . . is an opportunity lost of taking up a book with a purpose" (*The Choice of Books,* 35). On anxieties about nineteenth-century reading and idleness see Davidson, *Revolution and the Word;* Kerber, *Women of the Republic;* Sicherman, "Reading and Middle-Class Identity"; Zboray and Zboray, *Everyday Ideas,* 169–72, 178. See also Chapter 1.

69. Allen, "Novels Without a Purpose," 408.

70. Ohmann, *Selling Culture,* 255–56.

71. On the "uncertain and contested process" of canon formation reflected in the history of this series, see Casper, "Defining the National Pantheon: The Making of Houghton Mifflin's Biographical Series 1880–1900," 180.

72. "Changes Wrought by One Book," Beecher-Stowe clipping, Beecher-Stowe Collection.

73. An advertisement, possibly from the page of another book, pasted into the back cover of *Uncle Tom's Cabin* (Boston: Houghton Mifflin, 1888; NYPL). The ad continues: "It fixed the eyes of the nation and of the civilized world on the evils of slavery, presenting these so vividly and powerfully that the heart and conscience of mankind were thenceforth enlisted against them." "Recommended" reading lists often categorized *Uncle Tom's Cabin* as "historical" fiction. In his Preface to *The Virginian,* Wister uses *Uncle Tom's Cabin* to exemplify a "historical" novel "which presents faithfully a day and generation" (ix). Other commentators emphasized the book's role in shaping (not merely representing) historical events.

74. *Uncle Tom's Cabin,* Art Memorial edition, 24–25.

75. Burton, "The Author of 'Uncle Tom's Cabin,'" 699.

76. Cited in Fields, *Authors and Friends,* 181; "Days With Mrs. Stowe," 148. Among many twentieth-century citations, see G. Grant Williams, "Reminiscences of the Life of Harriet Beecher Stowe and her Family," 128.; Sandburg, *Abraham Lincoln: The Prairie Years and the War Years,* 385; Gossett, *Uncle Tom's Cabin and American Culture,* 344; Hedrick, *Harriet Beecher Stowe,* vii; the back cover of the Oxford World's Classic edition (1998).

77. *Uncle Tom's Cabin,* Art Memorial edition.

78. Winship notes that between 1886 and 1890 for example "a total of 109,495 copies were sold, providing Stowe nearly two and a half times the combined royalty . . . on all her other books published by the firm" ("The Greatest Book of Its Kind" 326).

79. Arthur Penn (pseud. Brander Matthews), *The Home Library,* 42. Cf. Rhodes, *History of the United States,* 284, n. 2.

80. Lyman Abbott, ed., *Hints for Home Reading.*

81. Conversely, numerous antebellum readers read the same copy. Parfait notes that "contemporary reviewers commonly computed between eight and 10 readers to a copy" (*A Publishing History of Uncle Tom's Cabin,* 87).

82. Knight, *History of the Work of Connecticut Women,"* 100.

83. *Uncle Tom's Cabin,* Art Memorial edition, 10; Higginson, "Harriet Beecher Stowe," a "Critical and Biographical Introduction" to *Uncle Tom's Cabin* (New York: Appleton, 1898), xiv.

84. Higginson, "Harriet Beecher Stowe, xiii–xiv. Higginson was exceptional in suggesting that the novel had begun some still unfinished business. Referring to the "brave effort . . . by [a greatly injured race] to raise itself," he noted that "it must still be many years . . . before the mission of 'Uncle Tom' is ended" (xiv). Despite this caveat, the edition as a whole stresses American progress. See Chapter 6.

85. Marshall, *Uncle Tom's Cabin Told To the Children,* vi.

86. Beadle, "Harriet Beecher Stowe," 286–87. On the centrality of "reunion" as a rallying cry toward the end of the century see Blight, *The Civil War in American Memory,* and Silber, *The Romance of Reunion.*

87. Knight, *History of the Work of Connecticut Women,* 94, 93. Further references to this discussion are included in the text.

88. Knight's report on the Stowe exhibit at the fair reflects her assumption that both Stowe's piety and her "message" (26) would constitute a problem for turn-of-century readers: Knight praises neither Stowe's religious nor her political aims, but rather her "unsectarian" Christianity (105), her "genius" (22, 26), and her success in representing "enduring 'flesh tints of the heart' " (27). In another typical formulation of the period, a review of a new edition (Houghton Mifflin, 1891) notes that "the issues upon which it was based have passed away forever[;] the younger generation of readers are little familiar with a work which passed into the mental make-up of all readers of an earlier day" (*New York Evangelist,* 62).

89. For discussions of the ideology informing the Chicago Exposition see Rydell, *All the World's a Fair;* Harris, de Wit, Gilbert, and Rydell, *Grand Illusions: Chicago World's Fair of 1893;* Domosh, "A 'civilized' commerce: Gender, 'race,' empire at the 1893 Chicago Exposition"; *Libraries and Culture* 41.1 Special Issue on the Woman's Building Library at the Columbian Exposition (Winter 2006).

90. In the 1890s Brander Matthews, Theodore Roosevelt, Thomas Wentworth Higginson and others waged an ongoing "Campaign for Literary Americanism." For a concise account, see Oliver, "Theodore Roosevelt, Brander Matthews, and the Campaign for Literary Americanism."

91. Indeed, the claim of literary greatness was so thoroughly defeated that throughout most of the twentieth century it became difficult to think of *Uncle Tom's Cabin* as "literature" at all. On other factors in the subversion of *Uncle Tom's Cabin* as "literature"

see Moers, *Harriet Beecher Stowe;* Arac, "Uncle Tom's Cabin vs. Huckleberry Finn"; Tompkins, *Sensational Designs.*

92. In the 1880s and '90s commentators defined realism as a sophisticated "high" taste. Nonetheless, historical romances had wide popular appeal. On the prestige of realism toward the turn of the century, see Glazener, *Reading for Realism;* Barrish, *American Literary Realism,* 16–47. On the appeal of popular romances in the same period see Hart, *The Popular Book;* Hochman, *Getting at the Author,* 1–10, 48–69; Smith, "Melodrama, Popular Religion, and Literary Value."

93. In 1852, George Sand set the tone for generations of criticism when she wrote of *Uncle Tom's Cabin:* "this book, defective according to the rules of the modern French romance, intensely interests everybody and triumphs over all criticisms" ("Introduction" to *Uncle Tom's Cabin* [Boston: Houghton Mifflin, 1896], 1). As we have noted, J. W. De Forest in his essay "The Great American Novel" proposed *Uncle Tom's Cabin* as the only worthy candidate for the title. Still, even De Forest suggested that "the comeliness of form was lacking" (28). In 1899, Florine McCray wrote as follows: "One commences to re-read this wonderful story with a view to its merits as literary art. But criticism, artistic standpoint, even the vehicle itself, is forgotten as one is swept away from all conventionalities and literary tenets upon the surging current of mighty feeling. *Uncle Tom's Cabin* has seldom been discussed as a mere work of art . . ." (98). In Barrett Wendell's *A Literary History of America, Uncle Tom's Cabin* is described as a "remarkable piece of fiction" despite its "artistic" faults (354).

94. In a letter to Harriet Beecher Stowe, Vice President Henry Wilson wrote as follows on July 2, 1874: "I send you my second volume. You will see on page 519 I have credited your great work with a huge influence" (Beecher-Stowe Collection, Radcliffe, Folder 259). See Wilson, *History of the Rise and Fall of the Slave Power in America,* 519; Eggleston, *A History of the United States and its People,* 296; Schouler, *History of the United States of America Under the Constitution,* 247; Rhodes, *History of the United States from the Compromise of 1850,* 284–85. Responding to a correspondent who asks whether *Uncle Tom's Cabin* had a role in causing the war, W. E. B. Du Bois cites Lincoln's words as quoted in Charles Stowe's biography of his mother. (Exchange of letters between P. Porohovshikov and W. E. B. Dubois, July 1935, October 25, 1935; November 1935; W. E. B. Du Bois Papers, U Mass Amherst, Reel 44). I am grateful to Claire Parfait for alerting me to this source.

95. See David Brion Davis, *The Emancipation Moment,* 22nd annual Robert Fortenbaugh memorial lecture; Sandage, "A Marble House Divided."

96. The inkstand was a gift to Stowe, "a testimonial to Mrs. Stowe from her English admirers in 1853" (Knight, *History of the Work of the Connecticut Women,* 93).

97. An image of the inkstand is reproduced at the head of the "List of Illustrations" in Charles Edward Stowe, *Life of Harriet Beecher Stowe,* xi. On the figure of the kneeling slave see also Albert Boime's reading of Thomas Ball's sculpture "Emancipation Group" (1874) in *The Art of Exclusion,* 17–18; Boulukos, *The Grateful Slave.*

98. See Rydell, *Grand Illusions,* 145–50.

99. Weimann, *The Fair Women,* 359.

100. Knight, *History of the Work of Connecticut Women,* 93. The books in the exhibit are partially preserved in the collection of the Connecticut Historical Society. In a letter of Sept. 30, 1893, Knight offered to donate the contents of the Connecticut women's exhibit to the Society; its corresponding secretary replied, in a letter of Oct. 2, 1893, that the Connecticut Historical Society "will gladly accept the gift" (Knight, 291). An acquisitions list of 1894 includes eleven volumes by Stowe, apart from *Uncle Tom's Cabin.*

101. *Uncle Tom's Cabin,* Art Memorial edition, 10.

102. Starling, *The Slave Narrative: Its Place in American History,* 308.

103. Unsigned, "What Susie Found at Tougaloo," 108; "Editor's Drawer," 971; George W. Cable, ed., "Strange True Stories of Louisiana. War Diary of a Union Woman in the South," 937.

104. See Young, *Disarming the Nation,* 36–37.

105. Parsons, "The Ornamentation Of Ponds And Lakes," 351; Welch, *Home History,* 137; "Editor's Literary Record," 780; Hamlin, "Pen Pictures of the Bosphorus," 494; White, "King Cole and His Band," 251; "Postal Communication, Past and Present," 284; Ralph, "Western Modes Of City Management," 710; "The Future of the British Empire," 387; Colomb, "The Battle-Ship of the Future"; Bradford, "Open Letters: Columbus's Day," 479.

106. An advertisement for *Girls Who Became Famous* by Sarah K. Bolton and two full pages devoted to the "Young Ladies' Library" suggest that the compiler was a girl or a young woman. The exclusive focus on white writers suggests that she was white. The year 1905 is the latest date to appear—noted on the reverse of the "frontispiece" page and toward the end beside a photograph of Theodore Roosevelt—"President of the United States 1905." The notebook is in the collection of Ellen Gruber Garvey. Many thanks to Ellen Garvey for sharing this source with me.

107. McBride, *How Dear to My Heart,* 3. Further references to McBride are included in the text.

108. On changes in theories of childhood and reading see Chapter 7.

109. Unsigned, *Publisher's Weekly,* no. 734 (Feb. 20, 1886) 284.

110. Alice Hamilton's reading, which was particularly intense and wide-ranging, is well documented. Perhaps her neglect of *Uncle Tom's Cabin,* during a lifetime of reading in which fiction figured prominently, can be partly explained by her father's "hatred of sentimentality," by his relation to the Civil War, or by her family's neglect of the "New England tradition" (despite its "receptive attitude to all sorts of books"). See Sicherman, "Sense and Sensibility," 205, 207; Hamilton, *Exploring the Dangerous Trades,* 25. Like other readers of the period, Hamilton mentions only the stage version of *Uncle Tom's Cabin,* which she notes deprecatingly, in passing (*Exploring the Dangerous Trades,* 145). Reading choices are always colored by both personal and cultural history; these are closely intertwined. Charlotte Perkins Gilman was Stowe's great-niece, and we might consider this in speculating why *Uncle Tom's Cabin* does not appear among the great variety of texts noted in her journal and why she only mentions it briefly in her autobiography: "Among our pleasantest visits were those at the new big house of Aunt Harriet Stowe in Hartford. She had built it to suit her eager fancy out of the proceeds of *Uncle*

Tom's Cabin" (*The Living of Charlotte Perkins Gilman*, 16). Yet the diminishing attraction of *Uncle Tom's Cabin* for white readers of the 1890s and early twentieth century is culturally typical and not explained by personal idiosyncrasies or family relations.

111. Locke, *This World, My Home*, 9.

112. Ibid., 75.

113. Rubin, *Songs of Ourselves*, 271.

114. In the penultimate chapter of the book, Locke writes: "So much there has been to test! It has been a dizzying age. I have been Eliza—*Uncle Tom's Cabin* Eliza [*sic*] crossing the river down at Ripley on the floating ice. With each step more slippery than the last, how sure was the shore? World after world has swept by me. To what end? To what good? The time to take inventory comes" (*This World, My Home*, 167).

115. Balestier, "Benefits Forgot," 52.

116. Lynn, *A Stepdaughter of the Prairie*, 81, 83, 118.

117. Wilson, *The Dark and the Damp*, 80. Further references to this edition are included in the text.

118. See also my Epilogue.

119. There has been little scholarly attention to children as part of Stowe's target audience. On *Uncle Tom's Cabin* as a children's book see Chapter 4.

120. Sanchez-Eppler, *Touching Liberty*, chap. 1.

121. *Female Life in Prison* by a Prison Matron (1862), 127. This book was apparently ghostwritten by F. W. Robinson, a hack journalist and novelist. With thanks to Clare Parfait for this source. *Uncle Tom's Cabin* seems to have influenced Marcus Clarke in writing the Australian convict novel *His Natural Life*. This narrative, which attacks the conditions in the British penal colonies, was first serialized in the *Australian Journal* in 1870–1872, subsequently published in book form, and often reissued. On Stowe's influence see *His Natural Life*, xxxi, n. 51; 611, n. 7. I thank Paul Eggert for this source.

122. "One day," she reports, "I got so engrossed in the part where Eliza braved the frozen river with her little son in her arms, I was indeed deaf to the world around me, the scalding tears falling on a pile of plates already inadequately wiped. I came smartly back to earth with a stinging swish from [my mistress's] walking stick across my behind" (cited in Burnett, *Useful Toil: Autobiographies of Working People from the 1820s to the 1920s*, 233). I thank Barbara Ryan for alerting me to this source.

123. Cited in Phillips, *Helen Hunt Jackson: A Literary Life*, 252.

124. Mizruchi, *The Rise of Multicultural America*, 321, n. 8.

125. Lewis, "What Life Meant to Me," 350. On Frances Hodgson Burnett's reading of *Uncle Tom's Cabin* see Introduction and Chapter 7.

126. Steiner, *Against the Current;* Tobenkin, *Witte Arrives*, 128. I am grateful to Shlomi Deloia for these references.

127. Although Jewish immigrants were considered not quite "white" in this period, the point holds. There is a vast literature on Jews and "whiteness." See especially Brodkin, *How Jews Became White Folks*, and Jacobson, *Whiteness of a Different Color*.

128. A letter to Harriet Beecher Stowe from a Serbian immigrant credits the book with sig-

nificant influence and attests to its value for another aspiring outsider. This letter, in the Beecher-Stowe collection of the Schlesinger Library at Radcliffe, is dated May 18, 1925. It is written on Columbia University Physics Department letterhead and signed by Michael J. Imim (family name is unclear). It describes the writer's experience of landing at Castle Garden in 1874, and being allowed into the United States partly on the strength of his "acquaintance" with Harriet Beecher Stowe through reading.

129. According to Barbara Sicherman, African American illiteracy declined to an estimated 70 percent by 1880, 45 percent by 1900, and 30 percent ten years later (*Well-Read Lives*). See also Kaestle, *Literacy in the United States;* Anderson, *The Education of Blacks in the South;* Robert Morris, *Reading, 'Riting, and Reconstruction.*

130. Johnson, *The Autobiography of an Ex-Colored Man,* 28. The anonymous publication of the *Autobiography* in 1912 was "met with speculation that the book was not entirely a fiction," as Karla F. C. Holloway points out (*Bookmarks,* 113). Further references to *Autobiography* are included in the text. See also my Epilogue.

131. The scrapbooks are in the William H. Dorsey Collection at Cheyney State College in Philadelphia. See also Lane, *William Dorsey's Philadelphia and Ours.* It is not clear whether the subject headings of the scrapbook were assigned by Dorsey or by the curator of the library. Dates and sources are sometimes handwritten on the clipping or scrapbook page—or not included. Sometimes there are no page numbers on the scrapbook leaves themselves, but in the case of the Harriet Beecher Stowe scrapbook, page numbers have been included on a background page, perhaps when the scrapbook was photographed. I include them here, when noted (there are no page numbers in the Booker T. Washington scrapbook). I am grateful to Ellen Gruber Garvey for alerting me to this source. For a fuller discussion of Dorsey, see her forthcoming *Book, Paper, Scissors: Scrapbooks Remake Print Culture.*

132. The last third of the scrapbook includes clippings about Henry Ward Beecher, his wife, and the death of Mrs. Elizabeth R. Tilton.

133. St. Paul *Globe* (Jan. 15, 1896); *Philadelphia Times* (Mar. 14, 1894). A letter to the editor by C. H. J. Taylor begins: "I have just read your editorial 'Is Booker T. Washington Correct?' At the risk of stirring up a hornet's next I am bound to say that the best thing Mr. Washington can do is stick close to Tuskegee. He is better prepared to turn out farmers, shoe makers, carpenters, cooks and seamstresses than he is for anything else." Attacking Washington's "dishonorable compromise," Taylor writes, "What the Negro desires to day is a Moses who will not lead him to the plow, for he knows the way there, but who will lead him to the point in this country where he can get all of his manhood rights under the Constitution. . . . Appropriations fabulous in amount can be had from legislatures for the purpose of educating the Negro to serve. It is only when the Negro calls for recognition as a citizen in proportion to his numbers modified by his education and tax paying qualification that an over whelming number of objections come to the fore. . . . The struggle will go on until before the law and in its operation the Negro shall be a full-fledged citizen to not only help to feed governors, but help to govern. We are all one people, not separate and distinct as are the fingers, on the Washington idea" (C. H. J. Taylor, "We Only Want our Rights as

Citizens," Dorsey Clipping; article reprinted from the *Christian Recorder,* Dec. 21, 1889 [date unclear]). The *Christian Recorder* was an African American newspaper.

134. "'We'll Kill 1000 Niggers'—Tillman; South Carolina Senator Says Roosevelt Has Made it Necessary" (Dorsey clipping, Oct. 23, 1901). A page in Dorsey's scrapbook with the handwritten title "Roosevelt and Washington" also includes an article that provides historical perspective as follows: "When President Roosevelt invited Booker T. Washington to break bread with him at the White House Wednesday night, he was not overstepping the color line for the first time in his official career. He went even farther, while governor of New York." The article tells of "a colored baritone named Brigham" who spent a night at the "Executive Mansion" when Roosevelt heard of his being denied accommodation at "two or three of the best hotels" in Albany (Dorsey clipping, Oct. 19, 1901).

135. The scrapbook is in the Beecher-Stowe Collection at Schlesinger Library, Radcliffe, a gift of Mr. and Mrs. Lyman Beecher Stowe. While it is unclear who made the scrapbook there is good reason to suggest that the maker/owner was Charles Stowe, and I will refer to it as his throughout my discussion. Stowe's son Charles was very involved with his mother's legacy in these years. He published a biography, *Life of Harriet Beecher Stowe: Compiled from her Letters and Journals* in 1889. Later he co-authored *The Life of Harriet Beecher Stowe,* with Stowe's grandson Lyman Beecher Stowe. The scrapbook, which begins with obituaries of Calvin Stowe (1886), contains an 1889 review of a book by Florine Thayer McCray (*Life Work of the Author of Uncle Tom's Cabin*). The following words are underlined in the scrapbook clipping of the review: "It would be a pity if any should confound this catch-penny book with the forthcoming Life, or conclude that this will answer, for it is hardly possible that a second treatment of the subject will be as poor as this." If Charles Stowe himself did not underline these words, the marking was clearly the work of someone closely associated with him. The review appeared in *The Nation* (Nov. 7, 1889), Beecher-Stowe scrapbook.

136. Apart from accounts of Stowe's death, funeral, and achievement, (with overwhelming emphasis on *Uncle Tom's Cabin*), both scrapbooks include such lengthy magazine articles as James Lane Allen's "Uncle Tom's Cabin at Home in Kentucky" with illustrations by E. W. Kemble, from the *Century,* and Elizabeth Stuart Phelps, "Reminiscences of Harriet Beecher Stowe."

137. Dorsey clipping, "Mrs. Stowe's 84th Year. Greetings from Over the World for the writer of Uncle Tom's Cabin," 11. Cf. Beecher-Stowe clippings: "Mrs Stowe at Eighty"; "Mrs. Stowe's 81st Birthday"; "Mrs. Stowe's Birthday . . . 83rd Milestone of her Life's Journey"; "Her 84th Birthday; Mrs. Stowe at her Hartford Home"; "Mrs. Stowe's Birthday Quietly Celebrated Today at the Forest Street Home. . . . Today is the 84th anniversary of the birth of Mrs. Harriet Beecher Stowe."

138. Dorsey clipping. The article continues with the following heading: "Mrs. Stowe's Efforts in Behalf of Negro Emancipation Won her an Enduring Fame Throughout the Civilized World" ("Harriet Beecher Stowe Dead," 17).

139. Dorsey clippings: "Glad of Mrs. Stowe's Death," and "Gen. Johnson on Mrs. Stowe," both dated July 3, 1896 (no sources noted), 20.

140. Dorsey clipping: "An Enemy of 'Uncle Tom,'" *Philadelphia Bulletin* (April 8, 1898). The letter-writer appears to be referring to a new stage production. Two responses, by "H. H. W." and B. Barclay Simmons, are pasted on the same page of the scrapbook as the hostile letter. Simmons suggests that the letter-writer "deserves the lasting scorn and detestation of all lovers of truth and justice" (76).

141. Beecher-Stowe clipping. No source or date.

142. Dorsey clippings: "Knew the Characters of 'Uncle Tom's Cabin,'" *New York World* (July 2, 1896), 21; "Was a Slave With 'Uncle Tom'" (July 18, 1896), 27.

143. Dorsey Clippings. "'George Harris.' Funeral of Mrs. Stowe's Negro Hero" (Dec. 20, 1897), 69. This might be from a black paper, but no source is listed. Harris is counted "the most prominent figure in the novel" in "Knew the Characters of 'UTC'" from the *New York World* (a white paper). Another obituary of Clark carries the heading "An Old Negro Slave Dies" (Special Telegraph to *The Times* 1897), 69. Still another, "Lewis George Clark Buried" (*The Times*), notes "his body lay in State in the Main Street Auditorium for five hours, an honor never before shown to the memory of a colored man in Kentucky" (70). Another obituary, with a portrait of Lewis George Clark, is entitled "A Famous Man" (*St. Paul Appeal* [handwriting unclear], [Dec. 25, 1897], 78).

144. Stepto, "Sharing the Thunder," 149. Buell speaks of the "George Harris subplot" ("The Dream of the Great American Novel," 196).

145. Dorsey clipping. "An Old Negro Slave Dies," 69.

146. Dorsey clipping. "'George Harris'; Funeral of Mrs. Stowe's Negro Hero," 69.

147. Dorsey clippings. "Knew the Characters in 'Uncle Tom's Cabin" includes an interview with Norman Argo, but it foregrounds George's experience. Additional information about Clark appears in another article about Argo, with the headline "Was a Slave with 'Uncle Tom'" (July 18, 1896), 27.

148. Dorsey clipping. "An Old Negro Slave Dies," 69.

149. Numerous obituaries for Lewis G. Clark appeared: "George Harris Dead," *Kansas Semi-Weekly Capital* (Dec. 17, 1897), 7; *Kansas City Star* (Dec. 18, 1897) 7; "Original George Harris Dead, *Aberdeen Daily News* (Dec. 18, 1897), 2; "A Negro to Lie in State," *New York Times* (Dec. 19, 1897), 2; "Honors for a Kentucky Negro," *Los Angeles Times* (Dec. 19, 1897), A 12; "Kentucky Honors Uncle Tom. Body of George Clarke Lies in State to-Day, *Philadelphia Inquirer* (Dec. 19, 1897), 4; "Clark's Body Lying in State," *Dallas Morning News* (Dec. 19, 1897), 1; "Funeral of George Harris," *Idaho Statesman* (Dec. 20, 1897), 2; "Lewis George Clark," *Tacoma Daily News* (Dec. 22, 1897), 2. Articles identifying Clark as the source for George Harris—outlining Clark's life-history and present living conditions—appeared widely in the press during the 1880s and '90s as well. Examples include, "A Living Character of Uncle Tom's Cabin," *New York Tribune* (Oct. 24, 1880), 3; "City Intelligence. From 'Uncle Tom's Cabin,'" *Chicago Daily Tribune* (June 30, 1885), 5; "Of Uncle Tom's Cabin. Cincinnati Originals of some of Its Characters," *Aberdeen Daily News* (March 30, 1890), 4; "Rally to the Aid of L. G. Clark: Hero of 'Uncle Tom's Cabin' Not to Be Allowed to Suffer in Old Age," *Chicago Daily Tribune* (Nov. 30, 1895), 1; "The Many Original Uncle Toms," *Springfield (Mass) Republican,* rpt. *New York Times* (Nov. 30, 1895), 10;

"Inspired Harriet Beecher Stowe," *San Francisco Chronicle* (Jan. 8, 1896), 13. ""Funds for Lewis George Clark," *Biloxi Herald* (Jan. 2, 1897), 3.

150. *Puck,* vol. 48, issue 1248 (Feb. 6, 1901), 3.

151. Holloway, "A Visit to Uncle Tom's Cabin." Holloway is identified thus in a line beneath his name and city (362).

152. Strieby, "The Look Forward," 357.

153. Proctor, "Addresses at Annual Meeting: The Sons of 'Uncle Tom,'" 20.

154. McPherson, *The Abolitionist Legacy,* 391.

155. Ibid., 190–91.

156. Ibid., 193.

157. The final verse contains some attempt to excuse "Uncle Tom" for his benighted ways while affirming the speaker's own goals, but tensions remain:

> How small is the light that illumines his pathway,
> And his noonday how like to the darkness of night;
> Yet he keeps in the beam directing his footsteps,
> So must his intent be accounted for right.
> I would not, I dare not, sit in judgment upon thee,
> Tho' the light on thy path be less bright than on mine,
> But rather come to the fullness of duty
> In my life as thou hast so well done in thine. (lines 103–10)

158. McPherson, *The Abolitionist Legacy,* 194–95.

159. Writing of the American Christian foreign mission movement, Sarah Robbins notes that in the 1870s and 1880s the journal *Woman's Work* developed a "two-pronged strategy" for spreading "mission-based literacy." Reports on "how to" promote this goal were followed by reports on "the powerful impact" of successful efforts and their "positive social effects" ("Woman's Work for Woman," 264).

160. On "the pictorial turn" see Mitchell, *Picture Theory,* 11–13. For Mitchell this turn is a recent phenomenon, but it also seems eminently applicable to the late nineteenth-century explosion of images in books, magazines, and the press.

6. IMAGINING THE PAST AS THE FUTURE

1. Houghton Mifflin became Stowe's publisher in 1880. See Parfait, *The Publishing History of Uncle Tom's Cabin,* 131. Winship, "The Greatest Book of Its Kind."

2. On these developments see Frederickson, *Black Image in the White Mind;* Logan, *Betrayal of the Negro;* McPherson, *The Abolitionist Legacy;* Sundquist, *To Wake the Nations,* Part II, "The Color Line," esp. 233–49. Woodward, *The Strange Career of Jim Crow: A Commemorative Edition.*

3. On changes in the technology for reproducing images and the effect of these changes on periodical publishing see Scholnick, "*Scribner's Monthly* and the 'Pictorial Representation of Life and Truth' in Post–Civil War America." On technological changes in modes of illustration see also Watrous, *American Printmaking;* Harris, "Iconography and Intellectual History," 196–211. On photography see Trachtenberg,

Reading American Photographs, and Fryer, *Women's Camera Work.* On advertising see Garvey, *The Adman in the Parlor,* and Ohmann, *Selling Culture.*

4. Scholnick, "*Scribner's Monthly* and the 'Pictorial Representation of Life and Truth' in Post–Civil War America," 48.

5. See Chapter 5.

6. Knight, *History of the Work of Connecticut Women,* 22, 93.

7. Sollors, "Was Roxy Black?," 75.

8. Mitchell, *Picture Theory,* 3. On the relation of word and image see also Barthes, *Image, Music, Text;* Thomas, *Pictorial Victorians.*

9. On Oct. 30, 1851, the *Era* appeared without an installment of *Uncle Tom's Cabin,* which had been appearing weekly, with one exception, since June 5, 1851. Bailey printed an apology for the absent episode and a promise that the next installment "shall appear next week" (174). On the following page of the *Era,* the reader's letter appeared, under the heading "*Uncle Tom's Cabin.*"

10. "Reader's Letter," 175.

11. On "romantic racialism" see Frederickson, *Black Image in the White Mind.* On differences between Billings and George Cruikshank, the best-known British illustrator of Stowe's novels in the 1850s, see O'Gorman, *Accomplished in All Departments of Art;* Wood, *Blind Memory.*

12. Billings was not the only early illustrator to emphasize reading. A Routledge edition (London, 1853; illustrated by Phiz, Gilbert, and Harvey) includes books in two illustrations placed before the title page; of eleven illustrations in this edition, four include images of books. The frontispiece in the 1852 edition by the same publisher ("Uncle Tom Under Inspection") is removed in the 1853 reprint and replaced by "Uncle Tom Teaching the two Negro Women the Bible." Scenes of reading were regularly included in editions of *Uncle Tom's Cabin.* See also Chapter 2.

13. An inscription by Stowe in Kemble's illustrated edition expresses gratitude to "Mr Kemble . . . for his faithful and admirable work in illustrating 'Uncle Tom's Cabin'" (cited in P.G.H., Jr., "Edward Windsor Kemble," 296); but we cannot take Stowe's praise at face value. Her mind was quite eroded at this stage of her life, which complicates any conjecture about her view of Kemble's work. A newspaper article, "Mrs Stowe at Eighty" (1891) notes: "Time has made its greatest inroads on the face and the brain. Wrinkles there are in numbers yet the face is a bright one, and the eyes still retain some of their old luster and sparkle. But the mind has ceased to do its bidding. Her bodily health is superb and each fair day sees her taking long walks, though she is always accompanied by an attendant. No one outside of her family and neighbors see her, for the least thing outside of her quiet daily routine excites her and brings on almost complete exhaustion. She can no longer concentrate her thoughts for more than a few moments upon any one topic and her two devoted daughters let her find her pleasure in those things which appeal most to her" (Beecher-Stowe scrapbook clipping, Beecher-Stowe papers). According to Earl A. French and Diana Royce, "After the death of her husband in 1886, Harriet began to decline. In 1889 she was briefly ill. Perhaps she had a stroke. Thereafter, except for lucid moments, she had what Lyman

Beecher Stowe called a life of 'complete irresponsibility, idleness, and childlike happiness'" (*Portraits of a Nineteenth Century Family,* 66–67). See also Hedrick, *Harriet Beecher Stowe,* 397.

14. The same white boy, in different costumes, served as Kemble's model for both Huck and Jim (Sollors, "Was Roxy Black?," 77).

15. Martin, "Edward Windsor Kemble, A Master of Pen and Ink," 61.)

16. Cited in Briden, "Kemble's 'Specialty' and the Pictorial Countertext of *Huckleberry Finn,*" 2.

17. P.G.H., Jr. "Edward Windsor Kemble," 295.

18. On Kemble's "pen-and-ink style that dominated a major part of the so-called Golden Age of American illustration," see Martin, "Edward Windsor Kemble," 54–55.

19. *Literary World, a Monthly Review of Current Literature* 22 (September 1891), 336. Cited in Sonstegard, "Artistic Liberty and Slave Imagery: 'Mark Twain's Illustrator' E. W. Kemble Turns to Harriet Beecher Stowe," 509.

20. "Uncle Tom's Cabin Illustrated," 23, 2.

21. Rydell explores the "erotically charged commercialism" of the Midway Plaisance, which featured such performances as the Middle Eastern belly dance (*Grand Illusions,* 164–66)

22. For accounts of black literacy in the context of white literary culture, see Cornelius, *When I Can See My Title Clear;* Gates, *Signifying Monkey;* McHenry, *Forgotten Readers;* and the enduringly insightful Salvino, "The Word in Black and White."

23. On this tension see Blight, *Race and Reunion,* 373–79; Frederickson, *Black Image in the White Mind,* especially chap. 7; Logan, *Betrayal of the Negro.*

24. Francis Martin has "catalogued over 6,000 published drawings [by Kemble] from such magazines as *Century, Life, Colliers, Cosmopolitan, Harper's, Good Housekeeping,* and others. This figure probably represents about half of his total magazine production" ("Edward Windsor Kemble, A Master of Pen and Ink," 67, n. 19).

25. Sollors suggests that *Kemble's Coons* (1897) served this function ("Was Roxy Black?," 74).

26. Bernstein, "Dances with Things."

27. In *A Coon Alphabet* the only written words represented as produced or employed by black figures are misspelled or neutralized by the ineptitude of the figures making or using the writing. The letter M ("M is for mendicants / what's bofe blind an' lame . . .") pictures a black man and woman wearing signs that read "I iz blind AND KriPPuld" and "So iz I." The page for the letter X ("X is fo' 'Xerky,' de blackest dat grew, / he wished he was white—") features a young black man with a barrel of white-wash who soon "becomes" white by spilling it over himself. A sign on the wall reads "Wite WASHiN done clean HeaR" (the S in WASHiN is reversed). This ABC book proposes to amuse white children into learning their letters while reminding them that African Americans are illiterate, comic, foolish, and impervious to violence. The pages of *A Coon Alphabet* are unnumbered.

28. On white educational goals for African Americans at the turn of the century, see Davidov, *Women's Camera Work,* chap. 4; McPherson, *The Abolitionist Legacy;* Woodward, *The Strange Career of Jim Crow.* See also Fairclough, *A Class of Their Own.*

29. On the argument about Bible-reading for slaves and prohibitions on slave literacy generally see Monaghan, "Reading for the Enslaved, Writing for the Free," and Cornelius, *When I Can See My Title Clear.* See also Chapter 2.

30. There are exceptions, to be sure. The oft-reprinted Houghton Mifflin edition of 1896 includes some reading scenes. Still, there are both subtle and dramatic differences between these images and Billings's. The act of reading itself is deemphasized when an illustration of Eva and Tom at Lake Pontchartrain is given a caption that reads "'Uncle Tom,' Eva said, 'I'm going there'" (304) rather than "Little Eva reading the Bible to Uncle Tom" as in the illustration for the first edition. In another instance an image of Eva and Tom writing to Chloe draws attention to Tom's limitations by representing him heavily laboring to make readable signs, while an ethereal Eva looks on (276). The sense of parity and casual intimacy in Billings's illustration of these moments creates a different perspective.

31. "Tom and his Children" (Vol. I, 140); "The Youngest Urchin" (Vol. II, 56); "Tom Marketing" (Vol. II, 89). For additional disjunctures compare text and illustration on page 160 and 270 of Vol. I; 163 and 170 of Vol. II.

32. In 1952, an edition of *Uncle Tom's Cabin* issued by Dodd, Mead, and Company reprinted two illustrations by Kemble for which Langston Hughes wrote captions that restored some of Stowe's meaning. In the Houghton Mifflin edition of 1891, Kemble's full-page image of *Uncle Tom* was positioned near a conversation between St. Clare and Miss Ophelia regarding Mozart's requiem (Vol. 2, facing p. 172). By contrast, Hughes accompanies the image of Tom with Stowe's introduction to her hero: "He was a large, broad-chested, powerfully made man, of a full and glossy black . . . whose truly African features, were characterized by an expression of grave and steady good sense united with much kindliness and benevolence . . . respectable enough to be a bishop of Carthage, as men of color were, in other ages" (Dodd, Mead edition; 177. Ellipsis in text). Hughes transforms the emphasis of the 1891 caption, "Scipio in the Swamp," not only by providing a new one, "Slaves Who Ran Away," but also by adding the following historical contextualization: "Scipio ran away, killed three bloodhounds with his naked fists, but was captured and returned to slavery. Many others who ran away were not captured, and throughout the slave period various revolts flared up, some of them involving thousands of Negroes. This drawing by E. W. Kemble shows Scipio seeking freedom in the swamps" (Dodd, Mead edition, 241). In the 1891 edition, by contrast, the image of Scipio faces St. Clare's account of the way good treatment made Scipio "as submissive and tractable as heart could desire" after his thwarted escape (52). Langston Hughes's caption radicalizes Stowe's own description of Scipio by emphasizing his escape, not his return and subsequent devotion to his master.

33. Sonstegard, "Artistic Liberty and Slave Imagery: 'Mark Twain's Illustrator' E. W. Kemble Turns to Harriet Beecher Stowe," 509.

34. On the ethnological villages on the Midway Plaisance see Rydell in Harris et al., *Grand Illusions,* 157–65.

35. O'Gorman notes that Billings made these changes himself; he also points out that

Eva's figure is less womanly, more childlike in the second version (*Accomplished in All Departments of Art*, 53–54).

36. Wood, *Blind Memory*, 194.

37. Mitchell, *Picture Theory*, 78–80.

38. Sollors emphasizes the importance of going beyond "identifying 'bad' stereotypes" ("Was Roxy Black?," 80 and passim). For comments on Kemble's racism see Banta, *Imaging American Women*, 182; Briden, "Kemble's 'Specialty' and the Pictorial Countertext of *Huckleberry Finn*"; Fishkin, *Was Huck Black? Mark Twain and African American Voices*, 88; Boskin, *Sambo: The Rise and the Demise of an American Jester*, 127. See also Stephen Railton's comments on "Representing Jim" on the *Huckleberry Finn* website, http://etext.virginia.edu/railton/huckfinn/jiminpix.html.

39. "Uncle Tom's Cabin Illustrated."

40. Billings (like Stowe) includes scenes of fighting, chasing, and performing (Sam and Andy's antics, George fighting, Topsy trying on Miss Ophelia's clothes). But these are not the exclusive or even most frequently represented scenes of the 1850s. The most often reprinted scenes throughout the 1850s were Eva with Topsy and Eva with Tom. See also Chapter 3.

41. See Wood's analysis of this image (*Blind Memory*, 17–21, 33–36).

42. The plate "Slaves at Their Toil" has been carefully removed from one well-preserved copy of this edition in the collection of the New-York Historical Society. Perhaps a reader, or previous owner, wanted to possess (or destroy) the image.

43. Mitchell, *Picture Theory*, 5.

44. Unsigned review of *Uncle Tom's Cabin, Christian Union* (Jan. 23 1892).

45. Harris, "Iconography and Intellectual History," 198. Citing the historian Estelle Jussim, Harris suggests that "the heart of the iconographical shift was the disappearance of the 'sign function' of the reproduction; it became 'an optical illusion with surrogate power'" (198).

46. Mitchell suggests that pictures with words included "reflect . . . on . . . both the way we speak of pictures, and the way pictures 'speak' to us" (*Picture Theory*, 65–66). There are "places where pictorial representation displays itself for inspection [through self-reference] rather than effacing itself in the service of transparent representation of something else" (*Picture Theory*, 48).

47. George William Curtis (clipping in an envelope pasted into back cover of *Uncle Tom's Cabin* [New York: Houghton Mifflin, 1888], NYPL). Advertising copy for this edition creates the same emphasis on the moral, the historical, and the vivid: "The publication of this remarkable story was an event in American history as in American literature. It fixed the eyes of the nation and the civilized world on the evils of slavery presenting these so vividly and powerfully that the heart and conscience of mankind were thenceforth united against them" (clipping pasted into last page of volume).

48. On the neglect of slave narratives see Mitchell, *Picture Theory*, 189; Starling, *The Slave Narrative: Its Place in American History;* Andrews, *To Tell a Free Story*. Nina Silber suggests that "forgetfulness, not memory, [was] . . . the dominant theme in the reunion culture" (*The Romance of Reunion*, 4). See also my "Epilogue."

49. Plantation fiction of the period represented the South as a chivalrous, wealthy, and orderly society. See Silber, *The Romance of Reunion,* and Hart, *Popular Book.*

50. Allen, "Mrs. Stowe's 'Uncle Tom' at Home in Kentucky," 866. See also Chapter 5.

51. Trachtenberg, *Reading American Photographs,* 183, 187–89.

52. Ibid., 183.

53. Allen, "Mrs. Stowe's 'Uncle Tom' at Home in Kentucky," 854, 858.

54. Ibid., 858–59.

55. *Uncle Tom's Cabin,* Art Memorial Edition, 29.

56. Wonham, *Playing the Races,* 134.

57. Ibid., 8, 7. "In practice," Wonham suggests, "these purportedly antithetical categories of representation remain intimately related" (9).

58. Cited in P.G.H., Jr., "Edward Windsor Kemble," 296.

59. Elliott, *The Culture Concept: Writing and Difference in the Age of Realism,* xvii; xxvii and passim).

60. Higginson, "Critical and Biographical Introduction," xiv. Further references to this edition are included in the text.

61. These words appear on a cloudy page facing the color plate frontispiece: "Anne of Brittany and her Patron Saints."

62. Appleton issued forty titles in the "World's Great Books" series between 1898 and 1901. An advertisement from the *Chicago Daily Tribune,* Sept. 13, 1906, offers "remaining volumes" for $1.50. *Uncle Tom's Cabin* is not among them. The initial titles include Aeschylus, *Great Dramas;* Edmund Burke, *Orations and Essays;* Cervantes, *Don Quixote;* Marcus Tullius Cicero, *Orations and Essays of Marcus Tullius Cicero;* Richard Henry Dana, *Two Years Before the Mast;* Benjamin Franklin, *Autobiography, Poor Richard, Letters;* Montesquieu et al., *The Spirit of the Laws;* Benjamin Jowett and Josiah Royce, *Dialogues of Plato;* Edgar Allan Poe, *Selected Works of Edgar Allan Poe;* Alexis de Tocqueville and Henry Reeve, *Democracy in America.*

63. See Chapter 3.

64. Unsigned, "Biographical Sketch," *Uncle Tom's Cabin* (New York: Houghton Mifflin, 1896), x–xii.

65. Smith, "Melodrama, Popular Religion, and Literary Value," 226, 222. Wright's work relies on unambiguous distinctions between good and evil. As Smith notes, "the primary energies of Wright's work are melodramatic, investing a desacralized world with [profoundly personal] religious meanings . . . rather than providing a revolutionary social vision" (228).

66. The illustration of Eliza at the door of Tom's cabin appears on an unnumbered page after Higginson's "Introduction."

67. The portrait follows page 514.

68. In *A Key to Uncle Tom's Cabin* Stowe speaks of Henson as one of many "parallels" to Uncle Tom (26). As Marion Wilson Starling points out, "it was not until 1858 that the idea seems to have occurred to Mrs. Stowe to assign more importance to Josiah Henson's narrative" (*The Slave Narrative,* 239). On Henson in the role of "Uncle Tom"

and the "touch of the charlatan" about him, see Starling, 239–40. On Stowe's use of Henson's biography see also Andrews, *To Tell a Free Story* 122–23; 310, n. 35.

69. See also Chapter 5.

70. "Original Uncle Tom Dead," 3; " 'Uncle Tom' Dies: Negro Said to Have Been Original of Mrs. Stowe's Character Passes Away," 5.

71. *Uncle Tom's Cabin,* Art Memorial Edition, 11.

72. "The Levee at Baton Rouge" follows page 166; "The Planter's Home" follows page 388.

73. Barthes, *Image, Music, Text,* 28. As Mitchell notes, it is as if, "in cognitive terms, . . . the principal connotation or 'coded' implication [of photography] is that it is pure denotation, without a code" (*Picture Theory,* 285).

74. W. R. Thayer, "The New Storytellers and the Doom of Realism," 476.

75. Henry James, "A Small Boy and Others," 168.

76. *Uncle Tom's Cabin* (Eaton and Mains, 1897) 33; Grace Duffie Boylan, *Young Folks Uncle Tom's Cabin* (Chicago: Jamieson-Higgins, 1901), facing title page. A frontispiece illustration for a children's edition of 1908 (Robinson, *Uncle Tom's Cabin for Children*) pictures George Shelby and Tom with his slate, accompanied by the caption: "You white folks al'us does things easy." The frontispiece is signed H. S. Adams.

77. Boylan, *Young Folks Uncle Tom's Cabin,* 94.

7. SPARING THE WHITE CHILD

1. On *Plessy vs. Ferguson,* see Logan, *Betrayal of the Negro;* Painter, *Standing at Armageddon;* Woodward, *The Strange Career of Jim Crow.* Expiration of Stowe's copyright in 1893 facilitated a slew of reprints. Stowe's 85th birthday in 1896, and her death later that year, occasioned considerable publicity. See Chapters 5 and 6.

2. *Uncle Tom's Cabin* is number thirteen on a list of "The Best Hundred Books for Children" compiled in 1900 for the *Living Age* (132). See also George Edward Paul Hardy, *Five Hundred Books for the Young,* prepared for the committee on literature of the New York state teachers' association in 1892 (75). In 1931 W. E. B. Du Bois recommends *Uncle Tom's Cabin* to a father seeking books "about Negroes or written by Negroes" (Holloway, *Bookmarks,* 33; 36–37).

3. *Young Folks Uncle Tom's Cabin* was reissued with a variety of covers, in New York, Philadelphia, and Chicago. In 1901, an unsigned review of "Children's Picture Books" praised *Young Folks Uncle Tom's Cabin* for giving "the essential part of the original" with "strong and effective" illustrations (APS online pg. 219).

4. On *Uncle Tom's Cabin* as an antebellum children's book, see Introduction and Chapter 4. In the 1850s *Uncle Tom's Cabin* was advertised, reviewed, and read as a book for "all ages." Review excerpts in one of Jewett's advertisements for *Uncle Tom's Cabin* claim that "50,000 families are alternately crying and laughing [over the book]" (*Unitarian Monthly Magazine*); "Let every man, woman and child in America read this book" (*Religious Recorder, Syracuse*). The ad, published in *Norton's Literary Gazette* in 1852, is reprinted in Parfait, *Publishing History of Uncle Tom's Cabin,* 55.

5. On *A Peep into Uncle Tom's Cabin* see Chapters 2 and 4; on *Pictures and Stories* see Chapter 4. Stowe was involved with both of these editions to some extent. They were the only U.S. children's editions of the period except the pro-slavery version, *Little Eva: Flower of the South*. Despite reservations about certain sections, the felt need for special children's editions was small in the 1850s. By the time children's editions proliferated in the 1890s, the market for children's books in general had grown exponentially. Children's librarianship had become a profession, and the division between literature for children and books for adults had deepened. References to *Pictures and Stories* are included in the text.

6. *Young Folks Uncle Tom's Cabin* implicitly endorses the end of slavery—any other position would have been untenable in 1901. Small modifications of Stowe's text confirm this position (Mr. Shelby, for example, is more sympathetic to Eliza's flight here than in *Uncle Tom's Cabin* [45]). On the other hand, the slave system appears less cruel and more subject to legal correctives than in *Uncle Tom's Cabin*. Legree is said to be "in fear of the law, which he knew would deal terribly with him in the end" (148). In the antebellum *Pictures and Stories,* by contrast, the narrator notes: "There was no law to punish the wicked planter, because Tom was black" (30). *Young Folks Uncle Tom's Cabin* replaces Stowe's criticism of legalized injustice with an affirmation of the U.S. legal code. This change is in keeping with turn-of-the-century patriotic lessons for children. It is also among a range of textual changes that provide a "happier" ending. Unless otherwise noted, further citations from *Young Folks Uncle Tom's Cabin* are from this edition and are included in parenthesis in the text.

7. On the repackaging of *Uncle Tom's Cabin* for the 1890s, see Chapters 5 and 6. For other approaches to the way *Uncle Tom's Cabin* was read in the 1880s and '90s see Riggio, "*Uncle Tom* Reconstructed"; Arac, *Huckleberry Finn as Idol and Target,* chap. 4.

8. Uncle Rastus was the Cream of Wheat icon; Aunt Jemima has endured into the twenty-first century.

9. Thomas Gossett writes that in stage performances *after* the Civil War "the sole function of Topsy was to supply low comedy" (*Uncle Tom's Cabin and American Culture,* 380). By contrast, as Eric Lott notes, even in the dramatic version by George Aiken of 1853 "much of Topsy's role is taken up by Eva's effect on her, not her antics only" (*Love and Theft,* 221).

10. The periodical press often represented inhabitants of Africa, Guam, and the Philippines as primitive creatures, especially after publication of Rudyard Kipling's "White Man's Burden" (1899) and during the debate about annexation of the Philippines. One widely circulated image of a crouching little savage appears in the corner of an advertisement asserting that "Pears Soap" is "a potent factor in brightening the dark corners of the earth." On the popular hit song "All Coons Look Alike to me" (1896) and racial caricatures in magazines of the period, see Wonham, *Playing the Races,* esp. 72–89. On E. W. Kemble, the well-known illustrator of *The Adventures of Huckleberry Finn, A Coon Alphabet* and *Comical Coons,* and *Uncle Tom's Cabin,* see Chapter 6.

11. Morgan's illustrations also remove the *physical* closeness between the races so prominent in antebellum illustrations—he creates no images of Eva decorating Tom with

flowers, or resting her hand on his while reading the Bible. Where the two are pictured together Eva stands while Tom sits (in one frequently reproduced cover design) or sits in a chair, while Tom sits on the ground (in the scene at the lake). The illustration of Tom saving Eva from drowning represents Tom leaping from the ship, and Eva in the water—not in Tom's arms, as in Hammatt Billings's much-reprinted illustration of this scene. In illustrations for *Young Folks Uncle Tom's Cabin* even Eva and Topsy do not touch. The passages in which Eva hugs Mammy with joy upon returning from New Orleans are removed. These changes are in keeping with illustrations for full-length editions of the 1890s. See Chapter 6.

12. African American children may well have encountered the book in the course of its reprinting and its presence in school libraries.

13. Gail Schmunck Murray describes the "typical female protagonist" in the second half of the nineteenth century as "innately kind, cheerful, innocent and charitable" (*American Children's Literature and the Construction of Childhood,* 81). While such images may, as Murray suggests, provide an image "of what society might become" (81) they also diminish the agency and moral stature of children and, I argue, allay anxiety stirred by contemporary theories of about the unruly instincts of children.

14. Beginning with the 1890s, children's editions of *Uncle Tom's Cabin* downplayed religion and spirituality. In her "Introduction" for an edition of 1966, Anne Terry White emphasizes the importance of the novel as "a mighty force in bringing about the Civil War" (vii) but suggests that "boys and girls no longer read" the book. In order to put the novel "into a form acceptable to young readers" she simplifies the language and cuts "references to books, events, characters, and things outside a young reader's knowledge and understanding" (viii, ix). Religious allusions and concepts are central to the deleted material: "It adds nothing to story that the slave-trader Haley intends to repent before he dies—this only clutters"; "much [of Mrs. Stowe's religiosity] merely weighs down the story and is incomprehensible to young readers" (x, xi).

15. As Lydia Maria Child put it in The *Mother's Book* (1831): "The books chosen for young people should as far as possible combine amusement and instruction; but it is very important that amusement should not become a necessary inducement" (86). According to the anonymous woman author of *The Mother's Friend* (1834), "We must bear in mind that we have to train up those intrusted to us, not for a life of rewards, ease and pleasure; but for a world in which they will meet with pain, sickness, danger and sorrow." Antebellum children were to be schooled to "fortitude and self denial" ("*The Mother's Friend,* 126).

16. G. Stanley Hall, ""The Story of a Sand-Pile," 54. In Hall's influential scheme the "charms of play" are rooted in the "sphere of the imagination." "The Story of a Sand-Pile" was first published in *Scribner's Magazine* III (June 1888).

17. Gillian Brown, "Child's Play, "13–39; Sanchez-Eppler, *Dependent States,* 13, 17. On changing literary and behavioral norms in children's books see also Avery, *Behold the Child;* MacLeod, *A Moral Tale;* Lurie, *Don't Tell the Grownups.*

18. On the rise of children's librarianship as a profession, see Eddy, *Bookwomen: Creating an Empire in Children's Book Publishing;* Garrison, *Apostles of Culture;* Lundin, "Little

Pilgrims Progress: Literary Horizons for Children's Literature." Immigrants were the ideal target population for the project of expanding children's literacy in cities; African Americans are often absent from the discussion. See also Augst, "Faith in Reading: Public Libraries, Liberalism, and the Civil Religion"; Hochman, "Readers and Reading Groups."

19. See Soltow and Stevens, *The Rise of Literacy and the Common School;* Graff, *The Literacy Myth;* Sicherman, "Reading and Middle-Class Identity in Victorian America."

20. Murray, *American Children's Literature and the Construction of Childhood,* 83.

21. With the rise of progressive reforms that affirmed a "right to childhood," children were viewed less as economic assets to the family, more as emotional and symbolic resources. See Zelizer, *Pricing the Priceless Child;* Sanchez-Eppler suggests that "by the end of the century play—and the worlds of the imagination—. . . [became] cultural markers for what was wonderful about childhood, and thus culturally valuable play would be recognized as an attribute of middle-class affluence and leisure" ("Playing at Class," 41).

22. Judd, *The Palmer Cox Brownie Primer,* 34. The verses were reprinted from *St. Nicholas'* magazine.

23. One discussion expresses reservations about Little Lord Fauntleroy as "a little too philanthropic for so young a child" and suggests that he "is apt to induce a comparison with the supernaturally angelic Eva in 'Uncle Tom's Cabin'" ("Old-Fashioned Children," 821).

24. On changing approaches to childhood rights and privileges see Coontz, *The Social Origins of Private Life;* Zelizer, *Pricing the Priceless Child;* Finkelstein and Vandell, "The Schooling of American Childhood"; Sanchez-Eppler, "Playing at Class."

25. Fears about the over-indulged child were much expressed by educators and writers for children, such as Kate Wiggin, *Children's Rights: A Book of Nursery Logic,* 4, 11, 21. The issue is implicit in debates about child labor: "Opponents of child labor legislation defended the pragmatic and moral legitimacy of a useful child" (Zelizer, *Pricing* the *Priceless Child,* 67; see also 11–12, 59). Nonetheless what Zelizer calls the "useless" child was increasingly seen as a value, in a change that cut across class lines. For a recent argument on behalf of not asking "too little" of children see Spitz, *Inside Picture Books,* 145.

26. *Pictures and Stories from Uncle Tom's Cabin* devotes half the book to Harry's danger and escape. See Chapter 4.

27. From Lydia Maria Child's *Mother's Book* (1831) through Samuel Goodrich's Peter Parley tales, obedience is a crucial element of antebellum educational theory. Sympathetic representations of naughtiness were rare. For an overview see Wishy, *The Child and the Republic;* MacLeod, *A Moral Tale;* see also Chapter 4.

28. Locke's influence on child-rearing practices in the antebellum United States was formative. See Brown, *The Consent of the Governed;* Crain, *The Story of A;* Reinier, *From Virtue to Character.*

29. *Pictures and Stories,* like *Uncle Tom's Cabin,* creates a sustained emphasis on the separation of families, especially the sale of children. Eliza's flight, the sale of Tom, the introduction of Topsy into the St. Clare family are all framed in terms of the outrage that men, women, and even children can be sold.

30. *Uncle Tom's Cabin* places great emphasis on Topsy's past: "it is not for ears polite to hear the particulars of the first toilet of a neglected, abused child. . . . [I]n this world multitudes must live and die in a state that it would be too great a shock to the nerves of their fellow-mortals even to hear described. . . . When [Miss Ophelia] saw, on the back and shoulders of the child, great welts and calloused spots, ineffaceable marks of the system under which she had grown up thus far, her heart became pitiful within her" (354–55).

31. On the importance of "good" behavior, especially for girls, see Dawson "The Miniaturizing of Girlhood." On analogous gender differences in twentieth-century children's picture books see Spitz, *Inside Picture Books,* 48, 148, 160–61.

32. In one characteristic comment, Wiggin celebrates "the perfect self-forgetfulness of children" (*Children's Rights,* 43). The late nineteenth-century psychologist James Mark Baldwin contrasts the behavior of children, absorbed in a game, with the "wretched self-consciousness in us adults" ("About Children," 308). This piece was reprinted in 1895 as part of Baldwin's *Mental Development in the Child and the Race.* James Sully writes: "A child is one creature when he is truly at play, another when he is bent on astonishing or amusing you" (*Children's Ways,* 15). See also Brown, "Child's Play," and Steedman, *Strange Dislocations.*

33. Joel Chandler Harris's *Uncle Remus: His Songs and Sayings* was published in 1880. Raymond Hedin suggests that Harris made the potentially subversive tales acceptable to a white audience by creating "the loyal Uncle Remus and his young white listener, who finds the tales amusing and renders them fit for a child" ("Probable Readers, Possible Stories: The Limits of Nineteenth-Century Black Narrative," 192). The figure of the elderly story-telling slave recurs in Charles Chesnutt's conjure tales. First published in the *Atlantic,* these stories were read by their white audience as local color, the tales' bitterness obscured by the figure of the black "Uncle" who entertains white visitors with his recollections. On Chesnutt's failed effort to move beyond this frame see Brodhead, *Cultures of Letters.*

34. As Sarah Meer suggests, *Uncle Tom's Cabin,* including its minstrel effects, facilitates diverse identifications—"like the members of minstrel show audiences, *Uncle Tom's* readers inhabit several positions at once" (*Uncle Tom Mania,* 30). On the complex blend of responses elicited by minstrelsy see also Lott, *Love and Theft.* For discussions of children's reading which emphasize the value of fluid identifications see Lurie, "Pottery," 32. Ellen Handler Spitz recommends "cross-gendered reading" for children on the assumption that fluid identifications are possible and valuable (*Inside Picture Books,* 25).

35. In Stowe's text Eva notices the chains on the hands of the slaves as she walks around the boat which is traveling south—taking her home, taking the slaves to an auction. She lifts the heavy chains in her own small hands and grieves.

36. Children (like women) could display the wealth of the family through conspicuous consumption of nonfunctional, non-necessary, objects, including books. Zelizer notes that the practice of giving children spending money ("allowances") emerges in this period—and not just for the middle class (*Pricing the Priceless Child,* 103–5): "By teaching how to spend money wisely, the allowance would train children as efficient

shoppers" (104). While Stowe attacks slavery, she does not challenge capitalist values, as Gillian Brown, Lori Merish, and others have argued (Brown, *Domestic Individualism;* Merish, *Sentimental Materialism*). Anglo-American children's books affirmed capitalist and even consumerist values from early on. See Avery, *Behold the Child,* 56–58; Crain, "Spectral Literacy: The Case of Goody Two-Shoes." These values are still more emphatic at the turn of the century.

37. As Thorstein Veblen points out, a well-trained servant at the turn of the century was a valuable possession. What better training for a servant (in deference, unobtrusiveness, etc.) than a career in slavery. . . . For Veblen's discussion of servants see *Theory of the Leisure Class.* On early twentieth-century rewritings of American history that stress slave loyalty see Blight, *The Civil War in American Memory;* Silber, *The Romance of Reunion.* See also Boulukos, *The Grateful Slave.*

38. Black self-sacrifice was often featured in postbellum romances, as well as children's stories. See for example Bruce, *Uncle Tom's Cabin of To-Day.*

39. ". . . likeness in God's sight / For both are the children of his grace" (*P&S,* 20). As Alison Lurie points out, although death was a staple of nineteenth-century literature for children, it disappeared from children's books in the first half of the twentieth century (*Don't Tell the Grownups,* xiv). Eva's death remains in all children's versions, but her suffering and the social/symbolic cause of her illness—slavery—disappears from *Young Folks Uncle Tom's Cabin* and other editions of the period. The scene at the lake, much illustrated in the antebellum period, is central to Jane Tompkins's influential analysis of *Uncle Tom's Cabin;* an illustration of the scene appears on the cover of Tompkins's *Sensational Designs.*

40. The theme of religious belief all but disappears from *Young Folks Uncle Tom's Cabin.* Eva points toward the sky and "look[s] . . . like an angel," but this is a cliché with no religious emphasis; a passing reference to the "new Jerusalem" is not elaborated (98). Religious language is used for nonspiritual ends: when Uncle Tom reads a letter written by George Shelby, he says "He ain't but fourteen years old, and he kin send a letter here dat makes my heart sing glory tunes" (98). Discussing illustrations of *Uncle Tom's Cabin,* Jo Ann Morgan points out that "few artists after Billings gave Tom Christian attributes and no image ever again analogized Tom's final days as reliving the passion of Christ" (*Uncle Tom's Cabin as Visual Culture,* 97). The figure of Tom was progressively de-spiritualized and devitalized in illustrations and children's editions. See also note 14 and O'Gorman, *Accomplished in All Departments of Art,* 55.

41. In Stowe's text, Topsy's talent for mimicry, acrobatics, theft, and general mischief is mainly confined to the chapter which introduces her. Late in the novel we are told that she does not become "at once a saint" (443), but her progress is represented as steady, especially after the conversion scene in which Eva expresses her love. In *Young Folks Uncle Tom's Cabin,* by contrast, Topsy acquires neither literacy, religious feeling, nor self-control. In a concluding chapter, when Topsy returns to the Shelby plantation after the war, she is still referred to as "a girl," and to everyone's relief she still reverts to type: "Mrs Shelby looks with amused eyes at the girl, who was leaping and whirling, with shining teeth and eyes . . . this is the Topsy that I hoped to see" (166). In Stowe's

text, as in antebellum children's editions and antebellum stage productions, Topsy's function was only partly comic.

42. Lydia Maria Child, *Mother's Book*, 91. See also Chapter 4.

43. The Playground Association of America was founded in 1906 (Zelizer, *Pricing the Priceless Child*, 34). On the growing interest in age-appropriate toys and activities see Calvert, *Children in the House;* Cross, *Kids' Stuff.* On age-grading in schools see Finkelstein and Vandell, "The Schooling of American Childhood."

44. Drummond, *The Child: His Nature and Nurture*, 17. Elaborating the analogy between the child's development and that of "the race," Drummond writes: "In the history of the race instinct has gradually been replaced by intelligence. As it has been in the race so is it in every child. Nature never forgets her past, and so we find all the primitive forms of instinct reappearing in the child's play, and gradually by their exercise giving place to intellectual powers" (104–5).

45. G. Stanley Hall, "Childhood and Adolescence," in Strickland (112). First published in Hall, *Adolescence.*

46. Stowe's thematic emphasis on child-rearing practices has been much discussed. See Tompkins, *Sensational Designs;* Fisher, *Hard Facts;* Robbins, *Managing Literacy, Mothering America.*

47. At the turn of the century the *North American Review* cost 50 cents; the *Century* 35 cents; *Scribner's* 25 cents; and the *Ladies' Home Journal* 10 cents.

48. On fathers see Baldwin, "About Children," 310; on observers see G. Stanley Hall, "A Study of Dolls," 203; Royce, "The Imitative Functions and Their Place in Human Nature."

49. Baldwin, "About Children," 308. For Josiah Royce "the study of the imitative functions [is] probably the most important task in the psychology of the immediate future" ("The Imitative Functions," 141).

50. Royce, "The Imitative Functions," 138. Royce, James Baldwin, W. B. Drummond, and others emphasized the early beginnings of the need to imitate—babies and young children "copy" motions, facial expressions, and even emotions. Language acquisition too is understood as a form of imitation. See Baldwin, *Mental Development in the Child and the Race*, 403; Drummond, *The Child*, 136. Since the 1960s, linguists have complicated and even rejected the notion that language is acquired through imitation. See Fromkin, Rodman, and Hyams, *An Introduction to Language*, 343–44; Owens, *Language Development: An Introduction*, 207–25. In the antebellum period what William Alcott called the "universal principle of imitation" was a central tenet of educational theory (*The Young Wife*, 266). Compared to antebellum educators, G. Stanley Hall and others had relatively little to say about children's reading, but for Royce it is axiomatic that imitation of fictional models is crucial to a child's assimilation of possible roles: "what we call [a child's] real self is for his still chaotic and planless inner consciousness, so long as it is not set in order by his imitativeness, the same as to be nobody in particular. But to be a horse, or a coachman, or a soldier, or the hero of a favorite story . . . that is to be somebody" (142). I discuss antebellum ideas about imitation and children in Chapter 4.

51. James Baldwin, "About Children" 309. Similarly, W. B. Drummond writes, "The brain grows not only *after* the pattern of ancestral habit, but *to* the impressions of individual experience, and in this way provision is made, provision infinitely greater than is the case in any of the lower animals, for individual adaptation and response to environment and education" (*The Child,* 125).

52. Using hypnotic suggestion as an analogue for the dynamic which prompts a child to imitate, Royce addresses the "well-known and frequent tendency" by which a child accepts an adult's "unintended counter-suggestion" and imitates something "undesirable" (144). Indeed, for Royce, children "whose life seems to their parents or teachers a life of almost persistent refusal to imitate models . . . are of the utmost interest" ("The Imitative Functions,"144).

53. The popular "bad boy" fiction of this period suggests that a certain amount of mischief is a natural and acceptable part of boyhood; the "bad boy" of the tale is assured a respectable future in the end. On "bad boys" see Avery, *Behold the Child,* 184–210; Fiedler, *Love and Death in the American Novel,* 259–90; Mailloux, "The Rhetorical Use and Abuse of Fiction," 133–57.

54. Burnett, "The One I Knew Best of All," 76. On Burnett see also Introduction. On doll punishment see Wiggin, *Children's Rights,* 15; G. Stanley Hall, "A Study of Dolls," 178. For a recent perspective see Bernstein, *Racial Innocence.*

55. Drummond, *The Child,* 17; G. Stanley Hall, "A Study of Dolls," 187; on Freud's impact in the United States of this period see Hale, *Freud and the Americans.* Michelle A. Masse's discussion of the unsettling impact of Freud on the idea of the child is especially relevant here ("Constructing the Psychoanalytic Child"). Citing Steven Marcus, Masse notes that the publication of Freud's *Three Essays* (including "Infantile Sexuality") in 1905 marks the close of "that epoch of cultural innocence in which infancy and childhood were regarded as themselves innocent" (155).

56. On the representation of moral consciousness and reason in antebellum children's books see Wishy, *The Child and the Republic,* and MacLeod, *A Moral Tale.* Kate Wiggin attacks "intellectual precocity" and "moral precocity" (*Children's Rights,* 21–22). G. Stanley Hall laments "our urbanized hot-house life, that tends to ripen everything before its time" and challenges "the tendencies to precocity in home, school, church and civilization generally" (Hall, "Childhood and Adolescence" in Strickland, 103; Hall, *Adolescence,* cited in Strickland and Burgess, "G. Stanley Hall: Prophet of Naturalism," in Strickland, *Health, Growth, and Heredity,* 19).

57. Hall, "Childhood and Adolescence," 101.

58. Children are subject to violence, but the brutality is rarely their own. Tom Sawyer is one significant exception.

59. MacLeod, *American Childhood,* 123. Yet adult fiction about children, like theories of childhood, acknowledges complexity. Caroline Levander suggests that "The Turn of the Screw" asks "does the child have a moral sense?" and explores the idea of "infant depravity" (*Cradle of Liberty,* 140, 141). Late nineteenth-century psychologists often emphasize the inaccessibility of childhood, despite their claims of optimism. G. Stanley Hall writes: "Simple as childhood seems, there is nothing harder to know; and responsive as it is to

every influence about it, nothing is harder to guide" ("New Departures in Education" in Strickland, 96). "Adaptable as children are, their ways and thoughts are not as ours; and the adult can no more get back into the child's soul by introspection than he can pass the flaming sword and reclaim his lost Eden" ("Child Study and Its Relation to Education," 89). W. B. Drummond notes that "the child is not simply an immature man" (*The Child,* 21). Apparently the idea of children as different from adults required restating as late as 1915, even though, according to Philippe Ariès and others, the idea dates from the eighteenth century. See Ariès, *Centuries of Childhood.*

60. See James Mark Baldwin, "About Children," 308, 310; Drummond, *The Child,* 101.

61. According to this theory, as white children grow they reproduce evolutionary progress (ontogeny recapitulates phylogeny) and their superiority shines through. As Drummond puts this, "the irascibility and impulsiveness of children . . . illustrate very strikingly the analogy between the child and inferior races" (*The Child,* 116). Hall writes, " 'Child study' is closely related to the study of instinct in animals and to the rites and beliefs of primitive peoples" ("Child-Study and Its Relation to Education," 76).

62. Anne Lundin notes that "A growing gender division led to further classification of children's books by gender and age categories, the expansion of the juvenile market and the disappearance of a unified audience. . . . In the 1890s reviewers began in earnest to differentiate between boys' and girls' books" (142).

63. Coleman, "The Unsentimental Woman Preacher of *Uncle Tom's Cabin,*" 18.

64. On the "close parallel between womanly virtue and physical crippling" in fiction for girls, see MacLeod, " 'The *Caddie Woodlawn* Syndrome': American Girlhood in the Nineteenth Century," 115.

65. Palmer A. Cox expressed a culturally typical position when he said of his own work for children that it would "always have happy endings. . . . It is time enough for children when they get big to learn that a reckoning must be made in suffering and bloodshed" (cited in Murray, *American Children's Literature and the Construction of Childhood,* 100). Kate Wiggin suggests that stories for children should "deal with the positive" (*Children's Rights,* 96).

66. At least one edition (New York: Hurst & Co., 1901) ends when George brings Uncle Tom safely back to the Shelby plantation. All the other editions that I have seen— from the copyrighted Jamieson-Higgins edition of 1901 through an Albert Whiteman Co. reprint of 1956—include the additional chapter with the reconciliation scene.

67. *Little Black Sambo* is set in India and Sambo (despite his name) is an Indian child. But illustrations foreground the American context, and this popular book was much reprinted in the United States throughout the twentieth century. At least one edition combines the story of Little Black Sambo with the story of Topsy. ("Little Black Sambo" appears as the second story in an edition entitled *The Story of Topsy from Uncle Tom's Cabin* [Chicago: Reilly and Britton,1908]). *Little Black Sambo* became controversial in the 1960s and '70s, when educators and commentators grew increasingly aware of the book's racist potential. See Yuill, *Little Black Sambo: A Closer Look;* Hay, *Sambo Sahib: The Story of Little Black Sambo and Helen Bannerman.* Given the many

tame and boring children's books published in this period, Little Black Sambo's danger and his outwitting of fierce tigers may well have been especially appealing. Ellen Handler Spitz examines the enduring popularity of *Little Black Sambo* from a psychoanalytic perspective. See *Inside Picture Books,* 209–15. See also Sanjay Sircar's analysis of his own fond recollections of reading the book as a child growing up in India (Sircar, "Little Brown Sanjay and Little Black Sambo").

68. Children's periodicals such as *Harper's Young People* or *Youth's Companion* ran occasional stories about loyal slaves or about newly benign relations between the North and the South along the lines of what Nina Silber calls the "romance of reunion"; but such tales pay little if any attention to the painful aspects of slavery, some of which do retain a shadowy presence in *Young Folks Uncle Tom's Cabin.*

69. Stepto, "Sharing the Thunder," 142.

70. Although Amherstburg is in Canada, this edition does give George and Harry a role in a Western democratic capitalist state and emphasizes their qualifications for a middle-class life rather than confining them to missionary work in Africa. Amherstburg was an important stopping point in the Underground Railroad.

71. Boylan, *Kids of Many Colors.* Illustrations by Ike Morgan.

72. One review praises Boylan's "ingenuity and real inventive talent," emphasizing that the playful "happy company" is "full of frolic and fun" (Rev. of "Children's Picture Books," APS online pg. 219).

73. Boylan, *Kids of Many Colors,* 147.

74. The 1901 review of *Young Folks Uncle Tom's Cabin* responds to the "liberal" message of Boylan's text, and the reviewer notes: "It seems incredible that such fiction as this could ever have had even a remote foundation of fact in this land of ours" ("Children's Picture Books," APS online pg. 219).

75. Many editions of Frederick Douglass's narrative for children are available. The prolific Anne Terry White, who adapted *Uncle Tom's Cabin* for young readers in 1966, wrote *North to Liberty: The Story of the Underground Railroad* in 1972. See also Hildreth, *Memoirs of A Fugitive: America's First Anti-Slavery Novel,* adapted for children by Barbara Ritchie (1971), and Johnston, *Harriet and the Runaway Book* (1977). Serious and historically accurate books about slavery for children continue to appear.

76. "Aunt Mary," *A Peep into Uncle Tom's Cabin,* v. As Stephen Railton points out, this edition rewrites Stowe's text in part by omitting passages and chapters, deleting "the novel's references to race and interracial sexuality. 'Quadroon,' for example, never appears in the *Peep,* nor does 'The Quadroon's Story'" ("*Uncle Tom's Cabin* and American Culture," http://utc.iath.virginia.edu/childrn/peephp.html). In addition, as we have noted, the book is restructured to foreground Tom himself (see also Chapter 2, fig. 6).

77. Harriet Beecher Stowe, "Address from the Author of 'Uncle Tom's Cabin' to the Children of England and America," in "Aunt Mary," *A Peep into Uncle Tom's Cabin,* 3.

78. Hewins, *Books for the Young: A Guide for Parents and Children,* 77. *Uncle Tom's Cabin* is included in the section "History, Historical Biography, Tales and Novels" under the sub-heading "Modern History, United States." The list of thirty-three authors in the

section characteristically includes few writers of fiction, among them Cooper, Hawthorne, Edward Everett Hale, Washington Irving, Thackeray. Charlemae Rollins includes *Uncle Tom's Cabin* in *We Build Together: A Reader's Guide to Negro Life and Literature for Elementary and High School Use Prepared for the National Council of Teachers of English* in 1941 (see also Epilogue, n. 65).

79. The clipping is a scrap, with no headline, in the Beecher-Stowe scrapbook. No source or date appears on the article, but it notes that HBS is in "her 83rd year" (i.e., 1894). On this scrapbook see Chapter 5.

80. Beecher-Stowe clipping. No source or date appears on the article. Stowe's 85th birthday was in 1896.

81. See, for example, Sorby, *The Schoolroom Poets*. Sorby cites from letters written to Longfellow's daughter by children in a South Dakota classroom composed of poor immigrant students. The teacher's penciled comments on the letters suggest that Longfellow's "exemplary poetry and life" will help "to mitigate the children's 'broken' and 'miserable' backgrounds by exposing them to an Anglo-Saxon middle-class culture based on taste." Across the United States Longfellow was taught in schools as a poet who could "dissolve social difference by acting as a civilizing force" (Sorby, 29).

82. Beecher-Stowe clipping.

83. A segregated black public library, established in Tyler, Texas, in 1941, purchased the *Young Folks Uncle Tom's Cabin* for its collection (probably in 1953). The library had already bought an edition intended for "juvenile" readers in 1943, but that was a full-length *Uncle Tom's Cabin,* illustrated by James Henry Daugherty (New York: Coward, McCann, and Geoghegan, 1929). The decision to buy these books is all the more significant because the majority of the library's collection was acquired through donations—not purchased. I am grateful to Cheryl Knott Malone for this information.

84. Boylan, *Young Folks Uncle Tom's Cabin* (Chicago: Albert Whiteman & Co., 1942) 147.

EPILOGUE: DEVOURING *UNCLE TOM'S CABIN*

1. See for example Wiegand and Danky, eds., *Print Culture in a Diverse America;* Holloway, *Bookmarks;* Kelley, *Learning to Stand and Speak;* McHenry, *Forgotten Readers;* Sicherman, "Reading *Little Women*"; Sicherman, *Well-Read Lives;* Stewart, *Reading and Disorder;* Zboray and Zboray, *Everyday Ideas.*

2. McHenry, *Forgotten Readers,* 7.

3. Ibid., 14.

4. Mitchell, *Picture Theory,* 189. On the neglect of slave narratives after the Civil War (and for much of the twentieth century), see also Starling, *The Slave Narrative: Its Place in History,* and Andrews, *To Tell a Free Story.*

5. In an "Author's Prologue" for a second edition of *The Slave Narrative* Marion Wilson Starling writes: "Ten thousand pages of interviews [from the Federal Writers' Project] were stored in barrels in the basement of the Library of Congress, under the control of the chief librarian. The papers were off limits to scholars until 1944, when they

were released by Dr. Benjamin Botkin, the librarian whose book on the narratives—*Lay My Burden Down*—was published in 1945 by University of Chicago Press" (xiv).

6. Baldwin, *The Devil Finds Work*, 10, 14.

7. The phrase "faith in reading" figures in the title of Nord's *Faith in Reading* as well as Augst's chapter "Faith in Reading: Public Libraries, Liberalism and the Civil Religion," in *Institutions of Reading*.

8. Holloway, *Bookmarks: Reading in Black and White*, 135, 184. Further references are included in the text.

9. McHenry, *Forgotten Readers*, 104. Further references are included in the text.

10. Washington, *Up from Slavery*, 129.

11. Cited in Ovington, "Selling Race Pride," 114. On Johnson see also McHenry, *Forgotten Readers*, 11; Coulter, '*Take up the Black Man's Burden*'.

12. The novel's low cultural prestige vis-à-vis older literary forms lingered well into the twentieth century, as we have seen. When James Russell Lowell identified "The Five Indispensable Authors" in 1894, his list was comprised of Homer, Shakespeare, Dante, Goethe, and Cervantes. The selection was culturally typical (Lowell, "The Five Indispensable Authors"). In an address to the (black) Boston Literary and Historical Association in 1902, the Reverend Frank F. Hall cautioned his audience to avoid indiscriminate reading: "Don't try to enter into the companionship of too many books . . . but know something about the really great literature of Homer, Virgil, Dante, Shakespeare" (cited in McHenry, *Forgotten Readers*, 172). On efforts to control fiction-reading in the twentieth century see Garrison, *Apostles of Culture*; Radway, *A Feeling for Books*; Rubin, *The Making of Middlebrow Culture*; Hochman, "Readers and Reading Groups." On theories of child development that made reading for leisure, pleasure, and fantasy increasingly acceptable see Chapter 7.

13. Wells, *Crusade for Justice*, 22.

14. Golden, *Migrations of the Heart*, 8.

15. Ibid., 6, 4.

16. Richard Wright, whose maternal grandmother condemned fiction as sinful, discovered social commentary as well as writing he could emulate in the work of Lewis and Dreiser: "All my life had shaped me for the realism, the naturalism of the modern novel," he writes, "and I could not read enough of [these novels]" (*Black Boy*, 250). Wright aligns himself with fiction of social protest by citing such models. But in literary culture of the 1940s, Lewis or Dreiser ranked not only well below ancient and European classics, but also below Tolstoy, Dickens, and Flaubert—even below American "greats" such as Hawthorne, Melville, or Cooper. F. W. Mathiessen's *The American Renaissance* (1941) is a good index to academic taste of the period.

17. Pinckney, "Introduction" to *Uncle Tom's Cabin*, xxii.

18. In 1912 an advertisement for *The Crisis*, with the heading "ARE YOU INTERESTED IN THE NEGRO PROBLEM OR PART OF IT?," includes Charles Stowe's *Life of Harriet Beecher Stowe*. The advertisement was often reprinted (e.g., *The Crisis* 3.3 [January 1912], 125; [February 1912], 169; [March 1912], 217). An advertisement for "The Best Books"

which includes Stowe's biography appears in *The Crisis,* September 1912, 259; November 1912, 52; January 1913, 155. In 1931 a "Philadelphia correspondent" wrote to Walter White, secretary of the NAACP, describing himself as "a Negro father" and asking for books "about the Negro or written by Negroes." In response, W. E. B. Du Bois, editor of *The Crisis,* included Stowe's novel on a list of recommended titles (Holloway, *Bookmarks,* 33). For the full list see Holloway, 36–37.

19. Bolivar was particularly interested in preserving information about Philadelphia's African American heritage "in the face of exclusion from the city's efforts to document its past" (Welburn, "To 'Keep the Past in Lively Memory,'" 174). Bolivar's collection included the first edition of *Uncle Tom's Cabin,* and the Tauchnitz edition of *Dred* as well as several other works by Stowe. I thank William Welburn for this information.

   Other African American efforts to preserve material evidence of black history in this period include the work of Arthur Schomburg, historian, bibliophile, and co-founder of the Negro Society for Historical Research in New York (1911), as well as William Dorsey's scrapbook collection (preserved in the William H. Dorsey collection at Cheyney State University in Philadelphia). Dorsey devoted almost an entire scrapbook to newspaper clippings about Stowe. On Dorsey see Chapter 5.

20. On Hughes see also Chapter 6, n. 32.

21. Morrison made this point in an NEH Summer Seminar titled "Fiction and History" directed by Emory Elliott at Princeton in 1989.

22. Starling, "Author's Prologue" (reprinted from the first edition), *The Slave Narrative: Its Place in American History* (xxiv). Further references are from the 1988 edition and are included in the text.

23. On "the emancipation moment" see Chapter 5.

24. While Arac's claim is not exact, it accurately reflects the cultural climate of the 1940s (*Huckleberry Finn as Idol and Target,* 92). On editions of that decade, see Parfait, *The Publishing History of Uncle Tom's Cabin,* 224.

25. Johnson, *Autobiography of an Ex-Colored Man,* 28. Further references to this edition are included in the text.

26. Chesnutt, *The Journals of Charles W. Chesnutt,* 125. See also Brodhead, *Cultures of Letters,* 191–92.

27. Ida B. Wells, "Woman's Mission," 181.

28. On Terrell's enthusiasm for Stowe see Terrell, *A Colored Woman in a White World,* 233, and her pamphlet *Harriet Beecher Stowe: An Appreciation;* Sterling, *Black Foremothers: Three Lives,* 136; and Sicherman, *Well-Read Lives.* On African American responses to Stowe see also Spillers, "Changing the Letter"; Warren, "The Afterlife of *Uncle Tom's Cabin*"; Yarborough, "Strategies of Black Characterization"; and Bernstein, "'Never Born': Angelina Weld Grimke's *Rachel* as Ironic Response to Topsy." See also Introduction and Chapter 5.

29. Terrell, *Colored Woman in a White World,* 10.

30. Wells, *Crusade for Justice,* 10.

31. Ibid., 21–22.

32. Malcolm X abrogated his self-imposed ban on novels in order to read *Uncle Tom's Cabin* in prison, while seeking books "about black history." "I never will forget how shocked I was when I began reading about slavery's total horror," he writes. "Books like the one by Frederick Olmstead opened my eyes to the horrors suffered when the slave was landed in the United States. The European woman, Fannie Kimball [*sic*], who had married a Southern white slaveowner, described how human beings were degraded. Of course I read *Uncle Tom's Cabin*. In fact I believe that's the only novel I have ever read since I started serious reading" (Haley and Malcolm X, *The Autobiography of Malcolm X*, 176, 177).

33. Terrell, *Colored Woman in a White World*, 10. Further references to this edition are included in the text.

34. See Chapter 5.

35. Terrell, *Harriet Beecher Stowe: An Appreciation*, 3. Further references to this edition are included in the text. On the common critical practice of avoiding Stowe's emphasis on the brutal details of slavery in commentaries and paratextual material of the 1890s. see especially Chapter 5.

36. Stowe makes this point in a letter to Eliza Cabot Follen. The letter is reprinted in Harriet Beecher Stowe, *Uncle Tom's Cabin*, Ammons, ed. (1994), 413.

37. On Stowe's account of her sons' response see Introduction.

38. See, e.g., James Lane Allen, "Mrs. Stowe's 'Uncle Tom' at Home in Kentucky" (1887); Mrs. William Liddel L. Bruce's tale of devoted slaves in *Uncle Tom's Cabin of To-day* (1906). See also Chapters 6 and 7.

39. Gillman, "Pageantry, Maternity, and World History," 396–97.

40. Chesnutt writes: "Yesterday I went up to Mr. Harris and Stayed nearly all day. Played the organ, and read 1 vol 'Uncle Tom's Cabin.' It was no ways old to me, although I have read it before" (*The Journals of Charles W. Chesnutt* [Aug. 23, 1875], 50).

41. Johnson notes with satisfaction that most reviewers accepted *Autobiography of an Ex-Colored Man* as "a human document," although "there were some doubters," and adds that he "did get a certain pleasure out of anonymity that no acknowledged book could have given" (*Along This Way*, 238).

42. Ibid., 31, 5, 32.

43. See "Uncle Tom's Cabin and the Clansman." In this short piece Johnson attacks the "incalculable harm" likely to ensue from the newly released movie, *The Birth of a Nation*. He begins by criticizing a recent protest against a theatrical version of *Uncle Tom's Cabin*, which was to be performed in Atlanta. The play finally was allowed to appear, Johnson remarks bitterly, when it "was changed and given the Arcadian title of 'Old Plantation Days'[;] the offensive parts were expurgated, Simon Legree was transfigured into a sort of benevolent patriarch, Uncle Tom was made into a happy old darkey who greatly enjoyed being a slave and who ultimately died of too much good treatment, and so, a performance was given that was, no doubt, a great success, and offended nobody's sensibilities" (613). Johnson's ironic description of these editorial changes clearly reflect his understanding of Stowe's novel as strong medicine not only in its own time, but perhaps even more so in 1915. The black actor Charles Gilpin was

fired from a Hollywood production of *Uncle Tom's Cabin* in 1927 "because he refused to play Tom as a sentimental and harmless darky" (Douglas, *Terrible Honesty*, 87). On the widespread tendency of white commentators to neutralize *Uncle Tom's Cabin* by emphasizing its benign view of slavery, see Chapter 5.

44. Johnson, *Along This Way*, 238.

45. The idea that *Uncle Tom's Cabin* teaches Johnson's narrator "what I was and what my country considered me" seems to confirm Walter Benn Michaels's claim that certain African American texts (*Beloved* is his central example) promote an idea of history that, experienced as a kind of group "memory," becomes a ground of identity construction. Yet Johnson's narrator, like Terrell and other African Americans in the post–Civil War period, is drawn to *Uncle Tom's Cabin* by the very belief that, according to Michaels, Morrison's fiction (like Stephen Greenblatt's historicism) rejects: the belief "that we might learn from the past things that are useful in the present . . . [by] taking the past as an object of knowledge" ("You Who Never Was There," 6). Johnson's narrator, Terrell, and others collect information in order to understand the puzzling behavior of close relatives (unexplained words, silence, and shame) as well as the attitudes of white teachers and railway porters—in other words they seek, by knowing the past, to explain the present.

46. On *Uncle Tom's Cabin* as a children's book for white readers see Chapters 4 and 7.

47. Caroline M. Hewins, *Books for Boys and Girls,* 10. An earlier version, *Books for the Young* (1882), recommended *Uncle Tom's Cabin* without the caution. See also Chapter 4.

48. Stonequist, *Marginal Man,* 173, 171. Further references this edition are included in the text. I am grateful to Shlomi Deloia for alerting me to this source.

49. *The Leopard's Spots* and Dixon's *The Clansman* (1905) were the inspiration for *Birth of a Nation*. The other books on the "negro girl's" reading list are W. E. B. Du Bois, *Quest of the Silver Fleece* (1911); Jessie Fauset, *There Is Confusion* (1924); Gertrude Sanborn, *Veiled Aristocrats* (1923).

50. In discussing the eclectic booklist of J. Saunders Redding, distinguished African American teacher and scholar of American studies, Holloway emphasizes Redding's unexpected mention of "racially invidious" texts, such as Charles Carroll's *The Negro, Man or Beast* and Thomas Dixon's *The Leopard's Spots*. Although Redding's autobiography typically mentions a range of books that impacted on his childhood, his notation of books he has "hated" as well as "loved" makes his booklist exceptional in Holloway's account (177, 176). Redding's list, like the list of eight titles compiled by Stonequist's "negro girl," is heavily weighted toward books that highlight racial conflict. Such books play a special role on a black booklist; they impel black readers to "brood" over their own life situation, asking "what was fit for the Negro to do," and even imagining race-war.

51. On the conflict between Douglass and Delany regarding the implications of *Uncle Tom's Cabin* and its popularity at mid-century see Levine, *Martin Delany, Frederick Douglass, and the Politics of Representative Identity,* chap. 2.

52. See Introduction and Chapter 3.

53. Gates, "Introduction," *The Annotated Uncle Tom's Cabin,* xxix.

54. Spillers, "Changing the Letter," 30. White literary commentators have reinforced the idea of Stowe as a touchstone for "negro" writing. "Mrs. Stowe has *invented* the negro novel," George Eliot famously wrote ("Review of *Dred*"). The first review of Nella Larsen's *Quicksand* opens with the statement: " 'Quicksand' is not part of the tradition which began long ago when Mrs. Stowe pictured for us Simon Legree beating Uncle Tom . . ." (cited in Hutchinson, *In Search of Nella Larsen,* 275).

55. Crosely, "Reader's Guide" to Butler's *Kindred,* 272.

56. Baldwin, "Everybody's Protest Novel," 495.

57. Baldwin, *Notes of a Native Son,* 11.

58. Eckman, *The Furious Passage of James Baldwin,* 41. Eckman's biography of Baldwin is based largely on interviews. In a page of "Acknowledgements" she thanks those "who, by sharing with me their memories and experiences, helped me trace Mr. Baldwin's passage from Harlem to the present." Baldwin confirms his mother's account of reading *Uncle Tom's Cabin* in *The Devil Finds Work,* 14.

59. Baldwin, *The Devil Finds Work,* 14. See also Lauren Berlant's reading of this episode in Baldwin's "cultural formation" (*The Female Complaint,* 58; 58–60).

60. Throughout *The Devil Finds Work* Baldwin explores the question of aesthetic illusion and the way movies or books create the illusion of reality—or do not. See, e.g., 13–14, 25–26, 30.

61. Hurston, *Dust Tracks on a Road,* 39.

62. *"Uncle Tom's Cabin,"* Hurston writes in a letter to Alain Locke in 1943, " . . . typed the Negro for the North. Not knowing Negroes, they. . . . have the fixed idea that we should all be long-suffering Uncle Toms, or funny Topsys. When the real us shows up, there is disillusionment. Then the northerner finds that he is no more willing to live in close communion with a number of Negroes than the southerner" (*Zora Neale Hurston: A Life in Letters,* 490).

63. Wilson, *Patriotic Gore,* 4–5. On editions published between the Civil War and the Modern Library Edition, see Parfait, *The Publishing History of Uncle Tom's Cabin.* See also see Chapters 5, 6, and 7.

64. Pinckney, "Introduction," vii.

65. When the African American writer and librarian Charlemae Rollins included *Uncle Tom's Cabin* in *We Build Together: A Reader's Guide to Negro Life and Literature for Elementary and High School Use Prepared for the National Council of Teachers of English* in 1941, she offered the following explanation: "Although sentimental and overdrawn, [*Uncle Tom's Cabin*] was undoubtedly one of the moving forces of freedom. Negroes today feel that it is responsible for the well-known stereotype 'Uncle Tom,' a label given to Negroes who are unduly submissive, obsequious and servile. [However,] some Negro parents think that their children, in order to know the history of their own people, should read this book" (15). In the 1967 edition of *We Buiild Together, Uncle Tom's Cabin* does not appear in the index; it has been replaced by a biography of Stowe (Wise, *Harriet Beecher Stowe: Woman with a Cause*) and a fleeting mention of Anne Terry White's adaptation for children: "Mrs. White has substituted acceptable words

for objectionable ones, deleted diverting and irrelevant passages, and simplified sentence structure making the book more readable for young people" (Rollins and Edman, "Introduction," xxvii). On White's adaptation see Chapter 7, n. 14.

66. Howard, *Publishing the Family,* 230. For a range of approaches to the cultural situatedness of reader response. see Schweickart and Flynn, ed., *Reading Sites.*

Abbott, John S. C. *The Mother at Home, or Principles of Maternal Duty.* Boston: Crocker and Brewster, 1833.

Abbott, Lyman, ed. *Hints for Home Reading: A Series of Chapters on Books and Their Use.* New York: G. P. Putnam's Sons, 1880, 1892.

Abbott, Lyman, et al., ed. *The House and Home: A Practical Book.* New York: Charles Scribner's Sons, 1896.

Abel, Elizabeth. "Black Writing, White Reading: Race and the Politics of Feminist Interpretation." *Critical Inquiry* 19 (Spring 1993): 470–98.

"About the Slave Trade." *Slave's Friend* I, no. 2 (1836): 9–10.

"Act as Well as Feel." *Slave's Friend* III, no. 4 (1838): 3–4.

Advertisement. "Are You Interested in the Negro Problem or Part of It?" *The Crisis* 3.3 (January 1912): 125; (February 1912): 169; (March 1912): 217.

Advertisement. "The Best Books." *The Crisis* 4.5 (September 1912): 259; (December 1912): 52; (January 1913): 155.

Advertisement. "Caste, A Powerful Anti-Slavery Novel." *The Liberator* (November 23, 1855).

Advertisement. *Chicago Daily Tribune* (September 13, 1906).

Advertisement. "Dred." *The Liberator* (October 3, 1856).

Advertisement. "The Rag Picker, Or Bound and Free." *The Liberator* (October 12, November 23, 1855).

Advertisement. "Uncle Tom's Cabin." Pasted into the back cover of *Uncle Tom's Cabin.* Boston: Houghton Mifflin, 1888. NYPL.

Advertisement. "Wistar's Balsam of Wild Cherry." *National Era* (January 31, 1851): 123.

Advertisement. "Wister's Balsam of Wild Cherry." *National Era* (June 5, 1851): 91.

Alcott, William. *Familiar Letters to Young Men on Various Subjects.* Buffalo: Derby, 1850.

———. *The Young Wife.* 1837. New York: Arno Press, 1972.

Allen, Grant. "Novels without a Purpose." *Current Literature: A Magazine of Record and Review* XX (July–December 1896): 408.

Allen, James Lane. "Mrs. Stowe's 'Uncle Tom' at Home in Kentucky." *Century* 34 (October 1887): 852–67.

Anderson, James D. *The Education of Blacks in the South, 1860–1935.* Chapel Hill: University of North Carolina Press, 1988.

Andrews, William L. *To Tell a Free Story: The First Century of African American Autobiography, 1760–1865.* Chicago: University of Illinois Press, 1988.

Applebee, Arthur N. *The Child's Concept of Story.* Chicago: University of Chicago Press, 1978.

Arac, Jonathan. "Uncle Tom's Cabin vs. Huckleberry Finn." *Huckleberry Finn as Idol and Target.* Madison: University of Wisconsin Press, 1997.

Ariès, Philippe. *Centuries of Childhood: A Social History of Family Life.* New York: Vintage Books, 1962.

Augst, Thomas. "Faith in Reading: Public Libraries, Liberalism, and the Civil Religion." In Augst and Carpenter, ed., *Institutions of Reading.* 148–83.

Augst, Thomas, and Kenneth Carpenter, eds. *Institutions of Reading: The Social Life of Libraries in the United States.* Amherst: University of Massachusetts Press, 2007.

"The Author of 'Uncle Tom's Cabin' Dies Peacefully at Hartford—Close of a Remarkable Life." *Philadelphia Times* (July 2, 1896): 3.

Avery, Gillian. *Behold the Child: American Children and Their Books, 1621–1922.* Baltimore: Johns Hopkins University Press, 1994.

Badia, Janet, and Jennifer Phegley, eds. *Reading Women: Literary Figures and Cultural Icons from the Victorian Age to the Present.* Toronto: University of Toronto Press, 2006.

Bailey, Gamaliel. "Our Annual Letter." *National Era* (November 13, 1851).

Baldwin, James. *The Devil Finds Work.* New York: Dial Press, 1976.

———. "Everybody's Protest Novel" (1949). *Uncle Tom's Cabin.* Ed. Elizabeth Ammons. New York: Norton, 1994.

———. *Notes of a Native Son.* London: Michael Joseph, 1949.

Baldwin, James Mark. "About Children." *Century* 49.2 (December 1894): 308–10.

———. *Mental Development in the Child and the Race.* New York: Macmillan, 1895.

Balestier, Wolcott. "Benefits Forgot." *Century* 46.1 (May 1893): 51–63.

Balter, Leon. "On the Aesthetic Illusion." *Journal of the American Psychoanalytic Association* 47.4 (1999): 1293–1333.

Bannerman, Helen. "Little Black Sambo." *The Story of Topsy from Uncle Tom's Cabin.* Chicago: Reilly and Britton, 1908.

Banta, Martha. *Imaging American Women: Idea and Ideals in Cultural History.* New York: Columbia University Press, 1987.

"Barbadoes" [*sic*]. *Slave's Friend* IV, no. 1 (1839): 13.

Barrett, Wendell. *A Literary History of America.* New York: Scribner's, 1900.

Barrish, Philip. *American Literary Realism: Critical Theory and Intellectual Prestige.* New York: Cambridge University Press, 2001.

Barthes, Roland. *Image, Music, Text.* Trans. Stephen Heath. New York: Hill and Wang, 1977.

Bartlett, Frederic Charles. *Remembering: A Study in Experimental and Social Psychology.* 1932. Cambridge: Cambridge University Press, 1995.

Baym, Nina. *Novels, Readers, and Reviewers: Fiction in Antebellum America.* Ithaca: Cornell University Press, 1984.

Beadle, J. H. "Harriet Beecher Stowe." *Literature: An Illustrated Weekly Magazine* II, no. 52 (February 16, 1889): 285–88.

Beecher, Catharine E. "Preface." *The Mayflower or Sketches of Scenes and Characters Among the Descendents of the Pilgrims.* By Harriet Beecher Stowe. New York: Harper Bros., 1843. xii.

Beecher, Catharine E., and Harriet Beecher Stowe. *The American Woman's Home.* Hartford: Harriet Beecher Stowe Center, 2002; c. 1869.

———. *Principles of Domestic Science As Applied to the Duties and Pleasures of Home.* New York: J. B. Ford, 1870.

Beecher, Henry Ward. "The Strange Woman." *Lectures to Young Men.* Salem: John P. Jewett, 1846. 170–214.

———. "Tribute to Harriet Beecher Stowe." Address given June 14, 1882 at the birthday anniversary of Harriet Beecher Stowe. Pt. in *Modern Eloquence.* Vol. 1. Ed. Thomas Brackett Reed, Rossiter Johnson, Justin McCarthy, and Albert Ellery Berg. Philadelphia: J. D. Morris, 1901. 51–54.

Beecher-Stowe Collection 1798–1956. Schlesinger Library Radcliffe Institute for Advanced Study. Microfilm. Reel no. 5. Folders 377–409.

Beecher-Stowe Scrapbook. Beecher-Stowe Collection. Folder 396.

Beetham, Margaret. "Toward a Theory of the Periodical as a Publishing Genre." *Investigating Victorian Journalism.* Basingstoke: Palgrave Macmillan, 1990. 19–32.

Benjamin, Walter. "Children's Literature." *Walter Benjamin Selected Writings.* Vol. 2, 1927–1934. Trans. Rodney Livingstone and Others. Cambridge: Harvard University Press, 1999. 250–56.

———. "The Storyteller." *Illuminations.* Trans. Harry Zohn. New York: Schocken Books, 1969. 83–110.

———. "The Task of the Translator: An Introduction to the Translation of Baudelaire's *Tableaus Parisiens.*" Trans. Harry Zohn. *The Translation Studies Reader.* Ed. Lawrence Venuti. New York: Routledge, 2004. 75–82.

Bentley, Nancy. "White Slaves: The Mulatto Hero in Antebellum Fiction." *American Literature* 65.3 (1993): 501–22.

Berger, John. "Why Look at Animals." *About Looking.* New York: Pantheon, 1980.

Bergner, Gwen. "Black Children, White Preference: Brown v. Board, the Doll Tests, and the Politics of Self-Esteem." *American Quarterly* 61.2 (June 2009): 299–332.

Berlant, Lauren. *The Female Complaint: The Unfinished Business of Sentimentality in American Culture.* Durham: Duke University Press, 2008.

Bernstein, Robin. "Dances with Things: Material Culture and the Performance of Race." *Social Text 101.* 27.4 (Winter 2009.): 67–94.

————. "'Never Born': Angelina Weld Grimke's *Rachel* as Ironic Response to Topsy." *Journal of American Drama and Theatre* 19.2 (Spring 2007): 61–75.

————. *Racial Innocence: Performing American Childhood from Slavery to Civil Rights.* New York: New York University Press (forthcoming).

"The Best Book." *New York Evangelist* (June 5,1851): 92.

"The Best Hundred Books for Children." *Living Age* 225.2910 (April 1900): 132–34.

Bettleheim, Bruno. *The Uses of Enchantment.* New York: Knopf, 1976.

Bhabha, Homi K. *The Location of Culture.* New York: Routledge, 1994.

"Biographical Sketch." *Uncle Tom's Cabin.* New York: Houghton Mifflin, 1896. x–xii.

Blackford, Holly Virginia. *Out of This World: Why Literature Matters to Girls.* New York: Teachers College Press, 2004.

Blackwell, Alice Stone. *Growing Up in Boston's Gilded Age: The Journal of Alice Stone Blackwell, 1872–1874.* Ed. Marlene Deahl Merrill. New Haven: Yale University Press, 1990.

Bleich, David. *Subjective Criticism.* Baltimore: Johns Hopkins University Press, 1978.

Blight, David. *Race and Reunion: The Civil War in American Memory.* Cambridge: Harvard University Press, 2001.

Bloch, Dorothy. *"So the Witch Won't Eat Me."* New York: Houghton Mifflin, 1978.

Blondheim, Menahem. "'Public Sentiment Is Everything': The Union's Public Communications Strategy and the Bogus Proclamation of 1864." *Journal of American History* 89.3 (December 2002): 869–99.

Bloom, Harold. *The Anxiety of Influence: A Theory of Poetry.* New York: Oxford University Press, 1997.

Boime, Albert. *The Art of Exclusion: Representing Blacks in the Nineteenth Century.* Washington, D.C.: Smithsonian Institution, 1990.

Bolton, Sarah Knowles. *Lives of Girls Who Became Famous.* New York: T. Y. Crowell, 1886.

Bonilla-Silva, Eduardo. *Racism without Racists: Color-Blind Racism and the Persistence of Racial Inequality in the United States.* Lanham, Md: Rowman and Littlefield, 2006.

Borgstrom, Michael. "Passing Over: Setting the Record Straight in *Uncle Tom's Cabin.*" *PMLA* 118.5 (October 2003): 1290–1304.

Borus, Daniel. *Writing Realism: Howells, James, and Norris in the Mass Market.* Chapel Hill: University of North Carolina Press, 1989.

Boskin, Joseph. *Sambo: The Rise and the Demise of an American Jester.* New York: Oxford University Press, 1986.

Boulukos, George. *The Grateful Slave: The Emergence of Race in Eighteenth-Century British and American Culture.* New York: Cambridge University Press, 2008.

Boyeson, Hjalmar Hjorth. "Why We Have No Great Novelists." *Forum* II (February 1887): 615–17.

Boylan, Grace Duffie. *Kids of Many Colors.* Chicago: Jamieson-Higgins 1901.

————. *Young Folks Uncle Tom's Cabin.* Adapted for Children by Boylan. New York: Hurst, 1901.

———. *Young Folks Uncle Tom's Cabin.* New York: Chicago: Jamieson-Higgins, 1901.

———. *Young Folks Uncle Tom's Cabin.* Chicago: Albert Whitman, 1942.

Bradford, Edward A. "Open Letters: Columbus's Day." *The Century* 39.3 (January 1890): 479.

Briden, Earl F. "Kemble's 'Specialty' and the Pictorial Countertext of *Huckleberry Finn.*" *Mark Twain Journal* 26.2 (Fall 1988): 2–14.

Brodhead, Richard H. *Cultures of Letters: Scenes of Reading and Writing in Nineteenth-Century America.* Chicago: University of Chicago Press, 1993.

Brodkin, Karen. *How Jews Became White Folks and What That Says about Race in America.* New Brunswick: Rutgers University Press, 1998.

Brooks, Peter. *Reading for the Plot: Design and Intention in Narrative.* New York: A. A. Knopf, 1984.

Brown, Gillian. "Child's Play." In Levander and Singley, ed., *The American Child,* 13–39.

———. *The Consent of the Governed: The Lockean Legacy in Early American Culture.* Cambridge: Harvard University Press, 2001.

———. *Domestic Individualism: Imagining Self in Nineteenth-Century America.* Berkeley, University of California Press, 1990.

———. "Reading and Children: *Uncle Tom's Cabin* and *The Pearl of Orr's Island.*" In Weinstein, ed., *Cambridge Companion to Harriet Beecher Stowe.* 77–95.

Brown, Joshua. *Beyond the Lines: Pictorial Reporting, Everyday Life, and the Crisis of Gilded Age America.* Berkeley: University of California Press, 2002.

Bruce, William Liddel L., Mrs. *Uncle Tom's Cabin of To-Day.* New York: Neale Publishing, 1906.

Buel, Clarence Clough. "The Author of 'The Lady or the Tiger.'" *The Century Illustrated Monthly Magazine* XXXII (May–October 1886): 406. "The Making of America" http://cdl.library.cornell.edu/cgi-bin/moa/pageviewer?coll=moa &ro.

Buell, Lawrence. "Harriet Beecher Stowe and the Dream of the Great American Novel," In Weinstein, ed., *The Cambridge Companion to Harriet Beecher Stowe.* 190–202.

———. "The Rise and 'Fall' of the Great American Novel." *Proceedings of the American Antiquarian Society* 104.2 (October 1994): 261–83.

"The Buffalo Fugitive." *National Era* (August 28, 1851): 139.

"The Buffalo Outrage." *National Era* (August 28, 1851): 140.

Bullen, George. "Bibliographical Account of Uncle Tom's Cabin." In Harriet Beecher Stowe, *Uncle Tom's Cabin.* Houghton Mifflin, 1896. lxiii–lxxxii.

"The Burman Slave Girl." *Slave's Friend* III, no. 2 (1838): 5.

Burnett, Frances Hodgson. "The One I Knew Best of All: A Memory of the Mind of a Child." *Scribner's Magazine* XIII (January–June 1893).

Burnett, John. *Useful Toil: Autobiographies of Working People from the 1820s to the 1920s.* New York: Routledge, 1994.

Burton, Richard. "The Author of 'Uncle Tom's Cabin.'" *Century* 52.5 (September 1896): 696–703.

Butler, Judith. *Bodies That Matter.* London: Routledge, 1993.

"Butternut Sugar." *Slave's Friend* III, no. 4 (1838): 9–10.

Cable, George W., ed. "Strange True Stories of Louisiana. War Diary of a Union Woman in the South." *Century* 38.6 (October 1889): 931–47.

Calvert, Karen. *Children in the House.* Boston: Northeastern University Press, 1992.

Camfield, Gregg. "The Moral Aesthetics of Sentimentality: A Missing Key to *Uncle Tom's Cabin.*" *Nineteenth-Century Literature* 43.3 (1988): 319–45.

Carey, Alice. "Annie Clayville." *National Era* (June 12, 1851): 94.

Carey, Phoebe. "Bessie." *National Era* (November 13 [misprinted Nov. 31], 1851): 183.

Carson, Sharon. "Africana Constellations: African American Studies and *Uncle Tom's Cabin.*" *Approaches to Teaching Stowe's Uncle Tom's Cabin.* Ed. Elizabeth Ammons and Susan Belasco. New York: MLA, 2000. 162–71.

Casper, Scott E. "Antebellum Reading Prescribed and Described." *Perspectives on American Book History.* Ed. Casper, Joanne D. Chaison, and Jeffrey D. Groves. Amherst: University of Massachusetts Press, 2002.

———. "Defining the National Pantheon: The Making of Houghton Mifflin's Biographical Series 1880–1900." In Moylan and Stiles, ed., *Reading Books.* 179–222.

Castiglia, Christopher. "Abolition's Racial Interiors and the Making of White Civic Depth." *American Literary History* 14.1 (2002): 32–59.

Castiglia, Christopher, and Julia Stern. Introduction. "Special Issue: Interiority in Early American Literature." *Early American Literature* 37.1 (2002): 1–7.

Chartier, Roger. *The Order of Books.* Trans. Lydia G. Cochrane. Stanford: Stanford University Press, 1994.

———. "Texts, Printings, Readings." *The New Cultural History.* Ed. Lynn Hunt. Berkeley: University of California Press, 1989. 154–75.

Chesebro, Caroline. "Finis." *National Era* (September 4, 1851): 141.

Chesnut, Mary Boykin. *A Diary from Dixie.* Ed. Isabella D. Martin and Myrta Lockett Avary. New York: D. Appleton, 1905.

Chesnutt, Charles. *The Journals of Charles W. Chesnutt.* Ed. Richard H. Brodhead. Durham: Duke University Press, 1993.

Child, Lydia Maria. *Lydia Maria Child: Selected Letters 1817–1880.* Ed. Milton Meltzer and Patricia G. Holland. Amherst: University of Massachusetts Press, 1982.

———. *The Mother's Book.* Boston: Carter, Hendel and Babcock, 1831.

"Children's Letters." *Slave's Friend* I, no. 4 (1836): 13.

"Children's Picture Books." *Literary World: A Monthly Review of Current Literature* 1870–1904. December 1, 1901. APS online pg 219.

Clarke, Marcus. *His Natural Life.* Ed. Lurline Stuart. Queensland: University of Queensland Press, 2001.

Clover, Carol J. *Men, Women, and Chain Saws: Gender in the Modern Horror Film.* Princeton: Princeton University Press, 1992.

Cobb, Edith. *The Ecology of Childhood.* London: Routledge and Kegan Paul, 1977.

Cobb, Lynn. *Cobb's Toys: Pretty Stories for Pretty Children.* Second Series, no. 11. 1835. Elmira, N.Y.: Ransom Birdsall, 1838.

Coleman, Dawn. "The Unsentimental Woman Preacher of *Uncle Tom's Cabin*." *American Literature* 80.2 (June 2008): 265–92.

Colomb, P. H., Admiral. "The Battle-Ship of the Future." *North American Review* 157.443 (October 1893): 412–23.

"Colored Infant Schools." *Slave's Friend* III, no. 1 (1838): 13.

"Commitment for Treason." *National Era* (October 2, 1851): 158.

"Cone Cut Corners." Excerpt. *The Liberator* (September 14, 1855).

"Constance." "Thoughts at a Grave." *National Era* (September 25, 1851): 153.

Coontz, Stephanie. *The Social Origins of Private Life: A History of American Families, 1600–1900*. New York: Verso, 1988.

Cornelius, Janet Duitman. *"When I Can Read My Title Clear": Literacy, Slavery, and Religion in Antebellum South*. Columbia: University of South Carolina Press, 1991.

Cott, Nancy F. *The Bonds of Womanhood: "Women's Sphere" in New England, 1780–1835*. New Haven: Yale University Press, 1977.

Coulter, Charles Edward. *"Take up the Black Man's Burden": Kansas City's African American Communities, 1865–1939*. St. Louis: University of Missouri Press, 2006.

Cozans, Philip J. *Little Eva: The Flower of the South*. New York: Philip J. Cozans, 1853.

Crain, Patricia. "Spectral Literacy: The Case of Goody Two-Shoes." *Childhood and Children's Books in Early Modern Europe, 1550–1800*. Ed. Andrea Immel and Michael Witmore. New York: Routledge, 2006.

———. "Spectral Literacy: The Child in the Margin." Paper given at the American Antiquarian Society (April 28, 2006).

———. *The Story of A: The Alphabetization of America from The New England Primer to The Scarlet Letter*. Stanford: Stanford University Press, 2000.

Crosely, Robert. "Reader's Guide." In *Kindred*. By Octavia E. Butler. Boston: Beacon Press, 2003.

Cross, Gary. *Kids' Stuff: Toys and the Changing World of American Childhood*. Cambridge: Harvard University Press, 1997.

Cruse, Amy. *The Victorians and Their Books*. New York: Houghton Mifflin, 1936.

Anna Quincy Thaxter Cushing Diary, vol. II (April 1852–July 1853). American Antiquarian Society. Worcester, Mass.

Daneen, Wardrop. "'While I am Writing': Webster's Blue-Back Spelling Book, the Ell, and Frederick Douglass' Positioning of Language." *African American Review* 32.4 (1998): 649–60.

Darnton, Robert. "First Steps toward a History of Reading." *The Kiss of Lamourette: Reflections in Cultural History*. New York: Norton, 1996.

———. *The Great Cat Massacre and Other Episodes in French Cultural History*. New York: Basic Books, 1984.

Davidov, Judith Fryer. *Women's Camera Work: Self/Body/Other in American Visual Culture*. Durham: Duke University Press, 1998.

Davidson, Cathy N., ed. *Reading in America: Literary and Social History*. Baltimore: Johns Hopkins University Press, 1991.

————. *Revolution and the Word: The Rise of the Novel in America.* New York: Oxford University Press, 1986.

Davis, David Brion. *The Emancipation Moment.* Gettysburg, Pa.: Gettysburg College, 1983.

————. *Inhuman Bondage: The Rise and Fall of Slavery in the New World.* New York: Oxford University Press, 2006.

Dawson, Melanie. "The Miniaturizing of Girlhood." In Levander and Singley, ed., *The American Child.* 63–84.

"The Deaf, Dumb, and Blind." *Slave's Friend* III, no. 2 (1838): 4.

De Certeau, Michel. *The Practice of Everyday Life.* Trans. Steven Rendall. Berkeley: University of California Press, 2002.

De Forest. J. W. "The Great American Novel." *The Nation* VI. 132 (January 9, 1868): 27–29.

Dewey-Bliss Family Papers. Box 2. Folder 8. American Antiquarian Society, Worcester, Mass.

De Wit, Wim, James Gilbert, Robert W. Rydell, and Neil Harris. *Grand Illusions: Chicago World's Fair of 1893.* Ed. Neil Harris. Chicago: Chicago Historical Society, 1994.

Denning, Michael. *Mechanic Accents: Dime Novels and Working-Class Culture in America.* New York: Verso, 1987.

"Dialogue." *The Liberator* (May 9, 1851): 4.

Dickens, Charles. "A Witch in the Nursery." *Little's Living Age* XXXI (October, November, December, 1851): 245–52.

Dix, John Ross. *Transatlantic Tracings.* London: W. Tweedie, 1853.

Dobson, Joanne. "Reclaiming Sentimental Literature." *American Literature* 69.2 (June 1997): 263–88.

Domosh, Moma. "A 'civilized' commerce: Gender, 'race,' empire at the 1893 Chicago Exposition." *Cultural Geographies* 9.2 (2002): 181–201.

Dorris, Michael, and Emilie Buchwald, *The Most Wonderful Books: Writers on Discovering the Pleasures of Reading.* Minneapolis: Milkweed Editions, 1997.

William H. Dorsey Scrapbooks. William H. Dorsey Collection at Cheyney State University in Philadelphia.

Douglas, Ann. *The Feminization of American Culture.* New York: Knopf, 1978.

————. *Terrible Honesty: Mongrel Manhattan in the 1920s.* New York: Farrar, Straus and Giroux, 1996.

Douglass, Frederick. "The Narrative of the Life of Frederick Douglass, an American Slave." *The Classic Slave Narratives.* Ed. Henry Louis Gates, Jr. New York: New American Library, 1987. 255–331.

Drummond, W. B. *The Child: His Nature and Nurture.* London: J. M. Dent, 1915.

Du Bois, W. E. B., Papers, University of Massachusetts, Amherst. Microfilm, Reel 44.

Eckman, Fern Marja. *The Furious Passage of James Baldwin.* New York: M. Evans, 1966.

Eddy, Jacalyn. *Bookwomen: Creating an Empire in Children's Book Publishing, 1919–1939.* Madison: University of Wisconsin Press, 2006.

"Editor's Drawer." *Harper's New Monthly Magazine* 76.456 (May 1888): 970–74.

"Editor's Literary Record (Rev. of the book *Landscape Architecture*)." *Harper's New Monthly Magazine* 47.281 (October 1873): 775–80.

"Editor's Study." *Harper's Monthly Magazine* 103 (June 1901): 151–54.

Eggleston. Edward. *A History of the United States and its People.* New York: Appleton, 1888.

Eliot, George. Rev. of *Dred: A Tale of the Great Dismal Swamp.* By Harriet Beecher Stowe. *Critical Essays on Harriet Beecher Stowe.* Ed. Elizabeth Ammons. Boston: G. K. Hall, 1980.

Elliot, William. *Lectures to Young Men.* 1853. Boston: American Unitarian Association, 1858.

Elliott, Michael A. *The Culture Concept: Writing and Difference in the Age of Realism.* Minneapolis: University of Minnesota Press, 2002.

Erikson, Erik. *Childhood and Society.* 1950. New York: Norton, 1963.

"Extract from a speech delivered at the last anniversary of the British and Foreign A. S. [Anti-Slavery] Society in Exeter Hall, London, by Prof. Stowe of the United States." *The Liberator* (June 10, 1853): 99.

Fairclough, Adam. *A Class of Their Own: White Teachers in the Segregated South.* Cambridge: Harvard University Press, 2007.

"The Fall of Hungary." "By the Workshop Bard." *National Era* (August 15, 1850): 132.

Fanon, Frantz. *Black Skin, White Masks.* New York: Grove Press 1967.

Fiedler, Leslie. *Love and Death in the American Novel.* New York: Stein and Day, 1975.

Fields, A. B. (Annie Fields). *Authors and Friends.* 1893. New York: Harper and Bros., 1896.

———. "Days with Mrs. Stowe." *Atlantic Monthly* (August 1896): 145–56.

———. *Life and Letters of Harriet Beecher Stowe.* Cambridge: Riverside Press, 1897.

Annie Adams Fields Papers. Microfilm, Reel 2. Massachusetts Historical Society, Boston.

Finkelstein, Barbara, and Kathy Vandell. "The Schooling of American Childhood." *A Century of Childhood, 1820–1920.* Ed. May Lynn Stevens Heininger, Karen Calvert, et al. Rochester: Margaret Woodbury Strong Museum, 1984.

Fish, Stanley. *Is There a Text in This Class?: The Authority of Interpretive Communities.* Cambridge: Harvard University Press, 1980.

Fisher, Philip. *Hard Facts: Setting and Form in the American Novel.* New York: Oxford University Press, 1985.

Fishkin, Shelley Fisher. *Was Huck Black? Mark Twain and African American Voices.* New York: Oxford University Press, 1993.

Fiske, A. K. "Profligacy in Fiction: Zola's 'Nana,' Ouida's Moths." In Natalie Schroeder, ed., Ouida, *Moths.* New York: Broadview Press, 2008: 550–54.

Fliegelman, Jay. *Declaring Independence: Jefferson, Natural Language, and the Culture of Performance.* Stanford: Stanford University Press, 1993.

Fredrickson, George M. *The Black Image in the White Mind: The Debate on African-American Character and Destiny, 1817–1914.* New York: Harper, 1971.

"The Free Negro Girl's Message." *National Era* (January 24 1850): 1.

French, Earl A., and Diana Royce, eds. *Portraits of a Nineteenth-Century Family.* Hartford: The Stowe Day Foundation, 1976.

Freund, Elizabeth. *The Return of the Reader: Reader Response Criticism.* London: Methuen, 1987.

Fromkin, Victoria, Robert Rodman, and Nina Hyams. *An Introduction to Language.* Boston: Thomson Wadsworth, 2003.

Frow, John. "Afterlife: Texts as Usage." *Reception: texts, readers, audiences, history* Vol. 1 (Fall, 2008): 1–23. 10 May 2009. www.english.udel.edu/rsssite/Frow.pdf. http://copland.udel.edu/~pgold/webpage/RSSsite/rssjournal/html.

Fuss, Diana. *Identification Papers.* New York: Routledge, 1995.

"The Future of the British Empire." *The Living Age* 106.1367 (August 13, 1870): 385–408.

Garrison, Dee. *Apostles of Culture: The Public Librarian and American Society, 1876–1920.* Madison: University of Wisconsin Press, 2003.

Garrison, William Lloyd, "Preface." Douglass, *Narrative.* In Gates, ed., *The Classic Slave Narratives.* 243–51.

Garvey, Ellen Gruber. *The Adman in the Parlor.* New York: Oxford University Press, 1996.

———. *Book, Paper, Scissors: Scrapbooks Remake Print Culture* (forthcoming).

Gates, Henry Louis, Jr. Introduction. *The Annotated Uncle Tom's Cabin.* By Harriet Beecher Stowe. Ed. Gates and Hollis Robbins. New York: Norton, 2007. xi–xlvii.

———. Introduction. *The Classic Slave Narratives.* Ed. Gates. New York: New American Library, 1987. ix–xviii.

———. *The Signifying Monkey.* New York: Oxford University Press, 1988.

Geggus, David Patrick. "Slavery, War, and Revolution in the Greater Caribbean." *A Turbulent Time: The French Revolution and the Greater Caribbean.* Ed. David Barry Gasper and Geggus. Bloomington: Indiana University Press, 1997: 1–50.

Geist, Christopher E. "*The Slave's Friend:* An Abolitionist Magazine for Children." *American Periodicals* 9 (1999): 27–95.

Gilfillan, George. "Introduction." *The Bards of the Bible.* New York: D. Appleton, 1851. 7–15.

Gillman, Susan. "Pageantry, Maternity, and World History." *Next to the Color Line: Gender, Sexuality, and W. E. B. Du Bois.* Ed. Gillman and Alys Eve Weinbaum. Minneapolis: University of Minnesota Press, 2007. 378–416.

Gilman, Charlotte Perkins. *The Living of Charlotte Perkins Gilman: An Autobiography.* 1935. Madison: University of Wisconsin Press, 1990.

Gilmore, Michael T. "*Uncle Tom's Cabin* and the American Renaissance: The Sacramental Aesthetic of Harriet Beecher Stowe." In Weinstein, ed., *Cambridge Companion to Harriet Beecher Stowe.* 58–76.

Gilmore, William J. *Reading Becomes a Necessity of Life: Material and Cultural Life in*

Rural New England, 1780–1835. Knoxville: University of Tennessee Press, 1989.

Ginsberg, Lesley. "Of Babies, Beasts, and Bondage: Slavery and the Question of Citizenship in Antebellum American Children's Literature." In Levander and Singley, ed., *The American Child*. 85–105.

Ginzberg, Carlo. *The Cheese and the Worms: The Cosmos of a Sixteenth-Century Miller.* 1980. Trans. John and Anne Tedeschi. Baltimore: Johns Hopkins University Press, 1992.

Glazener, Nancy. *Reading for Realism: The History of a U.S. Literary Institution, 1850–1910.* Durham: Duke University Press, 1997.

Golden, Marita. *Migrations of the Heart: A Personal Odyssey.* New York: Doubleday, 1983.

Goldstein, Judith L. "Realism without a Human Face." *Spectacles of Realism: Gender, Body, Genre.* Ed. Margaret Cohen and Christopher Prendergast. Minneapolis: University of Minnesota Press, 1995.

Goldstein, Philip, and James L. Machor, *New Directions in American Reception Study.* New York: Oxford University Press, 2008.

Goodrich, Samuel. *Recollections of a Lifetime.* New York: Miller, Orton, & Mulligan, 1856.

Gossett, Thomas F. *Uncle Tom's Cabin and American Culture.* Dallas: Southern Methodist University Press, 1985.

Gould, Stephen Jay. *The Mismeasure of Man.* New York: Norton, 1981.

Graff, Harvey J. *The Literacy Myth: Literacy and Social Structure in the Nineteenth Century City.* New York: Academic Press, 1979.

"The Great American Novel." *The Nation* VI, no. 132 (January 9, 1868): 28.

Greenwood, Grace. "Dora's Children." *National Era* (June 12, 1851): 93.

Grimke, Sarah. "Juvenile Anti-Slavery Meeting in Boston." *Slave's Friend* III, no. 2 (1838): 12.

Gross, Robert. "Epilogue: Reading for an Extensive Republic." *A History of the Book,* Vol. 2. Chapel Hill: University of North Carolina Press, 2009.

Gustafson, Sandra M. *Eloquence Is Power: Oratory and Performance in Early America.* Chapel Hill: University of North Carolina Press, 2000.

Gutjahr, Paul C. *An American Bible: A History of the Good Book in the United States.* Stanford: Stanford University Press, 1992.

Hakutani, Yoshinobu. *Young Dreiser.* Cranbury, N.J.: Associated University Presses, 1980.

Hale, Nathan. *Freud and the Americans: The Beginnings of Psychoanalysis in the United States, 1876–1917.* New York: Oxford University Press, 1971.

Haley, Alex, and Malcolm X. *The Autobiography of Malcolm X.* New York: Grove Press, 1965.

Hall, David D. "Uses of Literacy in New England: 1600–1850." *Cultures of Print: Essays in the History of the Book.* Ed. Hall. Amherst: University of Massachusetts Press, 1996.

————. "A Yankee Tutor in the Old South." *New England Quarterly* 33.1 (March 1960): 82–91.

Hall, E. B. "The Fear of Being an Old Maid." *The Liberator* (May 16, 1851): 4.

Hall, G. Stanley. *Adolescence.* New York: D. Appleton, 1904.

————. "Childhood and Adolescence." 1904. In Strickland and Burgess, ed., *Health, Growth, and Heredity.* 99–113.

————. "Child Study and Its Relation to Education." In Strickland and Burgess, ed., *Health, Growth, and Heredity.* 74–90.

————. "New Departures in Education." In Strickland and Burgess, ed., *Health, Growth, and Heredity.* 93–98. First pub. *North American Review* (February 1885): 144–52.

————. "The Story of a Sand-Pile." In Strickland and Burgess, ed., *Health, Growth, and Heredity.* 53–68.

————. "A Study of Dolls." *Aspects of Child Life and Education.* 1907. Ed. Theodate L. Smith. London: Routledge, 1995.

Hallowell, Anna Davis, ed. *James and Lucretia Mott: Life and Letters.* Boston: Houghton Mifflin, 1884.

Halttunen, Karen. *Confidence Men and Painted Women: A Study of Middle-Class Culture in America, 1830–1870.* New Haven: Yale University Press, 1982.

Hamilton, Alice. *Exploring the Dangerous Trades.* Boston: Little, Brown, 1943.

Hamlin, Alfred D. F. "Pen Pictures of the Bosphorus." *The New England Magazine* 11.4 (December 1891): 484–501.

Hardy, George Edward Paul. *Five Hundred Books for the Young.* New York: Charles Scribner's Sons, 1892.

"Harriet Beecher Stowe Dead." *Philadelphia Times* (July 2, 1896): 3.

Harris, Neil. "Iconography and Intellectual History." *New Directions in Intellectual History.* Ed. John Higham and Paul Conkin. Baltimore: John Hopkins University Press, 1979. 196–211.

Harris, Susan K. *The Cultural Work of the Late Nineteenth-Century Hostess: Annie Adams Fields and Mary Gladstone Drew.* New York: Palgrave Macmillan, 2002.

————. *Nineteenth-Century American Women's Novels: Interpretive Strategies.* New York: Cambridge University Press, 1990.

Hart, James. *The Popular Book: A History of America's Literary Taste.* New York: Oxford University Press, 1950.

Hart, John S. *A Manual of American Literature: A Textbook for Schools and Colleges.* Philadelphia: Eldridge and Brother, 1872.

Hartman, Saidiya V. *Scenes of Subjection: Terror, Slavery, and Self-Making in Nineteenth-Century America.* New York: Oxford University Press, 1997.

Hay, Elizabeth. *Sambo Sahib: The Story of Little Black Sambo and Helen Bannerman.* Edinburgh: Paul Harris, 1981.

Hedin, Raymond. "Probable Readers, Possible Stories." In Machor, ed., *Readers in History.* 180–205.

Hedrick, Joan. *Harriet Beecher Stowe: A Life.* New York: Oxford University Press, 1995.

Hempstead, M. "Liberty Bells." *The Liberty Bell.* Boston: National Anti-Slavery Bazaar, 1851. 1–3.

———. "The Wanderer." *National Era* (April 24, 1851): 68.

———. "Who Is Free?" *Frederic Douglass' Paper* (January 14, 1853): 4.

Hendler, Glenn. *Public Sentiments: Structures of Feeling in Nineteenth-Century American Literature.* Chapel Hill: University of North Carolina Press, 2001.

"Henry Long Case." *The Liberator* (January 17, 1851): 10.

Hewins, Caroline M. *Books for Boys and Girls.* Chicago: American Library Association Publishing Board. 3rd ed., revised 1915.

———. *Books for the Young: A Guide for Parents and Children.* New York: F. Leypoldt, 1882.

———. *A Mid-Century Child and Her Books.* New York: Macmillan, 1926.

Higginson, Thomas Wentworth. "Critical and Biographical Introduction to *Uncle Tom's Cabin.*" *Uncle Tom's Cabin.* By Harriet Beecher Stowe. New York: Appleton, 1898.

Hildreth, Richard. *Archie Moore: The White Slave, or Memoirs of a Fugitive.* 1855. New York: Augustus M. Kelly, 1971.

———. *Memoirs of A Fugitive: America's First Anti-Slavery Novel.* Adapted for children by Barbara Ritchie. New York: Thomas Y. Crowell, 1971.

Hill, Walter B. "Uncle Tom without a Cabin." *Century* 27.6 (April 1884): 859–65.

Hochman, Barbara. *Getting at the Author: Reimagining Books and Reading in the Age of American Realism.* Amherst: University of Massachusetts Press, 2001.

———. "The Good, the Bad and the Literary: Edith Wharton's *Bunner Sisters* and the Social Contexts of Reading." *Studies in American Naturalism* 1&2 (Summer 2006): 128–43.

———. Introduction. "Introductory Essay for Charles Beecher's *The Incarnation: or Pictures of the Virgin and Her Son.*" By Harriet Beecher Stowe. *PMLA* 118.5 (October 2003): 1320–24.

———. "Readers and Reading Groups." *The Cambridge History of the American Novel.* Forthcoming.

———. "The Reading Habit and 'The Yellow Wallpaper.'" In Badia and Phegley, ed., *Reading Women* 129–48.

Hoffman, Frederick. "The Spread of Freud's Theory." *Freudianism and the Literary Mind.* Westport, Conn.: Greenwood Press, 1977.

Holland, Norman N. *Nine Readers Reading.* New Haven: Yale University Press, 1975.

Holloway, J. W. "A Visit to Uncle Tom's Cabin." *American Missionary* 48.10 (October 1894): 362–63.

Holloway, Karla F. C. *Bookmarks: Reading in Black and White.* New Brunswick, N.J.: Rutgers University Press, 2006.

Hooker, Isabella Beecher. *A Brief Sketch of the Life of Harriet Beecher Stowe by Her Sister.* Hartford: Plimpton MFC Co. Press, 1896.

Howard, June. *Publishing the Family.* Durham: Duke University Press, 2001.

"How Children Become Slaves." *Slave's Friend* I, no. 2 (1836): 5–7.

Howells, William Dean. *Criticism and Fiction*. New York: Harper and Bros., 1891.

———— *My Literary Passions*. New York: Harper and Bros., 1895.

Hunt, Peter. "Narrative Theory and Children's Literature." *Children's Literature Association Quarterly* 9.4 (Winter 1984–85): 191–98.

Hunter, Paul J. "The Loneliness of the Long-Distance Reader." *Genre* 10 (Winter 1977): 455–84.

Hurston, Zora Neale. *Dust Tracks on a Road*. New York: Harper, 2006.

————. *Zora Neale Hurston: A Life in Letters*. Ed. Carla Kaplan. New York: Doubleday, 2002.

Hutchinson, George. *In Search of Nella Larsen: A Biography*. Cambridge: Harvard University Press, 2006.

Irving, Mary. "Be Patient." *National Era,* (December 18, 1851): 201; (December 25, 1851): 205.

————. "To Daniel Webster." *National Era* (April 4, 1850): 55.

Iser, Wolfgang. *The Act of Reading: A Theory of Aesthetic Response*. London: Routledge, 1978.

————. *The Implied Reader: Patterns of Communication in Prose Fiction from Bunyan to Beckett*. Baltimore: Johns Hopkins University Press, 1978.

Jacobson, Matthew Frye. *Whiteness of a Different Color: European Immigrants and the Alchemy of Race*. Cambridge: Harvard University Press, 1998.

James, Henry. *A Small Boy and Others*. London: Macmillan, 1913.

Jameson, Fredric. *The Political Unconscious: Narrative as a Socially Symbolic Act*. Ithaca: Cornell University Press, 1981.

Jauss, Hans Robert. *Toward an Aesthetic of Reception*. Trans. Timothy Bahti. Minneapolis: University of Minnesota Press, 1982.

Johnson, James Weldon. *Along This Way*. 1933. New York: Da Capo Press, 2000.

————. *The Autobiography of an Ex-Colored Man*. 1912. New York: Penguin, 1990.

————. "Uncle Tom's Cabin and the Clansman." 1915. *Writings*. New York: Library of America, 2004. 612–14.

Johnston, Johanna. *Harriet and the Runaway Book: The Story of Harriet Beecher Stowe and Uncle Tom's Cabin*. New York: Harper & Row, 1977.

Judd, Mary C. *The Palmer Cox Brownie Primer*. Arranged from Palmer Cox's Brownie Books. New York: Century Co., 1906.

"Juvenile Association." *Slave's Friend* III, no. 3 (1838): 14–16.

Kaestle, Carl F. *Literacy in the United States: Readers and Reading since 1880*. New Haven: Yale University Press, 1993.

Kaplan, Cora. "*The Thorn Birds:* Fiction, Fantasy, Femininity." *Sea Changes*. London: Verso, 1986. 117–46.

Karcher, Caroline L. *First Woman in the Republic: A Cultural Biography of Lydia Maria Child*. Durham: Duke University Press, 1998.

Kasson, Joy S. "Narratives of the Female Body: The Greek Slave." *The Culture of Sentiment: Race, Gender, and Sentimentality in Nineteenth-Century America*. Ed. Shirley Samuels. New York: Oxford University Press, 1992. 172–90.

Kavenaugh, Jane. "The Lost Child." *National Era* (June 19, 1851): 98.

Keating, AnaLouise. "Reading 'Whiteness,' Unreading 'Race': (De)Racialized Reading Tactics in the Classroom." In Schweickart and Flynn, ed., *Reading Sites.*

Keen, Suzanne. *Empathy and the Novel.* New York: Oxford University Press, 2007.

Kelley, Mary. *Learning to Stand and Speak: Women, Education, and Public Life in America's Republic.* Chapel Hill: University of North Carolina Press, 2006.

Kelly, Gordon R., ed. *Children's Periodicals of the United States.* Westport: Greenwood Press, 1984.

Kerber, Linda K. " 'We Own that Ladies Sometimes Read': Women's Reading in the Early Republic." *Women of the Republic: Intellect and Ideology in Revolutionary America.* Chapel Hill: University of North Carolina Press, 1997. 233–64.

Kete, Mary Louise. *Sentimental Collaboration: Mourning and Middle-Class Identity in Nineteenth-Century America.* Durham: University of North Carolina Press, 2000.

Kinney, Mary B. "A Sibylline Trio." *Putnam's Monthly Magazine of American Literature, Science and Art* 3.18 (June 1869): 708–10. Making of America. Accessed Oct. 9, 2006.

Kirkham, E. Bruce. *The Building of Uncle Tom's Cabin.* Knoxville: University of Tennessee Press, 1977.

"Knew the Characters of 'Uncle Tom's Cabin.'" *New York World* (July 2, 1896): 21.

Knight, Franklin W. "The Haitian Revolution." *American Historical Review* 105.1 (February 2000): 103–15.

Knight, Kate Brannon. *History of the Work of the Connecticut Women at the World's Columbian Exposition,* Chicago 1893. Hartford, Conn.: Hartford Press, 1898.

Kohut, Heinz. "Introspection, Empathy, and Psychoanalysis: An Examination of the Relationship between Modes of Observation and Theory." 1959. *The Search for the Self.* Vol. 1. Ed. P. Ornstein. New York: International Universities Press, 1978. 205–32.

Kris, Ernst. *Psychoanalytic Explorations in Art.* New York: Schocken Books, 1971.

Lacey, Barbara E. "Visual Images of Blacks in Early American Imprints." *William and Mary Quarterly* 53.1 (1996): 137–80.

Lake, Joy Jordan. *Whitewashing Uncle Tom's Cabin: Nineteenth-Century Women Novelists Respond to Stowe.* Nashville: Vanderbilt University Press, 2005.

Lane, Christopher. *The Psychoanalysis of Race.* New York: Columbia University Press, 1998.

Lane, Roger. *William Dorsey's Philadelphia and Ours: On the Past and Future of the Black City in America.* New York: Oxford University Press, 1991.

Langley, Lester D. *The Americas in the Age of Revolution, 1750–1850.* New Haven: Yale University Press, 1996.

Lapsansky, Philip. "Graphic Discord: Abolitionist and Antiabolitionist Images." *The Abolitionist Sisterhood: Women's Political Culture in Antebellum America.* Ed. Jean Fagan Yellin and John C. Van Horn. Ithaca: Cornell University Press, 1994.

Leavis, F. R. *The Sense of an Ending: Studies in the Theory of Fiction.* New York: Oxford University Press, 1968.

Lee, Patty. "Ill Starred." *National Era* (July 17–October 9, 1851).

———. "James McCary and His Boy." *National Era* (December 4, 1851): 193.

———. "Light and Shade." *National Era* (July 10, 1851): 109.

Lefevre, Andre A. "Translation Studies Today." *Encyclopedia of Literary Translation into English.* Vol. 2. Ed. Olive Chase. New York: Fitzroy Dearborn, 2000.

Lehuu, Isabelle. *Carnival on the Page: Popular Print Media in Antebellum America.* Chapel Hill: University of North Carolina Press, 2000.

Lemon, Lee T., and Marion J. Reis. *Russian Formalist Criticism.* Lincoln: University of Nebraska Press, 1965.

Lerer, Seth. "Epilogue: Falling Asleep over the History of the Book." *PMLA* 121.1 (January 2006): 229–34.

"Letter from William Wells Brown." *The Liberator* (June 3, 1853): 97.

Levander, Caroline Field. *Cradle of Liberty: Race, the Child, and National Belonging from Thomas Jefferson to W. E. B. Du Bois.* Durham: Duke University Press, 2006.

Levander, Caroline F., and Carol J. Singley, eds. *The American Child: A Cultural Studies Reader.* New Brunswick: Rutgers University Press, 2003.

Leverenz, David. *Manhood and the American Renaissance.* Ithaca: Cornell University Press, 1989.

Levine, Robert Steven. *Martin Delany, Frederick Douglass, and the Politics of Representative Identity.* Chapel Hill: University of North Carolina Press, 1997.

———. "*Uncle Tom's Cabin* in Frederick Douglass's Paper: An Analysis of Reception." In Stowe, *Uncle Tom's Cabin.* Ed. Elizabeth Ammons. New York: Norton, 1994. 523–42.

Lewis, Sinclair. "What Life Meant to Me." Rpt. in *The Jungle.* New York: Norton, 2003.

"Liberty Ode." *National Era* (November 21, 1850): 188.

"The Life of Olaudah Equiano." *The Classic Slave Narratives.* Ed. Henry Louis Gates, Jr. New York: New American Library, 1987. 41–42.

"The Literature of Slavery." *The New Englander* X (November 1852): 591–92.

Lloyd, S. H. "The Slave–A Tableau." *National Era* (January 16, 1851): 9.

Locke, Walter. *This World, My Home.* Yellow Springs, Ohio: Antioch Press, 1957.

Logan, Rayford. *Betrayal of the Negro: From Rutherford B. Hayes to Woodrow Wilson.* New York: Collier, 1965.

Long, Elizabeth. "Textual Interpretation as Collective Action." *The Ethnography of Reading.* Ed. Jonathan Boyarin. Berkeley: University of California Press, 1990. 180–211.

Looby, Christopher. "George Thompson's 'Romance of the Real': Transgression and Taboo in American Sensation Fiction." *American Literature* 65.4 (1993): 651–72.

Lott, Eric. *Love and Theft: Blackface Minstrelsy and the American Working Class.* New York: Oxford University Press, 1995.

Low, Mary. *A Peep into Uncle Tom's Cabin.* Boston: John P. Jewett, 1853.

Lowell, James Russell. "The Five Indispensable Authors (Homer, Dante, Cervantes, Goethe, Shakespeare)." *Century* 47.2 (December 1893): 223–24.

Lubbock, John. *The Choice of Books*. Philadelphia: Henry A Hemus, 1896.

Luciano, Dana. *Arranging Grief: Sacred Time and the Body in Nineteenth-Century America*. New York: New York University Press, 2007.

Lundin, Anne. "Little Pilgrims Progress: Literary Horizons for Children's Literature." *Libraries and Culture* 41.1 (Winter 2006): 133–52.

Lurie, Alison. *Don't Tell the Grownups: Subversive Children's Literature*. New York: Little, Brown, 1990.

———. "Pottery." *New York Review of Books* LIV. 14 (September 27, 2007).

Lynch, John. *The Spanish American Revolution, 1808–1826*. New York: Norton, 1973.

Lynn, Margaret. *A Stepdaughter of the Prairie*. New York: Macmillan, 1914.

"M." "The Fugitive Slave Law." *The Liberator* (January 3, 1851): 4.

MacCann, Donnarae. *White Supremacy in Children's Literature: Characterization of African Americans, 1830–1900*. New York: Garland, 1998.

Machor, James L. "Fiction and Informed Reading in Early Nineteenth-Century America." *Nineteenth-Century Literature* 47.3 (1992): 320–48.

Machor, James, ed. *Readers in History: Nineteenth-Century American Literature and the Contexts of Response*. Baltimore: Johns Hopkins University Press, 1993.

Mackay, Charles. "The Storytellers." *The Liberator* (January 11, 1850): 4.

MacLeod, Anne Scott. *American Childhood: Essays on Children's Literature of the Nineteenth and Twentieth Centuries*. Athens: University of Georgia Press, 1994.

———. "'The *Caddie Woodlawn* Syndrome': American Girlhood in the Nineteenth Century." *A Century of Childhood 1820–1920*. Ed. May Lynn Stevens Heininger, Karen Calvert, et al. Rochester: Margaret Woodbury Strong Museum, 1984.

———. *A Moral Tale: Children's Fiction and American Culture, 1820–1860*. Hamden, Conn.: Archon Books, 1975.

Mailloux, Steven. "Misreading as a Historical Act: Cultural Rhetoric, Bible Politics, and Fuller's 1845 Review of Douglass' *Narrative*." In Machor, ed., *Readers in History*.

———. "The Rhetorical Use and Abuse of Fiction: Eating Books in Late Nineteenth-Century America." *Boundary 2* 17.1 (Spring 1990): 133–57.

Maingot, Anthony P. "Haiti and the Terrified Consciousness of the Caribbean." *Ethnicity in the Caribbean*. Ed. Gert Oostindie. Amsterdam: Amsterdam University Press, 2005. 53–80.

Malik, Rachel. "Horizons of the Publishable: Publishing in/as Literary Studies." *ELH* 75 (2008): 707–35.

Marshall, Henrietta Elizabeth. *Uncle Tom's Cabin Told to the Children*. New York: E. P. Dutton, 1904.

Marshall Family Papers. American Antiquarian Society.

Martin, Francis, Jr. "Edward Windsor Kemble, A Master of Pen and Ink." *American Art Review* III, no. 1 (January–February 1976): 54–67.

Martin, Jay. *Harvests of Change*. Englewood Cliffs, N.J.: Prentice Hall, 1967.

Masse, Michelle A. "Constructing the Psychoanalytic Child: Freud's 'From the History of an Infantile Neurosis.'" In Levander and Singley, ed., *The American Child*. 149–66.

McBride, Mary Margaret. *How Dear to My Heart*. New York: Macmillan, 1940.

McCoy, Beth A. "Race and the (Para)Textual Condition." *PMLA* 121.1 (January 2006): 156–69.

McCulloch, Lou W. *Children's Books of the Nineteenth Century*. Des Moines, Iowa: Wallace-Homestead Book Co., 1979.

McCray, Florine Thayer. *The Life-Work of the Author of Uncle Tom's Cabin*. New York: Funk and Wagnalls, 1889.

McGill, Meredith L. *American Literature and Culture of Reprinting: 1834–1853*. Philadelphia: University of Pennsylvania Press, 2002.

McHenry, Elizabeth. *Forgotten Readers: Recovering the Lost History of African American Literary Societies*. Durham: Duke University Press, 2002.

McPherson, James M. *The Abolitionist Legacy: From Reconstruction to the NAACP*. Princeton: Princeton University Press, 1975.

Meer, Sarah. *Uncle Tom Mania: Slavery, Minstrelsy, and Transatlantic Culture in the 1850s*. Athens: University of Georgia Press, 2005.

Merish, Lori. *Sentimental Materialism: Gender, Commodity Culture, and Nineteenth-Century American Literature*. Durham: Duke University Press, 2000.

"Meta." "Guard Thy Trust." *National Era* (August 28, 1851): 137.

Michaels, Walter Benn. *Our America: Nativism, Modernism, and Pluralism*. Durham: Duke University Press,1995.

———. "'You Who Never Was There': Slavery and the New Historicism, Deconstruction and the Holocaust." *Narrative* 4.1 (January 1996): 1–16.

Mitchell, W. J. T. *Picture Theory: Verbal and Visual Representation*. Chicago: University of Chicago Press, 1995.

Mizruchi, Susan L. *The Rise of Multicultural America: Economy and Print Culture, 1865–1915*. Chapel Hill: University of North Carolina Press, 2009.

Moers, Ellen. *Harriet Beecher Stowe and American Literature*. Hartford: Stowe-Day Foundation, 1978.

Monaghan, Jennifer E. "Literacy Instruction and Gender in Colonial New England." In Davidson, ed., *Reading in America*. 53–80.

———. "Reading for the Enslaved, Writing for the Free: Reflections on Liberty and Literacy." *Proceedings of the American Antiquarian Society* 108.2 (1998): 309–41.

Morgan, David. "For Christ and the Republic: Protestant Illustration and the History of Literacy in Nineteenth-Century America." *The Visual Culture of American Religions*. Ed. Morgan and Sally M. Promey. Berkeley: University of California Press, 2001.

Morgan, Jo Ann. *Uncle Tom's Cabin as Visual Culture*. Columbia: University of Missouri Press, 2007.

Morris, Charles. "The Story of the Book and A Key to the Characters." *Uncle Tom's Cabin*. Chicago: Thomson and Thomas, 1897.

Morris, Robert C. *Reading, 'Riting, and Reconstruction: The Education of Freedmen in the South, 1861–1870*. Chicago: University of Chicago Press, 1981.

The Mother's Friend, or, Familiar Directions for Forming the Mental and Moral Habit of Young Children. New York: Leavitt, Lord, 1834.

Mott, Frank Luther. *American Journalism: A History of Newspapers in the United States through Two Hundred and Fifty Years: 1690–1940*. New York: Macmillan, 1947.

———. *Golden Multitudes: The Story of Best Sellers in the United States*. 1947. New York: R. R. Bowker, 1966.

Moylan, Michelle, and Lane Stiles, eds. *Reading Books: Essays on the Material Text and Literature in America*. Amherst: University of Massachusetts Press, 1996.

"Mrs. Stowe's 84th Year." *Philadelphia Evening Star* 14 (June 1895): 11.

"Murder of Lovejoy." *Slave's Friend* III, no. 8 (1838): 4–5.

Murray, Gail Schmunk. *American Children's Literature and the Construction of Childhood*. New York: Twayne, 1998.

Nell, Victor. *Lost in a Book: The Psychology of Reading for Pleasure*. New Haven: Yale University Press, 1988.

"New Cure for Consumption." *National Era* (November 20, 1851): 188.

Nichols, Charles. "The Origins of *Uncle Tom's Cabin*." *Phylon Quarterly* 19.3 (Fall 1958): 328–24.

Noble, Marianne. *The Masochistic Pleasures of Sentimental Literature*. Princeton: Princeton University Press, 2000.

Nord, David Paul. *Faith in Reading: Religious Publishing and the Birth of Mass Media in America*. New York: Oxford University Press, 2004.

———. "Religious Reading and Readers in Antebellum America." *Journal of the Early Republic* 15.2 (Summer 1995): 241–72.

Norris, Frank. "The Novel with a Purpose." *The Literary Criticism of Frank Norris*. Ed. Donald Pizer. New York: Russell & Russell, 1976.

Nyong'o, Tavia. "Racial Kitsch and Black Performance." *Yale Journal of Criticism* 15.2 (2002): 371–91.

Obituary, Isabella Rose. *National Era* (July 31, 1851): 123.

Obituary, Mary Osgood. *National Era* (July 10, 1851): 110.

O'Gorman, James F. *Accomplished in All Departments of Art: Hammatt Billings of Boston, 1818–1874*. Amherst: University of Massachusetts Press, 1998.

Ohmann, Richard. *Selling Culture: Magazines, Markets, and Class at the Turn of the Century*. New York: Verso, 1996.

"Old-Fashioned Children." *The Living Age* (September 30, 1898): 818–24.

Oliver, Lawrence J. "Theodore Roosevelt, Brander Matthews, and the Campaign for Literary Americanism." *American Quarterly* 41.1 (March 1989): 93–111.

Ong, Walter. "The Writer's Audience Is Always a Fiction." *PMLA* 90 (1975): 9–21.

"Original Uncle Tom Dead." *San Francisco Chronicle* (March 10, 1903): 3.

Ovington, Mary White. "Selling Race Pride." *Publisher's Weekly* (January 10, 1925): 111–14.

Owens, Robert E., Jr. *Language Development: An Introduction.* Boston: Allyn and Bacon, 1996.

P. G. H., Jr. "Edward Windsor Kemble." *Book Buyer* 9.6 (July 1894): 293–96.

Painter, Nell Irvin. *Standing at Armageddon: The United States, 1877–1919.* New York: Norton, 1987.

Parfait, Claire. "The Nineteenth-Century Serial as a Collective Enterprise: Harriet Beecher Stowe's *Uncle Tom's Cabin* and Eugene Sue's *Les Mystères de Paris.*" *Proceedings of the American Antiquarian Society* 12, Part 1 (2002): 127–52.

———. *The Publishing History of Uncle Tom's Cabin, 1852–2002.* Burlington: Ashgate, 2007.

Parsons, Samuel, Jr. "The Ornamentation of Ponds And Lakes." *Scribner's Magazine* 9.3 (March 1891): 351–61.

Parton, James. "International Copyright." *Atlantic Monthly* (October 1867): 430–52.

Pawley, Christine. *Reading on the Middle Border: The Culture of Print in Late Nineteenth-Century Osage, Iowa.* Amherst: University of Massachusetts Press, 2001.

Peabody, Ephraim. "Narratives of Fugitive Slaves." *Christian Examiner* (July 1849): 61–92.

Penn, Arthur (pseud. Brander Matthews). *The Home Library.* New York: Appleton, 1883.

Phegley, Jennifer. " 'I Should No More Think of Dictating. . .What Kinds of Books She Should Read': Images of Women Readers in Victorian Family Literary Magazines." In Badia and Phegley, ed., *Reading Women.* 105–28.

Phelps, Elizabeth Stuart. "Mrs Stowe." *Chapters from a Life.* Ed. Phelps. Rpt. in *McClure's Magazine* VII, no. 1 (June 1896).

"Philadelphia Correspondence: The Christiana Tragedy." *National Era* (October 2, 1851): 158–59.

Phillips, Kate. *Helen Hunt Jackson: A Literary Life.* Berkeley: University of California Press, 2003.

Phillips, Wendell. *Speeches, Lectures, and Letters.* New York: Negro Universities Press, 1968.

———. "Letter From Wendell Phillips Esq." Douglass, *Narrative.* In Gates, ed., *Classic Slave Narratives:* 252–54.

Pinckney, Darryl. Introduction. *Uncle Tom's Cabin.* By Harriett Beecher Stowe. New York: Signet, 1998.

"A Pioneer Editor." *Atlantic Monthly* 17.104 (June 1866): 743–51.

Pitcher, Evelyn Goodenough, and Ernst Prelinger. *Children Tell Stories: An Analysis of Fantasy.* New York: International Universities Presses, 1963.

"The Poor Boy." *National Era* (September 18, 1851): 151.

Porter, Noah. *Books and Reading: What Books Shall I Read and How Shall I Read Them?* New York: Charles Scribner's, 1870, 1883.

"Postal Communication, Past and Present." *The Living Age* 174.2249 (July 30, 1887): 257–320.

Poulet, Georges. "Criticism and the Experience of Interiority." In Tompkins, ed., *Reader-Response Criticism*. 41–69.

———. "Phenomenology of Reading." *New Literary History* 1.1 (October 1969): 53–68.

"The Press." *The Liberator* (February 5, 1847): 4.

Price, Leah. "You Are What You Read." *New York Times Book Review* (December 23, 2007): 19.

Proctor, H. H. "Addresses at Annual Meeting: The Sons of 'Uncle Tom.' " *The American Missionary* 48.1 (January 1894): 19–22.

Putnam, George W. "The Northern Tournament." *National Era* (April 4, 1850): 52.

———. "To the Workingmen of America." *National Era* (April 17, 1851): 61.

Radway, Janice. *A Feeling for Books: The Book-of-the-Month Club, Literary Taste, and Middle-Class Desire.* Chapel Hill: University of North Carolina Press, 1997.

———. "Reading Is Not Eating: Mass-Produced Literature and the Theoretical, Methodological and Political Consequences of a Metaphor." *Book Research Quarterly* (Fall 1986): 7–29.

———. *Reading the Romance: Women, Patriarchy, and Popular Culture.* Chapel Hill: University of North Carolina Press, 1984.

Railton, Stephen. "Representing Jim." http://etext.virginia.edu/railton/huckfinn/jiminpix.html.

———."*Uncle Tom's Cabin* and American Culture." www.iath.virginia.edu/utc/children/peephp.html.

Ralph, Julian. "Western Modes Of City Management." *Harper's New Monthly Magazine* 84.503 (April 1892): 709–21.

Raser, Harold E. *Phoebe Palmer: Her Life and Thought, Studies in Women and Religion,* vol. 22. Lewiston, N.Y.: Edwin Mellen Press, 1987.

Raven, James, Helen Small, and Naomi Tadmor, eds. *The Practice and Representation of Reading in England.* New York: Cambridge University Press, 1996.

Reader Notebook. Ca 1900. Private Collection of Ellen Gruber Garvey.

"Reader's Letter." *National Era* (October 30, 1851): 175.

"Recent Literature: H. B. Stowe's Uncle Tom's Cabin." *Atlantic Monthly* 43.257 (March 1879): 407–8.

Reid, Mandy. "Racial Profiling: Visualizing Racial Science on the Covers of *Uncle Tom's Cabin,* 1852–1928." *Nineteenth-Century Contexts* 30.4 (December 2008): 369–87.

Reinier, Jacqueline S. *From Virtue to Character: American Childhood, 1775–1850.* New York: Twayne, 1996.

"A Remarkable Decision in the Supreme Court." *The Liberator* (January 31, 1851): 17.

Rev. of *Uncle Tom's Cabin,* by Harriet Beecher Stowe. *Christian Union* 45.4 (January 23, 1892). APS online pg. 169.

Rev. of *Uncle Tom's Cabin,* by Harriet Beecher Stowe. *New York Evangelist* 62.53 (December 31, 1891). APS online pg. 1.

Reynolds, David. *Beneath the American Renaissance: The Subversive Imagination in the Age of Emerson and Melville.* New York: Alfred A Knopf, 1988.

Reynolds, Larry J. *European Revolutions and the American Literary Renaissance.* New Haven: Yale University Press, 1988.

Reynolds, Moira Davison. *Uncle Tom's Cabin and Mid-Nineteenth-Century United States: Pen and Conscience.* Jefferson, N.C.: McFarland, 1985.

Rhodes, James Ford. *History of the United States from the Compromise of 1850 to the End of the Roosevelt Administration.* 1893. Vol. I. New York: Harper, 1896.

Rich, Motoko. "Using Video Games." *New York Times* (October 6, 2008): A 1.

Risman, Barbara. "Strategies for Interviewing Kids about Inequality." Unpublished lecture. Ben-Gurion University, Be'er-Sheva, Israel. January 2, 2007.

Richardson, Charles F. *The Choice of Books.* New York: American Book Exchange, 1881.

Riggio, Thomas P. "*Uncle Tom* Reconstructed: A Neglected Chapter in the History of a Book." *American Quarterly* 28.1 (Spring 1976): 56–70.

Riss, Arthur. "Racial Essentialism and Family Values in *Uncle Tom's Cabin*." *American Quarterly* 46.4 (December 1994): 513–44.

Robbins, Sarah. *Managing Literacy, Mothering America: Women's Narratives on Reading and Writing in the Nineteenth Century.* Pittsburgh: Pittsburgh University Press, 2004.

———. "Woman's Work for Woman: Gendered Print Culture in American Mission Movement Narratives." *Women in Print: Essays on the Print Culture of American Women from the Nineteenth and Twentieth Centuries.* Ed. James Philip Danky and Wayne A. Wiegand. Madison: University of Wisconsin Press, 2006. 251–80.

Robinson, F. W. *Female Life in Prison,* by a Prison Matron (Pseud.). London: Hurst and Blackett, 1862.

Roethier, Jacque. "Reading in Color: Children's Book Illustrations and Identity Formation for Black Children in the United States." *African American Review* 32.1 (1998): 95–105.

Rogers, Daniel T. "Socializing Middle-Class Children: Institutions, Fables, and Work Values in Nineteenth-Century America." *Journal of Social History* 13.3 (Spring 1980): 354–67.

Rohrbach, Augusta. "'Truth Stronger and Stranger then Fiction': Reexamining William Lloyd Garrison's *Liberator*." *American Literature* 73.4 (2001): 727–55.

Rollins, Charlemae. *We Build Together: A Reader's Guide of Negro Life and Literature for Elementary and High School Use.* Champaign, Ill: National Council of Teachers of English. Third Edition, 1967. First edition, 1941; second edition 1948.

Roos, Rosalie. Letter dated May 4, 1853. *North American Women's Letters and Diaries* (consulted October 2006).

Rose, Jonathan. "Rereading the English Common Reader: A Preface to a History of Audiences." *Journal of the History of Ideas* 53.1 (1992): 47–70.

Rosenblatt, Louise. *The Reader, the Text, the Poem: The Transactional Theory of the Literary Work.* Carbondale: Southern Illinois University Press, 1978.

Ross, Catherine Sheldrick. "Metaphors of Reading." *Journal of Library History, Philosophy, and Comparative Librarianship* 22.2 (Spring 1987): 147–63.

Roth, Sarah N. "The Mind of a Child: Images of African Americans in Early Juvenile Fiction." *Journal of the Early Republic* 25 (Spring 2005): 79–109.

Royce, Josiah. "The Imitative Functions and Their Place in Human Nature." *The Century Illustrated Monthly Magazine* (May 1894): 137–45.

Rubin, Joan Shelley. *The Making of Middlebrow Culture.* Chapel Hill: University of North Carolina Press, 1992.

———. *Songs of Ourselves: The Uses of Poetry in America.* Cambridge: Harvard University Press, 2007.

Ryan, Barbara, and Amy Thomas, eds. *Reading Acts: U.S. Readers' Interactions with Literature, 1800–1950.* Knoxville: University of Tennessee Press, 2002.

Ryan, Susan M. *The Grammar of Good Intentions.* Ithaca: Cornell University Press, 2003.

Rydell, Robert. *All the World's a Fair: Visions of Empire at American International Expositions, 1876–1916.* Chicago: University of Chicago Press, 1984.

Salter, Anne, and Judith Brook. "Are We Becoming an Aliterate Society? The Demand for Recreational Reading among Undergraduates at Two Universities." *College and Undergraduate Libraries* 14.3 (2007): 27–43.

Salvino, Dana Nelson. "The Word in Black and White." In Davidson, ed., *Reading in America.* 140–56.

Samuels, Shirley. "The Identity of Slavery." In Samuels, ed., *The Culture of Sentiment.* 157–71.

———, ed. *The Culture of Sentiment: Race, Gender, and Sentimentality in Nineteenth-Century America.* New York: Oxford University Press, 1992.

Sanchez-Eppler, Karen. *Dependent States: The Child's Part in Nineteenth-Century American Culture.* Chicago: University of Chicago Press, 2005.

———. "Doors onto Childhood." Paper given at "Home, School, Play, Work: The Visual and Textual Worlds of Children." Princeton University, February 12, 2009.

———. "Playing at Class." In Levander and Singley, ed., *The American Child,* 40–62.

———. *Touching Liberty: Abolition, Feminism, and the Politics of the Body.* Berkeley: University of California Press, 1997.

Sand, George. "Review of *Uncle Tom's Cabin.*" In Harriet Beecher Stowe, *Uncle Tom's Cabin* (Norton, 1994): 459–63.

Sandage, Scott A. "A Marble House Divided: The Lincoln Memorial, the Civil Rights Movement, and the Politics of Memory, 1939–1963." *Journal of American History* 80.1 (June 1993): 135–67.

Sandburg, Carl. *Abraham Lincoln: The Prairie Years and the War Years, One-Volume Edition.* New York: Harcourt Brace, 1939.

Scholnick, Robert J. "*Scribner's Monthly* and the 'Pictorial Representation of Life and Truth' in Post–Civil War America." *American Periodicals* 1.1 (Fall 1991): 46–69.

Schouler, James. *History of the United States of America Under the Constitution,* vol. V. New York: Dodd, Mead, 1891.

Schudson, Michael. *Discovering the News: A Social History of American Newspapers.* New York: Basic Books, 1978.

Schweickart, Patricinio. Rev. of *Reading Women,* ed. Janet Badia and Jennifer Phegley. *Victorian Studies* 48.4 (2006): 733.

———, and Elizabeth Flynn, eds. *Reading Sites: Social Difference and Reader Response.* New York: MLA, 2004.

Scudder, Horace. *Methods of Teaching.* New York: Houghton Mifflin, 1888.

Segal, Elizabeth. "'As the Twig Is Bent . . .': Gender and Childhood Reading." *Gender and Reading: Essays on Readers, Texts, and Contexts.* Ed. Elizabeth Flynn and Patricinio Schweickart. Baltimore: Johns Hopkins University Press, 1986.

"Selling Slaves by the Pound." *Slave's Friend* I, no. 1 (1836): 4.

Sheldrick Ross, Catherine. "Metaphors of Reading." *Journal of Library History* 22 (Spring 1987): 147–63.

Sherman, James. Introductory Remarks. *Uncle Tom's Cabin.* By Harriet Beecher Stowe. London: H. G. Bohn, 1852.

Shklovsky, Victor. "Art as Technique." In Lemon and Reis, ed., *Russian Formalist Criticism.* Trans. Lemon and Reis. 3–25.

Sicherman, Barbara. "Reading and Middle-class Identity in Victorian America: Cultural Consumption, Conspicuous and Otherwise." In Ryan and Thomas, ed., *Reading Acts. 137–60.*

———. "Reading *Little Women:* The Many Lives of a Text." *U.S. History as Women's History: New Feminist Essays.* Ed. Alice Kessler-Harris, Linda K. Kerber, and Kathryn Kish Sklar. Chapel Hill: University of North Carolina Press, 1995.

———. "Sense and Sensibility: A Case Study of Women's Reading in Late-Victorian America." In Davidson, ed., *Reading in America.* 201–25.

———. *Well-Read Lives: How Books Inspired a Generation of American Women.* Chapel Hill: University of North Carolina Press, 2010.

Sigourney, Lydia. "Mothers as Christian Teachers." *The Lady's Book* (January 1839): 1–4.

Silber, Nina. *The Romance of Reunion: Northerners and the South, 1865–1900.* Chapel Hill: University of North Carolina Press, 1993.

Silverman, Gillian. "Sympathy and Its Vicissitudes." *American Studies* 43.3 (Fall 2002): 5–28.

Silverman, Kaja. *Male Subjectivity at the Margins.* New York: Routledge, 1992.

Sircar, Sanjay. "Little Brown Sanjay and Little Black Sambo: Childhood Reading, Adult Rereading; Colonial Text and Postcolonial Reception." *The Lion and the Unicorn* 28.1 (January 2004): 131–56.

Sizer, Lyde Cullen. *The Political Work of Northern American Women Writers and the Civil War, 1850–1872.* Chapel Hill: University of North Carolina Press, 2000.

"The Slave Mother to Her Child." *National Era* (August 1, 1850): 121.

Smith, Charles J. "Reform Verses." *National Era* (January 31, 1850): 20.

Smith, Erin A. "Melodrama, Popular Religion, and Literary Value: The Case of Harold Bell Wright." *American Literary History* 17.2 (Summer 2005): 217–44.

Smith, Gail. "Reading with the Other: Hermeneutics and the Politics of Difference in Stowe's *Dred.*" *American Literature* 69.2 (June 1997): 290–313.

———. "The Sentimental Novel: The Example of Harriet Beecher Stowe." *Cambridge Companion to Nineteenth-Century Women's Writing.* Ed. Dale Bauer and Philip Gold. New York: Cambridge University Press, 2001.

Smith, Henry Nash. *Virgin Land: The American West as Symbol and Myth.* New York: Vintage Books, 1950.

Smith, Susan Belasco. "Serialization and the Nature of *Uncle Tom's Cabin.*" *Periodical Literature in Nineteenth-Century America.* Ed. Susan Belasco Smith and Kenneth Price. Charlottesville: University Press of Virginia, 1995. 69–89.

Smith-Rosenberg, Carroll. *Disorderly Conduct: Visions of Gender in Victorian America.* New York: Oxford University Press, 1986.

Sollors, Werner. "Was Roxy Black? Race as Stereotype in Mark Twain, Edward Windsor Kemble, and Paul Laurence Dunbar." *Mixed Race Literature.* Ed. Jonathan Brennan. Stanford: Stanford University Press, 2002. 71–87.

Soltow, Lee, and Edward Stevens. *The Rise of Literacy and the Common School in the United States: A Socioeconomic Analysis to 1870.* Chicago: University of Chicago Press, 1981.

Sonstegard, Adam. "Artistic Liberty and Slave Imagery: 'Mark Twain's Illustrator' E. W. Kemble Turns to Harriet Beecher Stowe." *Nineteenth Century Literature* 63.4 (2009): 499–542.

Sorby, Angela. *The Schoolroom Poets: Childhood, Performance, and the Place of American Poetry, 1865–1917.* Durham, N.H.: University of New Hampshire Press, 2005.

Spillers, Hortense. "Changing the Letter: The Yokes, the Jokes of Discourse, or Mrs. Stowe, Mr. Reed." *Slavery and the Literary Imagination: Selected Papers from the English Institute, 1987.* Ed. Deborah E. McDowell and Arnold Rampersad. Baltimore: Johns Hopkins University Press, 1989. 25–61.

Spitz, Ellen Handler. *The Brightening Glance: Imagination and Childhood.* New York: Pantheon, 2006.

———. *Inside Picture Books.* New Haven: Yale University Press, 1999.

Spufford, Francis. *The Child That Books Built: A Life in Reading.* New York: Henry Holt, 2003.

"St. Thomas and Antigua." *Slave's Friend* III, no. 1 (1838): 9–11.

Stanley, Harold. *Gamaliel Bailey and Anti-slavery Union.* Kent, Ohio: Kent State University Press, 1986.

Starling, Marion Wilson. *The Slave Narrative: Its Place in American History.* Washington, D.C.: Howard University Press, 1988.

Stauffer, John. *The Black Hearts of Men: Radical Abolitionists and the Transformation of Race.* Cambridge: Harvard University Press, 2002.

Steedman, Carolyn. *Strange Dislocations: Childhood and the Idea of Human Interiority, 1780–1930.* Cambridge: Harvard University Press, 1995.

Steig, Michael. *Stories of Reading: Subjectivity and Literary Understanding.* Baltimore: Johns Hopkins University Press, 1988.

Steiner, Edward Alfred. *Against the Current: Simple Chapters from a Complex Life.* New York: Fleming H. Revell, 1910.

Stephens, John, and Robyn McCallum. *Retelling Stories, Framing Culture: Traditional Story and Metanarratives in Children's Literature.* New York: Garland, 1998.

Stepto, Robert B. "Sharing the Thunder: The Literary Exchanges of Harriet Beecher Stowe, Henry Bibb and Frederick Douglass." In Sundquist, ed., *New Essays on Uncle Tom's Cabin.* 135–54.

Sterling, Dorothy. *Black Foremothers: Three Lives.* 2nd ed. New York: The Feminist Press, 1988.

Sternberg, Meir. *Expositional Modes and Temporal Ordering in Fiction.* Baltimore: Johns Hopkins University Press, 1978.

Stevenson, Louis L. *The American Homefront: American Thought and Culture, 1860–1880.* Ithaca: Cornell University Press, 2001.

Stewart, David M. "Consuming George Thompson." *American Literature* 80.2 (June 2008): 233–63.

———. "Cultural Work, City Crime, Reading, Pleasure." *American Literary History* 94 (Winter 1997): 676–701.

———. *Reading and Disorder in Antebellum America.* Columbus: Ohio State University Press, 2011.

———. Rev. of *A History of the Book in America,* vol. 3: *The Industrial Book, 1840–1880,* ed. Scott E. Casper et al. *Resources for American Literary Study* 32 (2007): 321–24.

———. "Sensationalism." *U.S. Popular Print Culture, 1860–1920.* Ed. Christine Bold. New York: Oxford University Press, 2010 (forthcoming).

"Stolen Children." *Slave's Friend* III, no. 3 (1838): 2.

Stonequist, Everett V. *Marginal Man: A Study in Personality and Culture Conflict.* New York: Russell and Russell, 1937.

The Story of Little Eva. Boston: Dana Estes, 1902.

Stowe, Charles E. *The Life of Harriet Beecher Stowe Compiled From Her Letters and Journals.* Boston: Houghton, Mifflin, 1889.

Stowe, Charles E., and Lyman Beecher Stowe. *The Life of Harriet Beecher Stowe.* Boston: Houghton Mifflin, 1911.

Stowe, Harriet Beecher. *Collected Poems of Harriet Beecher Stowe.* Ed. John Michael Moran, Jr. Hartford: Transcendental Books, 1967.

———. *Earthly Care: A Heavenly Discipline.* Boston: American Tract Society, 1850.

———. "The Freeman's Dream." *National Era* (August 1, 1850): 121.

———. *House and Home Papers.* Published pseudonymously under Christopher Crowfield. Boston: Ticknor and Fields, 1865.

———. Introduction. *A Library of Famous Fiction: Embracing the 9 Standard Masterpieces.* New York: J. B. Ford, 1873. vii–x.

———. Introduction. *Uncle Tom's Cabin.* New York: Houghton Mifflin, 1896; c 1878. xxxi–lxi.

———. Introductory Essay. *The Incarnation.* By Charles Beecher. New York: Harper Brothers, 1849. iii–ix.

———. *A Key to Uncle Tom's Cabin.* 1853. Bedford, Mass.: Applewood Books, 1998.

———. "Literary Epidemics No. 1." *New York Evangelist* 13 (July 28, 1842): 235.

————. "Literary Epidemics No. 2." *New York Evangelist* 14 (July 13, 1843): 109.

————. *Pictures and Stories from 'Uncle Tom's Cabin'*. Boston: Jewett, 1853.

————. "Preface to the First Edition." 1852. *Uncle Tom's Cabin*. New York: Houghton Mifflin, 1896. lxxxiii–lxxxv.

————. Preface. *A Peep into Uncle Tom's Cabin*. Boston: Jewett, 1853.

————. *Uncle Tom's Cabin*. 2 vols. Ills. Hammatt Billings. Boston: John P. Jewett, 1852.

————. *Uncle Tom's Cabin*. 1 vol. Ills. Hammatt Billings. Boston: John P. Jewett, 1853.

————. *Uncle Tom's Cabin*. London: H. G. Bohn, 1852.

————. *Uncle Tom's Cabin*. 1 vol. Boston: John P. Jewett, 1853.

————. *Uncle Tom's Cabin*. London: Nathaniel Cooke, 1853.

————. *Uncle Tom's Cabin*. Ills. Phiz, Gilbert, Harvey. London: Cassell, 1853.

————. *Uncle Tom's Cabin*. New York: Hurst, 187–.

————. *Uncle Tom's Cabin*. New York: Houghton Mifflin, 1888.

————. *Uncle Tom's Cabin*. 2 vols. Ills. E. W. Kemble. New York: Houghton Mifflin, 1891, 1892.

————. *Uncle Tom's Cabin*. Ills. Jenny Nystrom-Stoopendaal. New York: Eaton and Mains, 1897.

————. *Uncle Tom's Cabin*. Adapted by Helen Ring Robinson. Philadelphia: The Penn Publishing Company, 1908.

————. *Uncle Tom's Cabin*. Ills. James Henry Daugherty. New York: Coward, McCann, and Geoghegan, 1929.

————. *Uncle Tom's Cabin*. Ills. Various artists. New York: Dodd, Mead & Company. 1952.

————. *Uncle Tom's Cabin*. New York: Penguin, 1987.

————. *Uncle Tom's Cabin*. Ed. Elizabeth Ammons. New York: Norton, 1994.

————. *Uncle Tom's Cabin*. New York: Oxford University Press, 1998.

————. *Uncle Tom's Cabin*. New York: Signet, 1998.

————. *Uncle Tom's Cabin: Art Memorial Edition*. Ills. Various artists. Chicago: Thompson and Thomas, 1897.

Streeby, Shelley. *American Sensations: Class, Empire, and the Production of Popular Culture*. Berkeley: University of California Press, 2002.

Strickland, Charles E., and Charles Burgess. "G. Stanley Hall: Prophet of Naturalism." In Strickland and Burgess, ed., *Health, Growth, and Heredity*. 26.

————. eds. *Health, Growth, and Heredity: G. Stanley Hall on Natural Education*. New York: Teachers College Press, 1965.

Strieby. "The Look Forward." *American Missionary* 39.12 (December 1885): 352–58.

Suleiman, Susan J., and Inge Crosman, eds. *The Reader in the Text: Essays on Audience and Interpretation*. Princeton: Princeton University Press, 1980.

Sully, James. *Children's Ways: Being Selections from the Author's 'Studies of Childhood' with Some Additional Matter*. New York: D. Appleton, 1907.

Sundquist, Eric. Introduction. *Frederick Douglass: New Literary and Historical Essays*. Cambridge: Cambridge University Press, 1990. 1–22.

————. ed. *New Essays on Uncle Tom's Cabin*. New York: Cambridge University Press, 1987.

———. *To Wake the Nations: Race in the Making of American Literature.* Cambridge: Harvard University Press, 1993.

Swisshelm, Mrs. "Letter to Country Girls." *The Liberator* (January 4, 1850): 4.

Tawil, Ezra. *The Making of Racial Sentiment: Slavery and the Birth of the Frontier Romance.* New York: Cambridge University Press, 2006.

Terrell, Mary Church. *A Colored Woman in a White World.* Washington, D.C.: Ransdell, 1940.

———. *Harriet Beecher Stowe: An Appreciation.* Washington, D.C.: Murray Bros. Press, 1911.

Thayer, W. R. "The New Storytellers and the Doom of Realism." *Forum* 18 (1894): 470–80.

"Thinking of U.T.C." *Puck* 48.1248 (February 6, 1901): 3.

Thomas, Julia. *Pictorial Victorians: The Inscription of Values in Word and Image.* Athens: Ohio University Press, 2004.

"Three Little Abolitionists." *Slave's Friend* I, no. 5 (1836): 2–3.

Thurman, Suzanne R. *"O Sisters Ain't You Happy": Gender, Family, and Community among the Harvard and Shirley Shakers, 1781–1918.* Syracuse: Syracuse University Press, 2002.

"To a Young Lady Who refused to give her name as a member of a Benevolent Society, because she thought her influence too small to be of any service." *Slave's Friend* III, no. 3 (1838): 13.

"To Juvenile Anti-slavery Societies." *Slave's Friend* III, no. 2 (1838): 11.

"To the Author of 'Uncle Tom's Cabin'." *The Liberator* (April 9, 1852): 4.

Tobenkin, Elias. *Witte Arrives.* 1916. New York: Frederick A. Stokes, 1968.

Tompkins, Jane P., ed. *Reader-Response Criticism: From Formalism to Post-Structuralism.* Baltimore: Johns Hopkins University Press, 1980.

———. *Sensational Designs: The Cultural Work of American Fiction, 1790–1860.* New York: Oxford University Press, 1989.

Trachtenberg, Alan. *Reading American Photographs: Images as History.* New York: Hill and Wang, 1989.

Trubey, Elizabeth Fekete. "'Success Is Sympathy': *Uncle Tom's Cabin* and the Woman Reader." In Badia and Phegley, ed., *Reading Women.* 53–76.

Twain, Mark. *Adventures of Huckleberry Finn.* Ed. Sculley, Bradley, et al. New York: Norton, 1977.

"'Uncle Tom' Dies: Negro Said to Have Been Original of Mrs. Stowe's Character Passes Away." *New York Tribune* (March 10, 1903): 5.

"Uncle Tom's Cabin Illustrated." *Literary World: A Monthly Review of Current Literature* 23.2 (January 16, 1892): APS online pg. 19.

"Uncle Tom's Cabin, the Story of the Story." *Weekly Champion and Press* (November 28, 1868): 1.

Vrettos, Athena. *Somatic Fictions: Imagining Illness in Victorian Culture.* Stanford: Stanford University Press, 1995.

Warner, Charles Dudley. "Uncle Tom's Cabin Half a Century Later." *Atlantic Monthly*

78 (July 1896). Rpt. in *Uncle Tom's Cabin*. Ed. Elizabeth Ammons. New York: Norton, 1994, 483–88.

Warner, William B. "Staging Readers Reading." www.english.ucsb.edu/faculty/warner/courses/w00/engl30/stagingreaders.ecf.8.99.htm.

Warren, Kenneth. "The Afterlife of *Uncle Tom's Cabin*." In Weinstein, ed., *The Cambridge Companion to Harriet Beecher Stowe*, 219–34.

Washington, Booker T. *Up from Slavery*. 1901. New York: Dover, 1995.

Watrous, James. *American Printmaking: A Century of American Printmaking, 1880–1980*. Madison: University of Wisconsin Press, 1894.

Watt, Ian. *The Rise of the Novel*. Berkeley: University of California Press, 1957.

Wayland, Francis. "Early Training of Children." *The Fireside Miscellany, and Young People's Encyclopedia* (February 1854): 60–61. www.merrycoz.org/articles/TRAINING.HTM.

Weimann, Jeanne Madeline. *The Fair Women*. Chicago: Academy Chicago, 1981.

Weinstein, Cindy, ed. *The Cambridge Companion to Harriet Beecher Stowe*. New York: Cambridge University Press, 2004.

———. *Family, Kinship, and Sympathy in Nineteenth-Century America*. New York: Cambridge University Press, 2004.

———. "*Uncle Tom's Cabin* and the South." In Weinstein, ed., *The Cambridge Companion to Harriet Beecher Stowe*. 39–57.

Welburn, William C. "To 'Keep the Past in Lively Memory': William Carl Bolivar's Efforts to Preserve African American Cultural Heritage." *Libraries and the Cultural Record* 42.2 (2007) 165–79.

Welch, Samuel Manning. *Home History. Recollections of Buffalo during the decade from 1830 to 1840, or fifty years since*. Buffalo: P. Paul & bro., 1891.

Weld, Theodore D. *American Slavery as It Is: Testimony of a Thousand Witnesses*. New York: Arno Press, 1968.

Wells, Ida B. *Crusade for Justice: The Autobiography of Ida B. Wells*. Ed. Alfreda M. Duster. Chicago: University of Chicago Press, 1970.

———. "Woman's Mission." *New York Freeman* (December 26, 1885). Rpt. in *The Memphis Diary of Ida B. Wells*. Ed. Miriam DeCosta-Willis. Boston: Beacon Press, 1995. 179–82.

Wendell, Barrett. *A Literary History of America*. New York: Scribners, 1900.

Wexler, Laura. "Tender Violence: Literary Eavesdropping, Domestic Fiction, and Educational Reform." In Samuels, ed., *The Culture of Sentiment*. 9–38.

Wharton, Edith. "Copy: A Dialogue." *Crucial Instances*. 1901. New York: AMS, 1969. 99–119.

"What Can We Do?" *Slave's Friend* I, no. 3 (1836): 8–9.

"What Susie Found at Tougaloo." *American Missionary* 42.4 (April 1888): 108–9.

Wheaton, Ellen Birdseye. *The Diary of Ellen Birdseye Wheaton* (1923). "North American Women's Letters and Diaries" www.alexanderstreet2.com/nwldlive/nawld.login.htm (consulted October 2006).

White, Anne Terry. *Uncle Tom's Cabin Adapted by Anne Terry White.* New York: George Braziller, 1966.

White, Charles Edward. *The Beauty of Holiness: Phoebe Palmer as Theologian, Revivalist, Feminist, and Humanitarian.* Grand Rapids: Frances Asbury Press, 1986.

White, Richard Grant. "King Cole and His Band." *The Galaxy* 22.2 (August 1876): 249–58.

Whittier, John Greenleaf. "On the Portrait of a Celebrated Magazine Publisher who has Lately Saved the Union and Lost a Contributor." *National Era* (April 4, 1850): 54.

———. "A Sabbath Scene." *National Era* (June 27, 1850): 102.

Wiegand, Wayne, and James P. Danky, eds. *Print Culture in a Diverse America.* Urbana: University of Illinois Press, 1998.

Wiggin, Kate. *Children's Rights: A Book of Nursery Logic.* Boston: Houghton, Mifflin, 1892.

Williams, G. Grant. "Reminiscences of the Life of Harriet Beecher Stowe and Her Family." *Colored American Magazine* 6 (1903). Rpt. in New York: Negro Universities Press (1969): 127–40.

Williams, Heather Andrea. *Self-Taught: African American Education in Slavery and Freedom.* Chapel Hill: University of North Carolina Press, 2005.

Williams, Linda. *Playing the Race Card: Melodramas of Black and White from Uncle Tom to O. J. Simpson.* Princeton: Princeton University Press, 2001.

Wilson, Edmund. *Patriotic Gore: Studies in the Literature of the American Civil War.* New York: Oxford University Press, 1962.

Wilson, Forrest. *Crusader in Crinoline: The Life of Harriet Beecher Stowe.* Philadelphia: J. B. Lippincott, 1941.

Wilson, Henry. *History of the Rise and Fall of the Slave Power in America,* vol. II. 1872. New York: Negro Universities Press, 1969.

———. Letter to Harriet Beecher Stowe, July 2, 1874. Beecher-Stowe Collection, Folder 259.

Wilson, Jock. *The Dark and the Damp: An Autobiography of Jock Wilson with Pen Sketches by the Author.* New York: E. P. Dutton, 1951.

Winnicott, D. W. *The Child, the Family, and the Outside World.* Baltimore: Penguin, 1969.

Winship, Michael. "'The Greatest Book of Its Kind': A Publishing History of 'Uncle Tom's Cabin.'" *Proceedings of the American Antiquarian Society* 109, Part 2 (1999): 309–32.

Wise, Winifred. *Harriet Beecher Stowe: Woman with a Cause.* New York: Putnam, 1965.

Wishy, Bernard. *The Child and the Republic.* Philadelphia: University of Pennsylvania Press, 1968.

Wister, Owen. *The Virginian.* New York: Washington Square Press, 1956.

Wittmann, Reinhard. "Was There a Reading Revolution at the End of the Eighteenth Century?" *A History of Reading in the West.* Ed. Guglielmo Cavallo and Roger Chartier. Trans. Lydia G. Cochrane. Cambridge, U.K.: Polity Press, 1999. 284–312.

Wonham, Henry B. *Playing the Races: Ethnic Caricature and American Literary Realism.* New York: Oxford University Press, 2004.

Wood, Marcus. *Blind Memory: Visual Representations of Slavery in England and America, 1780–1865.* New York: Routledge, 2000.

Woodward, C. Vann. *The Strange Career of Jim Crow.* New York: Oxford University Press, 2001.

Wright, Richard. *Black Boy.* New York: HarperCollins, 2005.

Yarborough, Richard. "Strategies of Black Characterization in *Uncle Tom's Cabin* and the Early Afro-American Novel." In Sundquist, ed., *New Essays on Uncle Tom's Cabin.* 45–84.

Young, Elizabeth. *Disarming the Nation: Women's Writing and the American Civil War.* Chicago: University of Chicago Press, 1999.

Yuill, Phyllis J. *Little Black Sambo: A Closer Look.* New York: Council on Interracial Books for Children, 1976.

"Zamor and Hinda." *Slave's Friend* III, no. 10 (1838): 1–13.

Zboray, Ronald J. *A Fictive People: Antebellum Economic Development and the American Reading Public.* New York: Oxford University Press, 1993.

Zboray, Ronald J., and Mary Saracino Zboray. "Books, Reading, and the World of Goods in Antebellum New England." *American Quarterly* 48.4 (December 1996): 587–621.

———. *Everyday Ideas: Socioliterary Experience among Antebellum New Englanders.* Knoxville: University of Tennessee Press, 2006.

Zelizer, Viviana A. *Pricing the Priceless Child: The Changing Social Value of Children.* Princeton: Princeton University Press, 1985.

Index

Page numbers in italics signify illustrations.